Revelation

Blackwell Bible Commentaries

Series Editors: John Sawyer, Christopher Rowland, Judith Kovacs

Revelation

The Apocalypse
of Jesus Christ

Judith Kovacs and Christopher Rowland

in collaboration with
Rebekah Callow

Blackwell
Publishing

© 2004 by Judith Kovacs and Christopher Rowland

350 Main Street, Malden, MA 02148-5020, USA
108 Cowley Road, Oxford OX4 1JF, UK
550 Swanston Street, Carlton, Victoria 3053, Australia

First published 2004 by Blackwell Publishing Ltd

Library of Congress Cataloging-in-Publication Data

Kovacs, Judith L., 1945–
   Revelation: the apocalypse of Jesus Christ / Judith Kovacs and Christopher
Rowland; in collaboration with Rebekah Callow.
     p. cm. – (Blackwell Bible commentaries)
Includes bibliographical references.
   ISBN 0-631-23214-1 (hardcover : alk. paper) – ISBN 0-631-23215-X
(pbk. : alk. paper)
   1. Bible. N.T. Revelation–Criticism, interpretation, etc. I. Rowland,
Christopher, 1947– II. Callow, Rebekah. III. Title. IV. Series.

BS2825.52.K69   2004
228'.07–dc22

2003018705

A catalogue record for this title is available from the British Library.

Set in 10 on 12½ pt Minion
by SNP Best-set Typesetter Ltd., Hong Kong
Printed and bound in the United Kingdom
by TJ International, Padstow, Cornwall

For further information on
Blackwell Publishing, visit our website:
http://www.blackwellpublishing.com

The editor and publisher wish to thank the following for permission to use
copyright material. McGinn, B., *Visions of the End, Apocalyptic Traditions in the
Middle Ages.* © 1998 Columbia University Press. Reprinted with permission of
the publisher.

In memory of our parents

Keith H. Tustison (1915–2002) *and*
Mary Carey Tustison (1915–1991)

Eric Rowland (1919–1994) *and*
Frances Mary Rowland (1914–1999)

Contents

Illustrations

The Blackwell Bible Commentaries series, the first to be devoted primarily to the reception history of the Bible, is based on the premise that how people have interpreted, and been influenced by, a sacred text like the Bible is often as interesting and historically important as what it originally meant. The series emphasizes the influence of the Bible on literature, art, music, and film, its role in the evolution of religious beliefs and practices, and its impact on social and political developments. Drawing on work in a variety of disciplines, it is designed to provide a convenient and scholarly means of access to material until now hard to find, and a much-needed resource for all those interested in the influence of the Bible on western culture.

Until quite recently this whole dimension was for the most part neglected by biblical scholars. The goal of a commentary was primarily if not exclusively to get behind the centuries of accumulated Christian and Jewish tradition to one single meaning, normally identified with the author's original intention. The most important and distinctive feature of the Blackwell Commentaries is that they will present readers with many different interpretations of each text, in such a way as to heighten their awareness of what a text, especially a sacred text, can mean and what it can do, what it has meant and what it has done, in the many contexts in which it operates.

The Blackwell Bible Commentaries will consider patristic, rabbinic (where relevant), and medieval exegesis as well as insights from various types of modern criticism, acquainting readers with a wide variety of interpretative techniques. As part of the history of interpretation, questions of source, date, authorship, and other historical-critical and archaeological issues will be discussed, but since these are covered extensively in existing commentaries, such references will be brief, serving to point readers in the direction of readily accessible literature where they can be followed up.

Original to this series is the consideration of the reception history of specific biblical books arranged in commentary format. The chapter-by-chapter arrangement ensures that the biblical text is always central to the discussion. Given the wide influence of the Bible and the richly varied appropriation of each biblical book, it is a difficult question which interpretations to include. While each volume will have its own distinctive point of view, the guiding principle for the series as a whole is that readers should be given a representative sampling of material from different ages, with emphasis on interpretations that have been especially influential or historically significant. Though commentators will have their preferences among the different interpretations, the material will be presented in such a way that readers can make up their own minds on the value, morality, and validity of particular interpretations.

The series encourages readers to consider how the biblical text has been interpreted down the ages and seeks to open their eyes to different uses of the Bible in contemporary culture. The aim is to write a series of scholarly commentaries that draw on all the insights of modern research to illustrate the rich interpretative potential of each biblical book.

John Sawyer
Christopher Rowland
Judith Kovacs

Preface

This commentary starts from the assumption that what people believe the Bible means is as interesting and important as what it originally meant. Ulrich Luz deserves gratitude for his part in putting the history of the interpretation and the influence of biblical texts (*Wirkungsgeschichte*) on the agenda of New Testament studies (Luz 1989: 95–9; cf. Patte and Greenholm 2000). His commentary on Matthew raises the question whether the time has come to devote much more attention to reception history. The task of the interpreter is not completed by historical exegesis, since 'one does not yet understand what the subject matter of the text *means* if one only understands what it *has meant*' (Luz 1989: 98). Interpretation is not to be confined to the scholarly elucidation of the text, for religious practice, suffering, song, poetry and prayer all have their contribution to make to understanding. As Luz indicates, 'biblical texts do not simply have one set, closed meaning but are full of possibilities' (Luz 1989: 98).

While reception history has received little attention in New Testament scholarship, it is not an entirely new endeavour. Notable examples include Schweitzer's unravelling of the influence of interpreters' own times and interests on the quest for the historical Jesus (Schweitzer 1961) and the exploration by Sanders (1977) of how Lutheran teaching has influenced the exegesis of Paul.

No one who has considered the history of the interpretation of the Revelation to John (referred to in this volume as 'the Apocalypse') will require any persuading of the great impact which this book has had down the centuries, initially on a Christian culture and more recently, in a more diffuse way and in a variety of contexts, on a much more secular age. Despite the general neglect of reception history by biblical scholars, those who set out to study the reception of the Bible quickly become aware of the enormous amount of scholarship that already exists. Much of what is contained in this commentary betrays our indebtedness to scholars in disciplines such as history, art history and literary studies who have studied the interpretation of the Apocalypse. We have not attempted to go afresh over ground so ably covered by others better qualified to judge and interpret texts that come from periods outside the limits of our expertise. The debt to a host of writers on the Apocalypse, particularly Bernard McGinn, Richard Emmerson, Marjorie Reeves, Kathleen Firth, C. A. Patrides, Joseph Wittreich, Arthur Wainwright, David Burr, Christopher Burdon, Morton Paley and Gertrud Schiller, will be readily apparent from the bibliographical citations. One particular word of appreciation is in order, to Charles Helms, whose unpublished doctoral dissertation (Oxford, 1991) has been an invaluable resource for the pre-Constantinian church fathers, especially for textual references. Since this work is not generally available, we have not given specific page references to it.

Given the immense influence of the Apocalypse on literature, art, theology, politics and popular culture, the decisions about what to include in this commentary have been difficult. Needless to say, it has been necessary to be selective about which interpreters and which writings to cite and discuss. Our aim is to give a representative sampling of different types of interpretation and of material coming from different periods of history. It is hoped that the major figures and the main types of interpretation have been fairly represented. Compared with earlier periods, there is relatively little on the modern period, and in particular not much on modern historical criticism. This is partly because this is so widely available in other commentaries and partly because the main hermeneutical options were already well established before the modern period (that is, before the end of the eighteenth century and the work of J. G. Eichhorn). Cost prevented us from including more pictorial representations. This is a particularly rich area, for the understanding of which the Apocalypse has been remarkably well served (Schiller 1990 and 1991; Carey 1999; Emmerson and McGinn 1992; see also the many plates in Van der Meer 1978 and Grubb 1977 and the websites noted in the bibliography, after the primary sources).

This commentary takes the form of an extended introduction to the Apocalypse and to the main types of interpretation of the book through the centuries, followed by examples of specific interpretations, arranged according to the chapters of the Apocalypse. The chapters on specific chapters of the Apocalypse are each divided into two parts. The first, entitled 'Ancient Literary Context', provides some historical context, noting especially links with the Hebrew Bible, Jewish and Christian apocalypses, and other ancient texts. The second, entitled 'The Interpretations', comprises the bulk of each chapter and is subdivided according to the major themes of the biblical chapter. The two parts of the book are intended to complement one another. The introductory chapter, with its typology of interpretations and survey of influential interpretations, offers a framework for the more diffuse commentary that follows. The body of the commentary, in its presentation of material of diverse types and periods, is more like an anthology (in this respect reflecting earlier commentaries like that of Beatus of Liébana). We have sought to ensure a balance between making clear the dominant types of interpretation down the centuries and conveying particularities of many different interpretations. In order to give readers a better idea of the particular flavour of various appropriations, we have included extensive quotations, especially from poems, songs and other literary works. To provide more cohesion, we have chosen a few interpreters and works for special emphasis, referring to them at various points in the commentary. These include Origen, Victorinus, Tyconius, Augustine, Joachim of Fiore, Peter John Olivi, Hildegard of Bingen, the *Geneva Bible*, John Bale, John Milton, John Bunyan, William Blake, the *Scofield Reference Bible,* and African-American songs.

Unless a particular translation has been specified, biblical texts are quoted from the NRSV. To help readers with the welter of names and to provide a chronological orientation, the 'Biographies and Glossary' contains brief biographies, with dates, of most interpreters cited, as well as explanations of certain writings, movements and terms. This is followed by a bibliography in three parts, containing primary and secondary sources and websites. The first part list editions and translations from which quotations in the text are taken and points readers to primary texts that are generally available – for example, the collected works of Milton and other poets, the various anthologies that have now made the history of interpretation of the Apocalypse more widely available, and the English translations of the church fathers in the two multi-volume series The Ante-Nicene Fathers (abbreviated ANF) and The Library of Nicene and Post-Nicene Fathers. Works discussed for which translations can be found in ANF include (with volume and page numbers): Barnabas, i.133–52; Justin Martyr, *Dialogue with Trypho*, i.194–270; Irenaeus, *Against the Heresies*, i.309–567; Tertullian, *Against Marcion, The Resurrection of the Flesh* and *Scorpion's Sting*, iii.269–475, 545–94, 633–48; Hippolytus, *Commentary on Daniel* and *The Antichrist*, v.177–91, 204–19; Cyprian, *Testimonies*, v.507–57; Methodius, Banquet, vi.309–55; Lactantius, *Institutes*, vii.244–55; Victorinus, *Commentary on the Apocalypse*, vii.344–66; Origen, *Commentary on John* and *Commentary on Matthew* (parts), ix.297–408, 413–512. Medieval sources (for example, the works of Joachim of Fiore and Peter John Olivi) are not so easily available, though enough is published on websites and in anthologies to offer readers the opportunity to follow up some of the more important themes. The influential commentary on the Apocalypse by the fourth-century church father Tyconius is not longer extant. Modern readers are dependent on the extensive quotations from Tyconius that are preserved by writers like Beatus of Liébana, the source of many of the references to Tyconius in this book (see Steinhauser 1987).

Following the Bibliography is a summary of allusions to the Hebrew Bible/Old Testament found in the marginal notes of the widely used Nestle–Aland 26th edition of the Greek New Testament, arranged by chapter and biblical book. Although John's vision offers no explicit biblical citations, the various attempts to track its relation to earlier biblical books is an important part of the book's interpretation.

We are indebted to Bernard McGinn and Richard Bauckham, who read an earlier draft of the commentary and offered helpful suggestions. To Rebekah Callow we owe a special word of thanks. She laboured hard over a period of many months to assemble much of the data which we used as the basis of our commentary. We are delighted to be able to pay tribute to her diligence and patient contribution to our work. Thanks are also due to Abram Ring for preparing the index, to Jean van Altena for her careful editing of the text, and to Kip Gresham, a Cambridge artist who has produced a series of half-tone prints in the Apocalypse, for his generous permission to use two of them. The Arts and Humanities Research Board granted additional leave which has greatly facilitated the completion of this project. This is acknowledged with grateful thanks. Thanks are also due to Clare Hall, Cambridge University, for providing a stimulating and congenial setting for a year's research leave.

Abbreviations

ANF   Ante-Nicene Fathers
CPW   *The Complete Poetical Works of Samuel*
                                    Taylor Coleridge
CSEL   Corpus Scriptorum Ecclesiasticorum
                                    Latinorum
PL   Patrologia Latina
SC   Sources Chrétiennes
SNTSMS   Society of New Testament Studies
                                    Monograph Series
TU   Texte und Untersuchungen
WUNT   Wissenschaftliche Untersuchungen zum
                                    Neuen Testament

Alexander the Minorite, *Expositio*   *Expositio in Apocalypsim*
Andrew of Caesarea, *Comm.*   *Commentary on the Apocalypse.*
Augustine, *Serm.*   *Sermons*
Beatus, *Comm.*   *Commentary on the Apocalypse.*

Preface	*Preface to the Commentary on the Apocalypse*
Brightman, *Rev. of Rev.*	*Revelation of the Revelation*
Cyprian, *Test.*	*Testimonies*
Fort.	*Fortunatus, An Exhortation to Martyrdom*
Vir.	*The Dress of Virgins*
Epiphanius, *Pan*	*Against All the Heresies*
Eusebius, *HE*	*Ecclesiastical History*
ExodusR	*Exodus Rabbah*
Hippolytus, *Antichrist*	*On the Antichrist*
Hippolytus, *Daniel*	*Commentary on Daniel*
Ignatius of Antioch, *Ephes.*	*Letter to the Ephesians*
Irenaeus, *AH*	*Against the Heresies*
Dem.	*Demonstration of the Apostolic Teaching*
Joachim of Fiore, *Comm. Jer.*	*Commentary on Jeremiah*
Expositio	*Expositio in Apocalypsim*
Lib. Conc.	*The Book of Concordances*
Justin, *Apol.*	*Apology*
Dial.	*Dialogue with Trypho*
Minucius Felix, *Octav.*	*Octavius*
Peter Olivi, *Lectura*	*Lectura super Apocalypsim*
Origen, *Comm. Jo.*	*Commentary on John*
Comm. Matt.	*Commentary on Matthew*
Comm. Rom.	*Commentary on Romans*
Hom. Gen.	*Homilies on Genesis*
Hom. Jer.	*Homilies on Jeremiah*
Hom. Num.	*Homilies on Numbers*
Schol Ap	*Scholia on the Apocalypse*
Tertullian, *Dress*	*De cultu feminarum*
Resurr.	*Treatise on the Resurrection*

Introduction

THE APOCALYPSE IN HISTORY: THE PLACE OF THE BOOK OF REVELATION IN CHRISTIAN THEOLOGY AND LIFE

On the day after the deaths of thousands of people in the World Trade Center in New York City, a British tabloid newspaper had a single caption to accompany its terrible picture: 'APOCALYPSE'. One word was considered sufficient to epitomize the destruction, the cataclysm and the sheer horror it inspired, and the book of Revelation, the Apocalypse, otherwise so neglected and despised, provided a way of evaluating this awesome event. In the popular view, Apocalypse *is* about cataclysm, death and destruction, or, as another paper described the events of that day in September 2001, 'the end of the world'. It offers images that convey the magnitude and malignity of our experience, not only at a national, international and social level, but in individual lives as well.

At another time and in another place, in the north-east of Brazil in 1990, a group of campesinos were talking about their lives. One elderly man started speaking about the upcoming Brazilian elections and the campaigning going on in the state of Ceará. Without any prompting he described the candidates (particularly those on the right) as the representatives of the dragon of the Apocalypse, whose heads were manifested in corrupt practices, bribes and blandishments, whereas there was little but injustice for ordinary people and persecution by the large landowners of those who dared to stand up for a modicum of justice. It was a totally surprising, unaffected and spontaneous appropriation of the Apocalypse.

The original meaning of the word 'apocalypse', derived from the Greek *apokalypsis*, is in fact not the cataclysmic end of the world, but an 'unveiling', or 'revelation', a means whereby one gains insight into the present – for example, about the fallenness of a particular historical situation and the powers confronted there. It offers that alternative horizon which gives a different perspective. So, for example, John Howard Yoder envisions a new politics based on Rev 5 (Yoder 1972: 237), determined not by Caesar's rule, but by truth telling and love of the enemy. Seen from this perspective, the Apocalypse is not just for the community of the last days, but is applicable to every age, offering a way of seeing in our own history Eden and the Fall, Jerusalem and Babylon.

In a modern theological culture that both fears and eschews apocalyptic thinking, it may come as a surprise to find how influential, directly or indirectly, the Apocalypse has been on Western art, literature and theology. Through the centuries it has been read in a great variety of ways (Froom 1946–54; Elliott 1851; Wainwright 1993; Allo 1921; W. Bousset 1896; Charles 1910; Maier 1981). This commentary aims to give a representative sampling of different types of readings down the centuries. This introductory chapter includes the following: (1) an introduction to the Apocalypse which sets it in the context of Jewish and early Christian literature, especially apocalypses and visionary literature; (2) a classification of the main types of interpretation of the book that have emerged over the centuries; (3) the point of view and special emphases of this commentary; (4) a survey of some of the most influential interpreters and interpretations, including consideration of how the book has been represented in music, liturgy and art.

1   The Apocalypse in the Context of Jewish and Early Christian Literature

The Apocalypse and other apocalypses

The Apocalypse is a different sort of text in more ways than one. Few will need convincing that it differs substantially in form and content from most other parts of the New Testament. As the unique New Testament example of the genre apocalypse, it is profoundly indebted to Jewish apocalyptic ideas (Rowland 1982). Its angelology, heavenly voices and preoccupation with the hidden are precisely what we find in Jewish apocalypses such as Daniel, 4 Ezra (= 2 Esdras 3–14),[1] *1 Enoch* and the *Apocalypse of Abraham* (Charlesworth 1983; J. J. Collins 1979 and 1984). It reflects a distinctive use of prophecy parallel to, but in significant respects different from, other apocalyptic texts (Bauckham 1993a). As many commentators down the centuries have pointed out, the crucial chapter 5 shows the mutation of apocalyptic thinking as the result of the gospel.

While the Apocalypse has much in common with other apocalypses, it exhibits important differences, as a comparison with Daniel and 2 Esdras illustrates. The Book of Daniel has influenced John's vision from almost the first verse to the last: for example, the vision of 'one like the Son of Man' in chapter 1, the vision of the beast in chapter 13, and the description of the book as 'what is to take place after this' (Rev 1:19). Nevertheless, the differences are marked. Daniel is pseudonymous and was probably written in the second century BCE at the height of the crisis which threatened Jerusalem and its temple under the Seleucid king Antiochus IV. John's apocalypse does not claim authority through an apostle but on the basis of a prophetic call (1:9–20), although the author has the same name as the son of Zebedee, and the book was from a very early stage linked with the apostle (Justin, *Apol.* 28; *Dial.* 81). Irenaeus, an early witness to the book, claims it was written by the apostle John during the last years of the reign of the Roman emperor Domitian, who ruled CE 81–96 (*AH* v.30.3; i.26.3; cf. Eusebius *HE* ii.18; iv.8). This date still finds widespread acceptance (A. Y. Collins 1984: 54–83; L. Thompson 1990: 13–17; Roloff 1993: 16–19), although some assign a date prior to the destruction of the Jerusalem temple in CE 70 (Rowland 1982: 403) or assume two editions reflecting both dates (Aune 1997: lvi–lxx).

The Apocalypse also differs from Daniel in the form of its visions (a point noted by Luther in his Preface to the New Testament of 1530). Daniel's format of dream-vision followed by interpretation by an accompanying angel (e.g. Dan 7:15: 'one of those who stood by made known to me the interpretation of these things') is almost completely lacking in the Apocalypse. Rev 17, where one of the angels of the seven bowls accompanies John and explains the vision of Babylon, offers a solitary exception. The closest parallels are between Dan 7:9–14 and the vision of the heavenly court in Rev 4–5 – probably because both are indebted to Ezek 1 – and between the beasts in Dan 7:1–8 and Rev 13.

[1] The Jewish apocalypse 4 Ezra is printed in Christian Bibles as chs 3–14 of 2 Esdras, which has Christian additions in chs 1–2 and 15–16. In subsequent citations both the Jewish and the Christian parts of this text will be referred to as 2 Esdras.

A significant part of the book of Daniel concerns the royal court in Babylon. Young Jews are presented as positively encouraged by the foreign king and his entourage and as having to resist being co-opted into the culture of Babylon (Dan 1). The stories of the fiery furnace and the lions' den (Dan 3 and 6) are a reminder of the terrible consequences for those who refuse to conform. Even so, there is admiration for the Jews on the part of the king, and Nebuchadnezzar is depicted with a degree of sympathy. The situation is very different in the Apocalypse, which reflects a more suspicious and antagonistic attitude to the dominant power (Bauckham 1993b). The book offers a vigorous rejection of the power of empire and evinces satisfaction at the ultimate triumph of God's righteousness (14:11; 19:3). There is little sign of accommodation with Babylon (Rome). At the appropriate moment those within her have to 'come out of her' (Rev 18:4); meanwhile what is suggested is resistance. Indeed, accommodation may be a sign of apostasy (2:20).

The Apocalypse's imagery and its hope for messianic vindication and defeat of Rome parallels in many ways 2 Esdras (Stone 1990). The message of this late first-century Jewish text is that all things should be viewed in light of the *eschaton* ('the end-time'), although eschatological interests are to some extent eclipsed by another concern: the pervasiveness of evil. The book wrestles with the apparently merciless character of the divine purposes and with human frailty in the face of them. While it lacks the elaborate symbolism of the Apocalypse, there are several specific parallels. Both 2 Esdras and Revelation have separate visions that reflect two parts of Dan 7: the beasts emerging from the sea (2 Esdras 11–12; Rev 13) and the 'messianic' vision of Dan 7:13–14 (2 Esdras 13; Rev 1:13–17). Like the messiah in 2 Esdras 13, the Lamb stands on Mount Zion (Rev 14:1). In both texts there is a two-stage eschatology, a messianic reign followed by a new age. This twofold scheme, found in 2 Esdras 7:28–32; 5:45, possibly for the first time in such an explicit form, is evidence in a Jewish apocalypse of hope for a new age that is transcendent and beyond history. So also in the Apocalypse the vision of the new heaven and new earth (21–2) is preceded by the millennial messianic reign (20:4–6).

Apocalyptic themes in early Christian literature

Although it is the only work of its genre in the New Testament, the Apocalypse reflects an early Christian tradition of apocalyptic interpretation rooted in Jewish apocalyptic tradition (which was itself to continue into the kabbalistic tradition of Judaism). One feature of this tradition, its interest in eschatology (teaching about the end-time), has dominated popular perceptions of the

Apocalypse and featured in much of its interpretation and influence down the centuries. Passages such as Matt 24–5 par.; 1 Thess 4:13–5:11; 2 Thess 2:3–12; Rom 8:18–30; and 1 Cor 15:20–5 remind us of the importance of eschatological expectation among early Christians. Such hopes were not merely future but were in some sense anticipated in the common life and in what Christians saw happening in the world around them. This 'realized' dimension is signalled in the New Testament itself, where 1 John 2:18 is the earliest explicit example of the tradition of the Antichrist, the polar opposite of Christ expected in the last days – here applied to a catastrophic split in the life of the eschatological community, a situation the author could not comprehend except as a sign of the last days.

In Hebrews and Ephesians apocalyptic categories are utilized to express convictions about Christ's exaltation and its consequences. The cosmology and the notion of revelation found in apocalypses and mystical literature provides a convenient starting place for reflection on the revelation inaugurated by the exaltation of Christ. The glory of the world above that is to be manifested in the future has now become a present possession for those who acknowledge that the Messiah has come and has already made available the heavenly gifts of the messianic age.[2]

The Gospel of John is frequently regarded as an example of the type of Christianity which firmly rejected apocalyptic, but the main thrust of its message has a remarkable affinity with apocalyptic thinking. John Ashton rightly calls the gospel 'an apocalypse in reverse' (Ashton 1991: 371; cf. Kovacs 1995). As in the Apocalypse, the goal is knowledge of the heavenly mysteries: in particular, the mysteries of God's person. Much of what the Fourth Gospel says relates to this theme, though here the quest for the highest wisdom of all, the knowledge of God, comes not through visions and revelations but through the Word become flesh, Jesus of Nazareth (Rowland 1996: 1–23). The heavenly mysteries are to be sought not in heaven but in Jesus, the one who has seen the Father and makes the Father known (cf. John 14:9).

The Apocalypse and visionary literature

The Apocalypse is also part of a broader visionary tradition evident not only in apocalypses but also in prophets such as Ezekiel and in other Jewish and

---

[2]   The contrast between 'above' and 'below' which is so typical of apocalyptic texts is well captured in the vision of the Woman Clothed with the Sun in the Trier Apocalypse, where there is a contrast between the extraordinary sign on in heaven while on earth soldiers are coming towards, and threatening, John the seer (Van der Meer 1978: 97 below 140).

early Christian texts. The christophany at its opening, the visions of heaven, the dirge over Babylon, the war against Gog and Magog, and the vision of the New Jerusalem – all exhibit the influence of the written forms of ancient prophecies on the more recent prophetic imagination of John of Patmos. The contribution of the first chapter of Ezekiel, the vision of the *merkabah* or heavenly throne of God, to the visionary vocabulary of John is evident in two crucial passages (Rev 1:13–20 and ch. 4), as well as in the references to thrones divine and demonic that form a *leitmotiv* throughout the book. The Dead Sea Scrolls found in Cave 4 demonstrate the importance of this *merkabah* tradition: for example, the fragment 4Q405 is dependent on Ezekiel and Isaiah, and was probably influenced by the same visionary tradition to which John belongs. Another example of this tradition, closely related in many respects, is the *Apocalypse of Enoch* (= *1 Enoch*, a work much emphasized in the Ethiopian Church; see Cowley 1983), many fragments of which were discovered in Cave 4 (Nickelsburg 2001). The heavenly ascent and vision of God in *1 Enoch* 14 displays many parallels with Rev 4, as does the similar vision in the *Apocalypse of Abraham* 18.

Many strands of the New Testament refer to visions and revelations, including the accounts of Jesus' baptism and the conversion of Paul (Mark 1:9–11; 9:2–3; Gal 1:12, 16; Luke 10:16; Acts 9; 10:11–16; and 2 Cor 12:2–4; Rowland 1982: 358–402; Lane Fox 1986: 375–418). In the first century CE Philo used the allegorical interpretation of Scripture to foster the ascent of the soul to the divine (Goodenough 1935). Similarly, in many Jewish and early Christian texts a concern to ascertain the deeper meaning of Scripture is linked with the language of vision (Fishbane 1985 and Boyarin 1994). The 'oracular', enigmatic words of prophetic and apocalyptic texts are susceptible to new interpretation as hermeneuts seek to 'divine' their meaning. Paul's letters testify to the conviction that the Scriptures, the fountain-head and embodiment of tradition and the basis of a community's identity, are now read in light of the new experience of the Spirit (Gal 3:2–4). The meaning of the Scriptures can be fully understood only with that Spirit-inspired intuition that flows from acceptance of the messiah (2 Cor 3:1–18). What is required is revelatory insight which will enable the enlightened reader to pierce beyond the letter of the text to discern its inner meaning. This is similar to the way the Teacher of Righteousness at Qumran, 'to whom God made known all the mysteries of his servants the prophets' (*1QpHab* 7.1), opened up the enigmatic prophetic oracles with his mystical insight. For Paul a mystery of ultimate importance had been revealed in Christ, and it is subsequently amplified by other divine mysteries (cf. 2 Cor 12:2–4). Paul's letters are an example of how the spirit of mystery and revelation recurs in New Testament theology (Rom 11:25; 16:25; 1 Cor 2:7; 15:51; Bockmuehl 1990; Becker 1980).

2   Differing Patterns in the Reception of the Apocalypse: A Summary

A striking example of the great diversity in the reception history of the Apocalypse is the contrast of the interpretations of the seventeenth-century independent Baptist Hanserd Knowlys and his contemporary Anne Wentworth. Knowlys follows conventional Protestant exegesis of his time, interpreting the book as an eschatological scenario and a critique of the Roman Catholic Church (Knowlys, *Exposition* 169 in Newport 2000: 31). Wentworth, a Baptist who had been ejected from her home by her abusive husband, sees in the book the promise of a great Day of Judgment when her husband and his co-persecutors will be judged. She uses the images of Jerusalem/Zion and Babylon (Rev 17–18 and 21–2) to interpret her own dire situation: 'the word of the Lord came unto me, and said: Zion and Babylon they did fight it out, And Zion did whole Babylon rout: And wounded Babylon very deep, That Zion might rejoyce and no more weep' (Hobby 1988: 50; for further discussion, see below, 189). Wentworth finds Babylon in a society based on patriarchy in which a woman who rebels against harsh treatment finds herself socially destitute. What is most striking is the fact that not only are the interpreters contemporaries, but there is every likelihood that the Knowlys mentioned in Wentworth's text as one of her persecutors is none other than the interpreter of the Apocalypse, who used the book as religious sanction for his anti-catholic sentiments.

This coincidental connection highlights the variety in approaches to the Apocalypse. Both interpreters use the image of Babylon, but there the similarity ends. For Knowlys the biblical text is a source to be expounded and interpreted. His interest is detailed textual exposition. To Wentworth, on the other hand, the Apocalypse is a text that empowers and provides imagery for her own visions. She is emboldened to speak out because of the prophetic gift bestowed on her, just as was John on Patmos. Her interpretation is an explicit 'actualization', a reading in relationship to new circumstances (Houlden 1995) which uses the apocalyptic images to address the specific circumstances in which she found herself.

All this is a reminder that the Apocalypse, no less than the Bible as a whole, hardly offers an unambiguous message. William Blake's witty aphorism 'Both read the Bible day and night/But thou readst black where I read white' (*The Everlasting Gospel*, notebook section, lines 13–14) is a salutary reminder to us as we embark on a study of the reception history of the Apocalypse, which has served many different agendas, those of revolutionaries and radicals as well as those of quietists and supporters of the status quo. In what follows an overview is offered of the main types of interpretation.

At the risk of oversimplification, it is possible to plot the differing inter-pretations of the Apocalypse along two axes. One is chronological and includes the various ways in which the images are linked with past, present and future persons and events. The other plots interpretations according to the degree to which they exemplify decoding, on the one hand, or actualization, on the other (see fig.1).

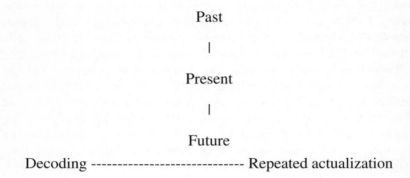

Decoding involves presenting the meaning of the text in another, less allusive form, showing what the text *really* means, with great attention to the details. Actualizing means reading the Apocalypse in relation to new circum-stances, seeking to convey the spirit of the text rather than being preoccupied with the plethora of detail. Such interpretation tends to regard the text as mul-tivalent, having more than one meaning (Wheelwright 1962: 92; Ricoeur 1969: 15 in Perrin 1976: 28–30).

The Apocalypse only occasionally prompts the reader to 'decode' the meaning of the apocalyptic mysteries (17:9; cf. 1:20 and 4:3). In this respect it is different from its Hebrew Bible counterpart, the book of Daniel, which is replete with detailed elucidation of its visions. None the less, some have sought precise equivalence between every image in the book and figures and events in history, resulting in a long tradition of 'decoding' interpretation. An image is seen to have one particular meaning, and the interpreter assumes that if the code is understood in its entirety, the whole Apocalypse can be rendered in another form, and its inner meaning laid bare. Meaning is confined as the details of images and actions are fixed on some historical personage or event. For example, the Spiritual Franciscans saw Saint Francis as the angel with the living seal of Rev 7:2, and Hal Lindsey sees in Rev 9 a description of an all-out attack of ballistic missiles on the cities of the world (1970: 87–102). Joseph Mede (1632) saw the seven seals as providing the key to the exact sequence of ages in the divine plan for history, while J. G. Eichhorn, a pioneer of historial criticism, interpreted the Apocalypse as a cryptic description of the history of John's day – for example, decoding the imagery of Rev 9:13–15 as a reference to the destruction of Jerusalem in CE 70.

There is a peculiar form of 'decoding' in which individuals 'act out' details of the text, in effect decoding the text once and for all in that person. For example, Joanna Southcott's understanding of her prophetic vocation was determined by the narrative of Rev 12, as she regarded herself as the incarnation of the Woman Clothed with the Sun (Hopkins 1982; Brown 2002). Similarly, the leaders of the Münster commonwealth in 1534 saw themselves as the two witnesses in Rev 11.

Actualizing interpretations take two forms. In one form the imagery of the Apocalypse is juxtaposed with the interpreter's own circumstances, whether personal or social, so as to allow the images to inform understanding of contemporary persons and events and to serve as a guide for action. Such interpretation has deep roots in the Christian tradition, going back at least to the time of Tyconius and Augustine (Fredriksen, in Emmerson and McGinn 1992: 20–37; Dulaey 1986). In contrast with 'decoding', it preserves the integrity of the textual pole and does not allow the image or passage from the Apocalypse to be identified solely with one particular historical personage or circumstance. The text is not prevented from being actualized in different ways over and over again. An example is understanding the book's images as an allegory of the struggles of the individual soul, in which the Apocalypse serves as a model of the progression from despair and darkness to the brilliance of the celestial city. This pattern lies behind two of the great literary texts that describe a 'spiritual journey': Dante's *Divine Comedy* and Bunyan's *Pilgrim's Progress*. Both are deeply indebted to the Apocalypse, for their narrative form as well as for particular images (Herzman in Emmerson and McGinn 1992: 398–411).

Secondly, there is the appropriation by visionaries,[3] where the words of the Apocalypse either offer the opportunity to 'see again' things similar to what had appeared to John or prompt new visions related to it. So in the visions of Hildegard of Bingen, many details of John's text reappear. Others, such as William Blake, exhibit a less direct relationship to the letter of the text. In his works the images and symbols of the Apocalypse appear in a different guise,

---

[3] Note the fourfold character of vision set out by Richard of St Victor (helpfully set out by Dronke 1984: 146): physical sight which contains no hidden significance; a mode of sight such as when Moses beheld the burning bush; seeing through visible things to the invisible; and, finally, contemplation of the celestial without the mediation of any visible figures. On Hildegard's description of the character of her visionary experience, see Dronke 1984: 168–9.

woven into the tapestry of Blake's own visionary world and incorporated into his idiosyncratic mythopoiesis.

Approaches to the Apocalypse can also be plotted on a chronological axis, according to whether they emphasize the past, present or future. In the Apocalypse itself, past, present and future are interrelated: eschatological visions (Rev 6–22) grow out of the past (Rev 5) and have an import for life in the present (Rev 2–3). The same is true in many interpretations – for example, in those of Joachim of Fiore and Joseph Mede. None the less, there are different emphases. Some interpret the Apocalypse mainly as a book about the past. From the earliest references to the book in the second century CE, John's vision has been linked to the social and political realities of late first-century Asia Minor, with its imperial cult. This approach is typical of historical-critical interpretation since the Enlightenment, which has antecedents in the interpretations of Grotius and other sixteenth-century interpreters. Roman Catholic theologians such as Luís de Alcázar responded to Protestant actualizing interpretations with an approach called 'preterism', which sees most of the Apocalypse as a description of the past of the Church.

Interpretations that emphasize the meaning of the Apocalypse for the present time include the two types of actualization just described. An emphasis on the present also characterizes some 'decoding', interpretations: for example, the references to contemporary controversies in the notes in the *Geneva Bible* ('decoding' in that it limits the reference of the Apocalypse to only one set of events). In the other, 'actualizing', interpretations, the book is seen as applicable to every age. It offers that alternative horizon, functioning as a lens through which one can see one's own situation afresh (Yoder in Pipkin 1989: 69–76; Yoder 1972: 237). So, for example, during the political crisis of the USA torn apart by the Vietnam War, William Stringfellow (1977) uses the Apocalypse's stark contrasts between Jerusalem and Babylon as an interpretative key to understand present reality.

Other interpretations are called 'futurist' because they see the book primarily as a prophecy of the events of the end-time. For example, up to the end of the second century, Rev 20–2 had wide influence among those called chiliasts or millennialists (after the Greek and Latin words for 1,000, respectively), who looked for God's thousand-year kingdom to be established on earth. The book's meaning for the future was also emphasized by sixteenth-century Roman Catholic theologians such as Cornelius of Lapide and Francisco Ribera, in another response to Protestant readings. In some forms of twentieth- and twenty-first-century North American eschatological expectation, the Apocalypse is seen to offer an elaborate blueprint for the events of the end-time. Varieties of this kind of interpretation are named after their various views about the millennium, the thousand-year messianic reign (see below, chapter on

Rev 20). These include pre-millennialism, which holds that the second coming of Christ will take place before the millennium, and post-millennialism, which teaches that Christ's appearance will take place only at its end. (Amillennialism involves the rejection of a literal future messianic reign on earth, a view often associated with the name of Augustine, which takes various forms.)

Finally, interpretations differ in whether they are responses to individual passages or images (for example, artistic portrayals of the Lamb or the Whore of Babylon or uses of individual images by poets) or interpretations of the book as a whole. Among the latter, some, like Alexander the Minorite in the mid-thirteenth century, read the Apocalypse as a sequential account of human history (Lerner in Emmerson and McGinn 1992: 60). Others understand parts of the book (particularly the sequences of seals, trumpets and bowls) as reca-pitulations or repetitions. From Victorinus and Tyconius onwards it has been widely assumed that certain passages should be seen as running concurrently. Joseph Mede, for example, regarded the seals and the trumpets as so closely related in their subject matter that they must refer to events taking place at the same time.

3　Point of View: Distinctive Emphases of this Commentary

While this volume aims to give a representative sampling of different types of interpretation of the Apocalypse, allowing different interpreters to speak for themselves without being subjected to editorial judgement, it has a distinctive point of view. In a time when the most prominent interpretations of the book emphasize its meaning for the past (historical criticism) or the future (prog-nostications of the *eschaton*), we aim to round out the picture by calling atten-tion to interpreters who seek to articulate the book's meaning for the present. Thus, alongside well-known examples of decoding interpretations, we present less known interpreters (church fathers, prophets and poets) who respond to the visionary character of the Apocalypse through actualizing interpretations.

The contrasting types of interpretation outlined in section 2 above presup-pose quite different understandings of the nature of exegesis, of which we shall need to be aware as we proceed (Boxall 2002). No book in the Bible raises the question of the nature of the exegetical task more acutely than the Apocalypse. The conventional assumption that a detailed, verse-by-verse explanation of a biblical text is what is required and expected already weights the answer in a particular direction. If one compares such detailed expositions of the text with the poetic and imaginative appropriations of it, there may at first sight seem to be no contest. After all, it is Mede (and after him the editors of the *Scofield*

Reference Bible and modern historical scholars) who attends carefully to the detail of the text and, by comparisons within the Apocalypse and to other prophetic texts of the Bible, offers some kind of overall explanation. The visionaries, poets and artists represent an altogether more oblique relationship with the text, hardly pausing to offer a justification for their interpretations. The biblical text is a springboard for other revelations, or a creative frame of reference for understanding their world. If we view exegesis as the close reading of the text, then this cannot be counted as exegesis. But the question is whether the Apocalypse is a text to be interpreted and deciphered or a text to be used and actualized.

Since the Enlightenment, there has been a growing interest in the location of the Apocalypse within the ancient world, which has led to intensive investigation of parallels between the book and other sources now extant from antiquity (see e.g. Aune 1997, 1998a and b; Hemer 1986). This has enabled us to imagine something of what life may have been like for those who converted to the way of life of a minority group with Jewish affinities. Historical scholarship has also helped articulate a critical perspective on interpretations that apply the Apocalypse in too facile a way to the contemporary world. Nevertheless, it is good to remember that in the Apocalypse references to ancient persons and situations are refracted through the visionary imagination.

Later visionaries who make use of the Apocalypse are attuned to something important in the text. Given the many references to visions in early Christian texts, it would be an excessively suspicious person who would deny that authentic visions lie behind some or all of these literary records. This is especially true of the Apocalypse itself. It is likely that actual visions, rather than literary artifice alone, have prompted the words we now read. When John the visionary on Patmos speaks of being 'in the spirit on the Lord's day' (Rev 1:10), he beckons interpreters to consider what is written in a way different from how they might consider the work of a mere collector of traditional material, requiring of them different interpretative techniques (Rowland 1998). Even if conjectures may be made about the significance of the time (the Lord's day) and the place (possibly, though not certainly, in exile) of the visions, it is impossible to know precisely what led to John's dramatic meeting with the heavenly 'one like the Son of Man' (1:13).

There may be signs of the seer's later reflection on his visions in verses like 17:9. Nevertheless, the explanation in such verses has the effect of complicating, rather than explaining, the detail of the visions. Perhaps the visions have been rearranged according to a certain 'narrative' sequence, starting with disaster and ending up with divine triumph (though there remain the abrupt changes and interruptions that have taxed interpreters down the centuries; see Lowth 1753). We should be careful not to assume, however, that order rather than chaos suggests later reflection. Even a brief acquaintance with the world of dreams indicates that sequence, and even certain moments when the dreamer 'stands back' from the dream, can be part of a visionary experience.

To characterize the pre-modern interpretations of the Apocalypse as *eisegesis* ('reading into the text') and compare them unfavourably with the exegesis ('reading out of the text') of modern scholars creates too sharp a divide (so Newport 2000: 21–3). An approach to visionary texts like Ezekiel 1, Isaiah 6 or the Apocalypse that stimulates a later reader to 'see again' what the biblical prophet saw in his vision might in fact offer an understanding of the text that is more faithful to the text than the results of patient historical exposition. Of course, such a use of the prophetic or visionary text is not without its difficulties and dangers (for further discussion, see below, 'A Hermeneutical Postscript'). The imagery opens the door to exegetical possibilities, whether via intertextual links within the book itself or those within the canon as a whole. This ambiguity irritates those who seek from Holy Scripture a clear message. As Tyndale recognized: 'The Apocalypse or Revelations of John are allegories whose literal sense is hard to find in many places' (2000: 157).

If what we have in this text is the written account of a vision or visions which came to John, even at different times, it becomes very difficult to describe any intention of the author, other than at most the ordering of the visions and their dissemination. John did not set out to write a literary work in an apocalyptic genre. Whatever the origin of the book's various components may have been, their function and juxtaposition are not the product of the visionary's conscious intention. And if the focus of interpretation is shifted away from the intention of the author, then reception history turns out to have particular importance; for then John's place is similar to that of the one who receives his visionary text. Both visionary and reader are in the position of interpreters. So, the 'afterlife' of the text, its reception by those who found in this visionary text an inspiration for their own visions or who have pored over it, seeking to use their interpretative skills to unlock its mysteries, is an integral part of its exegesis, as important as what the recipient of the vision and the original hearers may have understood it to mean.

An exposition of the Apocalypse that concentrates exclusively on the question 'What did this verse mean?' may miss the distinctive insight offered by later visionaries, who are inspired by the text to new imaginative insights or prophetic pronouncements. This was something recognized in debates about prophecy and apocalypse at the end of the eighteenth century. Herder, Hölderlin and Coleridge for example, sought to rekindle in their own writing the spirit of the Apocalypse (Shaffer 1972; Burdon 1997: 86–7, 146–52). Whether in Hölderlin's attempt to link his own work as a poet to the mystical insight of the seer of Patmos, Herder's recognition that reading the book is a means of being open to the converting power of Christ, or Coleridge's reaction against the historicism of Eichhorn, we find the same grasp of the dreamlike quality of this text, and the same search for appropriate ways of engaging with it. Eichhorn had viewed the book's symbols as a cloak for early Christian history, concerned with the Jewish revolt of CE 66–70 and the fall of Jerusalem. Coleridge responds, albeit in a comment on Ezekiel, raising his voice in favour of the poetry of prophecy and vision:

> It perplexes me to understand, how a Man of Eichhorn's Sense, Learning and Acquaintance with psychology could form, or attach belief to, so cold-blooded an hypothesis. That in Ezeckiel's [sic] Visions, Ideas or Spiritual Entities are presented in visual Symbols, I never doubted; but as little can I doubt, that such Symbols did present themselves to Ezekiel in Visions – and by a Law closely connected with, if not contained in, that by which sensations are organized into Images and mental sounds in our ordinary sleep. (Coleridge, *Marginalia* ii.410 in Burdon 1997: 146; Shaffer 1972: 89)

To focus exclusively either on the detailed analyses of the text of the Apocalypse or on poetic and prophetic actualizations of it would be to ignore important parts of the book's reception history. In the specific commentary which follows, this will be recognized, and the tension among different interpretations maintained.

4   The Reception of the Apocalypse: Survey of Important Interpretations and of Artistic Representations

The early Christian appropriation (Helms 1991 and Daley 1991)

An important part of the reception history of the Apocalypse is its textual history (Aune 1997: cxxxvi–clx; Hoskier 1929; Schmid 1955–6). Much work in this area has been devoted to the search for the original text, a task greatly complicated by the book's peculiar Greek, which is much influenced by Hebrew (Mussies 1971). Later writers tried to deal with difficulties by correcting John's syntax and smoothing out the style. The most famous textual variant, known as early as the end of the second century CE (through Irenaeus), occurs in 13:18, where some early versions read 616 instead of 666. Other significant textual variants include 1:5, where the Authorized Version reads 'and washed us from our sins in his own blood', while most modern translations follow the earliest manuscripts and translate 'freed us from our sins by his blood' (so NRSV). This requires only a small change in the Greek, but leads to a significant difference in understanding of the death of Christ.

Despite the reputation of the Apocalypse as a book designed for martyrs, evidence of its direct influence on the early martyrologies is less than might be expected (Musurillo 1972). The popularity of apocalyptic ideas among groups such as the second-century prophetic movement called Montanism led to a growing suspicion of the book. Apocalypticism, with its urgent eschatological expectation and its critique of worldly power, was a thorn in the flesh of the wielders of ecclesiastical power in the centuries that followed, not least because it was a central component of Christian experience and self-definition from the very start (McGinn 1992). Questions about the book's authorship are not confined to the modern period but go back to the early centuries of the Church, when anti-Montanist polemic led writers like Dionysius of Alexandria to question its apostolic origin. Dionysus even suggested, based on its this-worldly eschatology, that it might have been written by the heretic Cerinthus. In the East the book was not read in the Divine Service, as is still the case in Eastern Orthodoxy (see Averky 1985: 37). Such negative responses to the book are evident in later discussions as well. Luther and Zwingli both questioned the book's apostolic origin (Backus 1998 and 2000; cf. a modern discussion in Massyngberde-Ford 1975). In our own time doubts about the traditional view that the Apocalypse has the same author as the Johannine Gospel are widespread, with the consensus being that it was written not by the apostle John but by an unknown prophet named John who lived in Asia Minor (modern Turkey).

There is, however, evidence of a more positive appropriation of the book by patristic authors. In the struggle with Gnosticism, the Apocalypse's insistence on the materiality of the resurrection and this-worldly eschatology are echoed in Justin (*Dial.* 80), Irenaeus (*AH* v.26.1–36.3) and Hippolytus (*Daniel* 4.23.1–6; Cerrato 2002), all of whom had a chiliastic expectation of the coming of a kingdom of earthly bliss, as described in Rev 20. This view was shared by Victorinus of Poetovio, whose commentary on the Apocalypse, written around the year 260 (Dulaey 1993; Victorinus 1997; Matter in Emmerson and McGinn 1992: 38–40), is the earliest we have (an earlier commentary by Hippolytus has been lost). Victorinus' work was preserved thanks to Jerome, who issued a revised edition of it in 398, in which the chiliastic elements were removed. Variant versions of the commentary have come down to us, some with and some without Jerome's changes (this is reflected in the varying modern editions and translations, to which reference will be made in the bibliographical citations as Victorinus 1916 and 1997, and ANF vii).

A very different interpretation of the Apocalypse was promoted by Tyconius (d.c. 400) and then by Augustine, having been anticipated in part by

Origen in the third century. A pioneering exegete, Origen was the first to explicitly reject the chiliastic interpretation of the Apocalypse. He emphasizes the book's meaning for the present, focusing especially on what it teaches about Christ and about the spiritual life of the believer. Since the key event of redemption has already happened in Christ's incarnation and passion, Christians stand in the last times. What remains is a gradual process of ascent and return to God through an indefinite number of aeons, which is determined by the moral progress of the creature, not by the fall of this or that kingdom (in Monaci 1978: 148–9; cf. Anselmetto 1980; Mazzucco 1980). Tyconius, too, stressed the contemporary more than the eschatological import of the visions (Fredriksen in Emmerson and McGinn 1992: 24–9; Dulaey 1986), as he used the book to interpret the struggles between his persecuted, minority church (the Donatists) and the 'great church'. Although Tyconius' commentary on the Apocalypse is no longer extant, its pervasive influence is evidenced by the many citations in authors such as Bede and Beatus of Liébana (both eighth century; Steinhauser 1987). His ethical/ecclesial reading is combined with a reverent agnosticism about the exact time of the last days. Tyconius claims that a biblical text has a dual perspective, as is appropriate for a Bible with two testaments.[4] So he writes about Rev 21:4:

> This Jerusalem he says is the church, which he [John] sums up (*recapitulat*) from the passion of Christ up to the day in which it rises again and will be crowned unvanquished in glory with Christ. He mixes together two times, now present, now future, and it is more fully declared with how much glory [the church] is taken up by Christ and separated from all attacks of evil. (Quoted in Beatus, *Comm.* 12.2.1)

His hermeneutics of the Apocalypse and his general biblical hermeneutics were closely intertwined. The seven interpretative rules outlined in his *Book of Rules* allow the possibility of multiple reference (Babcock 1989); for example, a reference to Christ may include his 'Body' the Church (see 1 Cor 12:27; Eph 5:23) or vice versa. So, by the principle he calls 'the head and the body', the beast of Rev 13 has a double aspect. It symbolizes the devil but also his 'members', some of whom are in the Church: 'In the beast there are many members: sometimes devils, sometimes wicked priests, sometimes wicked people, sometimes false "religious" (*religiosos*)' (Beatus, *Preface* 5.17). The particular can suggest a general principle. Numbers may have a deeper symbolic significance, and sequential narratives may actually offer repetitions of the

---

[4]   This kind of dialectic is akin to the apocalyptic hermeneutics of Melchior Hoffmann in the sixteenth century; see Deppermann 1987: 242–3 and below, 21.

same event. Such interpretative rules parallel in several key respects *mutatis mutandis* what one finds in the emerging rabbinic rules (*middoth*) attributed to Hillel and Ishmael (Fishbane 1985).

For Tyconius the biblical text is a tool that facilitates moral and spiritual discernment. His hermeneutical method allows him to apply even obviously eschatological passages to the present life of the Church. Present and future are always mingled. Seeing the world as divided into two opposed societies, represented by the Whore of Babylon (Rev 17) and the New Jerusalem (Rev 21), he finds references to them throughout Scripture. The struggle between the demonic and the divine is evident in both the individual and society. Like many other interpreters, Tyconius viewed the final days of the world as a time of tribulation and persecution. It would be similar to what the Donatists were experiencing in Africa in his own days, which prefigured the end. When the time of the Antichrist's revelation finally comes, his true adherents will be revealed. The three and a half days of Rev 11:9 refer to the 350 years that must elapse between Christ and the revelation of the Antichrist (Beatus, *Preface* 5.6).

Tyconius interprets the millennial kingdom of Rev 20 as referring to the time of the Church between the two advents of Christ. Thus Satan has already been bound, and the saints are already enthroned with Christ. All the blessings are already available in the Church (Daley 1991: 127–30). Augustine, who at first followed a millennialist reading, in later years was influenced by Tyconius, for example in his understanding of Rev 20 (Fredriksen in Emmerson and McGinn 1992: 29–35). Through him the Tyconian interpretation influenced many later interpreters. For Augustine the Apocalypse is a source of insight into the present life of the Christian and also the *eschaton* (for further discussion, see below on Rev 20 and 21); but he does not interpret it as giving a blueprint for church history or world history, or as a means of calculating the time of the end. His approach to empire in *The City of God*, where he contrasts the 'city of God' with the 'city of the world' (Van Oort 1991), has much in common with the dualistic and suspicious attitude evident in earlier Christian apocalyptic interpretation.

The Joachite revolution

The Tyconian-Augustinian approach to the Apocalypse dominated interpretation for centuries (Wainwright 1993: 36–44). But the later Middle Ages saw the emergence of another influential reading, by the monastic reformer Joachim of Fiore (c.1135–1202). Joachim saw the Apocalypse as a hermeneutical key to both the entire Scriptures and the whole of history (Daniel in Emmerson and

McGinn 1992; cf. Lee, Reeves and Silano 1989; McGinn 2000: 74–109). He broke decisively with the Augustinian tradition in two ways. First, he opened up new possibilities for readers of the Apocalypse to discern their place in God's saving purposes as set out in Scripture, and, secondly, he saw human history the arena of the fulfilment of God's eschatological purposes. His interpretation reflected an optimistic view of what was happening in his own time and emboldened later groups and individuals to see themselves as participants in the imminent *eschaton*.

There are several threads which run through Joachim's complex hermeneutic. The Old and New Testaments are closely related: everything which happened in the former has its actuality in its own time but is also a sign pointing to a future happening in the new dispensation, which is (or will be) a fuller disclosure of God's purpose for humanity. The book of history is sealed with seven seals and cannot be opened until the Lion of the tribe of Judah opens it (Rev 5). God's purpose remains hidden throughout the seven periods of Old Testament history and can be understood only after the Incarnation ushers in the new age. One part of Scripture serves as a model for interpreting the whole (a principle Joachim calls *concordia*, or 'agreement'). He divides the Apocalypse into eight parts: 1:1–3:22 (letters to the seven churches); 4:1–8:1 (the opening of the seals); 8:2–11:18 (the trumpet blasts); 11:19–14:20 (the two beasts); 15:1–16:17 (the seven bowls); 16:18–19:21 (the destruction of the Babylon); 20:1–10 (the millennium) and 20:11–22:21 (the New Jerusalem). These correspond to the seven periods of the Church, followed by eternity. The seven seals, for example, have two interpretations, one relating to the seven ages of Israel and the other to the periods of the Church.

To Joachim the numbers two, three and seven have apocalyptic significance, and in the various sequences of seven, the sixth assumes great importance. This preoccupation with the penultimate period is characteristic of exegesis in the Joachite tradition: it is the period of the Antichrist which immediately precedes the fulfilment of the final age of the Spirit. Thus the sixth letter, to the angel of the church at Philadelphia (Rev 3:7–13), is a prophecy of the coming sixth age to begin soon after the year 1200, when a pope will be sent to renew the Church. Joachim incorporates these patterns of seven into an overarching trinitarian view of history: the age (*status*) of the old covenant belongs to the Father; the age of the Son began with the New Testament and continues through Joachim's day; and the coming age is that of the Holy Spirit, to be characterized by an outburst of spiritual activity in the form of monastic renewal. That time was imminent. The opening of the sixth seal (Rev 6:12–16) would begin a time of persecution and exile parallel to that experienced by the Jews in Babylon, which would purify the Church. The seventh era, begun by the opening of the seventh seal, would be the era of the Holy Spirit, when seeds sowed long before would come to fruition. The silence in heaven described in Rev 8:1 reflects this sabbath age of history. Thus the Apocalypse offers the key to the reading of the Bible as a whole and to the interpretation of history.

In some ways this interpretation resembles that of earliest Christianity, where the earnest expectation of God's reign on earth dominated Christian hope. How it gives eschatological significance to the present is well exemplified by the most daring of the commentators in the Joachite tradition, Peter Olivi (c.1248–98), who used Joachim extensively in his *Lectura in Apocalypsim* (Burr 1993 and 2001). The book was investigated and condemned by the papacy in 1326, in part because of its enormous popularity, particularly among Beguins and radical Franciscans who sought to keep Francis' rule of poverty literally (Potesta in McGinn 2000: 110; Burr 2001). What is remarkable about Olivi's exegesis is his emphasis on the sixth period, in which he places himself, as the beginning of the time of renewal; he identifies Francis of Assisi as its inaugurator. Immersed in the conflict over poverty which dominated the early history of the Franciscan order, Olivi sees the forces of evil concentrated in a worldly Church, a present, or at least imminent, reality, which he identifies with the Whore of Babylon (Rev 17). Such views contributed to the intense social upheavals of the later Middle Ages, which were fired in part by apocalyptic revivals (Cohn 1957). One example is the prophetic ministry of Girolamo Savonarola (1452–98) in Florence. His visions were combined with practical politics as he instituted a reformation which was to herald the new age, with life in Florence as its harbinger (Weinstein 1970). Unlike the Taborite revolution earlier in the same century and the one in Münster half a century later, this reform was not attended by violence, but it did end tragically for Savonarola (Cohn 1957: 205–22, 252–80).

The Reformation and the early modern period

The Apocalypse did not dominate the interpretative horizons of the principal reformers (Backus 2000). Nevertheless, its importance in the sixteenth century should not be underestimated (Bauckham 1978; Firth 1979; Hill 1990, 1993). Luther initially relegated the book to a subordinate place within the canon of the New Testament, outlining his reasons in words that echo much earlier (and later) assessments in the Christian tradition. He believed that it was neither 'apostolic or prophetic' because 'Christ is not taught or known in it', and 'to teach Christ is the thing which an apostle above all else is bound to do' (*Preface to the New Testament*, 12 (1520), in Backus 2000). In the later editions of his New Testament, from 1530 onwards, he subtly modified his view because he recognized the usefulness of the Apocalypse for anti-Catholic polemic. The pope, he came to believe, was the Antichrist (cf. Rev 13 and 17), a view held also by Calvin (Firth 1979: 13).

Such interpretations proved very useful in the ideological struggle with Rome (Scribner 1994). Protestant interpretations of the Apocalypse in England are pervaded by a sense of the providential nature of their age and of the life-and-death struggle in which the fledgling Protestant realm of England was engaged. This is evident both in the poetry of Edmund Spenser and the more overtly apocalyptic interpretations of John Bale (1495–1563) and Thomas Brightman (1562–1607). Bale offered a refinement of the Augustinian appropriation of the two cities doctrine (Bale (1849): 252), whereas Brightman's use of the Apocalypse (taken up later by Joseph Mede) is very much in the tradition of Joachim of Fiore, as he aims to understand the sequence of the periods of history and the position of the present Tudor state in God's providential ordering (Bauckham 1978; Firth 1979: 32–68, 150–79). Reaction to such application of the Apocalypse to contemporary history is reflected in Roman Catholic commentators like Francisco Ribera (1537–91), Luís de Alcázar (1554–1613) and Robert Bellarmine (1542–1621), who resorted to preterist or futurist interpretations in order to counteract this 'actualizing' method of interpretation (Wainwright 1993: 62–3; Armogathe in McGinn 2000: 190–1), though Bellarmine did claim that the demonic figure who rules over the pit in Rev 9:11 refers to Luther and Lutheranism (in Newport 2000: 69).

A witness to the interpretation of the Apocalypse in the early Calvinist tradition is provided by the notes in the *Geneva Bible*, which explore the relevance of the text for events and threats of the day (London 1578; cf. Hill 1993: 56; Firth 1979: 122). The book's Reformed protestant leanings are everywhere apparent, and it makes clear how the Apocalypse was used in the ecclesiastical struggle of the time. A similar approach is found in the sermons on the Apocalypse by the Swiss reformer Heinrich Bullinger (1504–75, for an example see Bauckham 1978: 298–320). The notes may have been influenced by Bale's writing (Bale 1849: 249–640; Firth 1979: 80 and Bauckham 1978: 45). The notes were supplemented in the 1602 edition by material from the commentary by Francis Junius (Bauckham 1978: 141–6; Daniell 2003: 369–75). As may be expected, Rome is identified with the Antichrist (see comment on Rev 13). The notes contain some distinctive interpretations, for example the locusts of Rev 9:3 are 'worldlie suttil Prelates, with Monkes, freres, cardinals, Patriarkes, Archbishops, Doctors, Bachelors and masters which forsake Christ to maintain false doctrine'.

The *Geneva Bible* sees the Apocalypse as a crucial tool for 'the true kings and priests in Christ' by which may be disclosed 'the wicked deceit' in their midst (on 16:12). It is a call to believers to act in a way appropriate to their election. Given that this hortatory reading of the Apocalypse rejects extremist interpretations, such as those of the radical Reformation groups known as the Anabaptists, it is strange that the Apocalypse has a less favoured position in the lectionary of the Calvinist-influenced *Book of Common Prayer* than the Apocrypha does (Brightman 1915: I.51). The admonitory opening words of the *Geneva Bible*'s comments on the Apocalypse, 'Read diligently; judge soberly and call earnestly to God for the true understanding hereof', may reflect a widespread suspicion of the way the book might be used once it was in the hands of ordinary people, in the vernacular (Backus 2000; Barnes 1988).

Though Thomas Muentzer (c.1485–1525), who was active in the Peasants' Revolt, is the archetypal apocalyptic revolutionary, there is very little appeal to the Apocalypse in his writings. He does use the angel with a sickle of Rev 14:14 to describe his own activity of social purging. He uses other passages, such as the vision of the two witnesses in Rev 11, only to support his sense of vocation, as coming 'in the spirit and power of Elijah'. Muentzer was, however, sympathetic towards dreams and visions as an important means of knowing the ways of God, and he believed that the Holy Spirit could give the elect a clear understanding of their difference from the wicked. The Apocalypse was used extensively in the writings of the Anabaptist sympathizer Melchior Hoffman (c.1500–1534), who influenced the radicals who sought to set up God's millennial kingdom on earth in the city of Münster (Deppermann 1987). He saw the Apocalypse as the key to the understanding of history, whose secrets had been revealed to himself. In approaching Scripture, Hoffman used the principle of 'the cloven claw' – that is, engagement with contradictions in Scripture and its ambiguities – by which Scripture as a whole becomes a kind of apocalypse, a sealed book that can be opened only by someone who is identified with Christ and thus has that special knowledge necessary to understand its true meaning. This emphasis on 'contraries' anticipates the hermeneutics of William Blake (*The Marriage of Heaven and Hell* 4 in Blake 1993: 141–93; and on Hoffman, Deppermann 1987: 242–3).

In the sixteenth century, radical Protestant groups called Anabaptists were known for their emphasis on prophetic inspiration and their challenge to ecclesial polity. An opportunity arose to translate Anabaptist ideals into political reality in the establishment of the 'New Jerusalem' in Münster, Germany (Cohn 1957; G. H. Williams 1962; Stayer 1972). Taken over initially by conventional means, Münster became a magnet for Anabaptist sympathizers, who established an eschatological commonwealth with an explicit apocalyptic colouring, from which Catholics and Lutherans who refused rebaptism were expelled (Wainwright 1993: 91–2). Some of the leaders' actions were marked by capricious ruthlessness, justified through a claim to ultimate authority bestowed by apocalyptic experience. Nowhere is this better exemplified than in the conviction that led one of the leaders, Jan Matthijs, to become literally a lamb led to the slaughter (cf. Rev 5) as he went out to defeat the surrounding armies of the bishop, only to be slaughtered before the eyes of the horrified Münsterites. The experiment ended in a chaotic and enthusiastic messianism and an orgy of antinomianism, which was violently suppressed, becoming a paradigm of reformation which friends and foes alike viewed with horror. Münster is an unusual example of the use of the Apocalypse in the practice of a millenarian politics (compare the more recent example of the Branch Davidian community at Waco), which did not remain at the level of utopian idealism but led to violent attempts to establish an eschatological theocracy (Walzer 1985: 120). In the wake of the catastrophic defeat at Münster, a less activist form of Anabaptism emerged, with Menno Simons laying the foundations for an Anabaptism more suspicious of apocalypticism (Klassen 1992).

Parallel to that of the Anabaptists in some ways is the use of the Apocalypse in the radical politics of the period of the English Civil War in the seventeenth century (Hill 1972, 1993; Firth 1979: 242). This is best exemplified in the social radical Gerrard Winstanley (1609–76) who, with others called 'Diggers', asserted the common ownership of the land, on the basis of a belief that the earth was a common treasury (Sabine edn 190–7, 230–6). Here the rule of the Beast (Rev 13) is seen not as an eschatological reality but as something evident in the political arrangements of the day. Professional ministry, royal power, the judiciary, and the buying and selling of the earth correspond to the four beasts in the book of Daniel (Sabine edn 251–8; Bradstock 1997; Rowland 1988: 102–14). An echo of this radical appropriation of the Apocalypse was to permeate English religion through an individualistic, spiritual reading of the apocalyptic narrative, evident, for example, in Bunyan's *Pilgrim's Progress*, written when the revolutionary politics of the mid-seventeenth century were on the wane and the hope of the establishment of a commonwealth of the saints on earth had receded (Hill 1989). In early North American exegesis we find an apocalyptic tradition that focuses particularly on the expectation of the coming earthly kingdom of Christ, after the four great empires of the world (R. Bloch 1985: 9–11, 7–1; Smolinski in Stein 2000: 36–71).

In the seventeenth century, alongside the use of the Apocalypse in radical religion, there was detailed exposition of the book, carried out in a more measured and less heated atmosphere, which was to encourage a long tradition of apocalyptic speculation. The most important representative was Joseph Mede (1586–1638), a fellow of Christ's College, Cambridge, whose work had enormous influence on subsequent generations (Firth 1979: 240; Elliott 1851: 487–95). Mede saw in the book a series of 'synchronisms' or recapitulations, with several passages relating to the same period of history. He calculated a period of 1,260 years from the rise of the papacy (dated to 365) to its overthrow some time in the seventeenth century (Firth 1979: 221). Mede's *Clavis Apocalyptica* (*The Key of Revelation*) is divided into two parts; the first, more important part provides the hermeneutical key based on synchronisms, and the second gives an example of how to apply it. Many in the seventeenth century thought Mede's own application of his method pointed to imminent fulfilment within a generation or two (though Mede himself was always extremely guarded about this).

Mede's emphasis on 'synchronisms' anticipates interpretative approaches that have had wide currency in modern scholarship, and it also resembles to some extent the recapitulative method of earlier interpreters such as Victorinus and Joachim of Fiore. His work was frequently quoted in subsequent centuries. Similar in approach (and explicitly indebted to Mede's work) are the writings on the Apocalypse by the Cambridge mathematician Isaac Newton (1642–1727). They are detailed and exhaustive attempts to demonstrate divine providence, what Mede called the marvellous orderliness in the history of Church and world, epitomized in the books of Daniel and Revelation and paralleled in the physical world (Burdon 1997: 37–51; Tannenbaum 1982).

William Blake and his contemporaries

As already mentioned, the Apocalypse has also been read in existential terms, with its conflicts related to the spiritual life of the individual. This interpretation is evident among Romantic poets (Abrams 1973: 47; Butler 1981), although the tendency to see in the book an account of universal history, with references to contemporary events, had a new lease on life at the time of the French Revolution (Burdon 1997). Throughout his life the poet Samuel Taylor Coleridge (1772–1834) retained a fascination for the Apocalypse (Shaffer 1972). Like his contemporary Joseph Priestley, he saw its prophecy fulfilled in the French Revolution. He also recognized the biblical prophecies and visions as effusions of kindred, poetic spirits, a view shared by William Blake (1757–1827; Erdman 1977; Mee 1992; Burdon 1997) and by the German poets Herder (1744–1803) and Hölderlin (1770–1843; Shaffer 1972: 145–90). These poets sought to re-create the prophetic inspiration in their own poetry. William Blake, for example, is one of the most biblically based poets, seeing himself as a prophet, even though his writings are often only loosely related to the Bible. Although they contain numerous verbal allusions to the Apocalypse, there is rarely any explicit attempt to interpret it. Instead, we see in Blake's own poetry and illustrations an expression of the apocalyptic spirit which inspired the biblical writers, with biblical images woven into the fabric of his poetry.

Recent study indicates that Blake was part of a prophetic movement in late eighteenth-century England, of which Richard Brothers (1757–1824) and Joanna Southcott (1750–1814) are the best examples (Mee 1992; Hopkins 1982; Brown 2002; Harrison 1979). We find also in the work of Robert Browning (1812–89), particularly his long poem *Sordello*, the kind of prophetic challenge which is stated more explicitly in Blake's apocalyptic prophecies (Woolford and Karlin 1996). Blake stands in a long tradition of Apocalypse interpretation in which text and illuminations are juxtaposed, as for example in medieval manuscripts of the commentary by Beatus of Liébana. Although Blake does not illustrate the biblical text itself, he seeks to reproduce the experience of apocalypse in the pictures and writing of his illuminated books (Blake 1991–5). In twentieth-century poetry and fiction, the indirect effect of an apocalyptic ethos has been emphasized by a succession of literary critics (Kermode 1999; Bethea 1989).

Deciphering the Apocalypse: the eschatological synthesis of modern fundamentalism

The interpretation of the Apocalypse as a repository of prophecies concerning the future has existed from the beginning of the exegesis of the book, reaching a high point in the influential interpretation of Joseph Mede. The last 200 years have seen a growing trend toward eschatological interpretation. What distinguishes this modern interpretation from Mede's is that it sees the Apocalypse as one piece of a larger biblical jigsaw, the whole of which provides resources for constructing the exact sequence of events in the last days. John Nelson Darby (1800–82), Anglican clergyman and leader of the Plymouth Brethren, interpreted the book as unfulfilled prophecy, a reading followed by the widely influential *Scofield Reference Bible*, first published in 1909. Also in this tradition is the best-selling popular book by Hal Lindsey, *The Late Great Planet Earth* (1970: 117–19, 173–4), which reflects the peculiar fears of the late twentieth century. Here the decline in religious and moral life, castigated in the Laodicean letter (Rev 3:14–22), is understood to refer to the twentieth century and viewed as a sign that the end is near.

Such interpretation, in which eschatological passages from different parts of the Bible (e.g. Daniel and Revelation) are woven together, encourages confidence that the elect will enjoy a miraculous rescue through the 'rapture', Christ's return to take the elect to himself (the idea is based on 1 Thess 4:17 and Luke 17:34; Mojtabai 1987: 146–60, 178–82; Boyer 1992 and in McGinn 2000: 140–78). The Apocalypse is seen to contain prophecies of contemporary institutions (e.g. the United Nations, the European Union; and in Adventist interpretation the USA is identified with the second beast of Rev 13). Part of the eschatological scenario is the final conversion of Jews to Christ, a mixture of eschatological hope and practical politics that is at least as old as Oliver Cromwell, who in the 1650s allowed the Jews back into England because he saw their return as part of the eschatological events dawning in his day (Newport 2000; Numbers and Butler 1987).

Loosely related to the interpretation of the *Scofield Reference Bible* are the ten novels in the 'Left Behind' series by Tim LaHaye and Jerry Jenkins (1995–2002, with four more planned; 'left behind' refers to people left behind on earth after the true believers have been suddenly snatched up in the rapture). The novels have been enormously popular in North America, with 35 million copies sold in seven years. They portray the Antichrist appearing as a political leader, promising peace and prosperity. He takes over the United Nations and establishes a totalitarian world empire based in Iraq, the new Babylon. During the seven-year period of the tribulation, which follows the rapture, people can still become Christians, but they must endure the terrors of the end-time portrayed in the seals, trumpets and bowls of Rev 6–9 and 15. The novels depict a group of newly converted believers, called the 'Tribulation Force', as they deal with a world in turmoil and prepare for the last battle against the Antichrist (Rev 16:16). Many of their adventures are based on specific parts of the Apocalypse: for example, in the first volume, *Left Behind*, the conversion of a member of the Tribulation Force begins when he reads the promise of Jesus' second coming in Rev 22:20 (p. 122), and volume 9, *The Desecration*, begins with a reference to the seven bowls of wrath of Rev 16:1–2 (p. xiii).

Historical interpretations that relate the Apocalypse to its ancient context

Since the Enlightenment, the rise of historical scholarship has led to a perspective on the Apocalypse that focuses more on past meaning than on present use, emphasizing detailed textual analysis and comparison with other ancient sources. Current scholars follow early modern interpreters like Hugo Grotius (1583–1645), who argued that the book's meaning was almost entirely related to the circumstances of John's own day (cf. the Roman Catholic preterist interpreters discussed above). Historical study attends to issues such as the reasons why John was on Patmos, the extent to which his visions presuppose persecution of Christians, whether Domitian's or Nero's reign is the setting, and how to evaluate the earliest external testimony (W. Bousset 1896; Swete 1906; Charles 1910, 1920; Farrer 1949, 1964; Caird 1966; Massyngberde-Ford, 1975; A. Y. Collins 1976, 1979, 1984, 1996; Court 1979; Sweet 1979; Rowland 1982, 1993, 1998; L. Thompson 1990; Bauckham 1993a, 1993b; Roloff 1993; Schüssler Fiorenza 1993, 1999; Aune 1997, 1998a, 1998b; Murphy 1998; Beale 1999; Barker 2000; Boxall 2002). Studies of social and economic conditions in first-century Asia Minor (Ramsay 1904; Hemer 1986) and comparison with other early Christian sources for that region (Lieu 1997; Trebilco 1991) have illuminated the general background of the text.

Perhaps the most distinctive contribution of modern historical study has been source-critical study. The recognition of inconsistencies led Grotius to think that the book was written at different times in John's life, a view that has undergone many variations. In the twentieth century R. H. Charles, doyen of source critics of apocalyptic texts, is the most important proponent of this approach (Charles 1910, 1920; see the latest and most comprehensive treatment of the modern scholarship on the Apocalypse, including source criticism, in Aune 1997). This approach may be contrasted with the evaluation of disjunctions and inconsistencies by eighteenth-century writers like Lowth (1753) and Bengel (1740/1857), who see them as typical features of prophetic books (Burdon 1997: 51, 76).

In the last few decades of the twentieth century, biblical exegetes began to use the social sciences, especially in the study of Paul and the gospels. Sociological study has had some influence on study of the Apocalypse (Thrupp 1970; Malina and Pilch 2000), though less than one might have expected, particularly since the rise of sectarianism and its ideology has been a major concern of the emerging discipline of sociology of religion (Esler 1995). A sectarian origin has often been posited for the Apocalypse and similar texts which see the world in terms of stark contrasts (Hanson 1974; Cook 1995; J. J. Collins in J. J. Collins 2000: 129–62). The book has been viewed as a myth for an oppressed community, which found itself confronted with the 'dissonance' between its beliefs and the socio-political realities of a militant Roman Empire, a means by which the reader could overcome the contradiction between the present, with its threat of persecution, and the hoped-for life of bliss. The connection with millenarian movements is discussed by Norman Cohn (1957), who also explores the social psychology of a dualistic mind-set. A social-psychological perspective is evident also in the work of Adela Collins, who discusses reading as a way of dealing with aggression, bringing about catharsis and displacement of difficult emotion (A. Y. Collins 1984). To some extent she follows in the footsteps of C. G. Jung, who juxtaposed the gospel and the Apocalypse as examples of different and unresolved aspects of the human personality (Jung 1984).

The influence of the Apocalypse in twentieth-century theology and philosophy (Bull 1995)

The emphasis on the influence of Jewish eschatological ideas on New Testament texts in the works of Weiss (1971, originally published in 1892) and Schweitzer (1961, first published in 1913) was to spill over in dramatic form into post-First World War theology in Karl Barth's commentary on Romans (first edition Barth 1919; cf. McCormack 1995; Gorringe 1999). For Barth, eschatology is central; but by this he means not so much the imminent expectation of God's reign in the world as the critical 'revelation' breaking in upon humanity. That which comes from beyond demands an attitude to the data of God's revelation which differs from the human hubris prevalent since the Enlightenment. Bringing about the ultimate crisis, it demands of a chastened humanity a reception in humility. Barth's theology offered a stark alternative to the world of destruction and devastation of 1918, and the compromises that contributed to it, which provoked an acute pessimism about humanity's resources to build a better world. Following the ancient apocalypses, Barth repudiated human attempts to comprehend God (natural theology). Divine revelation, an 'unveiling' or apocalypse, is the only basis for understanding anything about God (1958: 28).

Contemporary with Barth and equally committed to the eschatological inheritance of the Jewish tradition, but with a very different assessment of it, is the Marxist philosopher Ernst Bloch. Rehabilitating the perspectives of Joachim of Fiore, Thomas Muentzer and Gerrard Winstanley, Bloch aimed to rehabilitate that millenarian, apocalyptic/utopian inheritance on the fringes of orthodox Christianity. His mammoth book *The Principle of Hope* (E. Bloch 1986; Hudson 1982) explores how longing for a future age of perfection has coloured the whole range of culture in both East and West and contributed to Marxism as well as to the Judaeo-Christian tradition (though Bloch's views are tangential to the mainstream Marxist tradition and have been received with considerable skepticism by other Marxists; see Kolakowski 1978).

Bloch's work is echoed in a more attenuated form in the later writing of Theodor Adorno (1974; cf. Wiggerhaus 1994) and Walter Benjamin (1970). Adorno exhibits a pessimistic messianism, in which the present inadequacies are to be viewed 'in the messianic light' (Adorno 1974: 247). One of Benjamin's final works, 'Theses on the Philosophy of History' (written in 1940), though not an apocalypse in the sense of a vision or an audition, is an exercise in apocalyptic hermeneutics. It exemplifies the countercultural, non-conformist perspective of apocalypticism in the context of a disenchanted and pessimistic world. The work is full of a prophetic foreboding about the death and destruction perpetrated by evil in the name of civilization:

> This is how one pictures the angel of history. His face is turned towards the past. Where we perceive a chain of events, he sees one single catastrophe which keeps piling wreckage upon wreckage and hurls it in front of his feet. The angel would like to stay, awaken the dead, and make whole what has been smashed. But a storm is blowing from Paradise; it has got caught in his wings with such violence that the angel can no longer close them. This storm irresistibly propels him into the future to which his back is turned, while the pile of debris before him grows skyward. This storm is what we call progress. (Thesis VII, Benjamin 1970: 249)

Both of these philosophers were close friends of Gershom Scholem, the great pioneer of modern study of Jewish apocalypticism and mysticism (Biale 1982), who called attention to neglected aspects of the eschatological tradition and of its political potential. In the light of Bloch's work it is not surprising that some Christians and Marxists influenced by this utopian tradition have been united in a quest for a new social order in this world, based on peace and justice. Like those of Benjamin and Adorno, however, such efforts display a decidedly pessimistic tone, in that they consider social and political upheaval as the necessary prelude to significant change (McLellan 1987). A different interpretation is given by theologian Dietrich Bonhoeffer, writing in the 1930s. In a warning against a selective reading of biblical texts, he appeals to the Apocalypse in his challenge to the Church to be an advocate for the oppressed minority, the Jews, summoning it to be 'a community which hears the Apocalypse' (Bonhoeffer 1965: 324).

Modern liberationist interpretation

There is much evidence of the power the Apocalypse has among the grass-roots groups influenced by late twentieth-century liberation theology. Exponents of liberation theology look for the fulfilment of God's purposes in history and facilitate the use of the Bible to interpret contemporary social and political realities and to foster change that benefits the poor and the marginalized (Rowland 1999). Read from this perspective, the Apocalypse, which refuses to accept that the dominant powers are the ultimate point of reference, offers hope but also stimulates resistance. Apocalyptic discourse, which consists of picture and symbol as well as words, asks the reader to participate in another way of speaking about God and world, a way more readily understood by those whose approach is not primarily through the rationality of the academy. It taps wells of human response in those whose experience of struggle, persecution and death have taught them what it means to wash their robes and make them white in the blood of the Lamb (Rev 7:14). Allan Boesak, a Reformed minister active in the anti-apartheid struggle in South Africa, found in the Apocalypse a message of comfort and a resource for protest. While John writes about the political situation in first-century Asia Minor and how the Church should respond to it, his book is also prophecy that does not receive its full and final fulfilment in one given historical moment. What was true in the time of John is proved to be true over and over again in history, and this is why the Apocalypse continues to be relevant. The Apocalypse meant God's final judgement on the corrupt political and religious systems of oppression (Boesak 1987: 29). The liberationist perspective is also apparent in the marginal notes of the *Bíblia Sagrada* published in Brazil (1990; cf. Mesters and Orofino 2002), whose introduction explicitly promotes the relationship between text and 'our reality', which is qualified by the communal context of reading (Mesters 1993: 3–16 and 1989).

Two other interpreters ought to be mentioned in this context: Jacques Ellul (1977) and William Stringfellow (1973 and 1977). In works that are marginal to the mainstream of modern biblical exegesis, they show how the Bible, and particularly the book of Revelation, challenges ideology by its unmasking of the principalities and powers (see also the trilogy on the principalities and powers by Wink: 1984, 1986, 1993).

The Apocalypse in liturgy and biblical lectionaries

From medieval times, the triple Sanctus of 4:8 (cf. Isa 6:3) has been an essential part of the eucharistic liturgy, and occasional liturgical use is made of other parts of the book. For example, Rev 21 figures in medieval liturgies for the dedication of Churches (see below, 236). Compared with other New Testament books, the Apocalypse does not feature prominently in Christian lectionaries, lists of biblical texts chosen for public reading on Sundays and feast-days. In Eastern Orthodox Churches the book is not read in the Divine Service (Averky 1985: 37). In the West, however, texts from the Apocalypse are appointed for several holy days and for several Sundays following Easter. In the Roman Catholic Breviary, the whole of the book of Revelation is read as part of the Office of Readings for weeks two to five of Eastertide (The Divine Office 1974: ii: 506–601). Four canticles, so-called, from Revelation are also used in the Roman Catholic Divine Office: Rev 4:11; 5:9, 10, 12 in Evening Prayer on Tuesdays and also in the Common of Several Martyrs and the Common of One Martyr; Rev 11:17–18; 12:10b–12a for Evening Prayer on Thursdays and Evening Prayer I and II of the Ascension; Rev 15:3–4 for Evening Prayer on Fridays and for Evening Prayer I of Pentecost, Evening Prayer II of the Common for the Dedication of a Church (except during the Easter season), and for the Common of Men Saints; Rev 19:1, 2, 5–7 for Evening Prayer II on Sundays (including Easter and Pentecost), and Evening Prayer I and II (during the Easter season) for the Common for the Dedication of a Church.

The lectionary in *The Book of Common Prayer According to the Use of the Episcopal Church* 1977 appoints Rev 12:7–12 for St Michael and All Angels (29 Sept.), Rev 7:2–4, 9–17 for All Saints' Day (1 Nov.) and Rev. 21:1–7 for Holy Innocents (28 Dec.). The medieval feast of Holy Innocents also featured a reading from the Apocalypse alongside the gospel reading from Matt 2:16–18, but the text was from Rev 14, not 21 (Flanigan in Emmerson and McGinn 1992: 334–7). The reading from Rev 7 for All Saints' Day can be traced back to medieval times (Flanigan in Emmerson and McGinn 1992: 334–5) and is continued in the Roman Catholic Church today. In the North American *Revised Common Lectionary* 1992, formulated by representatives of 25 Protestant denominations, this text is read on All Saints' Day in the first year of a three-year cycle, while Rev 21:1–6a is read in the second year. This common lectionary also appoints Rev 21:1–6a, with its promise of a 'new heaven and a new earth', for reading on New Year's Day of every year. The Roman Catholic *Lectionary for Mass for Use in the Dioceses of the United States* 1998 contains one additional reading from the Apocalyse: Rev 11:19a; 12:1–6a, 10ab, for the feast of the Assumption of the Blessed Virgin Mary (15 Aug.).

For regular Sunday services, the *Revised Common Lectionary* 1992 suggests the following texts for the second through seventh Sundays after Easter in the third year of a three-year cycle: Rev 1:4–8; 5:11–14; 7:9–17; 21:1–6; 21:10, 22–22:5, 22:12–14, 16–17, 20–1. The Roman Catholic lectionary (1998) and the Episcopal *Book of Common Prayer* (1977) have virtually the same readings for these Sundays. One exception is that both include an additional reading from the Apocalypse, appointing Rev 1:9–19 (or 1:1–19) for the second Sunday after Easter; in these Churches Rev 1:4–8 is read in the second year of the three-year cycle, on the last Sunday of the Church year. Another divergence is that the Episcopal Church appoints Rev 19:1, 4–9, not Rev 21:1–6, for the sixth Sunday after Easter.

In the Church of England's *Book of Common Prayer* the Apocalypse is appointed for reading at Morning and Evening Prayer in November and December, but several chapters are omitted, including chapters 9, 13 and 17 (Brightman 1915: i.51). In the *Alternative Service Book* of 1980 the following passages are prescribed for the Sunday Eucharist over the two-year cycle: Rev 4; 21:1–7; 21:22–2:5; 1:10–18; 19:6–9; 3:14–end; 7:2–4, 9–end. In addition, the following passages are prescribed for holy days and other festivals: 21:1–7; 12:7–12; 7:2–4, 9–end; 14:14–end.

The Apocalypse in music

The heavenly hymns of praise in the Apocalypse have been a resource for musicians and hymn writers down the centuries. Best known are perhaps two choruses from Handel's *Messiah* (1742, libretto by Charles Jennens): 'Worthy is the Lamb that was slain' (Rev 5:12) and the 'Hallelujah Chorus' (Rev 19:6; 11:15; 19:16). Isolated verses from the Apocalypse have been given musical settings, partly because of their use in the liturgy (Flanigan in Emmerson and McGinn 1992: 333–51). The sixteenth-century English composition by Thomas Weelkes, 'I heard a voice from heaven!' (see Rev 19:1) is just one example of a setting in which a text is given a new interpretation as the awesome context of the destruction of Babylon is left behind. The papal approval of the feast of the Immaculate Conception in 1476 led to the composition of votive antiphons based on Rev 12:1, a text long associated with Mary (Stratton 1994; Pesce 1997: 311–12; Blackburn 1999). Two passages from the Apocalypse (4:11 and 14:13) conclude Brahms' *German Requiem* (1867), which is based on a collection of scriptural texts.

The vision of the angel proclaiming 'There will be no more delay' in Rev 10:6 is the inspiration for Olivier Messiaen's *Quartet for the End of Time*, written in 1940 while he was a prisoner of war. Contemporary is Karl Weigl's Fifth Symphony ('The Apocalyptic'), written in 1945 in memory of F. D. Roosevelt and composed in exile from the Nazi terror in the 1930s. The final movement, entitled 'The Four Horsemen', complements an earlier movement inspired by the Golden Calf story in Ex 32.

The only setting of the whole Apocalypse is Franz Schmidt's oratorio *The Book with Seven Seals*, first performed in Vienna in 1938. Schmidt describes the breaking of the first seal as the proclamation of the Christian message which is followed by chaos, reflecting a pattern of interpretation that goes back at least to Victorinus (Schmidt 1938, and see below on Rev 6). Even this work represents a selective choice of texts. Significant omissions, in light of their political component and the time in which the oratorio was written, are chapters 13 and 17. Schmidt acknowledges that he has omitted the negative pole in the Babylon/Jerusalem contrast in order to bring out the importance of the positive image of Jerusalem and the triumph of good over evil.

William Walton's roughly contemporary *Belshazzar's Feast* (1931), whose libretto by Osbert Sitwell is indebted to Rev 18, foretells the imminent destruction of Babylon. Using the musical styles of the marginalized (such as jazz),

Walton evokes the shifts of the text between the sadness of the elites that 'that great city' has been destroyed (Rev 18:22–3) and paeans of praise that express raw delight: 'Babylon the great is fallen. Hallelujah!' (Rev 18:2; 19:1; a point also brought out in Boesak 1987: 121–2).

Hymns inspired by the Apocalypse include 'O what their joy and their glory must be', based on a text by the medieval theologian Peter Abelard, and 'Lift your heads, ye friends of Jesus' by Charles Wesley. Images from Revelation are particularly prominent in African-American spirituals, especially in relation to two themes: (1) images from the plague sequences used to describe the dramatic end of life's trials at the time of the Last Judgement; (2) images of the New Jerusalem (chs 21–2) with its 'golden streets' and the 'tree of life', in descriptions of the heavenly joys that await the believer at the end of the earthly pilgrimage. Also frequently mentioned are the suffering Lamb (ch. 5), the white robes (6:11; 7:9, 13–14) and the 'book of life' (20:12).

Artistic representations of the Apocalypse

Over the centuries the Apocalypse has had particular appeal for artists. Artistic interpretation includes the iconography of ecclesiastical architecture, illuminations and woodcuts that accompany the text, and painted panels and drawings of individual themes. There are cycles of scenes from the Apocalypse in church murals, stained glass, vault carvings and tapestries (Schiller 1990, 1991; James 1931; Kirschbaum 1968; Emmerson and McGinn 1992; Rowland 1993; Wright 1996; Boxall 2002; for plates see also Van der Meer 1978 and Grubb 1997). Among the most prominent motifs (see discussions in the relevant chapters below) are John on Patmos (Rev 1), the visions of the heavenly thrones of God and the Lamb (Rev 4–5), the four horsemen (Rev 6), the beast from the abyss attacking the two witnesses (Rev 11), the Woman Clothed with the Sun and Michael battling the dragon (Rev 12), the Last Judgement (Rev 20) and the New Jerusalem (Rev 21–2).

In early Christian art individual motifs from the Apocalypse begin to appear after the official recognition of Christianity by Constantine and the formulation of the Nicene Creed in 325 (Kinney 1992: 201–2). Themes such as the 'heavenly liturgy', with the majestic Christ on the throne, the four living creatures, the 24 elders and the book with seven seals (Rev 4–5), and the Lamb on Mount Zion (Rev 7 and 14) serve to glorify Christ and celebrate the victory of Christianity (Schiller 1990: 116). These motifs, along with the New Jerusalem of Rev 21–2, are featured in the triumphal arches and apses of Churches, especially in fifth- to ninth-century Roman churches such as Saint Paul Outside the Walls, Saints Cosmas and Damian and Saint Prassede, and in San Vitale in

Ravenna (Schiller 1990: 116–17; Van der Meer 1978: 32, 54, 57–8, 62). They also figured on the facade of old Saint Peter's (Kinney 1992: 204). The motif that appears most frequently, in a great variety of media, consists of the Greek letters Alpha and Omega, used to describe Christ in Rev 1:8, 17, and 21:6 (Kinney 1992: 201–2; Van der Meer 1978: 33–4). Notably absent in early Christian art are representations of the plague sequences (Rev 6–9; 15–16).

It is a matter of debate at what point artists began composing connected cycles of illustrations (Schiller 1990: 117; Kinney 1992: 201), but considerable evidence of this tradition survives in lavishly illustrated Apocalypse manuscripts from the ninth to the fourteenth centuries (see articles by Williams, Klein and Lewis in Emmerson and McGinn 1992). In the ninth century the Apocalypse began to be produced as a separate book, an honor shared only by the four gospels and the Psalms. This development was influenced by commentaries on the book written in the eighth and ninth centuries, and perhaps also by the introduction of readings from the Apocalypse into the liturgy in certain locales (Schiller 1990: 118). The earliest such surviving manuscript, the Trier Apocalypse, produced near Tours, France, around the year 800, has a cycle of 74 full-page illustrations (Trier, Staatsbibliothek, MS 31; Schiller 1990: 142–4; Van der Meer 1978: 92–100). In comparison with the surviving early Christian depictions, we find here more emphasis on demonic powers and on scenes of judgement (e.g. Rev 14:14–20 and 20:11–15). The present import of the book is expressed by the addition of contemporary figures as witnesses to scenes from the text. The Cambrai Apocalypse (Bibl. Munic. MS 386) is a copy of the Trier manuscript, made at the beginning of the tenth century (Schiller 1990: 144).

While many Apocalypse manuscripts were commissioned by monasteries, the genre also appealed to royal patrons, who followed early Christian emperors in seeing their own rule as a reflection of the world rule of Christ (Schiller 1990: 147). One early example is the splendid Bamberg Apocalypse (Bamberg, Stadtsbibliothek MS Bibl. 140), which was probably commissioned by the German emperor Otto III around the year 1,000 (Schiller 1990: 147–9; Mayr-Harting 1991). Its 50 illustrations are notable for their expressiveness and their depiction of violent action. Coiling beasts inspire terror, while wide-eyed human figures express their horror or adoration as the events of the book unfold (Van der Meer 1978: 102–7).

A special place in the manuscript tradition is occupied by Spanish manuscripts of the tenth through the thirteenth centuries which illustrate the commentary on the Apocalypse composed in 776 by the monk Beatus of Liébana (J. Williams 1994 and in Emmerson and McGinn 1992: 217–33; Schiller 1990: 119–35; Van der Meer 1978: 109–27). The illustrations in these manuscripts, which reflect Beatus' commentary as well as the biblical text, are characterized by bands of vivid colours and lively depictions of fantastic animals. Beatus, writing in Christian northern Spain at a time when most of the country was occupied by Muslims, draws heavily on such earlier sources as Tyconius and Victorinus. His interpretation emphasizes ecclesiology and christology, reflecting a particular concern to combat the adoptionist christology of followers of Bishop Eliphandus of Toledo (Matter in Emmerson and McGinn 1992: 45–6). The popularity of the Apocalypse in Spain can be traced back to the seventh century, when the book's exaltation of Jesus as God and as a world ruler was useful in the battle against Arianism. In 633 the Council of Toledo mandated preaching from the Apocalypse in the period between Easter and Pentecost and threatened with excommunication anyone who did not regard it as authoritative (Schiller 1990: 120–1).

Particular Beatus manuscripts to which reference will be made in subsequent chapters of this commentary include the Morgan (c.940–5), Girona (975), Madrid/Facundus (1047) and Osma (1086) Apocalypses (for a list of all the extant manuscripts, see J. Williams 1994: 1:10–11; Schiller 1990: 131–5). The Morgan Apocalypse (MS 644 in the Pierpont Morgan Library in New York) includes a personal note from the scribe and painter, a certain Maius, which gives a sense of how and why monastic leaders commissioned such manuscripts:

> Let the voice of the faithful resound, and re-echo! Let Maius, small indeed, but eager, rejoice, sing, re-echo and cry out!
>
> Remember me, servants of Christ, you who dwell in the monastery of the supreme messenger, the Archangel Michael.
>
> I write this in awe of the exalted patron, at the command of Abbot Victor, out of love for the book of the vision of John the beloved disciple.
>
> As part of its adornment I have painted a series of pictures for the wonderful words of its stories, so that the wise may fear the coming of the future judgment of the world's end. . . .
>
> Be glory to the Father and to his only Son, to the Holy Spirit and the Trinity from age to age to the end of time. (J. Williams 1991: 12)

One innovation in this manuscript is the addition at the beginning of pictures of the four Evangelists, which serves to claim for the Apocalypse the same authority enjoyed by the gospels (Schiller 1990: 125; J. Williams 1991: 167–8, fols 1v–4).

Another tradition of manuscript illustration, the Anglo-French, began around the year 1250 in England and continued through the fifteenth century, spreading to other countries, especially France (Schiller 1990: 242–3; Klein

1992: 188–92). An outstanding early example is the Trinity Apocalypse (Trinity College, Cambridge) dated to 1250–60 (Schiller 1990: 261–2; Van der Meer 1978: 152–70), which is known for its rich colours, use of gold leaf, and lively, graceful drawing. The luxuriousness of this manuscript suggests that it had a royal patron, often thought to be Eleanor, wife of King Henry III of England. Royal and noble figures, especially noble ladies, figure prominently in the illustrations: for example, in the miniature for Rev 13 a noble lady, perhaps Queen Eleanor herself, bravely wields a sword against the seven-headed beast (fol. 14v; Van der Meer 1978: 156). Elsewhere we see the founders of new monastic orders, Saints Francis and Dominic (fol. 28; Van der Meer 1978: 152). The Apocalypse is framed on either end by numerous scenes derived from apocryphal accounts of the life of the apostle John, which has the effect of locating the exile during which John receives the book's visions within the context of the rest of his life. The seer also appears in the margins of the framed scenes from the Apocalypse, a device that underlines their visionary character and links the book's spiritual vision to the experience of exile (S. Lewis 1995: 31–3).

Of the many other manuscripts in this Anglo-French tradition, which exhibit a common style and a similar selection of scenes, two other notable examples are Douce 180, commissioned by Eleanor's son Edward I (late thirteenth century, now in the Bodleian Library in Oxford) and the Cloisters Apocalypse (c.1320–30), one of the treasures of the Cloisters Museum in New York, whose illustrations of the plague sequences are particularly vivid (Deuschler, Hoffeld and Nickel 1971). Other manuscripts in this tradition served as models for the tapestries of Angers, France, created c.1375–83 (Schiller 1990: 268–71; Van der Meer 1978: 176–87). A later exemplar (c.1400–25) is the Flemish Apocalypse in the Bibliothèque Nationale in Paris (BN néerl. 3; Van der Meer 1978: 202–35; Schiller 1990: 314–18), the first illustrated Apocalypse from the Low Countries. Here scenes that are portrayed separately in other manuscripts are combined into 23 complex illustrations, one for each chapter of Revelation, plus an introductory page with scenes from the life of John. Also in this tradition, but with the addition of numerous innovative scenes, including a number from the life of the Antichrist, is the Wellcome Apocalypse, part of a larger work produced in Germany around 1425–50 (Schiller 1990: 319–22).

A very different kind of artistic representation is found in the *Book of Figures* of Joachim of Fiore, which contains 16 diagrams apparently drawn under Joachim's direction and collected after his death in 1202 (Joachim of Fiore 1953 [facsimile edition, ed. Tondelli, Reeves and Hirsch-Reich]; cf. plates in Reeves and Hirsch-Reich 1972; McGinn 1979: 103–11; Schiller 1990: 168–71). These detailed drawings, which incorporate explanatory words of Joachim, do not illustrate specific scenes of the Apocalypse but instead express in symbolic pictures the essence of the Calabrian abbot's views on history and eschatology.

The influence of the Apocalypse on ecclesiological architecture, evident as early as the fifth century, continues in the cathedrals, churches and monasteries of the Romanesque and Gothic periods, where images from the book appear in portals, carved capitals, vault bosses, stained-glass windows, wall-paintings, altar-pieces and other decorations (Christe in Emmerson and McGinn 1992: 234–58). Examples include the large east window in York Minster, England (1405–8), the west rose window in Sainte Chapelle, Paris (1485), capitals in the cloister in Moissac in southern France (c.1110; Schiller 1990: 64–6), bosses in the vaults of the cloister in Norwich Cathedral in England (c.1500), and Signorelli's frescoes in the cathedral at Orvieto in Italy (1499–1504). Earlier examples of frescoes, painted by Cimabue and by a follower of Giotto (c.1240), are found in the basilica of Saint Francis in Assisi (Schiller 1990: 272–85). These are interesting not only for their artistic quality but also because they reflect the apocalyptic self-understanding of the new Franciscan movement (see the discussion of Rev 7:1–3 and 8:1–2 below).

Church doorways often feature imagery taken from Rev 4–5, especially the 24 elders and the four living creatures surrounding the divine throne, in their presentation of the 'majesty of the Lord'. Examples include the royal portal in Chartres (c.1144–5), the south doorway in the abbey Church in Moissac (c.1120), and the 'doorway of glory' in Santiago del Compostela in Spain (1186). In the Gothic cathedral in Rheims (c.1260–70), the south portal on the western façade and the corresponding inner doorway are unusual in that they portray a whole cycle of scenes, beginning with John on Patmos (Rev 1) and ending with the fall of the devil into the abyss (Rev 20:1–3). This recalls cycles found in manuscript illustrations, but here whole scenes are indicated by just one or two figures. As in the manuscript tradition, scenes from the apocryphal life of John complement those from the Apocalypse (Schiller 1990: 201–4).

Various elements combine to symbolize the New Jerusalem promised in Rev 21–2 and to present the Church as a gateway to the heavenly city (Wainwright 1993: 190). This theme is especially evident in the great chandeliers, or crowns of light, that began to appear in Germany and France around the year 1010 (Schiller 1990: 192–5; for further discussion, see below on Rev 21). A later example is the Pazzi Chapel in Florence, whose overall structure is determined by the Apocalypse (Barolsky 1995).

With the advent of the printing press, manuscript illuminations gave way to woodcuts illustrating the text. Best known are the 15 woodcuts by Albrecht Dürer (1497–8; Carey 1999; Smith 2000; Van der Meer 1978: 283–314), which began a new era in the book's illustration. They emphasize the visionary, other-worldly, character of John's experience, while at the same time showing the bored nonchalance of spectators as they casually watch the awesome incidents taking place in their midst. In the depiction of Rev 17 well-dressed people admire the Whore of Babylon (compare Lucas Cranach's portrayal in Luther's Bible, where the worshippers of Babylon include Ferdinand I, George of Saxony, Charles V and Johann Tetzel). This is also evident in the opening scene of John's persecution. When the terrible war in heaven takes place (Rev 12), there is tranquillity below on earth, where people have no comprehension of the spiritual battle being waged around them. It is only with the four horsemen (Rev 6) that a trace of fear appears, as royal personages, priests and prelates get trampled underfoot along with ordinary people. Dürer reflects some of the concerns that dominated exegesis in the Joachite tradition, where Saint Francis is identified with the angel of the sixth seal (Rev 7:2). In Dürer's portrayal of Rev 7 the angel from the sun holds a cross, perhaps suggesting Francis and the stigmata, and his emphasis on seals 5 and 6 and trumpets 5 and 6 may reflect emphasis on the penultimate, which is a distinguishing feature of the Joachite tradition. The appearance of trees in several of Dürer's portrayals brings to mind Joachim's *figurae* in which the Jesse tree plays an important role (Joachim of Fiore 1953; Reeves and Hirsch-Reich 1972; McGinn 1979: 109).

Both medieval manuscript illuminations and later woodcuts give contextual readings in which visions from the Apocalypse are used as an interpretative lens for viewing contemporary history. A well-known example is the depiction of the Whore of Babylon as papal Rome in Lucas Cranach's woodcuts for Luther's *Septembertestament* of 1522 (Van der Meer 1978: 308). These reflect the widespread iconic propaganda of the German Reformation, in which images inspired by the Apocalypse are pervasive (Scribner 1994: 148–89). The prominent place of Apocalypse illustrations in Luther's Bible of 1534 indicates the continuing role of artistic imagination in the exegesis of a controversial text (Martin 1983).

Over the centuries the Apocalypse has also inspired countless painted panels. These include altar-pieces such as that painted by Jan van Eyck for a chapel of Saint John in the cathedral of St Bavo in Ghent (Schiller 1990: 307–11; Van der Meer 1978: 236–57). Its central panel, known as the 'Mystical Lamb', exemplifies an interpretation that goes back to Tyconius and Augustine, which emphasizes relevance for the Church in the present time. Here the division between heaven and earth is transcended in the eucharistic feast, as the Lamb in the midst of the throne (Rev 5) is found on an altar on earth. Such eucharistic piety is paralleled in the central role which Dürer gives to the Lamb, whose blood is shed into a chalice held by a cardinal (plate 12, illustrating Rev 14, in Van der Meer 1978: 301). Another fifteenth-century altar-piece, a triptych made by Hans Memling for Saint John's Hospital in Bruges (1475–87), features numerous scenes from the life of John as well as the seer experiencing the vision on Patmos. Scenes that appear frequently in painted panels include John's vision in Rev 1 (e.g. Hieronymous Bosch, Staatliche Museen, Berlin, c.1500) and the Last Judgement (e.g. Fra Angelico, Museo di San Marco, Florence, c.1431; Grubb 1997: 86; and Wassily Kandinsky, private collection, 1910; Grubb 1997: 97). From the nineteenth century come two striking paintings that illustrate Rev 6:8: J. M. W. Turner's (1775–1851) *Death on a Pale Horse* (c.1825) manages to conjure up a scene of desolation following a cataclysm (Grubb 1997: 47), while William Blake's picture of the same title is more energetic (Grubb 1997: 48). Among twentieth-century painters, mention should be made of the apocalyptic character of the painting of Wassily Kandinsky (1866–1944), who felt himself led by a prophetic vocation in his artistic work (Heller 1983; Carey 1999: 276–9).

Ancient Literary Context

John's vision begins with the words 'Apocalypse (revelation) of Jesus Christ', indicating the origin and authority of what follows. It is the only time the term 'revelation' is used in the book, which is characterized either directly or indirectly as prophecy (22:18). The use of 'revelation/reveal' links this apocalypse with a range of texts written in the last centuries BCE and in late first century CE (the closest contemporary parallel is 2 Esdras (4 Ezra) 3–14). The description of John's vision as an 'apocalypse' (1:1) is distinctive as compared with the ancient Jewish texts that resemble it. Texts like *1 Enoch*, *2 Enoch*, and the *Apocalypse of Abraham* contain accounts of ascents to heaven and revelations concerning the divine mysteries, particularly with regard to the future (Rowland 1982; see above, 2). Links with biblical prophetic texts are obvious throughout (see the excursus for possible biblical allusions). The opening chapter includes a call vision (1:9–20) with affinities to Dan 10 and Ezek 1 and 9, affirming John's place in that prophetic tradition, though, as the occasional reference in

1:1, 5, 9 indicates, one that is influenced by Jesus Christ. John becomes an intermediary, like Enoch in *1 Enoch* 12–15. Indeed, in the later Johannine apocalyptic tradition, e.g. the *Third Apocalypse of John* (Court 2000: 108), John
becomes a key intermediary of heavenly secrets.

The terms 'revelation/reveal' (*apokalypsis*) are used occasionally in literature contemporaneous with Revelation to describe the unveiling of God or
divine secrets (M. Smith in Hellholm 1989: 9). For example, in the New
Testament *apokalypsis/apokalupto* is found in Simeon's song (Luke 2:32; cf. 1
Pet 1:11–12) and in contexts dealing with the eschatological revelation of
human secrets (Matt 10:26/Luke 12:2; Luke 2:35), divine secrets (Matt
11:25/Luke 10:21; Matt 16:17) or God (Matt 11:27). It is also central to Paul's
description of his conversion to the way of Jesus Christ (Gal 1:12), and he
also used it in reference to a future hope (1 Cor 1:7; cf. 2 Thess 1:7; 1 Pet 1:7;
1:13; 4:13). In Revelation the term 'apocalypse' is followed immediately
by a reference to the book as prophecy (1:3), suggesting that for John
prophecy and apocalypse are closely related (Mazzaferri 1989; cf. Barton 1986).
The vision of the 'one like the Son of Man' is paralleled in several ancient Jewish
texts, all of which are probably inspired by the vision in Dan 10:5–10 (Rowland
1985).

John's call has its closest parallel in a text (probably Jewish-Christian)
which in its original form is roughly contemporary, the *Ascension of Isaiah*
(6:10–12; Knight 1996). John's experience is linked with the Lord's day,
probably a reference to Sunday rather than the sabbath (cf. 1 Cor 16:2; Acts
20:7; Matt 28:1). This was the day when the Risen Lord had appeared to disciples in the past (Luke 24:13–35; John 20:1–29). Worship as the context for a
vision recalls the Temple vision of Isaiah (Isa 6). Worship was often seen as a
communion with heaven, in which the earthly saints join with the heavenly
hosts in lauding God, as when Isaiah witnesses the song of the seraphim.
Patmos has, at least temporarily, become sacred space, hallowed by the vision.
The tension between past, present and future, which plays a great role in interpretation of the Apocalypse, may reflect a liturgical sense of time, in which
different times seem inextricably mixed. What is expected in the future is experienced in the present celebration of the cult. John tells his readers that his
apocalyptic experiences occurred when he was 'in the spirit' on 'the Lord's day',
when in both heaven and earth the resurrection of Christ is celebrated. Paul
also repeatedly designates the parousia of Christ as 'the day of the Lord' (1
Thess 5:2; 2 Thess 2:2; 1 Cor 5:5; 2 Cor 1:14; Funk 1969b: 249–68). To celebrate the resurrection of Jesus on the Lord's day is to experience already
the day of the Lord (Flanigan in Emmerson and McGinn 1992: 340–1; cf.
Wainwright 1993: 253).

The Interpretations

This opening chapter offers interpretative clues regarding the character of the Apocalypse. According to the eighteenth-century Roman Catholic commentator Robert Witham, there are three ways of expounding its visions:

> The Visions are only to be fulfilled in Antichrist's time, a little before the End of the World . . .
> The visions may be applied to particular Events which happened in the first three of four Ages of the church, under the persecuting Heathens, by Constantine, and the succeeding Christian Emperors . . .
> Finally, 'by the great city of Babylon, is signified all wicked great Cities in the World, all the multitude of the wicked in all nations, their short and Vain Happiness; their Persecutions and oppressions of the good and faithful Servants of God, who live piously in this world, and who are call'd to be Citizens of the Celestial Jerusalem in the Kingdom of God' (*Annotations*, ii.510–11 in Newport 2000: 86)

It is the last of these options which Witham is inclined to accept.

For sixteenth-century writer John Bale, the Apocalypse has supreme value as a key to the nature of the Christian religion: 'He that knoweth not this book, knoweth not what the church is whereof he is a member' (Bale 1849: 252). Since all are citizens of either Jerusalem or Babylon (Rev 17:5; ch. 21), the true believer has to learn the nature of the two churches and take a stand with Abel rather than Cain (in Bauckham 1978: 60). Hildegard of Bingen similarly writes: 'And whoever tastes this prophecy and fixes it in his memory will become the mountain of myrrh [cf. Rev 21:10] and of frankincense, and of all aromatical spices, and the diffusion of many blessings; he will ascend like Abraham from blessing to blessing' (Hart and Bishop edn 536). Hildegard claims divinely given insight into the meaning of Scripture ('Scivias Declaration', Hart and Bishop edn 59), as does the sixteenth-century visionary Ralph Durden, who was given the 'gift of interpretation' (in Bauckham 1978: 188–9). Similarly, Joachim of Fiore finds in the Apocalypse the key to the inner meaning of Scripture and the whole history of salvation (in McGinn 1979: 99). The Apocalypse, according to Joachim, was no afterthought, a book to be tolerated but ignored, but rather the culmination of the whole of Scripture. David Koresh agrees: 'All the books of the Bible meet and end there. This is what we have learned over the years' (in Newport 2000: 212).

'what must soon take place . . . what is, and what is to take place after this': interpretative clues (1:1, 19)

Victorinus, living at a time when Christians were persecuted (he himself died a martyr), seems to have understood 'what must soon take place' (1:1) as a reference to his own time and to have taken the warnings and promises of the Apocalypse as addressed to his own church (Matter in Emmerson and McGinn 1992: 39; ANF vii.344). That sense of immediacy has presented problems for interpreters, nowhere more so than for those like the Millerites who had a detailed apocalyptic timetable for the end of the world and the consummation of scriptural promises. When Christ failed to return in 1843–4 as they had predicted, they searched the Scriptures and concluded that the error was not in the word of the Lord but in their own understanding of it (in Foster in Numbers and Butler 1987: 173–88). Such interpretation of experience through expectations based on authoritative texts has been a feature of prophetic and apocalyptic interpretation down the centuries. Failure of hopes to materialize often, as in this case, does not lead to abandonment of the hope but to questioning of human interpretative capacity and a channelling of eschatological enthusiasm into practical action (Foster in Numbers and Butler 1987).

'to the seven churches' (1:4)

The universal character of the vision is often noted. According to Victorinus, the seven stars (1:16) are the seven churches that John addresses (1916: 26.17, ANF vii.344), and together they represent the one church, as Paul also teaches by writing to exactly seven churches (Victorinus 1916: 26. 4–11). In the *Geneva Bible* likewise, the seven churches mean the church universal. According to Bede, 'the Apocalypse speaks of the seven churches of Asia which are really the one Church of Christ' (in Matter in Emmerson and McGinn 1992: 47). The *Scofield Reference Bible* says the message to the seven churches has a fourfold application: to the churches actually addressed; to all churches in all time ('so that they may discern their true spiritual state in the sight of God'); as exhortation to individuals; and, as a prophetic disclosure, to the seven phases of the *spiritual* history of the church (Scofield 1917: 1331–2).

'I, John, your brother, who share with you in Jesus the persecution . . . was on the island called Patmos' (1:9)

The location of John's vision and the reasons for John being on Patmos have been a matter for discussion, not least because of the long tradition that he was imprisoned there and subsequently released. John's situation and the nature of his vision are portrayed in the various artistic depictions. The christological significance of the attributes of the 'one like the Son of Man' has also received extensive attention, and John's vision prompted visionaries in succeeding centuries to look to him as their apocalyptic mentor, just as he followed in the footsteps of his visionary predecessors.

Patmos is an island off the west coast of Turkey, and the seven letters are addressed to communities in cities on the mainland. John writes little about himself. He mentions tribulation in 1:9, possibly suggesting persecution (cf. 7:14). Elsewhere this word is used in a general way for upheavals expected in the last days (Rom 8:35; Mark 13:18), so it does not necessarily imply systematic persecution, of which there is little evidence in this particular area in Domitian's time (L. Thompson 1990). Early Christian tradition had John in Ephesus confronting false teachers (Irenaeus *AH* ii.22.5). In the Johannine apocalyptic tradition, *The Second Apocalypse of John* (probably fourth century CE) has a revelation to John set on Mount Tabor, the mount of the Transfiguration, which is in some ways explanatory of eschatological features of the original Apocalypse (in Court 2000: 33). There is, however, a long tradition that John was persecuted; for example, Albrecht Dürer's sequence depicts an apocryphal story in which John is seated in a cauldron of boiling oil in front of the Roman emperor. According to second-century Christian tradition, after Domitian's death John returned from exile and lived until the age of Trajan (well into the second century CE; Irenaeus *AH* ii.22.5; iii.3.4).

Irenaeus dates the text to Domitian's reign and is the first to propound a view that continues to have wide currency, that the book's genre was chosen to conceal its real message, for fear of imperial retribution (*AH* v.30.3). In the middle of the second century Justin appeals to John and his vision to support belief in God's future reign on earth (*Dial.* lxxxi.4).

Robert Browning's poem 'Death in the Desert' (1864) explores the relationship among different writings attributed to John in the light of the challenges of higher criticism of the Bible pioneered by Renan and Strauss (Browning had recently read George Eliot's translation of Strauss's *Das Leben Jesu*). He offers the poem as a newly found manuscript recording the last words and death of John. The different periods of John's life coincide with three modes of knowing: from statement of what he heard and saw (the Apocalypse), to 'reasoning from his knowledge' (the Johannine epistles), to a final penetration of the essential meaning (the gospel), when 'what first were guessed as points, I now knew stars' (lines 135–75; Shaffer 1972: 191–224).

'I, John': doubts about the Apocalypse (1:9)

Positive testimony to the book's significance has to be balanced by a long tradition of suspicion that questions its origin and how it has been used. Erasmus
invoked the authority of 'very many very learned men', all of whom claimed
that the book lacks 'apostolic gravitas' and is no more than a history expressed
in figurative or allegorical terms. He claimed that John's repeating 'I, John' (1:9)
shows that he was drawing attention to himself rather than Christ. This
contrasts with the less direct self-references in the gospel of John and
with the writings of Paul, who also had visions but describes them as if they
were someone else's (cf. 2 Cor 12:2). While there were defenders of the book's
canonicity in the sixteenth century, the challenge of Erasmus caused much
suspicion (Backus 1998).

Martin Luther likewise famously denigrated the book's importance in his
original preface to *The German Bible*:

> About this book of the Revelation of John, I leave everyone free to hold his own
> ideas, and would bind no man to my opinion and judgement: I say what I feel.
> I miss more than one thing in this book, and this makes me hold it to be neither
> apostolic or prophetic. First and foremost, the Apostles do not deal with visions,
> but prophesy in clear, plain words, as do Peter and Paul and Christ in the gospel.
> For it befits the apostolic office to speak of Christ and his deeds without figures
> and visions but there is no prophet in the Old Testament, to say nothing of the
> New, who deals so out and out with visions and figures. And so I think of it
> almost as I do of the Fourth Book of Esdras, and I can in nothing detect that it
> was provided by the Holy Spirit. Moreover, he seems to be going much too far
> when he commends his own book so highly, – more than any other of the sacred
> books do, though they are much more important . . . Let every one think of it as
> his own spirit gives him to think. My spirit cannot fit itself into this book. There
> is one sufficient reason for me not to think highly of it – Christ is not taught or
> known in it; but to teach Christ is the thing which an apostle above all else is
> bound to do. (1522 *Preface to the New Testament* 12)

Luther takes a more positive approach in his 1546 *Preface to the New Testament*, however, where he offers advice about how to interpret the Apocalypse:

> The first and surest step toward finding its interpretation is to take from history
> the events and disasters that have come upon Christendom till now, and hold
> them up alongside of these images, and so compare them very carefully. If, then,
> the two perfectly coincided and squared with one another, we could build on
> that as a sure, or at least an unobjectionable, interpretation.

It is a book 'for our comfort' and 'for our warning'. He encourages readers 'to read this book and learn to look upon Christendom with other eyes than those of reason', thereby enabling them to do justice to its imagery. This is reflected in the way translations were illuminated and the imagery of the book informed popular culture of the Reformation period (Scribner 1994).

Luther's early doubts continue the qualms of certain church fathers who questioned the book's apostolic character. According to Eusebius *HE* iii.28.3, Dionysius of Alexandria regarded the expectation of a reign of God on earth as evidence of authorship by the heretic Cerinthus rather than the apostle John (in Backus 1998: 654). Luther's unease is also echoed by Tyndale, though in less trenchant form: 'The Apocalypse or Revelations of John are allegories whose literal sense is hard to find in many places' (2000: 156). Tyndale was deeply suspicious of allegorical exegesis. The preface to the *Geneva Bible* likewise urges: 'Read diligently; judge soberly and call earnestly to God for the true understanding hereof.' This is a tacit admission of the difficulties and threats posed by the book, something exemplified also in the severely circumscribed opportunities to hear it liturgically (Brightman 1915: i.51; see above, 29–31). Other criticisms of the book were occasioned by its use as licence for visions and dreams (Taves 1999: 18).

The vision of 'one like the Son of Man' (1:12–17)

The details of this vision of Christ have been understood as a mine of information about christological and ecclesiological matters. According to Irenaeus, Jesus' appearance as 'one like the Son of Man', with seven candlesticks, shows his sacerdotal nature and the glory he has received (*AH* iv.20.11). He wears priestly garments which Moses saw in a vision and copied in the vestures of the high priest. His feet of burning brass suggest the power of faith, which is tested and refined in the fire of the end of time (ibid.). Hippolytus links the vision with Daniel 10:5–21, claiming that Daniel sees the Lord but not in his perfect form (*Daniel* iv.36.5–6; cf. Rowland 1985). In *Antichrist* 12 he says that the eyes of Christ in 1:14 symbolize the prophets who foresaw both his suffering and his glory.

Despite his chiliastic views, Victorinus also emphasizes the meaning of the Apocalypse for the present, especially in the first six chapters, which describe the presence of Christ in the church and in Scripture. The Apocalypse is a recapitulation of all of Scripture, in which the resurrected Christ unlocks the meaning of the figures of the law (Victorinus 1997: 29–32). The vision of 1:12–20, for example, is an initiation into the mysteries of faith, encapsulating central points of christology and soteriology. It reveals Christ's double nature:

his divinity in his white head and shining face and his humanity in his priestly garment, which symbolizes the body of the incarnate one, offered as a sacrifice by the eternal priest. This vision also expresses the unity of Christ as head with his body the church: the white hair symbolizes the baptized, and the golden sash believers who drink pure milk of doctrine from the breast of Christ. The means by which humanity is united with Christ in the church are indicated by the two-edged sword (Scripture: law and gospel), the 'sound of many waters' (baptism), and the seven stars (the Holy Spirit; ANF vii.344–6). Chapters 2–3 then go on to show how Christ dispenses the sevenfold spirit (cf. Isa 11) to the universal church (ANF vii.346–7).

The two-edged sword (1:16) has its analogies in contemporary texts like Wis 18:16 and Heb 4:14. The Valentinian Gnostic text of the late second century, *The Gospel of Truth*, echoes Rev 1:16 in speaking of the divine Logos as a naked, two-edged sword which causes division between the spiritual and material within the individual person (26.1–15).

Lady Eleanor Davies, one of several women prophets in England in the 1640s and 1650s, identifies the figure of John's call vision (1:13) as a female divine being who will bring peace (drawing also on other scriptural texts like John 1, Isa 9:2 and Heb 7):

> She whose throne heaven, earth her footstool from the uncreated saying, I am A and O first and last, both beginning and ending, by whom all things were done: not without anything done or made; Trinity in Unity, of manhood the head; who of death have the keys, and of hell: than the Queen of the South a greater, born a greater not of woman: Malea, by interpretation, Queen of Peace, or She-Counsellor. And so much for this without contradiction, she his executioner made like unto the Son of God, the Ancient of Days' likeness: owner of the title of tithes, to whom the patriarch offered a tenth. ('The Appearance or Presence of the Son of Man' (1650) 7–8 Cope edn 174–81, in Hobby 1988: 28)

'the Alpha and the Omega . . . the first and the last' (1:8, 17; cf. 21:6; 22:13)

Origen uses 1:8 to argue that Christ shares in the Father's omnipotence (*First Principles* i.2.10; on Origen's interpretation of 'the Alpha and the Omega', see below, commentary on Rev 22:13). Joachim of Fiore broke with the medieval tradition of interpretation as he 'translated images into a kind of cosmic geometry', to borrow a phrase from Marjorie Reeves (in Reeves and Hirsch-Reich 1972: 38; cf. 46–7, 171, 192, and McGinn 1979: 104). In his later years Joachim complemented his literary expositions of the Apocalypse with 'figures' (*figurae*) that encapsulate his beliefs about history and salvation. In one, he uses the circle as symbol of the Godhead, indicating its trinity and unity (Joachim of Fiore 1953: plates 11a, 11b; cf. Reeves and Hirsch-Reich 1972: plate 26). The three overlapping circles show how the Trinity relates to history. At the far left are Alpha and Omega, as a kind of presupposition. The green circle on the left is that of the Father and is the time of the Old Testament; the middle, blue circle, that of the Son, interlocks with the two outer circles. The third circle is that of the Holy Spirit and indicates that the Spirit is from the Father and the Son since it overlaps with both the other circles. This third circle contains a reference to the 'Novum Testamentum', indicating that the New Testament is not superseded in the final age of the Spirit. Dante may have been aware of Joachim's *figura* in *Paradiso* 33.115–20:

> That light supreme, within its fathomless / Clear substance, showed to me three spheres, which bare / Three hues distinct, and occupied one space; / The first mirrored the next, as though it were / Rainbow from rainbow, and the third seemed flame / Breathed equally from each of the first pair. (In McGinn 1979: 106; cf. Herzman in Emmerson and McGinn 1992: 398)

Joachim also uses the Alpha and Omega in the 'psaltery with ten strings', a 'figure' that came to him in a mystical vision (1953: plate 13; Reeves and Hirsch-Reich 1972: plate 27, cf. pp. 46–58). After passing through a time of struggle to a higher plane of understanding, Joachim sang to God and began to understand the meaning of the words 'blessed are they who dwell in thy house' (Ps 84:4). He had striven to be an inhabitant of the city of God through his own efforts and had come to know 'inner peace' by the grace of vision (in Reeves and Hirsch-Reich 1972: 51–2; cf. McGinn 1979: 99 and 1985). The 'psaltery', like the Trinitarian circles, encapsulates the character of God, but here the angelic hierarchies are attached to the strings on one side of the diagram, with the gifts of the Spirit on the other. Milton also uses Alpha and Omega: 'In highth or depth, still first and last will reign' (*Paradise Lost* ii.324; cf. v.165). Karl Barth writes of Jesus as Alpha and Omega (1958: 463–516).

Depictions of John's call (1:9–11, 17–19)

Depictions of John's call bring out the various facets of its visionary character. Velasquez's painting emphasizes the moment of ecstasy: John's eyes are clearly focused on something beyond the picture (London, National Gallery). An open book with an empty page sits on his lap. It contrasts with large books at John's feet, perhaps representing the earlier Scriptures that are being supplemented by the revelation of Jesus Christ now taking place, thereby reminding us of the high authority which attaches to this particular book (cf. 22:18). In the portrayal of John's call in Paris BN lat. 11534, fol. 341 John's eyes are closed, and he is in ecstasy, as also in Giotto's work in the Cappella Peruzzi in Santa Croce Florence 1335 (in Van der Meer 1978: 25, 189). One is reminded of how Thomas Phillips (1807), when he painted William Blake (National Portrait Gallery, London, in Hamlyn and Phillips 2000: frontispiece; cf. Bentley 2001: 290–1), asked him to give rapt attention as if he were looking at a heavenly being. Velasquez's evocation of the ecstatic state is much more obvious, however (for a modern example of the depiction of a visionary trance see Stanley Spencer's painting *Sarah Tubb and the Heavenly Visitors* in Bell 1992: 110).

John on Patmos is often portrayed as a solitary figure on a rock: for example, in *St John on Patmos* by Hieronymus Bosch (Berlin Gemaeldegalerie). This is also emphasized by Victor Hugo in *Les Misérables*:

> We need not speak of the exile in Patmos who mightily assailed the world as it was with a protest in the name of an ideal world, a huge, visionary satire, which cast upon Rome-that-was-Nineveh, Rome-that-was-Babylon, and Rome-that-was-Sodom the thunderous light of his *Revelation*. John on his rock is the Sphinx on its pedestal; he is beyond our understanding; he was a Jew and a Hebrew. But Tacitus, who wrote the *Annals*, was a Latin, and, better still, a Roman. (1996: 888)

The rock also appears in an allusive reference in Dante's *Divine Comedy*, where Dante follows the Joachite tradition in linking the stigmata of Saint Francis with a seal of the Apocalypse. He describes the moment of Francis's receipt of Christ's stigmata: 'Then on the harsh rock between Tiber and Arno he received the last seal which his limbs bore for two years' (*Paradiso* 11.106–8). This points to the seal sequence of the Apocalypse (6:1–8:5) and also to John's situation on the rock of Patmos, where he is often shown marooned, as in Memling's altar-piece 'The Mystic Marriage of Saint Catherine' in Saint John's Hospital, Bruges, and in Dürer's woodcuts on Rev 10 and 14 (in Herzman in Emmerson and McGinn 1992: 406). Francis, like the apostle Paul (1 Cor 4:15; Gal 4:10; 6:17; Phil 3:10), became a bearer of Christ and a mediator of Christ's eschatological presence in the present, by bearing the marks of his death. That the angel in Dürer's depiction of Rev 7:2 holds a cross may reflect the identification of this angel with Francis, which became a feature of Franciscan interpretation of the Apocalypse, following Joachim (see below, 100, on Peter Olivi and Bonaventure). The *Divine Comedy* connects more generally with the Apocalypse in that it relates Dante's personal experience *and* God's plan for the cosmos: 'Apocalypse' involves the continual attempt to try to see things more and more from God's perspective (Herzman in Emmerson and McGinn 1992: 412).

Hieronymus Bosch also portrays John on a rock as he gazes up to a vision of the Woman Clothed with the Sun (Rev 12:1; Gemälde galerie, Berlin). She appears in a circular form in the top left-hand corner of the picture, as in several other contemporary depictions – for example, Hans Memling's altarpiece. In Bosch's picture John gazes in rapt attention at the vision of heaven, while around him, visible over his shoulder, are scenes of death and destruction (Rev 6:8–9, 16). While the visions John records are happening around him, his gaze is focused on almighty God. That gives perspective for everything else. A sharp contrast is set up between the violence below and the glory above. Also, John seems to be engaged in a kind of ecstatic automatic writing, an interpretation of what it means to be writing 'in the spirit' (in Blake 1991–5, Viscomi edn 42–3).

What most distinguishes Bosch's portrayal, however, is that John is accompanied by creatures, a bird (a raven, perhaps a parody of John's eagle or even a sign of death) and a little imp-like figure. The sublime moment is characterized as one of threat. The bird threatens to spill the ink, and the imp-like figure wears spectacles, evincing a certain donnish quality, and suggesting that the gently sceptical observer might have a question about the authenticity or validity of the vision.

One of the most remarkable openings of any sequence of illustrations of the Apocalypse is the frontispiece by Jean Duvet (1555) (see plate 1). Duvet's illustrations were completed at the end of his life, and he seems to have developed an affinity with the aged John who, according to tradition, died as an old man in the reign of Trajan (Eusebius *HE* iii.32.1). In the frontispiece Duvet represents himself as John on Patmos, with this inscription: 'Jean Duvet aged seventy has completed these histories in 1555'. An open book nearby is the Apocalypse of St John, and in the bottom left-hand corner is written: 'the sacred mysteries contained in this and the other following tablets are derived from the divine revelation of John and are closely adapted to the true letter of the text with the judgement of more learned men brought to bear.' Elsewhere Duvet writes: 'The fates are pressing; already the hands tremble and the sight fails, yet the mind remains victorious and the great work is completed.' His illustrations, then, involve a 're-seeing' of John's vision as one old man enters into the visions of another (cf. Hölderlin's fusing of his poetic inspiration with John's in 'Patmos', in Shaffer 1972: 303–9).

The sense of struggle amidst tribulation and temptation pervades Spenser's *The Faerie Queene*, in which the Red Cross Knight is introduced as 'faithful and true' (cf. Rev 19:11). He endures tribulations similar to those described in the Apocalypse and is led astray by 'antichrist' figures. Nevertheless he perseveres,

Plate 1   Jean Duvet as John on Patmos (Rev 1:9–20). British Museum, London.

learning greater discernment about the way of darkness and the way of light (in Sandler in Patrides and Wittreich 1984: 150). The progress of personal pilgrimage is also found in Ingmar Bergman's film *The Seventh Seal*; key existential moments are linked with the seven seals (Carey 1999: 334–5).

Interpretations that take the form of visionary appropriation

An example of a more general influence of the apocalyptic revelation is found in the *Apocalypse of John Chrysostom*, in which an early Christian theologian receives information about liturgical matters through a dialogue with Jesus Christ (fifth century CE, in Court 2000: 67–103). Hildegard of Bingen's *Scivias* contains a new vision inspired by John's (Hart and Bishop edn 482–3; Emmerson in Emmerson and McGinn 1992: 298).

John's apocalyptic vision also inspires Blake's visionary world and informs his understanding of his own political situation. Indeed, Blake explicitly links his own mythical world with the vision seen by John, much as Duvet does in his frontispiece. Blake makes this clear at the conclusion of the Eighth Night of *The Four Zoas* when he sees his own mythological creations as in direct continuity with the visionary apocalypticism of John (*Four Zoas* 8.597). Blake also looks back to Milton for inspiration, taking up and embodying the poetic genius of his predecessor in his *Milton*. The departed poet reappears, and the Muse has another opportunity, in Blake's writing, to express thoughts aright. Blake sees Milton's spirit enter into his left foot (*Milton* 14:49). In both appropriations the blurring of identity and time is apparent as the eternal and the temporal merge, and the mental dislocation this brings about is experienced by the reader. The effect is to plunge us into a kind of madness and make us see that what we regard as 'normal' is not the only imaginable way of reading, seeing, or thinking (so Essick and Viscomi in Blake 1991–5: 10). This may help explain John's own apocalypse, in which images and texts of the past are minted afresh in John's own vision. It is what happens when the prophet's visions are seen again at a different time and place, as David Halperin says about the appropriation of Ezekiel's vision of God's throne (*merkabah*) in later apocalypses: 'When the apocalyptic visionary "sees" something that looks like Ezekiel's merkabah, we may assume that he is seeing the merkabah vision as he has persuaded himself it really was, as Ezekiel would have seen it, had he been inspired wholly and not in part' (Halperin 1988: 71).

Ancient Literary Context

At first sight the seven letters seem similar to the phenomenon of epistolary exchange which was widespread in early Christianity, particularly between communities influenced by Paul ('Paul' or Ignatius wrote letters to several churches mentioned in the Apocalypse, such as Ephesus, Laodicea and Smyrna). The superficial similarity should not disguise the significant differences, however. While detailed investigation of the culture, archaeology and topography of the cities addressed in Rev 2–3 has suggested that John had an intimate knowledge of events, situations and persons in the various locations (Hemer 1986; and on the social and religious background Trebilco 1991 and Lieu 1997), these are largely hidden behind a biblical typology, with Balaam and Jezebel, two figures remembered for their wickedness (Num 25:1–3 and 1 Kings 21–2). The angels of the seven churches parallel the angelic representatives of individuals and nations which are a feature of Second Temple Jewish texts (LXX of Deut 32:8; Dan 10:13, 12:1; Matt 18:10; *Jubilees* 15:31–2; *1 Enoch* 89: 59–62; cf. Wink 1984, 1986, 1993).

The Interpretations

One specific concern of interpreters is the character and role of the angels. More generally, interpretations fall into three major types. Some emphasize the past, noting that here we are closer than perhaps anywhere else in the book to the reality of the first-century setting. Secondly, salvation-historical interpretations understand the different churches as a symbolic outline of ecclesiastical history. Thirdly, hortatory applications assume that the concerns of the seven letters are universally applicable, an assumption sometimes justified by seeing the number seven as a symbol of perfection.

The angels of the churches

A frequently discussed question concerns the identity of the seven angels. Primasius and Bede interpreted them as the ruling representatives of the people (in Swete 1906: 21). In the Apocalypse, however, outside the opening chapters, 'angels' are supernatural beings. Origen emphasizes the role of angels in God's providential plan. He compares the angels to masters who bear some responsibility for the activities of their pupils, attracting praise or blame. Not only every church, but also every person has a ministering angel (*Hom. Num.* 17.4; 20.3 in Monaci 1978: 146). Beatus of Lébbana compares how angels are linked with humans in Matt 18:10 and Acts 12:5 (1930: 87–90). According to Alexander the Minorite, the angels are bishops (*Expositio* 22–49 in Wainwright 1993: 54), a view popular in modern commentaries (cf. Aune 1997: 108–12). Some illuminated manuscripts portray the angels as the representatives or guardian angels of the churches, as in the Trier Apocalypse (in Quispel 1979: 38–40) and the illustration of the angel of the church in Sardis in the Girona Beatus (fol. 89v in J. Williams 1994: 2. illustration 309). Bullinger is in no doubt that the 'angels of the churches' are humans: 'And straightway [John] declareth what thing he understandeth by the candlesticks and stars, calling the candlesticks churches, and the stars angels of the churches. That is to wit, messengers, ministers and pastors' (in Bauckham 1978: 300).

A close interplay between heavenly and earthly is suggested by John's being commanded to write to the angels and by the role of angels in the upheavals that begin in Rev 6. This has its parallel in texts like the *War Scroll* (*1QM*) from the Dead Sea Scrolls, where angels join with humans in a last, critical battle. Few have understood the subtle interplay between angelic and human, natural and supernatural, as well as William Blake. His Continental Prophecies, *America* and *Europe*, blend the angelic and the human in describing historical events. Individual agents and social institutions are never sufficient to explain their significance (Doerrbecker in Blake 1991–5; Erdman 1977).

Interpretations focusing on first-century context: historical and geographical allusions

In Pergamum there was an altar dedicated to Zeus, surrounded by elaborate colonnades, and a temple dedicated to the goddess Roma, which may have influenced John's visionary imagination in 2:13 (Aune 1997: 182–4). The judgement of 'lukewarm' in the Laodicean letter has been explained by reference to the local water-supply which came from hot springs and arrived warm, and the eye salve in 3:18 is said to reflect the medical school and famous Phrygian eye powder (Hemer 1986: 186, 196). Attempts have been made to link various figures with individuals and events or to connect them with conflicts and disputes within the early Church. Jezebel's stance on idol-meat is akin to that of Paul in 1 Cor 8. Puzzlement about the identification of the Nicolaitans extends from ancient to modern commentators. Irenaeus thought they were followers of the Nicholas of Antioch mentioned in Acts 6:5 (*AH* i.26.3; iii.10.7). There was a group known by that name in the second century CE (Eusebius *HE* iii.29; Clement of Alexandria, *Stromateis* iii. 25). The *Scofield Reference Bible* offers an etymological explanation, based on *nikao*, 'to conquer', and *laos*, 'the people' (also linked with the word 'Balaam'; cf. Swete 1906: 28), and sees this as an early example of the division into 'priests' and 'laity', instead of the earlier equal brotherhood (cf. Matt 23:8). Similarly, the contrast between 'works' in Ephesus (Rev 2:6) and 'teaching' in Pergamum (Rev 2:15) is a sign of this emergence of a priestly perversion (Scofield 1917: 1332).

Salvation-historical readings

According to Victorinus, John's letters are for the whole church, not just for seven congregations, so the letters address all the different kinds of believers (1916: 30.12–32.12; ANF vii.344; cf. Wainwright 1993: 28). This type of interpretation is stated most clearly in Reformation times by Brightman, who saw in the letters references to the periods of church history from Christ to his own day. The church of Ephesus had a 'counterpane' in the apostolic church up to the time of Constantine. Smyrna corresponded to the time from Constantine to Gratian (382), and Pergamum to the next period, lasting until 1300, which was the type of the corrupt Roman Church. Thyatira represented the period from 1300 to 1520, Sardis the German Reformation, Philadelphia the churches in Geneva, and Laodicea the Church of England (in Firth 1979: 167; cf. Bullinger, *A Hundred Sermons upon the Apocalypse of Jesus Christ* in Bauckham 1978: 301).

Bonaventure, who emphasizes the decisive role of Saint Francis in salvation history, notes the significance of the number six in the Apocalypse. Thus the Philadelphian letter (3:7–13), as the penultimate, has particular importance (Burr 1993: 36–8 and further on Rev 7:1, below, 100 cf. Joachim of Fiore in McGinn 1979: 137). The pioneer of the rigorist Franciscans, Peter Olivi, whose life was dedicated to a strict interpretation of Francis's Rule, saw the 'synagogue of Satan' as a pervasive characteristic of God's people:

> Just as the synagogue, proceeding against Christ through Annas and Caiaphas, cast Him forth, so now the new synagogue, which is the 'congregation of Satan', in rejecting evangelical poverty, has cast out Christ in the persons of his apostles, those who practise true poverty. ('Commentary on Cecidit, cecidit, Babylon', *Lectura*, fol. 27r, in Lee, Reeves and Silano 1989: 23; cf. *Lectura* 246 in Burr 1993: 191, and further W. Lewis 1976)

Not surprisingly, the ecclesiastical authorities considered this an attack on the Church. This began a long tradition of identifying Babylon with the Roman Catholic Church, which was given particular impetus by the breakup of the church in the sixteenth century. So Rev 2:9 becomes for Luther a description of a life-and-death struggle, and for Protestants the 'Church of the Pope is the Synagogue of Satan' (*Ad Librum Ambrosii Catharini* 7 in Emmerson 1981: 215).

A variation on the salvation-historical interpretation is a reading of the various churches as types of contemporary religion. This is exemplified by Brightman, who takes 'hypocritical Sardis' in 3:1–6 to refer to Lutherans (*Apocalypsis* 87–123 in Wainwright 1993: 72), whereas 'Godly Philadelphia' of 3:7–13 represents the Calvinist churches in Europe and Scotland. He justifies his identification of the Church of England as Laodicea: 'We have such a mingle-mangle of the Popish Government with pure doctrine' and 'brave silken Ministers who glister as they go' and 'jet through the streets with troops like noble-men' (*Apocalypsis* 123–65 in Wainwright 1993: 72). In the *Geneva Bible* the letter to Pergamum is 'actualized' in the translators' day. Satan's throne in 2:13 is 'All towns and countries whence God's word and good living is banished, those places where the word is not preached sincerely, nor manners a right reformed'. The white stone in 2:17 is the election of those converted by sincere preaching, 'a token of God's favour and grace and a sign that one was cleared in judgement.' In 2:24 'the deep things of Satan' are false teachers. Perhaps inevitably, some of the Calvinists' opponents are mentioned: the Anabaptists, Libertines, Papists and Arians.

In a more systematic interpretation, the *Scofield Reference Bible* sees the messages as a preview of the *spiritual* history of the Church. Ephesus portrays its general state at the time of John; Smyrna, the period of the great persecutions; Pergamum, the Church settled down in the world, 'where Satan's throne is', after the conversion of Constantine, about CE 316. 'Thyatira is the papacy, developed out of Pergamum, with Balaamism (worldliness) and Nicolaitanism (priestly assumption) having conquered. As Jezebel brought idolatry into Israel, so Romanism weds Christian doctrine to pagan ceremonies. Sardis is the Protestant Reformation, whose works were not 'fulfilled'. Philadelphia is 'whatever bears clear testimony to the Word and the Name in the time of self-satisfied profession represented by Laodicea' (Scofield 1917: 1331–2). The spiritual significance of the Philadelphian church is emphasized also in the mystical interpretations of prophets like Jane Lead and others influenced by the mysticism of Jacob Boehme. Followers of the Philadelphians, who emphasized experience and vision, would be the sole survivors of a time of persecution (Smith in Ruether and McLaughlin 1979: 187; cf. Garrett 1987: 14). In September 1640 Henry Wilkinson preached in Oxford about God's threat to spew out 'lukewarm', Laudian England (in Capp in Patrides and Wittreich 1984: 109).

The sense of the weakness of an embattled community which interpreters find in the Philadelphian letter is exemplified in the way Jehovah's Witnesses use Rev 2–3 to interpret their spiritual ancestry. Like the Christians in Smyrna (2:10), John and his companions have been and continue to be 'tested'. Their faithfulness under trial marks them as God's own people. The persecution of Witnesses instigated by some of Christendom's leaders, which came to a head in 1918, was comparable to what the Christians in Smyrna received from the Jewish community there (*Watchtower Bible* 39; cf. the catalogue of the righteous Christians in the Anabaptist martyr narrative in Van Braght 1950). For the Millerites the period until the second coming of Christ was a time of trial for the faithful as they struggled to keep the true sabbath over against the rest of America (Newport 2000: 86).

Spiritual and hortatory interpretations

Down the centuries interpreters have found specific themes from the seven letters useful for moral exhortation and as guides for the spiritual life, as the following examples illustrate.

For Epiphanius, Thyatira is a doomed city, and what was predicted in 2:22–3 actually took place because of the city's toleration of Montanism (in Stonehouse 1929: 70; cf. Labriolle 1913: 196–220; Trevett 1995). The repeated appeal to 'listen to what the Spirit is saying to the churches' at the conclusion of the letters (2:7, 11, 17, 29; 3:6, 13, 22) pervades Hildegard's visions also: 'but let the one who has ears sharp to hear inner meanings ardently love My reflection and pant after My words, and inscribe them in his soul and conscience' (*Scivias* iii.1.18, Hart and Bishop edn 321; cf. ibid. 331, 354, 368, 385, 405, 421, 448, 469, 490, 511, 521, 536).

The threat to the Ephesian angel in 2:5 is taken up in a challenge posed by John Wesley:

> He hath given us long space to repent. He lets us alone this year also. But he warns and awakes us by thunder. His judgements are abroad in the earth. And we have all reason to expect that heaviest of all, even 'that he should come unto us quickly, and remove our candlestick of its place, except we repent and do the first works'. (Wesley 1975: 1.157–8 in Newport 2000: 139)

Following Rev 3:4–5, the reward of the spiritual life is portrayed as divesting and reclothing. According to Tertullian, the white garments in 3:5 are glorified bodies, the clothing of the soul (*Resurr.* 27.2 and *Scorpion's Sting* xii.10). In Bunyan's *Pilgrim's Progress* (1967 edn 56), this image is used by Christian, who speaks of crowns of glory to be given and garments that will make us shine like the sun in the firmament of heaven. As we read elsewhere in *Pilgrim's Progress*, this is not just a future eschatological experience but one enjoined now (1967 edn 82).

According to Irenaeus, Jesus' possession of 'the key of David' in 3:7 is not so much an eschatological as a present, christological reality (*AH* iv.20.2). Similarly, Origen views Christ as the 'door to the city of God' (*Hom. Num.* 25.6 in Mazzucco 1983: 71). In interpretations influenced by Joachim of Fiore there is less focus on christology; the one having David's key is the *pastor angelicus*, who would combine the powers of pope and emperor (Nicholas of Buldesdorf in Potesta in McGinn 2000: 131). The sense of privileged illumination is evident in Charles Wesley's use of 3:7: 'He who hath the key of David, who shuts so as no man can open, and opens so as no man can shut, hath taken off the seals, and opened to unworthy me in a very great, tho' not yet full, measure' ('Letter of Charles Wesley to an Unknown Correspondent', §2 in Newport 2000: 145).

The compromising, 'lukewarm' church is often called 'Laodicean' (cf. 3:16–17). Cyprian, the third-century North African writer who had himself given up a comfortable life, is especially critical of those who think they are rich in this world (*On Works and Alms*, ANF v.479). The sarcastic words to the angel at Laodicea are echoed in Hildegard's reproof to those who 'do not wish to tell [the Scriptures] or preach them, because they are lukewarm and sluggish in serving God's justice' (*Scivias* i and ii.10.7, Hart and Bishop edn 67,

479). Here, as often, the words of John's Apocalypse are taken up and form part of her own visions (cf. *Scivias* iii.8.5, using Rev 3:8, Hart and Bishop edn 427).

To Saint John of the Cross the supper with Christ who knocks on the door in 3:20 represents 'his own sweetness' which occasions the union between God and the 'Bride-Soul' (St John of the Cross 1979: 2:261 in Wainwright 1993: 20). Milton uses the verse in an eschatological invocation (see below, 132).

The use of 3:20 as an invitation to the spiritual life has a long history. Hildegard paraphrases:

> O you who faithfully love Me, your Savior, look and see how, wishing to aid you, I wait at the tabernacle of your heart, seeing what you have in the self-knowledge of your conscience, and with the breath of your memory I knock at your spirit that its goodwill may open and grant admission. And if then the faithful heart, which fears me, hears my knock, I join myself to him, embracing him and taking with him the unfailing food, since he offers me that sweet taste, himself, in his good works; therefore he too shall have that food of life in me, because he loves what brings life to those who desire justice. (*Scivias* i.2.25, Hart and Bishop edn 85–6; cf. ibid., p. 474)

This verse is also the subject of the famous Holman Hunt painting *The Light of the World* in Keble College, Oxford (interestingly titled given how the crucified Jesus faces exclusion). The painter might also intend an allusion to John 1:5: 'the light shines in the darkness, and the darkness did not overcome it' (cf. 1:9).

Revelation 4

Ancient Literary Context

This chapter has close affinities with the visions of God in biblical and contemporary Jewish texts. The ceaseless praise of verse 8, for example, echoes the song of the seraphim of Isaiah's vision:

Isaiah 6:3	Revelation 4:8
Holy, holy, holy is the LORD of hosts; the whole earth is full of his glory.	Holy, holy, holy, the Lord God, the Almighty, who was and is and is to come.

Interest in visions of God and God's throne is a central component of Jewish mysticism. This has a long history, from the return from exile in Babylon down to the Hasidic movements in our own day (Scholem 1955; Gruenwald 1978; Halperin 1988; Rowland 1982). It is highly probable that this was not only a matter of biblical interpretation but that the interpreter was led to 'see again' the vision of Ezekiel (Lieb 1991; Halperin 1988). In several Jewish apocalypses (e.g. *1 Enoch* 14; *Apocalypse of Abraham* 11–18) an ascent to heaven is followed by a vision of God dependent on the first chapter of Ezekiel and the related vision in Isaiah 6. The antiquity of visionary appropriation of these texts has been confirmed by the discovery of a fragmentary vision of God in the *Songs of the Sabbath Sacrifice* from Qumran (*4Q405* 20 ii.21–2, probably first century BCE; Vermes 1997: 228).

According to the earliest post-biblical code of Jewish law, the Mishnah (*Mishnah Hagigah* 2:1), involvement in mystical speculation or visionary activity was severely restricted by ancient Jewish teachers, who feared it could damage faith. So Jewish sources discourage ordinary readers from too deep a preoccupation with a text like Ezek 1 (Scholem 1955). Meditation on Ezekiel 1, which is set in Exile in the aftermath of a previous destruction of the Temple, would have been particularly apposite as the rabbis sought to come to terms with the devastation of CE 70. We know that Paul was influenced by apocalyptic ideas of ascent (2 Cor 12:2–4), and he emphasizes vision as the basis of his practice (Gal 1:12, 16; cf. Acts 22:17). Who was responsible for the visions of God found in apocalyptic texts of the Second Temple period, and in what circumstances the texts were written, is not certain. All are dependent on Ezek 1, and they contain both similarities to and differences from Rev 4. In *1 Enoch* 14:8–24 (at least third century BCE and probably much older), for example, more attention is devoted to the heavenly ascent, which probably reflects the layout of the Temple. In *4Q405* 20 ii.21–2, part of the *Songs of the Sabbath Sacrifice*, more attention is devoted to the movement of the divine throne-chariot, as in Ezek 1.

John's vision of God and of heavenly worship is different in one important respect: it is complemented by the emergence from the circle around the divine throne of a Lamb 'standing as if it had been slaughtered' (5:6). The depiction of the salvific agent as an animal has parallels in Jewish texts (Dan 8–9, *1 Enoch* 89–90, which has a ram, 2 Esdras 11–12, and 2 Esdras 11:37; 21:31, a lion), but in none of these texts do the animals appear in a vision of God in heaven. The closest analogy is Dan 7, where animals represent the kingdoms of the world, though here, in contrast to Rev 5, the divine agent takes the form of a human figure (as in Rev 1:13). More akin to the angelic appearances in texts like Dan 10 is the appearance of Christ in Rev 1:13, which is less obviously linked with the Cross than is Rev 5.

The Interpretations

Many interpretations involve use of the vision as a paradigm for later visionaries and mystics, although often without any direct acknowledgment. Details
of the vision explored by later interpreters include the relationship of the new
moment in God's revelation with the old covenant and the identity of the 24
elders. This chapter contains the first of many examples of heavenly hymns,
which have influenced Christian hymnody and liturgy (Prigent 1964).

Actualizing interpretations: visionary appropriations of John's vision

In 4:1 the door opening marks a new dimension to John's experience. This is
paralleled in a martyr account from the late second or early third century CE,
in which Satyrus and Perpetua ascend to heaven, where they are conducted
into a garden (*viridiarium*) and summoned to greet the Lord (*The Martyrdom
of Perpetua and Felicity*, tr. in Musurillo 1972: 121; cf. Crum 1913: 149, 152,
for evidence of the text's influence on early Montanism; cf. Rowland 1982:
392–402; Lane Fox 1986: 375–418).

Some interpreters describe their own visionary experience as the source of
complete clarity about the meaning of Scripture. So Hildegard writes at the
beginning of *Scivias* of heaven opening and 'a fiery light of exceeding brilliance'
which 'came and permeated my whole brain':

> Immediately I knew the meaning of the exposition of the Scriptures, namely the
> Psalter, the gospel and the other catholic volumes of both the Old and the New
> Testaments, though I did not have the interpretation of the words of their texts
> or the division of the syllables or the knowledge of cases or tenses. (*Scivias Dec-
> laration*, Hart and Bishop edn 59)

Such insight into the deeper meaning of the text did not come primarily by
study. Joachim of Fiore writes that the 'God who once gave the spirit of
prophecy to the prophets has given me the spirit of understanding to grasp
with great clarity in his Spirit all the mysteries of sacred scripture' (*Ten Stringed
Psaltery* 10 in McGinn 1979: 99–100). A sudden visionary experience at
Casamari was the source of his understanding of the Apocalypse:

> Having gone through the preceding verses of the Book of Revelation to this place
> (Rev 1:10: 'I was in the Spirit on the Lord's day') I experienced such great diffi-
> culty and mental constraint beyond the ordinary that it was like feeling the stone

that closed the tomb opposed to me . . . After a year, the Feast of Easter came round. Awakened from sleep about midnight, something happened to me as I was meditating on this book, something for which, relying on the gift of God, I am made more bold to write . . . Since some of the mysteries were already understood, but the greater mysteries were yet hidden, there was a kind of struggle going on in my mind . . . Then on the above-mentioned night, something like this happened. About the middle of the night's silence, as I think, the hour when it is thought that our lion of the tribe of Judah [5:5] rose from the dead, as I was meditating, suddenly something of the fullness of this book and of the entire agreement of the Old and New Testaments was perceived by a clarity of understanding in my mind's eye. The revelation was made when I was not even mindful of the chapter mentioned above. (*Expositio* 39 in McGinn 1998: 130; note also the visionary experience of Joachim's contemporary Raimon Llull 1993)

Indebtedness to the apocalyptic visionary tradition is also evident in Hildegard's vision of the throne of God: 'I saw a great mountain of the color of iron and enthroned on it One of such great glory that it blinded my sight . . . and above the cloud a royal throne, round in shape, on which One was sitting, living and shining and marvellous in His glory' (Hart and Bishop edn 67; cf. 73, 309, 482). Elsewhere she describes 'an image full of eyes on all sides' (*Scivias* i, Hart and Bishop edn 67; cf. *Scivias* ii.7.1, Hart and Bishop edn 67, 294).

In seventeenth-century England women visionaries such as Anna Trapnel and Anne Wentworth were inspired by the Apocalypse. Trapnel's visionary trance and prophetic denunciation of the failures of the Protectorate exhibit numerous parallels to the Apocalypse, while Wentworth's use of the Zion/ Babylon contrast in the context of domestic oppression reflects how the Apocalypse could help women find a voice (Hobby 1988: 104; cf. Trapnel 2000; Bradstock and Rowland 2002: 144–57). Like the ancient Jewish rabbis, many Christians have found such visionary experiences problematic, and they frequently caused suspicion or hostility. One theologian who offered an apology for their theological significance was Jonathan Edwards, who argued that such phenomena were a natural result of the 'intense exercises and affections of mind' in persons of 'particular constitutions' whose 'affections are so strong' (in Taves 1999: 35, 109, 124; cf. Smolinski in Stein 2000: 55–60).

A vision of the New Testament preaching: Victorinus

Continuing his interpretation of Rev 1–6 as a succinct presentation of the mysteries of christology and soteriology (see above, 45), Victorinus understands Rev 4–5 as a parable of Christian preaching (1997: 32; ANF vii.347–50). He explains the 'open door' of 4:1: 'The new testament is announced as an open door in heaven . . . Since the door is shown to be opened, it is manifest that previously it had been closed to men. And it was sufficiently and fully laid open when Christ ascended with His body to the Father into heaven' (ANF vii.347). When John in 4:1 hears again 'the first voice' he had heard before, this reveals that the same Spirit speaks in the prophets and the gospel: 'That is the Spirit, whom a little before [John] confesses that he had seen walking as the son of man in the midst of the golden candlesticks [1:12] and he now gathers from Him what had been foretold in similitudes by the law, and associates with this scripture all the former prophets, and opens up the Scriptures' (Ibid.).

The two stones mentioned in 4:3 are the two testaments and also the two judgments of God, and the rainbow and the sea of glass are the two covenants (Victorinus 1997: 64–7). The intermediaries between God and man are symbolized by the 24 elders and the four living creatures, the former indicating the testimony of the law and the prophets (and, on another interpretation, the 12 patriarchs and 12 apostles) and the latter the four gospels and also the four main phases of salvation: incarnation, passion, resurrection and ascension. The creatures' wings are the Old Testament prophecies (six times four equaling the number of OT books; for this division see Victorians 1916: 54.8–10 and 56.3–4). Just as a creature cannot fly without wings, the four living creatures, representing the gospels, cannot 'fly' without the prophecies of the Old Testament. The eyes on the inside and outside indicate the double sense, moral and prophetic, of Scripture.

Influence of Ezekiel's vision: the importance of the merkabah (throne-chariot)

Ezekiel's vision of God's throne borne on the four living creatures is the raw material for John's own vision, supplemented by distinctive features such as the 24 elders and motifs drawn from Isa 6. In literary and artistic interpretations, mutual influence among these biblical texts is evident. Although John's vision lacks the wheels from Ezek 1, they play an important role in Joachim's interpretation. The merkabah vision of Ezekiel becomes a hermeneutical key to the relationship between the Apocalypse and the other books of the Bible (e.g. the gospels). The 'wheels within the wheels' (Ezek 1:15–16) are used by Joachim to link the old and new dispensations and their related narrative accounts (1953: plate 15; cf. Reeves and Hirsch-Reich 1972: plate 28). Also the progression clockwise round the diagram marks the different stages of the life of Jesus from birth to ascension. A christological interpretation of Ezek 1 is apparent in Rev 5, paralleled in John 12:41–3, which claims that Isaiah saw the glory of Christ (cf. Justin, *Dial.* 126). Also important for emerging christology was the identification of the fiery figure on the throne (Ezek 1:26–8) with Jesus, probably presupposed already in Rev 1:13–17 (Rowland 1982: 94; Hurtado 1998). Similarly, the vision of Isa 6 is linked with Ezek 1 in the Bamberg Commentary on Isaiah (eleventh century; in Mayr-Harting 1991: plate 22).

That Blake connected Rev 4 and Ezek 1 is clear from his pictures *Ezekiel's Wheels* (Museum of Fine Arts, Boston) and *The Twenty Four Elders* (Tate Gallery, London), and from the unfinished sketches on the *Book of Enoch* (Butlin 1981: i.1079–83). *The Twenty Four Elders* merges Rev 4 and 5, with a prominent divinity holding the sealed scroll and a comatose Lamb barely visible in the midst of the encircling eyes and worshiping elders. This contrasts with the prominence given to the human in Blake's depiction of Ezekiel's vision, where the humanity in divinity is to the fore, rather than the strange elements so much emphasized in Ezekiel's vision.

A Beatus manuscript depicts the throne in heaven with God in a doorway on a seat, and below this a large circle, at the center of which is a lamb with a cross and a shrine surrounded by elders and the living creatures. Yin-yang shapes give an impression of movement (representing wheels, according to Van der Meer 1978: 110). An anthropological use of Ezek 1 is evident in Blake's portrayal and in Raphael's *The Vision of Ezekiel* (Pitti Palace, Florence), where throne and chariot disappear to be left with a human figure surrounded by cherubs. The African-American song 'Ezekiel saw the wheel' also introduces the human into Ezekiel's vision; 'ev'ry spoke was humankind' (in Johnson and Johnson 1954: ii.144).

Interpretations of special motifs

THE 24 ELDERS AROUND THE THRONE (4:4, 10–11)

The identity of the elders has been much debated, with interpretations including the 24 priestly courses of the old covenant and the representatives of both the old and the new Israel (e.g. Victorinus, see above). The heavenly scene from Rev 4 provides Dante with images for his description of the strange procession in *Purgatorio* 29.43–85 (line 82 mentions 2 elders). Milton describes the elders as 'amongst the enthroned gods on sainted seats' ('A Masque presented at Ludlow Castle' 11; cf. *Paradise Lost* iii.350–2 and 'Ad Patrem' 32–3). In Bunyan's *Pilgrim's Progress* Christian is promised that he will be united with elders and saints (1967 edn 56).

LIGHTNING, THUNDER, SEVEN TORCHES, SEVEN SPIRITS (4:5)

Irenaeus reflects a christological development linking the seven spirits with the Lamb (*Dem.* 9): they form a candelabra, which illuminates the heavens and is given to the divine Son. According to Victorinus, the lightning, voices, thunder and seven torches in 4:5 herald the advent of Christ and the announcement of a New Testament from heaven (1916: 56.16–18). The burning torches show that the gift of the Holy Spirit comes through the wood of the Cross (1916: 56.18–20). The *Geneva Bible* explains two contrasting implications of the scene: 'The Holy Ghost is as a lightning unto us that believe, and as a fearful thunder to the disobedient.' For Nicholas Buldesdorf, at the *eschaton* the candelabrum of the Church (Rev 4:5) would be returned to the synagogue, which had to be faithful to the Mosaic law and their fathers' traditions, for there would be no need of conversion to Christianity in the last days (*Testimonies of the Holy Spirit in Prophecies* in Potesta in McGinn 2000: 132). The Jews also play a significant role in Joachim's eschatological expectation (McGinn 1985: 33).

A wider influence of elements of Rev 4 may be detected in the Islamic traditions: 'Five lights emanate from the divine throne as holy spirits. These five lights are continuous with the Speaking (*natiqa*) Spirit which is God, and which shines into the hearts of Muhammad, Ali, Fatima, Hasan and Husayn, (*Apocalypse of Jabir* Umm. 83 in Arjomand in McGinn 2000: 259).

THE RAINBOW, THE SEA OF GLASS AND THE FOUR LIVING CREATURES (4:6–8)

Milton often uses imagery from this chapter: 'Orbed in a rainbow; and, like glories wearing,/Mercy will sit between,/Throned in celestial sheen' ('On the Morning of Christ's Nativity' xv.143–5; cf. *Paradise Lost* iii.517–20, v.713–15 (lamps of fire); for allusions in Byron, Coleridge and Shelley, see Paley 1999: 193, 274). He connects the ladder of Jacob stretched up to heaven (Gen 28:12) with the sea of glass: 'There always, but drawn up to heaven sometimes/ Viewless, and underneath a bright sea flowed/Of jasper, or of liquid pearl, whereon/Who after came from earth' (*Paradise Lost* iii.517–20; cf. vii.619). For Andrew of Caesarea (*Comm.* 10 in Averky 1985: 84) the sea of glass indicates the tranquillity of the future life as opposed to the stormy sea of this life, from which the Antichrist comes. So also the *Geneva Bible*: 'The world is compared to a sea because of the changes & unstableness.'

A similar sense of foreboding is conjured up by Shelley's subtle variations on Rev 4, 6 and 20:

> The Father and the Son
> Knew that strife was now begun,
> They knew that Satan had broken his chain,
> And, with millions of demons in his train,
> Was ranging over the world again.
> Before the Angel had told his tale,
> A sweet and creeping sound
> Like the rushing of wings was heard around;

> And suddenly the lamps grew pale –
> The lamps, before the archangels seven,
> That burn continually in heaven.
>
> (*The Poetical Works of Percy Bysshe Shelley*
> 2:299 in Paley 1999: 274; cf. the last lines of
> Blake's *Europe*: 'and with a cry that shook all
> nature to the utmost pole, call'd all his sons
> to the strife of blood')

By introducing proleptically elements from later chapters, he turns the glorious heavenly scene into a doomsday scenario.

Irenaeus initiated the interpretation taken up by Victorinus (see above) which links the four creatures of 4:7–8 with the four evangelists. The lion is Mark (lion roaring in the desert); the calf represents Luke (who narrates Zacharias offering sacrifice); the man is Matthew (who portrayed Jesus' fleshly lineage from Mary); and the eagle symbolizes John ('pointing out the gift of the Spirit hovering with His wings over the Church'). These four living creatures represent the universal nature of the fourfold gospel; just as there are 'four zones of the cosmos' and 'four principal winds' (*AH* iii.11.8, ANF i.428). Irenaeus is countering those who use only one gospel (Ebionites, Marcion and perhaps Cerinthus; *AH* iii.11.7–8). As manifestations of the Son and of the succeeding age of the Spirit, the creatures are different from all other creatures of heaven. Their fourfold praise shows the universal nature of worship and is the original pattern followed by Moses in Ex 25:31–40 (*AH* iii.11.18).

For Joachim the four animals stand for the four senses of Scripture. They also represent the four great works of Christ – the nativity, the passion, the resurrection and the ascension – and also the four orders of the Church: apostles (or pastors), martyrs (or deacons), doctors (or confessors), virgins and hermits (or contemplatives, *Lib. Conc.* 25v, 67v; *Expositio* 17–18 in Reeves and Hirsch-Reich 1972: 233; cf. Wainwright 1993: 151). These interpretations illustrate the role of numbers in Joachim's hermeneutical method. In a twelfth-century poem the breaking of the first seal (Rev 6:1) reveals the four living creatures, here identified as members of the church hierarchy: pope, bishop, archdeacon and dean (in Emmerson in Emmerson and McGinn 1992: 297). Milton, by adding wheels and eyes to the creatures' wings, links them with Ezek 1:

> 'but conveyed
> By four cherubic shapes, four faces each
> Had wondrous, as with stars their bodies all
> And wings were set with eyes, with eyes the wheels
> Of beryl, and careering fires between'
> (*Paradise Lost* vi.752–6)

The creatures figure in the communion of saints with a special day in the calendar of the Ethiopian Church (Cowley 1983).

THE SANCTUS: 'HOLY, HOLY HOLY' (4:8)

The Sanctus has long been an essential part of the eucharistic liturgy, as is seen already in the Roman rite of the late medieval period:

> It is truly meet and just, right and beneficial to our salvation, that we should at all times and in all places give thanks to You, O holy Lord . . . Through whom the angels praise Your majesty . . . With whom we, your supplicants, pray You to join our voices also praising You and saying: Holy, holy, holy Lord God of Hosts. Heaven and earth are full of your glory. (In Flanigan in Emmerson and McGinn 1992: 344–5; cf. Prigent 1964; for other echoes of the hymn see Dante, *Paradiso* 7.1–3, 26.69, and Milton, *Paradise Regained* iii.111)

While the immediate biblical source is Isa 6:3, the addition of 'heaven and earth are full of your glory' reflects the scene in Rev 4:8. Also prompted by the Apocalypse are a series of liturgical questions and answers found in the *Apocalypse of John Chrysostom* (fifth century CE; in Court 2000: 67–103).

The threefold praise of God also echoes in hymns sung today: for example, in words by the poet Reginald Heber (1783–1826), which allude also to the sea of glass of 4:6 and to the casting down of crowns (4:10–11), here an activity of all the saints:

> Holy, holy, holy! Lord God Almighty!
> Early in the morning our song shall rise to thee;
> Holy, holy, holy! merciful and mighty,
> God in three Persons, blessed Trinity.
>
> Holy, holy, holy! All the saints adore thee,
> casting down their golden crowns around the glassy sea;
> cherubim and seraphim falling down before thee,
> which wert, and art, and evermore shalt be.
> (*Hymnal* 1982: 362)

THE SCENE OF HEAVENLY WORSHIP (4:9–11)

This scene has its parallel in the ancient Jewish-Christian apocalypse, the *Ascension of Isaiah* (8:2 and 9:6). It inspired Bunyan's picture of the destiny of those who have persevered in the Christian life (*Pilgrim's Progress*, 1967 edn 56).

Anna Trapnel, one of the more remarkable prophetic voices of the Civil War period in seventeenth-century England, gives women an important place in her vision of the heavenly court, substituting them for the elders:

John thou wilt not offended be
That handmaids here should sing
That they should meddle to declare
The matters of the King.
John will not be displeased that
They should sit about the throne,
And go unto original
And nothing else will own. . . .
And the handmaids were promised,
Much of that spirit choice,
And it is, and it shall go forth
In a rare singing voice.
('Voice of the King of Saints'
(1657) 37, 54 in Hobby 1988: 33)

In an African-American spiritual the author looks forward to joining the worship of the elders: 'Deep River, my home is over Jordan. . . . /Walk into heaven and take my seat,/And cast my crown at Jesus' feet' (Johnson and Johnson 1954: i.100–3).

Revelation 5

Ancient Literary Context

This chapter has its closest analogies in visions such as those of Dan 7–8, where beasts represent world empires, a feature taken up later in Rev 13 and 17. In the present chapter, however, the beast, the Lamb, intrudes into the heavenly scene as agent, not object, of judgement. In Jewish apocalypses there are several types of vision (J. J. Collins 1984): a report by the seer of what he has seen in heaven, usually after a mystical ascent (e.g. *1 Enoch* 14), communication to the seer of divine secrets by an angel, with no vision account (as in 2 Esdras), and the dream vision in which the seer sees various objects (often animals) which are explained afterwards by an angel (Dan 7 and *1 Enoch* 89–90).

In the Jewish apocalypses the dream-vision, with its extravagant symbols and interpretation, is not usually merged with the heavenly ascent vision, as it is in Rev 4–5. The vision in Rev 4 is a good example of the first type of vision, but in Rev 5 language more typical of the symbolic vision (cf. Dan 7) is introduced into the heavenly vision. The use of animal imagery resembles *1 Enoch*

89–90, where animals represent humans. The awkwardness created by this combination, and also in the juxtaposition of the Lion and the Lamb in 5:4–5, point to the unique eschatological reality to which John seeks to bear witness. The Lamb has affected the normal apocalyptic conventions, and hitherto accepted patterns of discourse are shattered along with the understanding and course of history. The Lion of the tribe of Judah echoes Num 23:24, Mic 5:8 and Gen 49:9. Also relevant is 2 Esdras 11, where a lion reproves and destroys a great eagle, which represents the wicked power of Rome (11:37–12:3).

The Interpretations

Modern exegesis of this chapter almost universally regards it as the pivotal moment in the vision, in which history finds its meaning in the heavenly vindication of the Lamb that was slain. Ancient commentators like Victorinus said the same (1916: 60.10; 64.6–11). This chapter is important for another reason, because it is what gives a uniquely christological perspective to the apocalyptic scenes in the rest of the book (Caird 1966: 73; Massyngberde-Ford 1975, who claims the Apocalypse is essentially a Jewish vision, is an exception to this consensus; Barker 2000, on the other hand, thinks that the Apocalypse was a vision of Jesus himself). The theological significance attributed to this chapter is well illustrated by interpretations of the sealed book in 5:1. John's expression of grief (5:4, a rare moment when the impact on the visionary is noted) dramatizes the closed nature of the book. The seer's sadness is answered by a vision of the Lamb, who, he hears, is none other than the Lion of the tribe of Judah. What John hears is interpreted by what he sees. The fierce lion turns out to be a lamb. The christological significance of this is explored to the full by interpreters.

The sealed scroll (5:1)

Many are the speculations about the scroll (book) of 5:1, sometimes connected with the 'open scroll' of the angel in 10:8. Victorinus regarded the sealed book 'written within and without' as the Old Testament (1916: 64.6–9); the opening of the seals is the revelation of its true contents though Christ's death and resurrection. The four living creatures and the 24 elders in 5:8–9 represent both the new and the old covenants, which join together in singing a new song.

This song (5:9–11) indicates that with the incarnation, resurrection, seal of the Spirit and expectation of the kingdom, the new age has begun (1916: 66.2–11). The unsealing also points forward to the second coming of Christ (1916: 66.18–20) to which the message of the divine spirit, the rider on the white horse in 6:1–2, bears witness (1916: 68.1–13; ANF vii.350).

For Bullinger the sealed book contains 'all the counsels of God, all his works and judgements', sealed because the meaning of historical events is hidden from the world (*A Hundred Sermons* 159 in Bauckham 1978: 114). The sealed book contains 'the very destinies of the church' which are 'a sweet mystery' and 'a singular comfort to the faithful' (ibid. in Bauckham 1978: 303). The frontispiece to the Apocalypse in the Bible from Muiers-Granval, Tours (c.840), has the Lion and the Lamb on either side of an empty throne and below them the unveiling of the face of Moses by the living creatures, which symbolize the gospels (in Van der Meer 1978: 75, 78). Charles Wesley and Newton both identify the 'scroll' of Rev 5 with the book in Dan 12:4 (in Newport 2000: 128). The image of the scroll also influenced poets like Shelley and Blake. Shelley describes religion as 'a book sealed' ('England in 1819', line 11 in Paley 1999: 234), while for Blake the unsealing of the book is an indication of the moment when the false god of religion, law and hierarchy begins his tyrannous rule ('For Urizen unclasped his book', *Europe* 12.4 in Paley 1999: 66).

Joachim had two ways of interpreting the seal visions: as a description of events from the time of the patriarch Jacob to the Roman conquest of Israel, and as a portrayal of events beginning with the lifetime of Jesus. Seven periods or 'seals' form the old dispensation, with seven parallel periods in the new dispensation. In the sealed book, the whole of history is comprehended, and no one can loose its seals save the Lion of Judah (in Reeves and Hirsch-Reich 1972: 5–6). The Lion of Judah has been a potent image for Rastafarians, along with Rev 14:7 and 19:16 (in Barrett 1977: 104–5).

'I began to weep bitterly' (5:4)

The weeping of the seer finds a possible echo in the mystical writer Margery Kempe, who repeatedly writes of 'visionary' weeping, for her sins, for her bad attitude to God in the past, and when she contemplates the passion or sees the eucharist (Kempe 1985: 291; cf. Taves 1999: 111–12). Similar emotion and sensory perception are portrayed in this description of the Beguin visionary Na Prous Boneta:

> The Lord had given birth to her in the spirit and given her three gifts: the gift of tears or weeping whenever she stood at the aforementioned sepulchre; a greater

fragrance or odor than she had ever before smelled; and a gentle, sweet warmth as if a mantle had been thrown over her shoulders and wrapped around her. (in May 1965: 477–500; cf. Burr 2001: 230–6)

The Lion and the Lamb (5:5–7)

Not surprisingly, commentators see Jesus as the slain Lamb. According to Irenaeus, he is the only one who can see God and open the book (*AH* iv.20.2, 11). Hippolytus, like Victorinus, understands the sealed book as the Old Testament prefigurations (*Daniel* 20), which the Lamb opens so that the things spoken of him in secret might be 'proclaimed from the housetops' (cf. Luke 12:3). According to Cyprian, John sees the moment of the passion of Christ (*Test.* 11.15). Hildegard writes of seeing 'The Son of God, the strong Lion, who crushed fatal infidelity by the shining light of faith.' She emphasizes apocalyptic insight into the meaning of history: 'for it is by great fortitude that people believe through counsel what they cannot see with their bodily sight' (*Scivias* iii.8.15, Hart and Bishop edn 438). According to Bullinger, the receipt by the Lamb of the scroll in 5:7 means his receipt from God the Father of all power, both in heaven and in earth, an act which is a source of comfort (*A Hundred Sermons* 160 in Bauckham 1978: 303, 114–15).

The *Scofield Reference Bible* links this enthronement scene with Dan 7:13–14, noting that the Apocalypse adds what was hidden from Daniel: namely, that 'the kings and priests of the church age are to be associated with the Son of Man, the Lamb as it had been slain, in his reign on the earth' (Rev 5:9–10, Scofield 1917: 910, 1335–6). David Koresh seems to have thought of himself as the 'Lamb' who had the power to unseal the seven seals (in Newport 2000: 222; cf. Ralph Durden at the end of the sixteenth century, in Bauckham 1978: 188–91).

In a passage which is probably better known than any passage in the Apocalypse (at least in the English-speaking world), William Blake uses the image of the Lamb in an evocation of a better world and a prophetic challenge to create it. It occurs in a preface found in some versions of his little known poem *Milton* (sometimes known as 'Jerusalem', though it is to be distinguished from the later poem of the same name):

> And did those feet in ancient time
> Walk upon England's mountains green:
> And was the holy Lamb of God,
> On England's pleasant pastures seen!

And did the Countenance Divine,
Shine forth upon our clouded hills?
And was Jerusalem builded here,
Among these dark Satanic Mills?

Bring me my Bow of burning gold:
Bring me my Arrows of desire:
Bring me my Spear: O Clouds unfold!
Bring me my Chariot of fire!

I will not cease from Mental Fight,
Nor shall my Sword sleep in my hand:
Till we have built Jerusalem,
In England's green & pleasant Land.
Would to God that all the Lord's people
were Prophets.
                                    Numbers xi. 29v

Here several themes of the Apocalypse are brought together. The New Jerusalem of Rev 21 is not something remote or far off, but a present possibility; it may be built in England's 'green & pleasant land'. There is no disjunction between human activity and divine activity, no sense of 'leaving it all to God'. For Blake prophecy is not just a thing of the past but is the present vocation of all God's people.

The Lamb appears in several other poems of Blake, most accessibly in his *Songs of Innocence and Experience*. Just as in Rev 5 the sharp juxtaposition of the Lion of Judah and the Lamb that was slain challenges assumptions about the character of the Messiah, so Blake complements Christ's mercy in 'The Lamb' with his justice in 'The Tyger [*sic*]'. The poem presents the contrast confronting us all as we wrestle with the 'contraries' of life. The coming of Christ heralds not only the blissful salvation of the Lamb but also the wrath of the Tyger (*Songs of Experience*).

In *Jerusalem*, the last of Blake's major poems, the Lamb appears frequently as the goal from which Albion (who symbolizes the inhabitants of Britain) is alienated (7.59, 67, 69; 9.9; 12.40; 18.27; 20.9, 39; 24.2, 50, 53; 25; 27.6, 18, 65, 94; 36[40].51; 38[43].30; 40[45].15; 41[46].28; 50.10, 24, 30; 59.49; 60.38, 50; 62.30; 73.18; 77; 78.13–14, 18–19; 79.41, 51; 80.30, 65, 77; 82.7, 54; 83.15; 88.49–54; alternative plate numbers in brackets). Blake's poem, like the Apocalypse itself, is a complex unfolding of the state of alienation and the long tortuous path to redemption, for which he longs: 'Recieve the Lamb of God to dwell/In England's green & pleasant bowers' (*Jerusalem* 77). Blake contrasts the Lamb with the 'Abomination of desolation' (*Jerusalem* 7:69; cf. Dan 9:27; Mark 13:14). The Lamb offers an ever-present possibility for moral renewal, though the inhabitants of Britain are prevented from reaching that goal by their inability to recognize their true destiny (*Jerusalem* 9:9). Blake saw Jerusalem and the way of the Lamb emerging in his own work and abode in LAMBeth (*Jerusalem* 12:40). Albion's alienation from its true vocation is so far advanced that traces of the Lamb's presence are virtually extinguished (*Jerusalem* 24:80). In *Jerusalem* 27:6 the Lamb appears along with the Bride (see Rev 21:2). The sense of an apocalyptic struggle in which the Lamb is liberator and also the target of superhuman forces (as in Rev 5 and 17:14) is never far from Blake's poetic imagination (cf. *Jerusalem* 78:13–19). It is the prophet's role (and Blake certainly saw himself as a prophet) to hammer out a way of justice as a herald to the Lamb of God (*Jerusalem* 88:49–54).

John Howard Yoder, in a classic statement of an Anabaptist position which expresses a countercultural politics, offers Rev 5 as the paradigm for a Christian attitude to history (Yoder 1972: 237; cf. Pipkin 1989: 69–76; McClendon 1994: 97–102). What Rev 5 proclaims is the politics of the Lamb. John sheds tears in the face of the world's injustice, but the meaning of history is the formation, around the Lamb that was slain, of a new human race, international in character and determined not by Caesar's rule, which is based on violence (cf. Wengst 1987). The Lamb's suffering for the cause of right overturns the principalities and powers, as is stated in the hymnic proclamation in 5:9 which heralds the beginning of a new politics (Yoder in Pipkin 1989: 73–5).

Artistic representations of the Lamb

Many Beatus manuscripts contain lively illustrations of the Lamb in the midst of the throne. The Pierpont Morgan Beatus has the Lamb bearing a cross in the centre of a large circle, surrounded by the four living creatures (MS 644 (c.950) in Grubb 1997: 15). In van Eyck's painting *The Mystical Lamb* (1432), St Bavo, Ghent, in Seidel in McGinn 2000: 497–500), following in the tradition of Tyconius (see above, 16), the division between heaven and earth is transcended in the eucharistic feast. The Lamb in the midst of the throne is found on an altar on earth (cf. the Bamberg Bible, fol. 339v, where the Lamb is juxtaposed with a chalice). In his illustrations of the Apocalypse, Dürer brilliantly evokes the stark contrast between an idyllic earth and the apocalyptic, otherworldly, complexity of the heavenly scene (in Smith 2000: 20).

Given the supreme importance of the Lamb within the framework of Blake's long poem *Jerusalem*, it has a rather subordinate role in his picture *The Twenty-Four Elders* (Tate Gallery, London). It evokes Rev 4 especially (the rainbow, the worship of the elders and the four living creatures around the throne), but in a prominent position, though hardly highlighted, is a sleeping lamb. Placed immediately before the enthroned God, the Lamb has a sealed scroll in his right hand.

The seven spirits and the harp (5:6, 8)

The seven spirits of 5:6 are compared by Irenaeus to a candelabrum, which illuminates the heavens. When they are given to the Son, all heavenly creatures praise God as creator and sender of the Son (*Dem.* 9). Incense is offered to the slain Lamb in the midst of the throne (*AH* iii. 17.6; cf. Rev 7:17). The motif of seven eyes sent into all the world in 5:6 (which draws on verses like Zech 4:4) is taken up by Milton in *Paradise Lost* iii.534. For Victorinus, the harp of 5:8, which has strings stretched across a wooden frame, is a sign of the flesh of Christ stretched upon the wood of the Cross (1916: 66.11–13).

'they will reign on earth' (5:10)

The this-worldly promise in 'they will reign on earth' is picked up in the description of the millennial kingdom in 20:4–6 (see commentary thereon). This represents a markedly different kind of eschatology from the mainstream Christian tradition: a hope for this world rather than some transcendent realm (Cohn 1957; Rowland 1988; Bradstock and Rowland 2002). It is pointedly rejected by the *Geneva Bible*'s marginal gloss: the saints will reign, but 'Not corporally'. This exemplifies a fundamental division within the Christian world, ancient and modern, which does not run along ecclesiastical or denominational lines but concerns whether Christians believe that the kingdom of God involves a hope for the transformation of this world and its structures. A re-emphasis on the millennium has been a feature of some modern systematic theology (Moltmann 1996: 129–256).

Praise of the Lamb (5.11–13)

Milton links this heavenly scene with other biblical verses like Ps 68 to evoke the blessing of the Son of God (*Paradise Lost* iv.767–70, vi.886; xi.24). The hymn of 5:12, 'Worthy is the Lamb ... to receive power and wealth and wisdom and might and honour and glory and blessing' is set to music in Handel's *Messiah*, as is the praise of 5:13, 'blessing and honour, glory and power be unto Him'. In an African-American spiritual, the singer imagines joining the heavenly praises:

Want to go to heab'n, when I die . . .
To see God's bleedin' Lam' . . .
Den you raise yo' voice up higher . . .
an' you jine dat heab'nly choir . . .
To see God's bleedin' Lam'.

(Johnson and Johnson 1954:
ii.152–4; cf. references to the Lamb
in i.144, 173; ii.114–15, 138–9)

Ancient Literary Context

Chapter 6 begins one of three similar sequences of seven plagues (seals, 6:1–17; 8:1–2; trumpets, 8:2–9:21; 11:15; and bowls, 16:1–21). This ordered, enumer-ated progression links to contemporary Jewish and Christian texts in two ways. First, in the pronouncements of woe on an unrepentant world, it reflects a widespread tradition of disaster preceding the time of bliss (Dan 12:1; Mark 13; Matt 24; Luke 21). In Mark 13:8 the woes are described as 'birth pangs' (cf. Rom 8:22). Secondly, in some texts, particularly two apocalyptic texts roughly contemporary with the Apocalypse, 2 Esdras 5:1–12 and the *Apocalypse of Baruch* 25–7, there is a fixed quota of 'messianic woes' (see also *Jubilees* 23:31). This scheme of plagues or woes became a standard component of Jewish and Christian expectations of the future, and the term 'apocalyptic' is often asso-ciated with such catastrophes. The Apocalypse's seven woes are paralleled in the early Christian apocalypse, the *Vision of Paul*, where the pit of hell is a well that is sealed with seven seals (in Emmerson and McGinn 1992: 311).

The first four seals of Rev 6 are related to one another and may well be inspired by the four horses of Zech 1:8 and 6:1–3. In Revelation they are coloured white, red, black and pale green, whereas in Zechariah they are red, red, sorrel and white (1:8), or red, black, white and dappled grey (6:1–3). A quarter of the earth is to suffer death and famine, a combination familiar from prophetic sources (Jer 14:12; 15:2; 21:7; Ezek 5:12–15; 14:21; 33:27). The seals unleash catastrophes of various kinds with antecedents in Ex 9 and 14 and in prophetic texts (Isa 13:10; 50:3; Ezek 29:5; 38:19; Joel 2:10).

The Interpretations

For several reasons this chapter has always figured prominently in interpretation of the Apocalypse. First, it is intimately linked with the critical vision in Rev 5 where the Lamb takes the sealed book and then, in Rev 6, begins to open it. Secondly, its relationship with other sequences of seven in the book (the letters, trumpets and bowls) has led to both sequential and recapitulative interpretations. In the first of these the book is seen as unfolding in a neat linear sequence, and in the second, more common reading, the various sequences are regarded as repetitions of what has already been unfolded in the first sequence. Thirdly, the prominent position of the opening of the first seal (reinforced by similar imagery in Rev 19:11) has given Rev 6 a peculiar place in the history of interpretation. The following examples focus on: the first rider, who sits on the white horse; the nature of the sequences of seven; 'actualizations' in which the images of the Apocalypse are used to interpret past, present and future history; the souls under the altar; and, finally, the effects of the apocalyptic catastrophe, which prompts a reaction of utter terror in the face of the enormity of the death and destruction.

The rider on the white horse: the first seal (6:1)

CHRISTOLOGICAL INTERPRETATIONS
In the *Second Apocalypse of John* 18 (fourth century CE) the opening of the seals is interpreted to refer to the final judgement that follows victory over the Antichrist (in Court 2000: 43). Victorinus, however, begins a long tradition of interpretation when he identifies the rider on the white horse as Christ, or the Christian gospel (suggested by the rider of 19:11). His coming is the revelation of the meaning of the Old Testament in the person of Jesus Christ: 'after our Lord ascended into heaven, he opened all things and sent the Holy Spirit, whose

words, like seals, reached the human heart through preachers and overcame unbelief . . . [T]he white horse is the word of preaching sent to the world with the Holy Spirit' (ANF vii.350). While the white horse is a positive symbol and the others are all negative, the four horses together represent one entity, the two sides of the character of God, mercy and judgement (Victorinus 1916: 68.10–11). The last three horses represent the wars, famines and pestilences announced in Matt 24:14. The third seal and the black horse signify famine, particularly in the time of the Antichrist, while the pale horse, Death, is the 'devouring' or final damnation of impious souls. The fifth seal (6:9–11) serves a different function, describing the souls of the saints under the altar in the underworld (1916: 70.1–4; 72.2–5; 74.10–11).

This christological interpretation of the first seal is picked up in the Trier Apocalypse (early ninth century; in Klein in Emmerson and McGinn 1992: 176), where the rider on the white horse is pictured separately from the other three. The Beatus manuscript at Osma (c.1086, Burgo de Osma, Archivo de la cathedral I, fol.151) has the rider on the white horse with the sword coming out of his mouth (cf. 19:11), separated from the other riders (in Van der Meer 1978: 114). For Andrew of Caesarea the removing of the first seal is the sending into the world of the holy apostles. Like a bow, they direct the preaching of the gospel against demons. The black horse symbolizes lamentation over those who have fallen away from faith in Christ (*Comm.* 15 in Averky 1985: 95). The christological interpretation of the first rider is also evident in this interpretation from 1789: 'the whiteness showing the Church's purity and the bow the victory of the gospel, so the breaking of the first seal prophesies the spread of the gospel in the apostolic age' (Bryce Johnston in Burdon 1997: 83–4). Coleridge combines Rev 5 and 6 in his evocation of apocalyptic themes: 'And all that were and had the spirit of life, / Sang a new song [cf. Rev 5:9] to him who had gone forth, / Conquering and still to conquer!' (*Osorio* (1797) in *CPW* 2:596–7 in Paley 1999: 118).

THE RIDER AS THE UNMASKING OF VIOLENCE BY THE GOSPEL OF THE LAMB

An influential exploration of the impact of the gospel on human culture is that of René Girard (1987), who claims that human cultures have their origin in that basic human tendency of rivalry and the imitation of violent behaviour. Such conflicts of desire are resolved by the murder or scapegoating of an arbitrary victim. Myths grow up which narrate such murders from the perspective of the killers, with the accompanying sacrificial rites providing an outlet for the actual violence generated by mimetic desire. In the New Testament, particularly the gospels, however, we have a story of a victim and a killing told from the perspective of the scapegoated person, and asserting his innocence. This has the effect of unmasking all cultures that are based on violence.

Humanity is challenged to imitate the renunciation of violence advocated and practised by Jesus (Rowland 1998: 606). The earliest commentator on the Apocalypse, Victorinus of Poetovio, comes close to this view when he interprets the rider on the white horse as the gospel's effect on a violent world.

Thus one way of reading Rev 6, following Girard, is to regard it as the unmasking of human culture by revealing the vindication of the Lamb who was slain. The story of Jesus' death is a revelation of the false consciousness encouraged by the scapegoat mechanism and the violence it institutionalizes. The gospel offers an alternative pattern for human *mimesis*. This in turn provokes a violent reaction. Whatever value we attach to this approach to the Apocalypse, it shows how a modern interpreter committed to non-violence can read even this most violent book as 'carrying out subversion' and 'supplying the secret motive force of all subsequent history' (Girard 1997: 209).

The seven seals

Bede represents those who see the seven seals as depicting stages in the development of the Church. The white horseman of the first seal represents the purity of the primitive Church, and the following three horsemen represent three successive wars against the Church. The woes of the sixth seal are the final earthly trials under the Antichrist, and the 'silence in heaven for about half an hour' (8:1) is the brief time of rest between the coming of the Antichrist and the Last Judgement (in Lerner in Emmerson and McGinn 1992: 54). Bernard of Clairvaux plays with the idea that the four horsemen are parables of the four ages of the Church, changing their order to correspond with historical realities: first the age of persecution (red horse), then a time of peace in the Church (white horse), then hypocrisy (black horse), then the Antichrist (the pale horse, *Sancti Bernardi Opera* vi.87–8 in Rusconi in McGinn 2000: 298).

Heinrich Bullinger writes of the sealed book in Rev 6 that the calamities are sent for humanity's health, 'since they are not sent without [God's] providence and disposition'. They are for human edification:

> We miserable mortal men, environed with sinful flesh, ought to learn, that we should acknowledge also the justice of God in all his works, and not murmur at his government and most rightful judgments: but rather to worship God, to submit us unto him, to praise his righteousness, and give thanks for his most holy government, and to cry with the prophet, Thou art just, O Lord, in all thy ways, and holy in all thy works [Ps 145:17]. (In Bauckham 1978: 303)

Pointing out that the number seven means perfection, he describes the three sequences: the seals indicate 'all manner of calamities by the just judgement of

God poured out on the world', whereas in the trumpets John 'comprehendeth all heresies in the world'. The bowls 'comprehendeth again all manner and the most full plagues of God' (in Bauckham 1978: 305, 311).

Anselm of Havelberg combines ecclesiological themes with a historical framework in an interpretation of the seals that was to have many echoes in subsequent writing (see below on Lambert and Bale):

First seal: the purity of the apostolic Church (The first rider is 'Christ ruling the Church and humiliating and casting down the proud with the bow of apostolic teaching');
Second seal: persecution under the pagan emperors from Nero to Constantine;
Third seal: major heresies after Constantine;
Fourth seal: age of false Christians and hypocrites who 'confess Christ publicly but deny him by their deeds';
Fifth seal: martyred Christians in all ages;
Sixth seal: time of the Antichrist and end of the world;
Seventh seal: heavenly bliss.
(In McGinn 1998: 114–15; cf. Emmerson 1981: 19; Morrison in Emmerson and McGinn 1992: 356–9)

In Book 3 of the *Liber de concordia*, Joachim worked out a systematic presentation of the seven seals as seven periods of the old covenant, with seven corresponding periods of the new covenant. The seven seals and their opening would take 42 generations (cf. Matt 1:1–17), with an average of six generations each. The sixth in the sequence was of particular importance. Jesus was conceived in the sixth month, and the letter to the church at Philadelphia is emphasized (see above, commentary on Rev 3:7–13). In stressing penultimacy throughout his interpretation, Joachim picks up a recurring theme of the Apocalypse. He looks forward to a future pope of the sixth period, who will be sent as an emissary from 'Jerusalem' to 'Babylon', to renew the Church, which is oppressed by the sixth and seventh heads of the dragon (in Daniel in Emmerson and McGinn 1992: 81–2).

Joachim's emphasis on the penultimate is a reminder that there is clearly a space for a this-worldly reformation, as is signified by the space between the heads and the dragon's tail in his *Book of Figures* (1953: plate 12; cf. Reeves and Hirsch-Reich 1972: plate 21 and p. 146; McGinn 1979: 134 and see discussion below, 141). In his scheme of three ages or 'stages' (of Father, Son and Spirit), the third age of the Spirit does not supersede that of the Son. Rather, the first two 'states' are embodied in the third. Joachim's emphasis on the second coming of Christ has two dimensions: a 'middle advent' (which followers of Francis of Assisi, in the light of Joachim's interpretation of the Apocalypse, saw fulfilled in his coming) and a future coming. This resembles the view of the Apocalypse and other New Testament writings according to which Christ comes both as present judge (Rev 2–3, especially 2:16) and in the future (19:11).

Joachite themes had a widespread influence, evident, for example, in Jaroslav Vrchlicky's remarkable poem, which expresses nineteenth-century Czech nationalism and hoped-for freedom:

> The only and third Kingdom of the Spirit will come,
> When all riches and possessions and gold,
> Jewels, base wealth will be mere mire,
> When the poor in goods will be rich in spirit,
> And the world comes alive with the bustle of eternal spring
>
> With trembling joyous ear I listen to him. . . .
>
> I know he tells the truth, for from one side here
> I look at Sodom and Rome,
> And from the other side I look in anger
> At Byzantium and Gomorrah, and I weigh up their error and guilt,
> And I do not wonder that the world lies in shadows.
>
> He rides into the world like a fiery wedge. . . .
>
> The kingdom of the Father has been – that was the flaring of sweet stars;
> The kingdom of the Son has been – that was the smiling of the moon;
> The kingdom of the Spirit is to come – an unperishing sun . . .
> The kingdom of laws, suffering and anxiety has been;
> The kingdom, of mercy, faith and discipline has been;
> Now the kingdom of love will come, the Kingdom of eternal love! . . .
>
> A 'hallelujah' sounds through the expanses of the worlds . . .
>
> Now the eternal gospel [cf. Rev 14:6] transmits its glowing flame;
> Now the true freedom of human souls will begin,
> The freedom which will victoriously trample all chains into the dust. . . .
> Joachim of Fiore, prophesy this golden age.
> (Jaroslav Vrchlicky, *Vecne evangelium* in Reeves 2001: 323; this poem was
>   set to music by Janáček; cf. also Reeves and Gould 1987)

In the sixteenth century the interpretation of the seven seals as a historical sequence reappears in the following scheme of Francis Lambert which influenced John Bale and others:

First seal: outpouring of the Spirit at Pentecost and apostolic mission through the Roman world.

Second seal: Roman emperors persecuted Christians; few heresies in the
    church.
Third seal: peace given to church by Constantine followed by many heresies.
Fourth seal: After the suppression of these errors, Satan corrupted the papacy
    with 'worldly ambition, by spreading the hypocritical monastic lie, as well
    as by persecuting the Church outwardly through the armies of Islam.'
Fifth seal: the persecution of the saints in all ages, though their affliction by
    the papacy has been especially acute since the seventh or eighth century.
Sixth seal: revival of the gospel (Lambert thought this had been going on for
    the last 100 years but that the sixth age would conclude with a fearful per-
    secution.)
Seventh seal: millennium on earth, within history.
(In Fairfield 1976: 74–5; cf. Bauckham 1978: 23–9, 258–64)

In *The Image of bothe churches* Bale follows a similar pattern, minus the chiliasm, agreeing with Lambert and the long tradition of interpreting the Apocalypse as a mirror of church history. Bale thinks that the Apocalypse showed
how the purity of the early church had gradually grown rotten, and yet how
God had always kept his truth alive in a faithful few. The church, begun in a
pristine state with the apostles' preaching at Pentecost, had lost spiritual vigour
after Constantine, as is evident in the laziness and worldly ambition of popes.
Bale did not, however, adopt the view of the Lollards and of Thomas Muentzer
('Sermon before the Princes' in G. H. Williams 1957: 49–70; Muentzer 1988:
226–9) that the church had been irredeemably corrupted. In the third period
(the third seal), he says, the church's problems continued, and the collapse of
the church took place in the next period (the fourth seal). With the opening
of the sixth seal, which Bale links directly with Wyclif, there was a revival of
the gospel. This sense of renewal in the sixth period is typical of the Joachite
tradition. Lambert had seen the sixth age (his own) as a reawakening of true
preaching, but he predicted at the end of the period a horrible persecution, the
42 months when the dragon would make war on the saints and overcome them
(Rev 13:5–7), leading to the seventh age, the millennium on earth (20:4–6).
Bale played down imminent eschatological expectation and stressed the presence of the Beast already at work in the world. Keen to dampen dangerous
enthusiasm, he poured scorn on the Anabaptists (particularly those of the chiliastic variety, as in the Anabaptist commonwealth of 1534 in Münster; cf. Cohn
1957: 261; Deppermann 1987). Although he acknowledged the possibility of a
future 1,000-years' peace (in Firth 1979: 43), Bale put a much higher value on
the Reformation already happening in his own time.

The *Geneva Bible* represents a more general form of this scheme, without
much historical specificity. The white horse 'signifieth innocence, victory, &

felicity which should come by the preaching of the Gospel. He that rideth on the white horse is Christ.' The rider on the red horse 'signifieth the cruel wars that ensued when the Gospel was refused'. Hence the earthquake in 6:12 'signifieth the change of the true doctrine, which is the greatest cause of motions & troubles that come to the world'. The Sun's darkening means 'the traditions of men', and the moon turning to blood signifies that 'the Church was miserably defaced with idolatry & afflicted by tyrants'. When the stars of heaven fell (6:13), 'doctors & preachers depart from the truth'. In *The Christian's Complete Family Bible* (1739) the four horsemen are said to preview the early history of the church from its period of purity and conquest during the age of Christ and the apostles (the rider on the white horse) to more troubled experiences and persecutions at the hands of the Romans (in Newport 2000: 7).

Joseph Mede's *Clavis Apocalyptica* attempts to show how the various plague sequences relate to one another. In some instances the seals, trumpets and bowls overlap (though the bowls are less emphasized). The first six seals are grouped together to cover the time to Constantine. The opening of the seventh seal and the sounding of the first trumpet coincide (Rev 8:1–7), and the first four trumpets tell the story of the decline of the Roman Empire (8:1–12). While Constantine arrived on the scene during the sixth seal, the major change in the fortunes of the Empire came with the death of Theodosius the Great (395) and the permanent division of the Empire into east and west. At that time the first trumpet sounded, and this period lasted until about 410. The second trumpet (8:8–9) heralds the sacking of Rome by Alaric, and the third (8:10–11) the deposition of Emperor Romulus Augustulus by Odoacer in 476. The fourth trumpet (8:12) coincided with Belisarius and the Ostrogothic wars (which Mede dates to 542). The last three trumpets (9:1–20; 11:15–19) tell of the wars of persecution waged by the arch-enemies of Christendom, the Saracens (from 630), the Turks (from 1080), until finally the Antichrist of Rome will appear. With the defeat of the Antichrist the seventh trumpet ushers in the millennium (in Firth 1979: 220). For Mede the sequences relate specifically to the history of empire and then, beginning in chapter 10, to the life of the Church from the time of the apostles onwards. Mede, a Cambridge academic, was much consulted up to the time of his death immediately before the English Civil War in 1641. His notion of how the sacred text related to historical events was influential, as was his idea that the last things are already being fulfilled (in Firth 1979: 213–28).

Actualizations: the seven seals and interpreters' own experience

Tyconius takes the four horsemen to refer to the church and the influence of the devil in it. The first horseman is Christ, and the first horse is the church.

The other three are the devil or his minions; for example, the black horse refers to the 'spiritual famine' in the church (with the rider of this horse being false prophets). The sun's darkness in 6:12 means that 'the splendour of doctrine' is obscured for unbelievers. Tyconius interprets the sixth seal (6:13) to refer to disturbing of the faithful. In the last struggle with the Antichrist, those who seem holy will be shaken off by the church just as a fig-tree, moved by the wind, sheds unripe figs. The current struggle in the church in Africa gives the world an example of the future revelation of the Antichrist (in Beatus, *Preface* 4.1.41).

The visionary Na Prous Boneta, a radical Franciscan follower of Peter Olivi, links the text closely with her own experience. An outspoken critic of the contemporary papacy, she was sentenced to death in 1325. She claimed that the Lord God told her that she opened the sealed book of the Apocalypse 'which Blessed John said he had seen sealed with seven seals' (in Potesta in McGinn 2000: 119; cf. May 1965; Burr 1997 and 2001: 230–7). More recently, David Koresh believed that the breaking of the first seal prophesied his own ministry (in D. Thompson 1996: 293–7).

An example of particular identifications of the awesome beasts of death and destruction is Frederick II's identification of the monstrous red horse of 6:4 with the pope. This illustrates how apocalyptic images could be used by both sides, temporal and spiritual, in political and ecclesial struggles (in McGinn 1998: 175; cf. McGinn in McGinn 2000: 88–9; D. Thompson 1996: 73). Olivi identified Saint Francis with the angel of the sixth seal (7:2–3). His appearance heralded a persecution, inspired by the Antichrist, of the evangelical 'status' (*Lectura*, fols 83v–84r in Lee, Reeves and Silano 1989: 22–3). Olivi interprets the earthquake of the sixth seal (6:12) as the 'spiritual upheaval represented by conversions to the Franciscan order on the one hand and carnal opposition to it on the other in the time of the mystical Antichrist; to the Albigensian crusade' (*Lectura* 394–408, 817 in Burr 1993: 109, 135).

The apocalyptic character of his own time is evoked by the convert to the Spiritual Franciscans, Jacopone da Todi. His poem on the Antichrist ('Lauda' 50) draws on Rev 6 (and also 12:9, 15; 13:16–17) to situate church and society of his own day in the time of decadence which precedes the *eschaton*:

> Now it will be clear who has faith!
> I see the prophesied tribulation
> Thundering on every side.
> The moon is black, the sun darkened;
> I see the stars fall from heaven
> The ancient Dragon seems to be unleashed,
> And I see the whole world follow him,

He has drunk up the waters on all sides;
He hopes to swallow the River Jordan,
To devour the people of Christ.
The sun is Christ who now gives no sign
To strengthen his servants.
We see no miracle that supports
Faith in the people. . . .
So the moon is the darkened church
Which in the night shone upon the world,
Popes and cardinals and their court,
Light is turned into darkness;
The whole of the clergy
Has galloped off and taken the wrong way.
O Lord, who can escape?
The stars that are fallen from heaven
Are all the religious orders.
Many have departed from the right path
And entered on the dangerous road.
The waters of the flood have risen up,
Covered the mountains, flooded everything.
Help, God, help us to swim!
I see the whole world upset
And cast in ruins,
Like a man in frenzy
To whom no one can give a cure
Whom the doctors have given up for lost,
Because neither spell nor science can help.
So we see the world in its last turmoil.
I see all the people signed with the
Mark of the ancient Dragon,
And he has divided the signs into three parts:
He who escapes from one, will be given pain by another,
Discomfited them and killed many:
There are few who wish to resist. . . .
Because no other has been as bad as this,
Nor will there be any as strong.
The saints had great fear of it
(Of coming to take such a reward!);
To feel secure is to feel foolish.

> (Tr. by McGinn from the edition of F. Agenbo in
> McGinn 1998: 217–18)

Another interpretation that relates the four horsemen to periods in the life
of the Church is found in the prophetic ministry of Savonarola in late fifteenth-

century Florence, here with the added conviction that the climax of the sequence is about to take place. The white horse represents the time of the apostles, the red the time of the martyrs, the black that of the heretics, and the pale horse the present, the period of lukewarm Christianity, in which the Church has languished for a long period but that is soon to end. As God's prophet, Savonarola heralded the renovation of the Church (in Weinstein 1970: 161–3).

Coleridge thought the events of the French Revolution were predicted in the Apocalypse, as he makes clear in a marginal note to a passage in his 'Religious Musings' which refers to the fifth and sixth seals as well as to Rev 17:

> Rest awhile,
> Children of wretchedness! More groans must rise,
> More blood must stream, or ere your wrongs be full.
> Yet is the day of retribution nigh:
> The Lamb of God hath opened the fifth seal:
> And upward rush on swiftest wing of fire
> The innumerable multitude of Wrongs
> By man on man inflicted! Rest awhile,
> Children of wretchedness! The hour is nigh;
> And, lo! The great, the rich, the mighty Men,
> The Kings and the chief Captains of the World,
> With all that fixed on high like stars of heaven
> Shot baleful influence, shall be cast down to earth,
> Vile and down-trodden, as the untimely fruit
> Shook from the fig-tree by a sudden storm
> Even now the storm begins
> The abhorred Form,
> Whose scarlet robe was stiff with earthly pomp.
> Who drank iniquity in cups of gold,
> Whose names were many and all blasphemous,
> Hath met the horrible judgement! Whence that cry?
> The mighty army of foul Spirits shrieked
> Disinherited of earth! For she hath fallen
> On whose black front was written Mystery;
> She that reeled heavily, whose wine was blood;
> She that worked whoredom with the Demon power
>   ('Religious Musings' 65–6)

The apocalyptic character of Coleridge's times is also expressed by the cartoonist James Gillray, who portrayed Death on a pale horse as William Pitt (*Presages of the Millenium* [sic] in Wainwright 1993: 178; cf. Paley 1999: 141–2; Carey 1999: 247).

In the twentieth century, the distinguished biblical exegete Adolf Deissmann applied the awesome images of Rev 6 to the situation of Germany in the First World War. He regarded the terrible apocalyptic images as relating not to one particular war but to the ongoing struggle between light and darkness, in which Germany had a God-given role. Its soldiers had to be 'faithful until death' (Rev 2:10). The horses of the Apocalypse were positive pointers towards the good things Germany was achieving in the First World War. That such an application comes from a respected member of the biblical studies fraternity helps to explain the indignation felt by theologians like Karl Barth about the theological establishment's support for the First World War (in Wainwright 1993: 171; cf. Gorringe 1999: 24–74).

Catastrophes (6:3–8)

Milton describes the grim threat to the life of paradise in words that echo 6:7–8: 'Close following pace for pace, not mounted yet / On his pale horse: to whom Sin thus began. / Second of Satan sprung, all-conquering Death.' (*Paradise Lost* x.589–91). Coleridge alludes to 6:8 in a description of corrupt society nearing its end: 'And the Devil thought of his old friend / Death, in the Revelation' ('The Devil's Thoughts' in Paley 1999: 147). Shelley refers to the black horse of 6:5 ('A black Tartarian horse of giant frame / Comes trampling over the dead'), though its rider, an angel robed in white with a sword, is more reminiscent of Rev 19:11 (*The Revolt of Islam* 249–503 in Paley 1999: 256; cf. ibid. 221, 239; see also Shelley's 'The Mask of Anarchy' 30–3). In *Prometheus Unbound*, a poem shot through with allusions to Rev 6 and 8:7–12, Shelley has Prometheus addressed as an apocalyptic saviour who will 'quell this Horseman grim' (lines 780–8 in Paley 1999: 260; cf. Burdon 1997: 174–80). Byron makes an explicit allusion to 6:8: 'The Giant steed, to be bestrode by Death, / As told in the Apocalypse' ('Manfred' II.ii.1 in Paley 1999: 193). The pale horse of 6:8 stimulates Hildegard's imagination: 'Then I looked to the North, and behold! Five beasts stood there. One was like a dog . . . another was like a yellow lion; another was like a pale horse; another like a black pig; and the last like a grey wolf' (*Scivias* iii.11, Hart and Bishop edn 493). The sombre tone of 6:4 evokes in Christina Rossetti a surprising response, a hymn to love ('The Face of the Deep' 201 in Wainwright 1993: 211).

The fifth seal: the souls under the altar (6:9–11)

These verses have provided evidence for an interim state before the coming of Christ during which the souls of martyrs rest peacefully and look forward to vindication (C. E. Hill 1992). According to Tertullian, the martyrs go directly to heaven (*On the Soul* 55.5; *Scorpion's Sting* xii.8–11), while others must wait for the general resurrection. But even the martyrs must wait for their glorified bodies (*Resurr*.38). This eschatological scheme has a parallel in the *Ascension of Isaiah*, a late first- or early second-century CE Jewish-Christian text. In the seventh heaven Isaiah sees the righteous as part of the heavenly host, who have heavenly garments but still must wait for their crowns and thrones of glory (9:6–12). That the martyred souls are told to wait until their number is complete (Rev 6:11) confirms for Hippolytus that the delay of the *eschaton* is determined by God: if the martyrs have to wait, others should, too (*Daniel* iv.22.4). Augustine brings this text into his discussion of the 1,000-year reign of the saints in 20:4–6 (see below, 207), using it to show that even in times of persecution the saints continue to reign with Christ, and that this will also be true in the short tribulation after Satan is released (20:7; *City of God* xx.13).

In the Bamberg Apocalypse the robes received by the martyrs under the altar include liturgical stoles, perhaps suggesting that they are seen as the priests to God as mentioned in 1:6; 5:10; 20:6. While most interpreters understand the imagery metaphorically, for Adventists the white robes of 6:11 are regarded not as metaphors for faith, but as actual garments (Doan in Numbers and Butler 1987: 128–9, 137).

The Protestant triumph at the Reformation, in particular the accession of Elizabeth I to the throne of England, is seen by Thomas Simmons as a fulfilment of the cry for vengeance (in Newport 2000: 60; cf. Spenser's *The Faerie Queene* in Sandler in Patrides and Wittreich 1984: 159). For Nicholas Ridley the martyrdoms of the Reformers hasten the end (in Bauckham 1978: 148). Such views anticipate modern discussions of the political theology of the Apocalypse and its emphasis on synergism with the divine (A. Y. Collins 1996: 198–217). The cry for vengeance also echoes in Milton's 'Avenge O Lord thy slaughtered saints' (Sonnet xv, 1655, line 1). Langland paraphrases these verses: 'To those who sullied us and shed our blood – as it seemed, unmade us: Revenge the blood of the just!" (*Piers Plowman* xvii.293).

Catastrophes of the sixth seal (6:12–17)

Again and again, interpreters emphasize the awesome effects of the apocalyptic seals on the world's inhabitants. In the *Quran* the earthquake of the hour, the smoke, the rolling up of the sun, and the movement of mountains are probably based on the sixth seal (99:1–3 in Arjomand in McGinn 2000: 239). John Bale likens the emergence of religious reform to the earthquake that shook parts of England in the year that Wyclif was condemned (in Firth 1979: 42–3).

Shakespeare's *King Lear* echoes 6:15: 'the wrathful skies / Gallow the very wanderers of the dark, / And make them keep their caves' (III.ii. 43–5 in Wittreich in Patrides and Wittreich 1984: 192). Marlowe's Faustus cries: 'Mountains and hills, come, come and fall on me / And hide me from the heavy wrath of God' ('Doctor Faustus' xix.152–3 in Patrides in Patrides and Wittreich 1984: 236, n. 76; cf. Rev 6:13). In Milton's *Paradise Lost* the fallen Adam pleads with nature to hide him from the face of God (ix.1088–90; cf. x.723–4; vi.840–3 in Patrides and Wittreich 1984: 227, 265). Coleridge's poem 'Religious Musings' (cited earlier in this chapter) links 6:13, 15 to the outbreak of the French Revolution (lines 329–34; likewise Blake, in his early poem *The French Revolution* 74–8 in Paley 1999: 46–7, 112).

Charles Wesley's hymnody is redolent with images from Rev 6, as in the following example (which alludes also to Rev 7; 19:11; and 20:11–15):

> Lift your heads, ye friends of Jesus,
> Partners in his patience here,
> Christ to all believers precious,
> Lord of Lords, shall soon appear:
> Mark the tokens
> Of his heavenly kingdom near!
>
> Hear all nature's groans proclaiming
> Nature's swift-approaching doom!
> War and pestilence and famine
> Signify the wrath to come;
> Cleaves the centre,
> Nations rush into the tomb.
>
> Close behind the tribulation
> Of these last tremendous days.
> See the flaming revelation.
> See the universal blaze!
> Earth and heaven
> Melt before the judge's face!
>
> Sun and moon are both confounded,
> Darken'd into endless night,
> When with angel-hosts surrounded,
> In his Father's glory bright
> Beams the Saviour.
> Shines the everlasting light.
>
> See the stars from heaven falling
> Hark on earth the doleful cry,
> Men on rocks and mountains calling,

While the frowning judge draws nigh,
Hide us, hide us
Rocks and mountains from his eye!

With what different exclamation
Shall the saints his banner see!
By the monuments of his passion,
By the marks received for me
All discern him
All with shouts cry out, 'Tis he!

Lo! 'Tis he! Our heart's desire
Come for his espoused below
Come to join us with his choir,
Come to make our joys o'erflow:
Palms of victory,
Crowns of glory to bestow.

Yes, the prize shall now be given,
We his open face shall see;
Love, the earnest of our heaven,
Love our full reward shall be,
Love shall crown us
Kings through all eternity.
(In Newport 2000: 142–5)

Writing a century or so before, the Welsh hymn writer Morgan Llwyd links this text with Rev 4:6 and Dan 7:9–10:

Before one houre before day is darke
that great Ecclypse is neare
one fierce and farewell storme and then
the evening will be cleare . . .

Sing on a brittle sea of glasse
Sing in a furne of fire
In flames wee leap for joy and find
a cave a singing quire
('The Summer' in N. Smith 1994: 269)

Echoes of this chapter are also found in the African-American Blind Willie Johnson's songs, for example in 'John the Revelator':

Who that a-writin?
John the Revelator

> What John a-writin 'bout?
> About the revelations of the seven seals.
> The stars and heavens gonna all come down
> The dead's gonna rise from under the ground.
> The sea's gonna boil and cause a flood.
> The moon's gonna drip on away with blood.
> The sun's gonna tremble and hide her face.
> The rock's gonna cry 'no hiding place'.
>   (1930, www.ibiblio.org/jimmy/folkden/Revel)

Many spirituals use images from the plague sequences, such as falling stars and darkening of sun and moon (6:12), falling rocks (cf. 6:16; 8:8), fire from heaven (8:5, cf. 20:9) and trumpets (8:2–9:20; 11:15–19; cf. 1 Cor 15:50) to describe the dramatic end of the present situation. In these interpretations, the plagues are linked more directly with the scenes of judgement and reward (Rev 20–2) than is the case in the Apocalypse itself.

> My Lord, what a mornin', My Lord, what a mornin'.
> My Lord, what a mornin', When de stars begin to fall . . .
> You'll hear de trumpet sound, to wake de nations under ground
> Lookin' to my God's right hand, when de stars begin to fall
>   (Johnson and Johnson 1954: i.162–3)

> My Lord says he gwineter rain down fire
>   (Ibid. ii.28)

> De moon run down in a purple stream,
> De sun forbear to shine,
> And every star disappear,
> King Jesus shalla be mine.
> An' ev'ry po' soul dat never did pray'll,
> be glad to pray dat day.
>   (Ibid. i:150–1)

> O rocks don't fall on me. . . .
> O in-a dat great great judgment day . . .
> De sinners will run to de rocks and say
> Rocks and mountains don't fall on me.
> When ev-ahry star refuses to shine . . .
> De trumpet shall soun' And de dead shall rise
>   (Ibid. i. 164–6)

Other songs play on the image of kings seeking in vain for refuge in rocks and mountains (6:15–16):

Dere's no hidin' place down dere. . . .
Oh I went to de rock to hide my face,
De rock cried out, 'No hidin' place.' . . .
Oh de rock cried 'I'm burnin' too' . . .
I want to go to hebben as well as you.

(Ibid. i.74–5)

In dat Resurrection Day, sinner can't fin' no hidin' place
Go to de mountain, de mountain move;
Run to de hill, de hill run too,
Sinner man trablin' on trembling groun'
Po los' sheep ain't nebber been foun'.

(Ibid. i.167–9)

Artistic representation

Dürer's illustration of the sixth chapter of the Book of Revelation (Smith 2000: 32–3) shows a pope, a bishop and ordinary priests and monks among those who will call in vain on the mountains and rocks to hide them (in Cohn 1957: 84). His depiction (dated 1497–8) of the four horsemen as a quartet establishes a reading that was to have enormous influence (see plate 3). As we have seen, in many patristic and medieval interpretations a distinction is made between the first horseman, symbolizing the advent of Christ and the spread of the gospel, and the rest. Beginning with Dürer, however, many artists have closely linked all four horsemen. A modern exception to this is J. M. W. Turner in his *Death on a Pale Horse* (Tate Gallery, London), which focuses on the fourth horse, portraying it in typical late Turner style as a shadowy figure emerging from smoke, with a skeleton draped over it. This contrasts with William Blake's depiction of the same subject (Fitzwilliam Museum, Cambridge), where *Death on a Pale Horse* is accompanied by the black horse, and a sense of movement is created by the scroll of history unfolding above the horsemen as they surge forward (see plate 4). Kip Gresham incorporates into his depiction of the Four Horsemen the opening of the sixth seal, where 'the sun became black as sackcloth' (6:12).

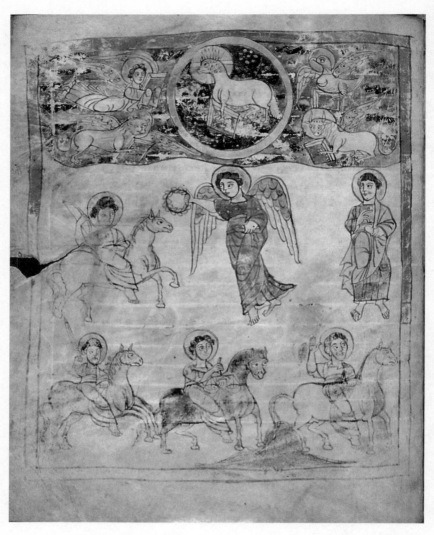

Plate 2   The Four Horsemen of Rev 6:1–8. Trier Apocalypse, Stadtsbibliothek, Trier.

Plate 3 Albrecht Dürer, The Four Horsemen of Rev 6:1–8. Fitzwilliam Museum, Cambridge.

Plate 4   William Blake, *Death on a Pale Horse* (Rev 6:7–8). Fitzwilliam Museum, Cambridge.

Plate 5   Kip Gresham, *The Four Horsemen* (Rev 6:1–8, 12).

Ancient Literary Context

The two-part vision of the assembly of the people of God, with its counterpart in Rev 14, has its roots in biblical passages which predict an assembly of the dispersed Israelites in Zion (Isa 2; Mic 4; Ezek 37:12; Deut. 30:2), although Rev 7 adds a wider membership, the second multitude which none can number (7:9). More explicitly than elsewhere in the New Testament, the beginning of the vision indicates a clear role for Jews in that eschatological assembly, with nothing said about their conversion to Christianity (a possibility only ambiguously suggested in Rom 11:25, and even then as a change of opinion from Paul's earlier uncompromising statements such as 1 Thess 2:15). The assembly of the elect is a key feature of 2 Esdras 13, an apocryphal text whose influence persisted into the early modern period (Hamilton 1999), and it was an important component of Second Temple eschatological belief (Sanders 1985: 95–7).

It is Rev 7 and passages such as Rev 2:13 and 13:16 that suggested that the Apocalypse is a martyr text reflecting the specific concerns of a time of official persecution. In particular, it has often been linked with a supposed persecution at the end of the reign of Domitian, although recent interpreters point out that there is actually little evidence of an empire-wide persecution at that time (L. Thompson 1990; Rowland 1982: 403–12).

This chapter illustrates a phenomenon that recurs in the Apocalypse: the interruption of a sequence at a point just before its completion (cf. 9:13–19). In Rev 17:10, for example ('five have fallen, one is living, and the other has not yet come'), the sixth in the sequence corresponds with the present time and lends weight to six as a penultimate number that points to the immediate situation. Joachim of Fiore made great interpretative play with this, giving special emphasis to the number six in the sequences of sevens. Such interpretation captures a perspective of many early Christians, who saw themselves as a privileged generation, living at a special moment in the divine economy, between the time of Jesus and his coming in glory (cf. 1 Cor 10:11 and 7:29–31). Throughout the New Testament the word 'tribulation' (*thlipsis*, 7:14) is used to describe an ordeal which is to come immediately before the fulfilment of God's saving purposes; in Col. 1:24, for example, it indicates suffering that is already afflicting the young Christians.

The Interpretations

One issue in interpretations of this chapter has been the identity of the angel from the sun, which assumed great importance in Franciscan exegesis, following the tradition of Joachim of Fiore. The presence of different groups in the vision, those sealed on the forehead and the multitude which none can number, has provoked debate about their identity. Finally, in the complex eschatological scenario of judgement and escape for the elect that certain modern Christian groups construct on the basis of a mosaic of scriptural passages, the reference to the 'great tribulation' has provided a particularly important link with other parts of Scripture.

Restraining the four winds (7:1–3)

The restraining of the winds serves to forestall the outbreak of chaos on earth (cf. 8:2–5). Similarly, the *Syriac Apocalypse of Peter* says: 'Thereupon shall I order the four winds, and they shall be let loose one in the direction of the other' (in W. Bousset 1999: 247). The opening verse of Rev 7 has inspired poetry by Donne and Milton, both of whom link it with the trumpet blasts that begin in 8:2 and the judgement scene of 20:11–15.

> At the round earth's imagin'd corners, blow
> Your trumpets, Angells, and arise, arise
> From death you numberlesse infinities
> Of Soules, and to your scattered bodies goe,
> All whom the flood did, and fire shall o'erthrow,
> All whom warre, dearth, age, agues, tyrannies,
> Despaire, law, chance, hath slaine, and you whose eyes,
> Shall behold God, and never taste death's woe
>   (John Donne, 'Holy Sonnets' vii.1–4; cf. Milton,
>   *Paradise Lost* iii.326–9 in Emmerson and McGinn
>   1999: 427–8)

The angel from the east (7:2)

The angel ascending from the east has been variously identified and in all cases given eschatological significance. Thus for Victorinus he is Elijah the prophet, the precursor of the Antichrist (1916: 82.4–5; 112.1–3; ANF vii.351–2; cf. Mal. 4:5, 6; Mic 5:5, 6). Alexander Minorita describes the reign of Constantine as the 'angel ascending from the sun' (in Wainwright 1993: 54). It is the interpretation of Joachim of Fiore, who predicts the arrival of a saintly pope, that has had the most profound effects, however:

> In this generation [the forty-second generation in the Church] first of all the general tribulation will be completed and the wheat carefully purged of all tares, then a new leader will ascend from Babylon [that is, Rome], namely a universal pontiff of the New Jerusalem, that is, of the Holy Mother the Church. . . . The Lord of hosts will already begin to reign over the whole earth. (In McGinn 1998: 134–5, cf. 196–221; Wainwright 1993: 51)

According to the radical Franciscan Peter Olivi, the angel of the opening of the sixth seal is Francis. Olivi builds on Joachim's interpretation of 7:2 and then argues that this is Francis, describing him as 'the renewer of the evangelical life and rule which is to be promoted and glorified in the sixth and seventh periods':

> Just as our most holy father Francis is, after Christ and under Christ, the first and principal founder and initiator and exemplar of the sixth period and its evangelical rule, so he, after Christ, is primarily designated by this angel. Thus,

as a sign of this fact, he appeared transfigured in a fiery chariot in the sun in order to show that he had come in the spirit and in the image of Elijah, as well as to bear the perfect image of the true sun, Christ. (*Lectura* 414–17, tr. D. Burr, 119, www.fordham.edu/halsall/source/olivi. html; cf. McGinn, 1998: 209)

Even among those Franciscans who in other respects espoused a less radical interpretation, this view is widely held. Thus Bonaventure suggested that the sixth day of creation heralds the age of clear teaching when there will be a prophetic existence. It was necessary that a single order come in this time, of a prophetic disposition reflecting Christ, whose head would be 'the angel ascending from the sun having the seal of the living God,' who is fully conformed to Christ. Bonaventure was clear that this 'angel' had already come in the person of Francis (*Collationes in Hexaemeron* 16:16 in McGinn 1998: 201; cf. Burr 1993: 38; for the identification with Francis see also Na Prous Boneta, in Potesta in McGinn 2000: 120; Burr 2001: 230–6). This identification of the angel with Saint Francis also seems to be reflected in a fresco by Cimabue in the apse of the upper basilica in Assisi, where the interlude of Rev 7:1–3 is given prominent billing. To earlier representations of this text Cimabue adds a medieval city wall and cityscape, thus emphasizing the relevance of the eschatological vision to the present time. The four angels of 7:1, shown close together in frontal pose with open wings, express the temporary restraining of the winds' destructive power (Schiller 1990: 276–7). A seventeenth-century pair of figurines, in which a stigmatized Francis is embraced by an angelic Christ (in the Museu de Arte Sacra de São Paulo, Brazil), may be influenced by the identification of Francis with the angel in Rev 7:2.

In the Elizabethan age, Bale suggests that the angel is Elizabeth: 'She is that Angel, as saint John doth him call, / That with the Lord's seal doth mark out his true servants. . . .' (*King Johan* 11.2671–9 in Bauckham 1978: 129). For Bale (1849: 332) the angel is also 'betokening the prophets, apostles and all just preachers'.

The sealing on the foreheads (7:3–4)

According to Charles Wesley, the sealing on the foreheads is a sign to the elect not to fear the wrath which is to be revealed. The intervention of the 'preventing' angels (7:1) will result in gathering the elect from the four corners of the earth, unto a place of safety on the earth (Letter of Charles Wesley in Newport 2000: 146–7). The sealing played a significant role in the practice of radical Anabaptists, including Hans Hut and the Münster Anabaptists, who baptized adults by making a mark with water (the *THAU* or a cross) on the heads of those who would be part of the 144,000 elect (in Snyder and Huebert-Hecht 1996: 73, 250). Joachim links the marking with Ezek 9:

> Now is the time for the elect to weep over the imminent destruction of that youngest Babylon lest perchance we share in her sins and be forced to partake of her punishments, as if we did not have the letter Thau written on our foreheads [Ezek 9:4–6; Rev 7:4] and were not able to avoid her threatening destruction. ('Letter to the Abbot of Valdona' in McGinn 1998: 118)

There is a less positive kind of marking, 'of weakness and woe', in Blake's prophetic gaze on his day. As the poet goes through the streets of London, he says: 'I wander thro' each charter'd street. / Near where the charter'd Thames does flow / And mark in every face I meet / Marks of weakness, marks of woe' ('London' in *Songs of Experience*, plate 46, Blake 1991–5; E. P. Thompson 1993: 181–2).

The 144,000 of the tribes of Israel (7:4–8)

According to Pseudo-Methodius, the 144,000 in 7:4 are Christian martyrs killed in the persecution of the Antichrist (in Alexander 1980: 45). In another interpretation they are the Jews who are the first to hear and believe; Victorinus believed that Elijah who is to come would bring about the conversion of many Jews (1916: 82.4–5; 112.1–3; 140.8; ANF vii.351–2; cf. the Arabic fragment of Hippolytus in Prigent 1973: 320). Irenaeus, who also interprets the 144,000 of Jews who will be saved, discusses the absence of the tribe of Dan in the list in 7:5–8 (*AH* v.30.2; cf. Lactantius, *Institutes* vii.17; W. Bousset 1999: 172–3). The point of the precise numbering is explained by Langland in terms of a distinction between heaven and hell: 'Heaven has even number and hell is without number' (*Piers Plowman* xx.270). In the Middle Ages an indefinite number was perceived as imperfect and threatening.

The multitude who have washed their clothes and made them white in the blood of the Lamb (7:9–17)

The closest parallel to 7:9 is 2 Esdras 13:12–13: 'After that I saw the man come down from the mountain and summon to himself a different, peaceful, company. He was joined by great numbers of men, some with joy on their faces, others with sorrow, some coming from captivity, and some bringing others to him as an offering' (*Revised English Bible*). Modern scholars regard the core of this work (chs 3–14) as roughly contemporary but independent of the Apocalypse. But the Jesuit interpreter Luís de Alcázar (in *Vestigatio arcane sensus in Apocalypsi* in Hamilton 1999: 226) suggested that 2 Esdras was written after Revelation and borrowed from it.

According to Hippolytus, the multitudes who survive the great tribulation are Gentile Christians raised up on the last day (in Prigent 1973: 320). Tertullian explains the multitude who have washed their clothes and made them white in the blood of the Lamb (7:14) as those who have triumphed over the Antichrist: 'The uncleanness, indeed, is washed away by baptism, but the stains are changed into dazzling whiteness by martyrdom' (*Scorpion's Sting* xii.9–11, ANF iii.646). Foxe relates 7:14–15 to 'the persecuted forerunners of the Reformation' (in Firth 1979: 77). Milton associates the multitude holding palm branches (7:9) with the angelic struggle which saw the forces of Satan defeated and the triumphant Christ returned to the Father's side:

> With jubilee advanced; and as they went,
> Shaded with branching palm, each order bright,
> Sung triumph, and him sing victorious king,
> Son, heir, and Lord, to him dominion giv'n,
> Worthiest to reign: he celebrated rode
> Triumphant through mid heav'n.
> > (*Paradise Lost* vi.884–9; cf. Milton's
> > description of sanctified humans in
> > 'At a Solemn Music' 14: 'With those
> > just spirits that wear victorious palm')

The theme of victory over the supernatural powers has a long history in Christian theories of atonement (Aulen 1931). In a visionary appropriation Hildegard sees those who 'stand in the presence of this light, a multitude of white-clad people, a cohort of people in the presence of God's justice, shining with faith and well and honourably constituted in good works' (*Scivias* ii.7, Hart and Bishop edn 294).

The vision of the great multitude has inspired hymn writers, most famously John Mason Neale in his translation of Bernard of Cluny's (c.1100–50) poem 'Jerusalem the Golden'. The third stanza explicitly recalls the end of Rev 7:

> There is the throne of David,
> And there, from care released,
> The shout of them that triumph,
> The song of them that feast;
> And they, who with their leader
> Have conquered in the fight,

> For ever and for ever
> Are clad in robes of white.
> (*Hymns Ancient and Modern*
> 1983: 184; *Hymnal 1982*: 624)

The special robes of 7:9, 13–14 (cf. 6:11; 16:15) are mentioned often in African-American spirituals:

> I got a robe, you got a robe,
> All o' God's Chillun got a robe.
> When I get to heab'n I'm goin' to put on my robe,
> I'm goin' to shout all ovah God's Heab'n.
> (Johnson and Johnson 1954: i.71)

> I know my robe's gwinter fit me well . . .
> I tried it on at de gates of hell.
> (Ibid.i.99; cf. i.118–19; ii.68–71; ii.84–5; ii.105–7:
> 'Oh Yes! Wait 'til I git on my robe')

The great tribulation (7:14)

The great tribulation of 7:14 has been a central feature of some modern eschatological interpretations. According to the *Scofield Reference Bible*, it is the period of unexampled trouble in the last days, focused on Jerusalem and the Holy Land and involving the Jews who will have returned to Palestine. Its duration is three and a half years, or the last half of the seventieth week of Dan 9:24–7. It involves the cruel reign of the 'beast rising out of the sea' (Rev 13:1) but will also be a period of salvation. An elect number out of Israel is sealed for God (Rev 7:4–8), and, with an innumerable multitude of gentiles (Rev 7:9), they are come 'out of the great tribulation [NRSV: "ordeal"]' (Rev 7:14), which will be immediately followed by the return of Christ in glory (Scofield 1917: 1337).

In the notes on Dan 9:24–7 the *Scofield Bible* constructs a complex eschatological schema that uses various elements from the Apocalypse and hinges on the 'great tribulation' of Rev 7:14. There are to be 70 weeks of seven years each (Dan 9:24). The messiah's coming, predicted in Dan 9:25, was fulfilled in the birth and manifestation of Christ. Then comes the destruction of the city of Jerusalem, fulfilled in CE 70, followed by the time 'unto the end' (Dan 9:26). When this time of the Church will end is nowhere revealed. The seventieth and last week of history, only seven years long, is described in Dan 9:27. The 'prince who is to come' (Dan 9:26) will covenant with the Jews and allow them to restore their temple sacrifices for seven years, but in the middle of that time he will break the covenant. The last three and a half years (see Dan 7:27) are identical with the 'great tribulation' of Rev 7:14 (cf. Matt 24:15–28), the 'time of trouble' (Dan 12:1) and the 'hour of temptation' (Rev 3:10). It is brought to an end by Christ's parousia, Armageddon, the millennium, the defeat of Satan, and resurrection and judgement (Scofield 1917: 994–5, cf. 1137 and 1350–1). Influenced by this scenario are the ten novels in the 'Left Behind' series by Tim LaHaye and Jerry Jenkins (see above, 25), whose second volume is called *The Tribulation Force* (1996).

Revelation 8

Ancient Literary Context

The sounding of the trumpet has a long history within the Bible: it is a sign of crisis, marking decisive moments in the nation's life (Lev 25:9) and also the judgement of God (Joel 2:1). In Matt 24:3, 1 Thess 4:16 and 1 Cor 15:52 it forms part of the eschatological scene as Jesus returns to gather the elect. As indicated in the commentary on Rev 6, the pronouncements of woe on an unrepentant world reflect a tradition widespread in Jewish and Christian texts of the period, in which disaster precedes the time of bliss (see Dan 12:1; Mark 13; Matt 24; Luke 21).

The Interpretations

Interpretations of Rev 8 reflect many of the typical interpretative moves evident in the reception of other parts of the Apocalypse. Commentators are attentive to the wider context, whether the relation to the seals and bowls or to images elsewhere in the Bible. Some view the succession of trumpet blasts as a clear sequence which reflects the unfolding of the divine purposes in history, an interpretation with a long history that had particular force at times of crisis such as at the Reformation. The tendency to relate individual aspects of the vision to specific events, whether in the past or in the interpreter's own world, has many examples. Individual features of this chapter which prompted significant interpretative traditions include the eschatological silence, the heavenly throne room and the images of destruction (interpreted as threats to the people of God from heresies within the Church and persecution from without). The chapter's images invite graphic portrayal, evident in the vivid illustrations in medieval commentaries. These exploit sensuous elements in the text (smell and sound, for example) which stand alongside the visionary's intense experiences of awe and terror to evoke the rapture of worship and awe before the divine honour.

Early interpretations as witness to inner-biblical interpretation

Characteristic of early interpretations is the use of typology. Commenting on 8:8, 12, Hippolytus contrasts the mountain cast into the sea, the sea changed into blood and the darkness cast over the land, seen as signs of God's judgement over the whole world, with the darkness over Egypt (Ex 10:22–3) and the water-become-blood (Ex 7:20), which brought only partial destruction. Similarly, in 8:11 the water changed into wormwood signifies how the water of pagans becomes bitter, even as the water-become-blood chastised the Egyptians in the past. But by means of another kind of wood (which Hippolytus identifies as the cross in *Antichrist* 61), God will provide sweet waters and save the Christians, as he did the Hebrews at Massah (Ex 17:6–7, in Prigent 1973: 325; cf. Gwynn 1888: 401). Victorinus' approach is attentive to the wider structure of the vision. The trumpet blast is the word of power, and what is revealed briefly in the trumpet sequence is shown at greater length in the bowls of Rev 16. Both visions show that the marks of the Antichrist are evident in the empire of Babylon and in the Roman emperors, as well as in the figure to come in the last days (1916: 84.14–86.12).

Silence in heaven: a sabbath rest for the people of God (8:1–2)

The eschatological silence is reminiscent of the cultic silence before God (Ps 46:10; Zech 2:13; *Letter of Aristeas* 95). In 2 Esdras 7:30 the universe returns to silence after the upheavals of the last things. For Ignatius of Antioch, silence symbolizes the salvific mystery (*Ephes.* 15.19), and for Victorinus it begins the everlasting rest, though this is partial because it is interrupted (1916: 84.14, ANF vii.352). Anselm of Havelberg says that, as the last of seven, this seal represents the seventh state of the Church, 'the silence of divine contemplation, the renewal of the year of jubilee, and the celebration of the eighth day of infinite beatitude' (in McGinn 1998: 116). For Bede the opening of the seventh seal, accompanied by silence, symbolizes a period of peace to follow the time of the Antichrist (the sixth seal). He compares the opening of the seventh seal to the quiet of Christ's rest on the sabbath following his crucifixion, which was followed by the glory of the resurrection. Similarly, the time of peace after the Antichrist will be followed by the glory of the second advent (*Explanatio Apocalypsis* 1.8, PL 93:154 in Emmerson 1981: 103–4; cf. Lerner in Emmerson and McGinn 1992: 54).

Joachim of Fiore surmised that the silence of the seventh seal would last about half a year because an 'hour' was a 'time' and a 'time' was a year (*Lib. Conc.* 3.2.7 in Lerner in Emmerson and McGinn 1992: 59; cf. Reeves and Hirsch-Reich 1972: 123). The opening of the seventh seal and the ensuing silence have great importance in Joachite interpretation, where they signify universal tranquillity and peace in both church and world. For example, Arnold of Villanova, a radical exponent of Joachim's ideas, writes of the blessedness of that time of 'universal tranquillity and peace in the Church, in which the truth shall be recognized throughout the entire world, and Christ shall be adopted', and 'there shall be one shepherd and one sheepfold [John 10:16]' (in Lee, Reeves and Silano 1989: 31–2; Burr 2001: 111–12). That millennial element is also evident in Bale, who suggests that the seventh seal means the overthrow of Babylon and the Antichrist and the binding of the dragon for 1,000 years (in Firth 1979: 43). Milton also captures the ultimate significance of that moment of silence in *Paradise Lost*, where it follows God's asking whether there has ever been a love like that of the divine Son in his redeeming the world: 'And silence was in Heaven: on Man's behalf, / Patron or intercessor none appear'd' (iii.218–19).

Ingmar Bergman's film *The Seventh Seal* begins and ends with a citation of Rev 8:1–2, and at the film's climax one of the characters reads the description of the first three trumpets (8:7–11). The verses from the Apocalypse provide the backdrop for the story of Antonius Block, a knight returning to Sweden from the Crusades in mid-fourteenth century, when the Black Death was raging in Europe. Adapting a theme from medieval paintings, and alluding to the fourth rider of Rev 6:8, Bergman portrays a personified Death who accompanies Block on this travels and engages him in a game of chess, in which what is at stake is Block's own life.

Imagery of the heavenly throne room (8:1–5)

The apocalyptic character of spontaneous 'this-worldly' worship is well exemplified by a description of Methodist worship in early nineteenth-century New Jersey, which echoes imagery of 8:1–5:

> At ten o'clock, the trumpets sound again to summon the people to public worship; the seats are all speedily filled and as perfect a silence reigns throughout the place as in a Church or Chapel; presently the high praises of God sound melodiously from this consecrated spot, and nothing seems wanting but local elevation to render the place a heaven indeed. (Elaw, *Memoirs* 65–6 in Taves 1999: 107)

Milton plays on the chapter's images in describing heaven: 'Temper'd soft tunings, intermix'd with voice / Choral or unison; of incense clouds, / Fuming from golden censers, hid the mount' (*Paradise Lost* vii.598–600; cf. xi.17–20). A more threatening side to the image is found in the suggestion that David Koresh considered this passage as a prophecy that his last act on earth would be to start an eschatological fire (cf. v. 5) (in D. Thompson 1996: 299).

The seven trumpets (8:6–9:20; 11:15–19)

THE TRUMPETS AS A KEY TO HUMAN HISTORY

Some think the seven trumpets symbolize a sequential unfolding of divine purposes in history: for example, English interpreters who think that the visions of the Apocalypse describe events to appear in strict historical sequence (so Keach, *Antichrist Stormed*, Preface to ii in Newport 2000: 38). Brightman applied the trumpet visions to enemies who attacked the Church beginning in about 300. The first four sounded before the year 607. The fifth trumpet, the first of the greater trumpets, indicates the apostasy of Muhammad, who fell like the star from heaven, and at the same time the dealing of Pope Boniface III with the emperor Phocus. The locusts also have two meanings. They represent Saracens in the East and monks in the West (a frequent identification of negative images in the Apocalypse by sixteenth-century Protestant interpreters). The sixth trumpet, said to last from 1300 until 1696 at the latest, adds the Turkish Empire to the list of enemies and foretells its rise and fall (Brightman in Firth 1979: 168–9; a similar historical approach is found in Alsted, see Wainwright 1993: 68; cf. Bossuet in Newport 2000: 72 and Wainwright 1993: 64).

Napier interprets both trumpets and bowls to refer to particular past events. So the first trumpet (8:7) and first bowl (16:2) refer to the destruction of Jerusalem in CE 70. The second trumpet (8:8–9) and second bowl (16:3) represent the translation of the Empire to the East in CE 316 (Constantine and Pope Sylvester I), the third trumpet (8:9–11) and third bowl (16:4) refer to Totila's burning of Rome in 561, and the fourth trumpet (8:12) and fourth bowl (16:8) to the coronation of Charlemagne in 806. The fifth trumpet (9:1) and bowl (16:10) refer to Zadok the dominator of the Turks (1051), the sixth to Osman (1296), and the seventh to the Reformation in 1541 (*A Plaine Discovery* 8 in Firth 1979: 144). John Bale takes the angel in mid-heaven (v. 6) to refer to particular servants of God such as Joachim, Savonarola (Bale 1849: 349 in Firth 1979: 44).

In Joseph Mede's *Clavis Apocalyptica* 59 the first four trumpets tell the story of the decline of the Roman Empire. Constantine arrived on the scene during the sixth seal (6:12–19), but the major change in the fortunes of the Empire came with the death of Theodosius the Great (395) and the permanent division of the Empire into East and West. At that time the first trumpet sounded (8:7), and this period lasted until about 410, when the second trumpet sounded (8:8–9) with the sacking of Rome by Alaric I. The last three trumpets (9:1–20; 11:15–19) tell of the wars of persecution waged by the arch-enemies of Christendom, the Saracens from 630, the Turks succeeding them (1080), and then the Antichrist of Rome. With the defeat of the Antichrist the seventh trumpet ushers in the millennium (in Firth 1979: 219–20). Joseph Priestley echoes Mede in thinking that the first trumpet represents the invasion of the Goths under Alaric in 395; the second the coming of the Vandals c.407–55, and so forth. The locusts are the Saracens under Muhammad and the period of 'five months' (9:5) is from c.612 to 762 (*Works* 1:459 in Newport 2000: 130; cf. the similar Adventist interpretation of John Loughbrough in Anderson in Numbers and Butler 1987: 79–80).

THE TRUMPETS AS PREDICTIONS OF THE POLLUTION OF THE CHURCH

According to the *Geneva Bible*, the seventh seal and what follows it represent the corruption of doctrine and the 'sects & heresies' which are brought into the church as a result. This ecclesiastical interpretation has many echoes in texts of the sixteenth century (Firth 1979: 44 on Bale; Bauckham 1978: 305 on Bullinger). Occasionally, these images are linked with more specific figures or movements. The fourth angel's trumpet blast (8:12) with the blocking of a third part of the sun signifies that because Christ is the sun of justice, those who 'boast of their works and merits obscure Christ and tread his death under foot' (*Geneva Bible*). In similar vein, Luther interprets the hail and fire with blood of the first trumpet as a judgement on the doctrine of works-righteousness, which 'had to be the first doctrine in opposition to the gospel, and it also remains the last'. In his introductory notes on the Apocalypse, Luther interprets the third angel who caused the great star to fall (8:10–11) as Origen, the falling star 'who embittered and corrupted the Scriptures with the philosophy of reason' (Luther 1546 *Preface to the New Testament* in Pelikan in Patrides and Wittreich 1984: 10–11, 81). The 'ships' destroyed in 8:9 are the 'Churches of mystical Babylon', which is Rome, according to Knowlys (*Exposition* 102 in Newport 2000: 35). The star from heaven (8:10), he wrote, is Nestorius, the fourth-century heretic, whose theological errors on matters such as original sin, justification and election were subsequently prevalent in Catholicism (in Newport 2000: 32–5).

THE TRUMPETS AS PREDICTIONS OF SPECIFIC HISTORICAL EVENTS

Felgenhauer claimed that the comet of 1618 had ushered in the time of the seventh trumpet in Revelation, that the year 1648 was the time of the first judgement (20:4), while the second (20:11–12) was announced by the comet of 1652 (*Bonum Nuncium Israel* in Hamilton 1999: 222). According to Lewis Mayer, the falling star is Louis XVI (in Burdon 1997: 102). Coleridge, in his notes to Eichhorn's commentary on the Apocalypse, suggests similarities between the situation preceding the fall of Jerusalem in CE 70 (to which he thinks John alludes) and the French Revolution: 'The 4 first Trumpets of Revelation 8:13 denote the Evils that preceded, and prepared the way for, the Outbreak of the Zealot terrorism' (*Marginalia* 2:509–10 in Paley 1999: 152). Hal Lindsey suggests that the biblical writers did not fully understand their own visions (an approach similar to that of the *Habakkuk Commentary* from the Dead Sea Scrolls, which claims to set forth for the first time the true meaning of the prophet's words). The hail and fire mixed with blood (8:7), he claims, are missiles as they appeared to John's first-century eyes, and John's image of horses with lion-like heads and fire pouring from their mouths represent 'some kind of mobilised ballistic missile launcher' (Lindsey 1978, 23, 130, 131, 132, 141 in Boyer 1992: 127, 332).

OTHER INTERPRETATIONS OF THE TRUMPET BLASTS

A vision of the Anabaptist prophet Ursula Jost from c.1539 (a time of enormous upheaval in southern Germany in the aftermath of the Peasants' Revolt) contains clear echoes of the Apocalypse, especially Rev 8:7 (vision 32 in Snyder and Huebert-Hecht 1996: 284). Milton regards the falling star of 8:10 as Satan (not unsurprising given Isa 14:14, *Paradise Lost* ii.706–11; other possible allusions in *Paradise Regained* iv.618–21; *Paradise Lost* iv.1–12, the latter more closely linked with Rev 12:7). A mingling of the various eschatological elements is evident in these passages, and also in John Donne's 'At the round earth's imagin'd corners' (discussed above, 100). Shakespeare's *Henry VI Part II* refers to the trumpet visions:

> O let the vile world end,
> And the promised flames of the last day
> Knit earth and heaven together!
> Now let the general trumpet blow his blast,
> Particularities and petty sounds
> To cease!
>
> (v.ii.40–5 in Emmerson in
> McGinn 2000: 426–7)

At the end of the first act of Shelley's *Prometheus Unbound*, four spirits who address Prometheus echo the dire images of Rev 8 ('On a battle-trumpet's blast'). Reflecting despair with religion, they are 'from the dust of creeds outworn'. The voices coming from the mountains, the springs, the air and the whirlwinds resemble the judgements delivered by the first four trumpets on earth, sea, springs and sun, moon and stars (Rev. 8:7–12, *Prometheus* i.694–751 in Burdon 1997: 175–6; Paley 1999: 255–75).

Various images from the Apocalypse, including the consequences of the fourth trumpet in 8:12, are linked in Charles Wesley's hymn 'Lift your heads, ye friends of Jesus' (Newport 2000: 142, see above, 90–1). The trumpets also echo in African-American spirituals, in allusions to the fire (8:5), thunder and lightening (8:7), and the effect of the plagues on trees (8:7; cf. 7:1):

> Steal away, steal away . . . to Jesus.
> Steal away home, I ain't got long to stay here. . . .
> My Lord, He calls me,
> He calls me by the thunder,
> The Trumpet sounds withina my soul . . .
> Green trees a bending,
> po' sinner, stands a trembling,
> the trumpet sounds withina my soul.
> I ain't got long to stay here.
>
> (Johnson and Johnson 1954: i.114–17)

> Gimme dat ol' time religion . . .
> It's good enough for me. . . .
> It will do when de world's on fiah . . .
> An it's good enough for me.
>
> (Ibid. i.76–7; cf. ii.28–9; i.136: 'Where shall I be
> when de firs' trumpet soun'?')

Revelation 9

Ancient Literary Context

After the first four trumpets in Rev 8, the introduction to the last three trumpet blasts in 8:13 suggests that their consequences will be particularly disastrous. Two of these are described in Rev 9, the third in 11:15–19. Various themes echo the Hebrew Bible: for example, 9:20 echoes Pharaoh's hardness of heart, and the longing for death in 9:6 recalls Job's plea to be released from his torment (Job 3:21; cf. Gen 4:13–16; Luke 23:30; Rev 6:15–17). The loathsome and frightening character of swarms of locusts (vv. 3–11) had been used as an image of judgement and destruction (Joel 2:1, 25). In the Apocalypse the hostile creatures become more terrible: they are armoured horses ready for battle (9:7). The locusts' king is Abaddon, the destroyer (9:11, from the Hebrew word meaning 'destruction'; cf. Job 26:6; Prov 15:11). More generally, this chapter's vivid portrayal of the threat of evil recalls the Jewish and early Christian tradition of the two ways, one leading to life and the other to perdition (Prov 2; Matt 7:13–14; *Didache* 1).

The Interpretations

Interpretation of Rev 9 is like that of Rev 8, in that the last trumpet visions are often taken to refer to periods of history, and also in the linkage of specific images with particular individuals (a move encouraged by the description of the bottomless pit in 9:2). The awesome and terrifying images of this chapter lend themselves to polemical denunciations of opponents.

Victorinus sees universality in the four corners of the altar of God (9:13), which he interprets as the four corners of the earth and the four winds (ANF vii.352–3). A universal dimension is also evident in Bale's interpretation of 9:14–15 as symbolizing the preaching of the gospel in the whole world, in the sixth age of the Church (1849: 359). In Europe this had begun with Wyclif: 'And as these angels are loosened in this quarter of the world, so shall they be in all other quarters, the Lord appointing their times' (*The Image* 13 in Bauckham: 1978: 71; cf. Firth 1979: 32–68). The fallen star of 9:1 is 'the true spiritual Church falling into worldliness' (Bale 1849: 350; cf. Firth 1979: 44).

The Beguin Na Prous Boneta sees in 9:1 both mercy and judgement. The angel with the keys of the abyss (9:1,11) is the Holy Spirit inspiring Na Prous, who follows in the footsteps of her mentors: Francis, symbolized by the angel with the seal of the living God (7:2), and Peter John Olivi, the angel clothed with the sun (10:1). The abyss will not be a threat for those who believe her words, but will open for those who disbelieve them (in Potesta in McGinn 2000: 120; Burr 2001: 230–6).

The *Geneva Bible* manifests an ecclesial interpretation in its explanation of the fifth angel and the fallen star as 'the Bishops and ministers, which forsake the word of God, & so fall out of heaven, & become Angels of darkness'. The key of the bottomless pit is the 'authority chiefly committed to the Pope in sign whereof he beareth the keys in his arms'. The locusts symbolize false ministers:

> Locusts are false teachers, heretics, and worldly futile Prelates, with Monks, Friars, Cardinals, Patriarchs, Archbishops, Bishops, Doctors, Bachelors & Masters which forsake Christ to maintain false doctrine. (In Firth 1979: 44; cf. later Knowlys, *Exposition* 205, and Witham, *Annotations on the New Testament of Jesus Christ* 2:463 in Newport 2000: 30, 85)

The trumpet sequence as a key to human history

Hippolytus interprets the four angels of 9:14–15 as Persians, Medes, Assyrians and Babylonians, and links them with the seven-headed dragon of chapter 12 (whose heads are kings of Persia, Mede, Assyria, Babylon, Alexander, his generals and Rome). One purpose of this interpretation is to condemn the present, persecuting Empire, which is depicted as the willing instrument of the Antichrist (*Daniel* iii.9.10 in Prigent 1972: 402). Bale thinks that the time from Innocent IV to Julius II (thirteenth to sixteenth centuries), the fall of the papacy, was the 'kingdom of locusts' (9:3–11); the final period extended from Julius II to Paul IV (sixteenth century) 'and all the times of their successors unto the judgement of Christ' (*The Pageant*, Dedication 102–3 in Firth 1979: 79). The *Geneva Bible* takes the loosing of the four angels (9:14–15) to mean 'the enemies of the East country, which should afflict the Church of God, as did the Arabians, Sarasines, Turks, & Tartarians'. Other commentators take 9:1–11 as 'a vision of the birth of Islam' (*Christian's Complete Family Bible* 1739, on Rev 9, in Newport 2000: 7). Similarly, Whiston regards the sixth trumpet or second woe as 'a most lively Description of the Turks, and of the Miseries they have brought upon Europe' (*Essay* 176–93 in Burdon 1997: 53; see also Foxe and Napier in Firth 1979: 94–5, 143–4). The preoccupation with the East anticipates modern interpreters who understand 9:14–16 as a portrayal of the Sino–Soviet alliance. Lindsey writes of 9:18 as a 'terrifying prophecy about the destiny of this Asian horde which will wipe out a third of the earth's population' (1970: 82 in Boyer 1992: 167).

The application of images to specific individuals

From the perspective of radical Franciscans such as Arnold of Villanova, the star falling from heaven (9:1) points to Thomas Aquinas, who fell from the height of divine truth to the earth: that is, into a dark, cloudy and ignorant conception. The key of the abyss is insight into the depths of inferior wisdom – that is, worldly philosophy – which Aquinas then manifested in his philosophical writings (in McGinn 1998: 225). For Osorius, a Jesuit writing in 1595, the angel of the fifth trumpet (9:1) is Ignatius Loyola. This illustrates how the Joachite approach to the Apocalypse continued to pervade even Counter-Reformation interpretation (in Firth 1979: 162; cf. Wainwright 1993: 61 on the view that the falling star is Luther; see above, 100, for the way in which Francis is linked with the angel of the sixth seal). The beast from the pit in 9:11 is Luther and Lutheranism, according to Bellarmine (in Newport 2000: 69; cf. Reeves 2000: 276; Wainwright 1993: 61). For Coleridge this image offered the opportunity for a pun on the word 'Pitt' (William Pitt was Prime Minister in England at the time, in Paley 1999: 142, 152).

Visionary appropriation

In addition to offering a colourful resource for vilifying opponents, the terrible images of this chapter have invaded later visionary imaginations. For example, in his poem *Milton* Blake invests Milton with poetic/prophetic power: 'Then first I saw him in the Zenith as a falling star, / Descending perpendicular, swift as the swallow or swift; / And on my left foot falling on the tarsus, entered there' (*Milton* 14:48–50, illustration in Blake 1993: plate 29). Blake, like Paul of Tarsus on the Damascus road, undergoes a dramatic spiritual experience which, he thinks, enables to him to recapitulate and redeem the earlier fallen prophetic genius, for Milton's inspiration was not wholly beneficial ('Milton was a true Poet and of the Devil's party without knowing it': *The Marriage of Heaven and Hell* 6). The power which enters him has been distorted in its values (particularly rationalism and the espousal of chastity: *Milton* 19 [21]: 10:13) and needs the redemptive power of Blake's poetic genius to save it from false paths (in Paley 1999: 81). The role of Lucifer in Milton's *Paradise Lost*, potentially great but in fact deeply flawed, is exploited by Blake in his mixture of admiration and contempt for his fallen hero.

Literary and artistic representations

Abaddon/Apollyon, the angel of the bottomless pit (9:11), appears in the poetry of Milton (*Paradise Lost* iv.624) and Coleridge ('Skeltoniad' in Paley 1999: 151). For Bunyan, Apollyon is a foul fiend whom Christian meets in the Valley of Humiliation (*Pilgrim's Progress*, 1967 edn 102).

In the illustration in the Cambrai Apocalypse an eagle is at the top, placed with the sun in a heaven separated by a sharp line from all that is below. On the next storey down are the seven angels, one blowing his trumpet, and through this storey streams the wake of the falling star, which lies holding its key at the mouth of the pit on the lowest level. The pit's bottomlessness is represented by a flight of steps leading towards the viewer, and beside it are the emerging locusts and the seer himself. The fact that the writer is included in the picture (as he usually is in medieval Apocalypses, as well as in the opening depictions of Dürer's and Duvet's sequences) shows that the illustrator is giving an interpretation of what John wrote, not simply trying to reproduce what John saw (in Burdon 1997: 20). The spatial contrasts that are so important for the Apocalypse itself (see 4:1 as well as 9:1) are picked up in the iconography. This is also clear in the demarcation between heaven and earth in the depiction of Rev 12:1 in the Trier Apocalypse (see below, 140).

Ancient Literary Context

A second interruption to a sevenfold sequence (cf. ch. 7) is the occasion for a renewed commission. This time John is told not only to 'write' and 'see' (cf. 1: 11) but also to prophesy about nations, peoples and languages (10:11). Allusions to the commission of Jeremiah (Jer 1:10) and Ezekiel's eating the scroll (Ezek 3:1–10) serve to articulate John's vocation. The sense of being part of a prophetic tradition, evident in the use of Ezekiel's vision to express John's own prophetic call, occurs occasionally in other apocalyptic texts (Frankfurter in VanderKam and Adler 1996: 129–96; Frankfurter 1992; Lieb 1991).

The Interpretations

This chapter has links with other parts of the book, in the mighty angel (cf. the 'one like the Son of Man' in 1:13 and 14:14), John's renewed commission (cf. 1:9–20) and the 'little book' (cf. the sealed book opened by the Lamb in ch. 5). The identity of the angel and of the little book and the mysterious fact that the content of the seven thunders is left unspecified (10:4) have provoked many ingenious explanations. The chapter is important because of its connection with chapter 5 (Bauckham 1993a: 81); Joseph Mede (among others) found here an interpretative key to the structure of the whole of the Apocalypse (in Elliott 1851: iv.492).

The mighty angel and the little scroll (book) (10:1–2)

Historical interpretation has identified this angel with significant figures of the past or present. For the *Geneva Bible*, the angel is Jesus, who 'came to comfort his Church against the furious assaults of Satan and Antichrist: so that in all their troubles, the faithful are sure to find consolation in him'. Alexander the Minorite identified the angels in 10:1, 8 with the emperors Justin and Justinian (*Expositio* 112, 153, 157, 162, 197, 299, 310, 384–5, 408–9 in Wainwright 1993: 54). In an obscure passage Joachim of Fiore seems to identify himself with the angel of Rev 10:1–2 (*Comm. Jer.* 23 in McGinn 1998: 163).

Peter Olivi identifies the angel with Francis, who 'appears in the fiery chariot transfigured into the sun so that it might be evident that he has come in the spirit and image of Elijah and at the same time that he bore the perfect image of Christ, the true sun' (*Lectura* in McGinn 1998: 208). This makes good exegetical sense in the context of Olivi's interpretation, which emphasizes the sixth, penultimate period (see above, 85), since the angel of 10:1 is associated with the sixth trumpet. After his death, Olivi's followers saw him as the near equal of Francis (McGinn 1998: 205), believing that he was the one above all others to whom the truth of Scripture and understanding of the Apocalypse had been revealed (Potesta in McGinn 2000: 119; Burr 1993; W. Lewis 1976: 79–82; Burr 2001). A report about Na Prous Boneta describes how she identified Olivi with the angel of 10:1, complementing Francis, who was the angel with the seal of the living God (Rev 7:2):

> Again, God told her [so she claims] that Saint John saw three angels the first of which bore the sign of the living God, and that was Saint Francis. The second had a face like the sun, and that was Brother Peter John [Olivi]. The third carried the keys of the abyss, and that was the Holy Spirit whom God gave to her. (In Potesta in McGinn 2000: 120; cf. Burr 2001: 230–6; www.fordham.edu/halsall/source/naprous.html)

For Bale the angel is a herald of the Reformation, the sixth age of Church, and the book (or scroll) is the Bible whose position was to be restored. The angel's feet are the two testaments, 'pillars of fire' (1849: 368; cf. Firth 1979: 46). Joachim of Fiore had compared the two testaments to everlasting pillars, the foundation on which the structure of the third age of the Spirit would be built, identified with the feet of the angel of Rev 10:1 (see also the extraordinary depiction of the angel in Dürer's woodcut of this passage). John Foxe sees the little book as 'the Scriptures, and the presentation to John [is] the restoration of Scripture to the Church'. The agency for this restoration was the revival in learning, and especially the discovery of printing (Foxe 1583: 4:252–3; 1587: 107 in Firth 1979: 103).

In the *Geneva Bible* the little book is 'the Gospel of Christ, which the Antichrist cannot hide, seeing Christ bringeth it open in his hand', and also the Holy Scriptures which the minister must receive from the hand of God. The command to take and eat the book 'signifieth that the ministers ought to receive the word into their hearts, and to have grave, deep, judgement and diligently to study it and with zeal to utter it' (words which echo the exhortation at the beginning of the Apocalypse in the *Geneva Bible*: 'read diligently, judge soberly, and call earnestly to God for the understanding thereof'). The sweet then bitter character of the book's words signify 'that albeit that the minister have consolation by the word of God, yet shall he have sore, & grievous enemies, which shall be troublesome unto him'. The little book is connected to the church by Joseph Mede (in Armogathe in McGinn 2000: 194) and with the book of Daniel by Houteff (*Shepherd's Rod* 1:16 in Newport 2000: 207).

Adventists used Rev 10 to come to terms with the 'great disappointment', the failure of the eschatological events to appear as predicted in 1844 (Numbers and Butler 1987; Garsted 1973). Often people with intense, unfulfilled expectations do not abandon their beliefs after some climactic disappointment but turn to other activities in compensation (so the 'cognitive dissonance' theory, explored by Gager 1975 in relation to the eschatological hopes of early Christianity). Thus the disappointed Millerites relate the bitterness of the 'little book' to their group's need to pick itself up and renew its mission:

> In eighteen hundred forty-four,
> We thought the curse would be no more.
> The things of earth we left behind,
> To meet the Saviour of mankind. . . .
> The day passed by – no tongue can tell
> The gloom that on the faithful fell.
> That what it meant they hardly knew
> But to their Lord they quickly flew.
> They searched the Word, and not in vain,
> For comfort there they did obtain.

> They found 'the bridge' they had passed o'er;
> Then they rejoiced and grieved no more.
> Their faith was firm in that blest Book,
> And still for Jesus they did look.
>   (*Recollections of Luther Boutelle*, Appendix
>   in Numbers and Butler 1987: 212; cf.
>   Butler in Numbers and Butler 1987: 199)

The voice of the seven thunders and the little book (10:3–4, 8–11)

In 10:3–4 John is not allowed to record the voice of the seven thunders. For Bale this is a warning to those 'which think that they can of their own will and industry declare such causes, unless God openeth unto them by his word or some evident sign as he hath done in this age most plenteously to many' (1849: 372; Firth 1979: 46). For the *Geneva Bible* the 'sealing up' suggests a particular way of reading the text, requiring diligence, not apocalyptic insight: 'Believe that that is written: for there is no need to write more for the understanding of God's children.' The thunders are 'the whole grace of God's Spirit bent . . . against Antichrist'. As to the voice of 10:8: 'As St. John understood this by revelation, so is the same revealed to the preachers to discover the Pope and Antichrist.' This contrasts with interpretation in terms of a subsequent revelation: for example, David Koresh's belief that he was the seventh angel of Rev 10:7 (in Newport 2000: 233). He linked the thunders with his Adventist predecessors, including prophets William Miller, Ellen White and Victor Houteff, and his own work with the seventh thunder, which reveals the mysterious content of the other thunders (in Newport 2000: 216).

The African-American spiritual 'In Dat Great Gittin up Mornin' brings together themes from different parts of Revelation, including the trumpets that unleash plagues (ch. 8), the advent of Christ in 19:11–16, the unleashing of Satan (20:7) and the Last Judgement (20:11–15). Identifying the figure of 10:2, who stands on both sea and land, as the angel Gabriel, it portrays the seven thunders (10:3–4) as the sound of his trumpet:

> I'm a goin' to tell you 'bout de comin' of de Saviour . . .
> Dere's a better day a comin' . . . In dat great gittin' up mornin' . . .
> De Lord spoke to Gabriel . . . Go look behin' de altar . . .
> Take down de silvah trumpet . . . Blow yo' trumpet Gabriel . . .
> Lord how loud shall I blow it . . . Blow it right calm an' easy . . .
> Do not alarm my people . . . Tell 'em to come to judgment . . .
> Gabriel blow yo' trumpet . . . Lord, how loud shall I blow it . . .
> Loud as seven peals of thunder . . . Wake de livin' nations . . .

Place one foot upon de dry lan' . . . Place de other on de sea . . .
Hell shall be un capp'd an' burnin' . . . Den de dragon shall be loosen'd . . .
Den you'll see po' sinner ris'in . . . den you'll see de worl' on fiah . . .
See de moon a bleedin' . . . See de stars a fallin' . . .
See de elements a meltin' . . . See de forked lightnin' . . .
Hear de rumblin' of de thunder . . . Earth shall reel an' totter . . .
See dem marchin' home to heav'n . . . Den you'll see my Jesus comin . . .
Wid all His holy angels . . . Take de righteous home to glory . . .
Dere dey live wid God forever . . . In dat great gittin' up mornin.
(Johnson and Johnson 1954: ii.40–3)

The command to 'look behin' de altar' appears to be an interpretation of actions in the heavenly sanctuary described in 8:1–3.

According to Protestant expositors, the command to John in 10:8–11 to take the 'little open book', eat it, and 'prophesy again' was a divinely ordained prophetic image of the Protestant Reformation, which opened the Bible to all. Victorian expositors of the historical school combined this interpretation with Joseph Mede's division of the Apocalypse into 'two principal prophecies', interpreting all history as divided into two eras, pre- and post-Reformation (Elliott 1851 in Carpenter and Landow in Patrides & Wittreich 1984: 312).

Prophesy again (10:11)

The new command is taken by Victorinus to refer to a new dimension of John's prophetic witness: John has been released from the mines of Domitian and is now free to go and speak his apocalypse 'before peoples, nations and languages' (ANF vii.353). The word 'again' is important for Mede, demonstrating to him that the previous prophecy of seals and trumpets refers to the same points in external history as does 'the other prophecy . . . of the open book' (in Burdon 1997: 34). So the following visions of the two-horned beast, the ten-horned beast, the woman in the wilderness, the lamentation of the witnesses, the harlot and the company of the sealed 'all synchronize with each other' (Cooper, *A Translation of Mede's Clavis Apocalyptica* 22 in Burdon 1997: 3, 34 and see above, 84, 110).

Ancient Literary Context

The two witnesses have the same power as Elijah (11:6; cf. 1 Kings 17:1) and Moses (11:6; cf. Ex 7:17–15:25). Elijah was to be the forerunner of the day of the Lord (Mal 3:1; 4:5; Matt 11:10). The threat against the witnesses marks the first appearance in the Apocalypse of the beast (11:7), which will be the focus of attention in 13:1–10 and 17:8; here he emerges from the 'bottomless pit' (cf. 9:1–2). Several themes in the chapter have led commentators to posit an earlier independent Jewish tradition, used by John and also by writers such as Hippolytus and Lactantius (Bousset 1999: 203–11). This is thought to include the coming of a single figure who exposes the Antichrist as a false messiah and is killed by him, followed by judgement. Elements in Rev 11 such as the resurrection and ascension of the witnesses would have been introduced by John to the Jewish tradition.

The *Apocalypse of Elijah* (in its present form a Christian apocalypse dating from the second or third century CE) has a passage (4:7–19) which resembles

Rev 11, with witnesses identified as Elijah and Enoch (in Charlesworth 1983: i.721–54; cf. Aune 1998b: 588–91; Frankfurter in VanderKam and Adler 1996: 129–96). It is often said that Lactantius (*Institutes* vii.17.1–3) identifies the witnesses in Rev 11 with Enoch and Elijah; actually he has a passage similar to Rev 11, but with only one unnamed prophet (in McGinn 1979: 61).

The evocation of hostile forces trampling the Jerusalem temple to the very threshold of the holy place (11:1–3) suggests the events of the last days of the siege of Jerusalem in CE 70 (recorded in graphic detail in Josephus' *Jewish War*), when Roman legionaries drew ever closer to the temple precincts. Either John's visionary imagination was suffused by the searing impact of this event, or, as early historical scholars suggested (Charles 1920: i.276–8; cf. Aune 1998b: 594–5), he made use of a Jewish oracle from the days before the fall of Jerusalem, when Zealots took refuge in the sanctuary and were inspired by a prophet who promised deliverance (Josephus, *War* vi.122, 285–7; cf. Luke 21:24). The pattern of prophetic witness, its cost and divine vindication is paralleled in Isa 53 and Wis 2–3, though without the explicit destruction of the rebellious city. In Rev 11 the complex of themes in which the holy city moves from being a beleaguered place to being juxtaposed with Sodom and Gomorrah, cities of rebellion (Gen 18; for their linkage with Jerusalem, cf. Isa 1:10), reminds the reader that iniquity is the property not just of Babylon (cf. Rev 17). The Beast is already at work in the midst of the children of light, as the letters in Rev 2–3 have made plain. The deliverance and liberation promised by the prophet in Josephus' account was very different from the lot of the witnesses in Rev 11.

The Interpretations

While many interpretations of this chapter follow patterns which have emerged in earlier chapters, distinctive elements such as the numbers, the indirect reference to the Jerusalem temple, and the specificity of the figures have encouraged a variety of identifications with figures past, present and future. As already mentioned, some have suggested the possibility of dependence on an earlier Jewish text about the temple. The linkage of the sanctuary with the church in patristic interpretation prefigures some modern exegesis (Bauckham 1993a: 84). The two witnesses have been identified with persons in an interpreter's own time, or, more often, with eschatological agents (Petersen: 1993). Similarly, the numerical calculations have been understood to point to specific historical moments or to the nearness of the decisive eschatological events, once the limited period is past.

General application: testing the Church (11:1–2)

Many patristic authors interpret the discussion of the temple in general terms, as referring to the church. According to Hippolytus, the temple is Christ's body, the church, and the holy city trampled down indicates a church persecuted by the Antichrist (in Prigent 1972: 402; cf. Achelis 1897: 229–38; similarly Ribera 1898: 35, 184–208, 284–301, 303, 374–8, 385 in Wainwright 1993: 62). Andrew of Caesarea (*Comm.* 30) sees the temple of the living God as the church in which rational sacrifices (cf. Rom 12:1) are offered, and the Temple court is the society of unbelievers (in Averky 1985: 127).

For Victorinus 11:1 refers to the measuring rod of the gospel, the norm by which one is to remain true to orthodox doctrine threatened by heretics like Valentinus, Cerinthus and Ebion. The death of two witnesses (11:9–10) reflects the deaths of prophets, both in the past and under the Antichrist (1916: 102.16–104.3; ANF vii.353–4). Augustine interprets the nations' raging against the Temple (11:2) as another reference to the unbinding of Satan (cf. 20:7), who will attack the faithful together with his allies (*City of God* xx.8).

According to Knowlys 'the great city' is London (*Exposition* 140 in Newport 2000: 33). He interprets the nations of 11:2 as the papists (*Exposition* 125 in Newport 2000: 31). For the *Watchtower Bible* the measuring of the Temple reflects the standards to be met by God's people (162–3).

Numerical calculation (11:2, 3, 9, 11)

This chapter is full of numbers: 42, 1,260, $3\frac{1}{2}$. The 1,260 days, or 42 months (11:2–3; cf. 12:6 and Dan 7:25; 12:7), and the three and a half days (11:7, 9) figure in apocalyptic calculations, with days sometimes being understood as years, and vice versa. Although Tyconius was largely responsible for opening up an ethical reading of the Apocalypse, he may have expected the millennium (the time of the church) to end very soon, for, he explains, 'the three and a half years during which the two witnesses of Revelation 11 give testimony were 350 years, beginning with Jesus' crucifixion' (*Rules* 5 in Burkitt 1894: 61; cf. Wainwright 1993: 35 and 233, n. 12). The period of 1,260 days indicates both the period of the Church and the eschatological persecution, showing thereby that the future is able to inform the present. Joachim equates the 1,260 years from Jacob to Zerubbabel with a parallel 1,260 in the new dispensation which are specifically stated to be years. He calculates 42 generations of 30 years each, implying the year 1,260 for the *eschaton*, though he draws back from precise prediction, warning that the final generation may not last exactly 30 years (in Reeves and Hirsch-Reich 1972: 137). According to Olivi, the 1,260 days indicate the duration of the mission to the Gentiles after the rejection of Christianity by the Jews (*Lectura* 643). For Bale, the 1,260 days, which run contemporaneously with the 42 months, represent a time of exile and persecution, and thus the tribulations of the true church in every age (Bale 1849: 254, 386; Fairfield 1976: 152–3; cf. Olsen 1973: 69–73).

A more specific interpretation of 'trample over the holy city for forty-two months' (11:2) is given by Foxe: the three and a half days in which the witnesses lie dead in the street (11:9) refers to the Council of Constance in 1414–18 and its condemnation of Jan Hus, since it met for nearly three and a half years (in Firth 1979: 103). Mede saw the 1,260 days as the years of papal oppression (in Wainwright 1993: 69).

The numbers have provoked a variety of mathematical calculations yielding dates for the eschatological events. For example, on the basis of 11:3 and 11:9–10, Pierre du Moulin (1624) arrived at the date of 1689 to mark the end of the beast's reign (*The Fulfilment of Prophecies* in Armogathe in McGinn 2000: 207). According to Sutcliffe, in about 1790 the 1,260-day prophecy of Rev 11:3 (cf. 13:5 and the 'time, and times and half a time' of Rev 12:14) came to an end (*Treatise* 21 in Newport 2000: 101). Thruston said the 1,260 years of papal power would end in 1866 and be followed by the millennium, 'a world for ever happy and a Christianity for ever pure' (*England Safe and Triumphant* 1:33; 2:349 in Wainwright 1993: 168). For Houteff the 1,260 days lasted from CE 538 to 1798 (*Shepherd's Rod* 2:227 in Newport 2000: 207). Gerrard Winstanley, before his 'Digger period' (i.e. his occupation of the common land in 1649), writes what is in fact a homiletical commentary on Rev 11, which he thinks outlines the battle against the dragon in his own life and that of his followers and typifies the three and a half ages in which the Church will be in captivity to anti-Christian power. This reflects Winstanley's sense of an ending overshadowing the events of his own day (*The Breaking of the Day of God*, Sabine edn 88), when the beast triumphs in humanity, as the life of the flesh or covetousness is manifested in the accumulation of private property, Adam's divisive legacy (*The New Law of Righteousness*, Sabine edn 175). He links the 42 months with the 1,260 days, implicitly reflecting the penultimacy of the sixth which is typical of Joachite exegesis (noted explicitly by Winstanley in *The Mysterie of God concerning the Whole Creation*, Sabine edn 82).

A dissenting note about such calculation is registered by S. T. Coleridge, reacting to the German exegete Eichhorn, who had said that the 1,260 days or 42 months represented simply a long period of calamity. In the margin of Eichhorn's commentary Coleridge complains that Eichhorn 'stands here on the very same [line of] Error, only at the other end of the line, as the prognosticating commentators'. In other words, the computation of periods of time, whether general or specific, is to be questioned (in Burdon 1997: 147–8; cf. Shaffer 1972: 17–96).

The two witnesses

The question of the identity of the two witnesses of Rev 11 has received many different answers. In Quodvultdeus, *The Book of the Promises and Predictions of God*, '*Half-Time*', chapter 13, Peter and Paul come in a sequence of pairs of witnesses beginning with Moses and Aaron and culminating in Elijah and Enoch at the time of the Antichrist (in McGinn 1998: 53–4; cf. Daley in McGinn 2000: 33; W. Bousset 1896: 108; Petersen 1993: 57, n. 189). As already mentioned, scriptural allusions in 11:6 suggest a connection with Elijah and Moses. A more general application is the *Geneva Bible*'s: 'By two witnesses he meaneth all the preachers that should build up God's Church, alluding to Zerubbabel & Jehoshua which were chiefly appointed for this thing, & also to this saying, in the mouth of two witnesses standeth every word [Rev 11:3–4].'

For Nonconformists of the seventeenth century, the two witnesses are faithful servants of God down through the ages: for example, the Waldensians and Albigensians (in Newport 2000: 39; cf. Bale 1849: 398, and Knowlys's 'ministers and saints of God' in Newport 2000: 31–2). In similar vein, Mede says that the witnesses are those who have preached the true (Protestant) faith in the 1,260 years (since 456), and who still preach it now (*Clavis Apocalyptica* ii.45–7). Their mission follows the type of ancient witnesses: 'according to the pattern of those famous pairs under the Old Testament, Moses and Aaron in the wilderness, Elias and Elisæus [i.e. Elijah and Elisha] under the Baalitical apostasy, Zorobabbel and Joshua under the Babylonian captivity' (in Patrides in Patrides and Wittreich 1984: 229). Winstanley interprets the witnesses christologically as references to Christ in the flesh and Christ in the mystical body of the saints in whom the spirit dwells: 'Those who will not worship without the establishment of a human power are none of his [Christ's] witnesses' (*The Breaking of the Day of God*, Sabine edn 88).

According to Beatus, the two witnesses of Rev 11 are the law and the gospel (*Comm.* 367–406 in Reeves in Patrides and Wittreich 1984: 44). This theme is paralleled in Millerite/Adventist interpretation (Oliver 1978: 53; cf. *Shepherd's Rod* 2:283 in Newport 2000: 207). In the Seventh-day Adventist Bible Commentary (7:801) the witnesses are the Old and New Testaments, which testify to Christ down through the ages, including the 1,260 years of the Antichrist (in Miller in Newport 2000: 158). Richard Brothers identifies the two witnesses with the apostolic gospels, Matthew and John, which are rejected by the apostate city, which he identified with London at the end of the eighteenth century (*A Revealed Knowledge of the Prophecies and the Times* (1794), 25–6).

Bunyan, inspired by the vivid scenes of Rev 11, says that the witnesses will be slain in a period when 'plots and conspiracies are laid against God's church all the world over, and . . . none of the kings, princes, or mighty states of the world will open their doors'. It is a time when the identity of the church will be so attenuated that there will be no living visible church of Christ, only a Church in ruins. Such events will be the signs of the last times (Bunyan 1862: ii.59, 63, 68 in Hill 1989: 330). In *Pilgrim's Progress* Bunyan describes the end of Faithful in terms reminiscent of the death and resurrection of the witnesses in 11:7–11 (1967 edn 136).

THE WITNESSES AS BIBLICAL FIGURES WHO WILL RETURN

According to Hippolytus, the Antichrist will rebuild the city of Jerusalem, restore the sanctuary, remove the two witnesses and forerunners of Christ (Rev 11:3), make war upon the saints, and desolate the world (in W. Bousset 1999: 44–6; cf. Prigent 1972: 396; Daley 1991: 39). For Lactantius a sign of the end of this age is God's sending of a great prophet (*Institutes* vii.17 in McGinn 1979: 61–2). A long tradition of interpretation has the two witnesses as Enoch and Elijah, neither of whom tasted of death (Tertullian, *On the Soul* l.5; Daley 1991: 153, 179–80, 203; cf. W. Bousset 1999: 203–9). Hildegard of Bingen (*Scivias* xi) mentions Enoch and Elijah (Hart and Bishop edn 496, 505; cf. Bauckham 1976 and 1978: 186; Newport 2000: 83). Victorinus sees one witness as Elijah, whose preaching will lead to the conversion of many Jews, and the other as Jeremiah:

> Many think that either Elisha or Moses is with Elijah, but they both have died. Jeremiah's death, however, is not found [in Scripture]. . . . For the very word which was given to him bears witness to this: 'Before I formed you in the womb, I knew you, and I made you a prophet to the nations' [Jer 1:5]. But Jeremiah was not a prophet to the nations; therefore since both words [Jer 1:5 and Rev 11:3] are divine, [God] must keep his promise and make Jeremiah a prophet to the nations. (1916: 98. 10–17, tr. J. Kovacs; cf. ANF vii.354)

In Islamic interpretation one of Muhammad's companions expected that he would return as 'a prophet like Moses' (cf. Deut 18:15). While it is unlikely that the Islamic material is directly dependent on the Apocalypse, this may reflect a belief common in late antiquity that Moses had not died and would return as one of the two unnamed witnesses of Revelation 11:1–13 (in VanderKam and Adler 1996: 181; cf. Arjomand in McGinn 2000: 247).

CONTEMPORARY ACTUALIZATIONS

Altogether more contentious and daring is the way certain interpreters saw these figures appearing in their own day. For some this reflects a conviction that the last days have come, for others (for example, Blake) a conviction that these images have an ongoing capacity to interpret the world. The Moses and Elijah link, which arises out of allusions in the text itself, is echoed by Joachim and extended to 'stand for two religious orders' (*Expositio* fols 106r, 146r, 148r in Wainwright 1993: 51; cf. McGinn 1998: 164–5). A particularly interesting illustration in this Franciscan tradition is found in the commentary of Alexander Minorita (Cambridge University Library MS Mm.V.31): two white-robed friars (described as 'predicatores') preach from their rostrums to ordinary people about the parable of Dives (the rich man) and Lazarus (Luke 16:19–31) (see plate 6). This parable of reversal challenges the conventional hierarchies and the rich of Alexander's world, whose heedless opulence is contrasted with the rigours of the Franciscan order (in Carey 1999: 83–4; cf. James 1931: 67).

The Beguin Na Prous Boneta (c.1297–c.1325) interpreted the two witnesses as her Franciscan mentors, Francis and Peter John Olivi. Although Olivi's work was condemned, and his memory vilified, he was highly regarded among popular movements like the Beguins. Na Prous sees Pope John XXII as the Antichrist and thinks Olivi's condemnation means the destruction of the gospel of Jesus Christ, as the following testimony to her views indicates:

> In that terrestrial paradise [probably a reference to Rev 20–1] Christ placed Elijah and Enoch, and that Elijah was Saint Francis while Enoch was Brother Pierre D'Jean [Peter John Olivi], both of whom bore witness to Jesus Christ. Saint Francis bore witness to the life of poverty instituted by Christ, while Brother Pierre D'Jean bore witness to the divinity in holy scripture, in which he discovered all the words of the saints and conveyed them in his writings through the power of the Holy Spirit given to him. Again, Christ told her, so she claims, that Antichrist killed Elijah and Enoch, that is, Saint Francis and Brother Pierre D'Jean, in the middle of the street, which street she said was holy scripture. (Paris Bibl. nat., Collection Doat, tome 27, fols 51v–79v in May 1965; cf. Burr 2001: 230–6; Potesta in McGinn 2000: 119)

In the fourteenth century Konrad Schmid and his closest associate had perished at the hands of the Church of Rome. Their followers were convinced that they would return again, this time to overthrow the Antichrist and preside over the Last Judgement (in Cohn 1957: 141–6). An illustration in the sixteenth-century Wittenberg Bible reflects Luther's own day. The measuring

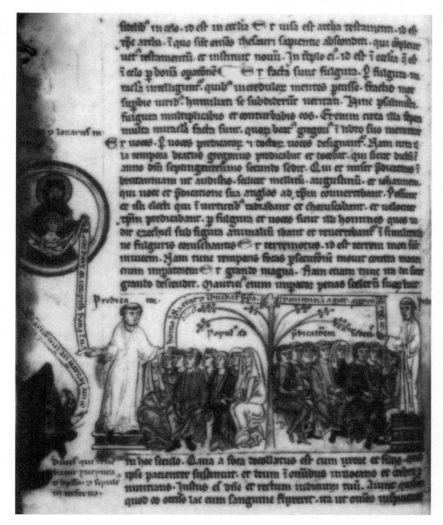

Plate 6   Marginal illustration in Alexander the Minorite's commentary on the Apocalypse: friars preaching as the two witnesses of Rev 11:3–6. Cambridge University Library.

of the temple by the two witnesses takes place before the Beast, who wears a papal tiara. The background is the Castle Church at Wittenberg with Luther's pulpit, and the witnesses are Protestant preachers with the fiery word of God proceeding from their mouths (in Scribner 1994: 175).

The German theologian Melchior Hoffman saw in the early Anabaptist preachers in Strasbourg 'the true Elijah who is to come before the last day', specifically identifying Enoch with Cornelis Poldermann or Caspar Schwenckenfeld. Hoffmann's apocalyptic ideas inspired those who set up the Anabaptist kingdom in Münster. Leaders such as Jan Matthijs thought the time had come to assemble the 144,000 of Rev 7 and 14, who would oppose the Antichrist, and Matthijs saw himself as the Enoch of the last days (in Deppermann 1987: 257, 336; cf. Cohn 1957: 261–70).

In the seventeenth century, during the English Civil War and its immediate aftermath, Mary Cary thinks the rising of the witnesses from the dead is realized in the creation of the New Model Army (in Capp in Patrides and Wittreich 1984: 112–13; cf. Capp 1972; Hill 1989: 51), and Ludowick Muggleton and John Reeve regard themselves as the witnesses who would oppose the Beast (in Hill 1990: 132–3; Underwood 1999). According to Benjamin Keach, the witnesses' resurrection is the reversal of a perilous situation, when in 1688 William of Orange, a 'glorious Instrument' in the hands of God, saved England from Roman Catholicism (*Distressed Sion Relieved* (1689) in Newport 2000: 40).

Similar in its interpretative method is Blake's identification of the witnesses with Wesley and Whitefield, the founders of Methodism. The Nonconformist Blake saw in these two religious figures kindred spirits, one symbolizing divine wrath, the other divine pity: 'But then I [apparently a reference to the Lamb] rais'd up Whitefield,/Palamabron rais'd up Westley [*sic*]/And these are the cries of the Churches before the two witnesses' (*Milton* 22 [24]:55–62 in Paley 1999: 75). While neither Wesley nor Whitefield would have shared Blake's political views, like him, they protested against the religion they considered oppressive.

The French Revolution provides the backdrop for Joseph Towers' interpretation of various images of chapter 11 (in Burdon 1997: 98). Another view of events in France is offered by Alexander Pirie, who denounced the Republic as 'the beast that ascendeth out of the bottomless pit' of 11:7 (*The French Revolution* in Paley 1999: 22).

The beast from the bottomless pit (11:7)

This image provokes both general and particular identifications, ranging from Alexander the Minorite's identification with Justinian's general Belasarius (in Wainwright 1993: 54) to John Bale's 'cruel, crafty, and cursed generation of Antichrist, the pope with his bishops, prelates, priests, and religious in Europe, Mahomet with his doting doucepers in Africa, and so forth in Asia and India, all beastly, carnal, and wicked in their doings' (Bale 1849: 392; cf. Wainwright 1993: 60, 95). Anti-Jewish and anti-Catholic sentiments have been tied with this figure. One of the most pervasive beliefs concerning the Antichrist is that he will be born a Jew and pretend to be the messiah (Pseudo-Alcuin, *In Apocalypsin* in Emmerson 1981: 79–83).

In the *Geneva Bible* the beast 'is the Pope which hath his power out of hell and cometh thence' and 'gaineth the victory, not by God's word, but by cruel war'. The interpretative possibilities opened up by the rebellious locations in 11:8 (Sodom, Egypt, and 'where their Lord was crucified') are taken by the *Geneva Bible* to mean: 'the whole jurisdiction of the Pope, which is compared to Sodom for their abominable shame, and to Egypt because the true liberty to serve God is taken away from the faithful: and Christ was condemned by Pilate, who represented the Roman power which should be enemy to the godly'. Coleridge sees William Pitt as one who has 'dug a pit into which he himself may be doomed to fall' (*Lectures* 1795: 12 in Paley 1999: 142, n. 130; cf. Pirie's association of the beast with the French Republic, discussed above).

The earthquake (11:13, 19)

The earthquakes are linked with particular events: for example, the invasion of Italy by the Goths (Alexander of Minorita in Wainwright 1993: 54), the end of popery in Britain (Keach, *Antichrist Stormed* in Newport 2000: 41; similarly Napier in *Plaine Discovery* 64–8, 145–9 in Emmerson 1981: 209), or the political 'earthquake' in France in 1789 (Burdon 1997: 98, 114; Newport 2000: 100; cf. Paley 1999: 21 on Joseph Priestley).

Perhaps most striking of all is Botticelli's *Nativity* (National Gallery, London), which represents the Incarnation as the symbol of a future divine event when 'angels will converse with men'. The inscription tells us that Botticelli believed himself to be painting at the time of the second woe of Apocalypse 11:14:

> I Sandro painted this picture at the end of the year 1500 in the troubles of Italy in the half time after the time according to the chapter of St. John in the second woe of the Apocalypse in the loosing of the devil [that is, the reign of the Antichrist] for three and a half years. Then he will be chained . . . and we shall see him trodden down, as in this picture. (In D. Thompson 1996: 114; cf. Reeves in Patrides and Wittreich 1984: 63; Weinstein 1970: 334)

The seventh trumpet (11:15–19)

For Napier the seventh trumpet and also the seventh bowl (16:17) represent the Reformation, which was a prelude to the decisive year 1688 when Napier calculated that Christ would appear (*A Plaine Discovery* 8 in Firth 1979: 144). Brightman thinks that the seventh trumpet blew in 1558 (*Rev. of Rev.* 388 in Firth 1979: 170). Benjamin Keach sees the seventh trumpet as the big turning point, indicating the arrival of William in 1688, which is the first stage in God's visitation upon the Antichrist (*Antichrist Stormed*, ch. 16 in Newport 2000: 39, 41, 144).

As so often in the appropriation of the Apocalypse we find William Blake taking up and using the images in new and different ways. Sceptical about the decadence and oppression he saw around him, Blake bitterly parodied the clarion call of progress in the scientific revolution pioneered by Newton:

> A Mighty Spirit leap'd from the land of Albion,
> Nam'd Newton; he seiz'd the Trump, & blow'd the enormous blast!
> Yellow as leaves of Autumn the myriads of Angelic hosts, fell thro' the wintry skies seeking their graves;
> Rattling their hollow bones in howling and lamentation.
>
> (*Europe* 13.2–5 in Paley 1999: 66)

Quite a different tone is evident in Milton's adaptation of the heavenly praise in verses 15–18:

> Thy kingdome is now at hand, and thou standing at the dore. Come forth out of thy Royall Chambers, O Prince of all the kings of the earth, put on the visible roabes of thy imperiall Majesty, take up that unlimited Scepter which thy Almighty Father hath bequeath'd thee: for now the voice of thy Bride calls thee, and all creatures sign to bee renew'd. ('Animadversions' in *The Works of John Milton*, ed. Frank A. Patterson III, 148, in Patrides in Patrides and Wittreich 1984: 220)

The temple in heaven (11:19)

In an interesting allegorizing interpretation, Hippolytus regards the opening of the temple in heaven, with attendant awesome noises, as the bodily resurrection of the Lord (in Prigent 1972: 402). While the earliest resurrection accounts (including the account in the apocryphal *Gospel of Peter*) do not describe such a scene, it is hinted at in Matt 27:52. Justin used the Apocalypse to argue that Christians are now the chosen people of God, since the Jerusalem temple has been removed to heaven (11:19), and a New Jerusalem comes down to earth (21:2). Victorinus sees the opening of the temple in heaven as both the first and second coming of the Lord (1916: 104.9–14).

This chapter provided an important resource for the Millerites to come to terms with the failure of their predictions in 1844. Ellen Harmon and James White reinterpreted the prophecies that had been used to claim 1844 as the year of eschatological fulfilment as references to Christ's cleansing the sanctuary in heaven (Rev 11:19) and his blotting out sins in advance of his second coming (Harmon and White in Stein 2000:118; and see above, 119–20). Thus they asserted that Christ's coming is an invisible event, hidden from human gaze, but none the less real (in Numbers and Butler 1987: 185).

Artistic interpretations

Depictions of the beast rising from the abyss to attack the two witnesses (11:7) vary widely, from the Trier Apocalypse's beast with teeth, claws and pointed ears to representations of the beast as horse-like, with a human face and long hair (Klein in Emmerson and McGian 1992: 159–99). Some illustrations portray a winged warrior or a king riding on a beast that tramples the two witnesses (in Emmerson 1981: 110). Even though the text may refer to only one beast, two or more beasts are sometimes portrayed. There is often a link with the locust-like beasts of 9:7–9, which were interpreted to be the forces of the Antichrist (e.g. the Trinity College Apocalypse, c.1242–5, the Cloisters Apocalypse, c.1320, and the Angers Tapestry of 1375–81).

The Gulbenkian Apocalypse portrays in a single picture a beast and a human Antichrist as separate figures. On the left of the picture, the Antichrist sits majestically, giving orders for Enoch and Elias to be executed, while two executioners carry out his command, and on the right, the beast from the abyss attacks the two witnesses, who lie defeated on the ground (Lisbon MS L.A., c.1255–65 in Emmerson 1981: 112; cf. Seidel in McGinn 2000: 473). The transformation of the beast into a human figure of a militaristic nature appears for the first time in a mid-tenth-century Beatus manuscript. The artist depicts a warrior wearing distinctive boots, blue-green leggings and a dark blue tunic with a yellow undergarment; he holds a huge sword with a long handle and decorated pommel. He seizes one of the witnesses by the hair, pulling his head down to lay bare his neck in the standard formula for execution. By substituting man for beast, and dressing him in familiar garments, the Antichrist is transformed into a figure recognizable as a human ruler (in Seidel in McGinn 2000: 473).

Ancient Literary Context

The abrupt transition to 'another sign in heaven', the Woman Clothed with the Sun pursued by the dragon, followed by war in heaven between the archangel Michael and Satan, introduces a complex of visions that has affinities with ancient popular culture and roots in earliest Christian mythology. Similarities between the Woman Clothed with the Sun and various figures, including Isis and Leto, the mother of Apollo, suggest that this image would have resonated with John's readers and hearers (A. Y. Collins 1976 and in J. J. Collins 2000: 408).

The war in heaven and Satan's ejection are both familiar themes in Jewish and Christian sources, as is the two-level drama, in which heavenly and earthly events are juxtaposed and closely related. The *War Scroll* (*1QM*) from the Dead Sea Scrolls describes elaborate preparations for a final battle in which spiritual and human forces join (cf. Dan 10:10–21; 21:1). In John's vision human endeavour is focused on prophecy, endurance and witness, rather than force of arms (12:11), though one should not play down the symbiotic relationship between human and divine initiative (A. Y. Collins 1996: 198–217; Bauckham 1993a). The struggle with, and the defeat of, suprahuman powers, in political and personal realms, is an important theme in early Christian writings (Eph 6:11–17; cf. Wink 1993; Aulen 1931). Luke 10:16 and John 12:31 (especially the variant form of this verse which has Satan cast down rather than merely cast out) are close parallels to Rev 12:7, and the story of the temptation of Jesus (Matt 4:1–11par.) belongs to the same theological complex. The theme is given particular force when, in Rev 12:18, the fall of Satan is specifically linked with the power of the Beast over ordinary mortals.

The Interpretations

The interpretations of this chapter cover the whole gamut of interpretative methods and exegetical possibilities. Frequent is the link with Jewish hope for a male messiah. In the illustration in the Bamberg Apocalypse, for example, the genitalia of the male child are pronounced, suggesting that it is really the male child who is to be the messianic king (in Mayr-Harting 1991: ii, colour plate 4; cf. Van der Meer 1978: 95). Compared with the rest of the Apocalypse, this passage is unusually prominent in Christian lectionaries because of its Marian connections and its association with the feast of Michael and all angels (in the *Revised Common Lectionary* of 1992, for example, Rev 12:7–12 is linked with Gen 28:10–17, Heb 1:5 and John 1:47–51). The Woman Clothed with the Sun has for centuries been associated with the Blessed Virgin Mary, but in earliest interpretation she was usually regarded as a symbol of the church. Thus it is not surprising that the vision is seen as guidance for the spiritual life, an approach evident in more secular times in the echoes of this chapter in literature and psychological aetiology.

This vision was given added weight after Pope Sixtus IV approved the feast of the Immaculate Conception of Mary in 1476, and this passage became one of the proper scriptural readings for the corresponding feast (Stratton 1994; Drury 1999: 174–5). It is probably no accident that in several depictions of John's visionary call (1:9–20) painted after this date, the Woman Clothed with the Sun Appears in the top left corner of the picture. We see this, for example, in Velasquez's portrayal of John on the island of Patmos (1618, National Gallery, London) and earlier in Hieronymus Bosch's *St John on Patmos* (Berlin Gemaeldegalerie) and in Hans Memling's altar-piece in Bruges (Saint John's Hospital). This also prompted votive antiphons to Mary (Blackburn 1999; cf. Pesce 1997). William Blake depicted this chapter, though, typically, he portrays the woman as being on the point of defeat in the face of the overwhelming presence of the dragon (Blake 1981: i.587–8).

The war in heaven between Satan and Michael has presented problems for Christian theologians, because the victor is an angel, which seems to threaten the unique rule of Christ. From an early period the text was thought to offer insight into the larger cosmic struggle between God and the forces of darkness, and it became a proof-text (along with passages like Isa 14) for a pre-mundane fall of Satan. As with other passages from the Apocalypse, the relationship of the various figures and images to human history has not been neglected.

The Woman Clothed with the Sun

THE WOMAN AS THE CHURCH

According to Hippolytus, the child is Christ, and the woman giving birth means 'that the Church, always bringing forth Christ, the perfect man Child of God, . . . becomes instructor of all the nations' (*Antichrist* 61, ANF v.217). This implies that Christ's incarnation, although a unique moment in history, is a continuing event through which the church becomes the universal teacher. The ecclesiological interpretation is also found in Tyconius, who suggests that the Woman Clothed with the Sun is the mystical body of Christ, contrasted with the company of the wicked in the mystical body of Satan, the Beast and Babylon (in Bauckham 1978: 57). The battle in Rev 12, Tyconius believes, refers in general to Christ's ongoing struggle with the devil, and in particular to the struggle going on in the church in his own time. The woman is an image of his own Donatist Church, pregnant with the gospel but persecuted by the devil, acting through the false (Catholic) Church (Balás and Bingham 1998: 114). Methodius interprets Rev 12 both as a guide for the Christian virgin who would imitate Christ, the 'Archvirgin', and as a symbol of the maternal Church, who is in labour until Christ is born in every one (*Banquet* 1.5). To Victorinus the woman is the ancient church of ancestors and prophets and saints and apostles, groaning with longing for the Christ. The sun points to the hope of resurrection, whereas the moon under her feet suggests the bodies of both Old and New Testament saints (1916: 106.1–4; 106.6–10; ANF vii.355). Her crown of 12 stars is the choir of ancestors of the old covenant (apparently an allusion to the choir of 24 elders in Rev 4:4, 10–11, of whom 12 are Old Testament figures (1916: 50.2–5). The devil's attempt to devour the child represents the temptation and passion of Christ (1916: 108.1–8).

For later Franciscan writers the woman is an image of the age of the apostles (*Breviloquium* in Lee, Reeves and Silano 1989: 133; cf. Brightman in Firth

1979: 169). Similarly, Bullinger calls her 'a figure of the faithful church' (Bauckham 1978: 306). According to the *Geneva Bible*, the moon under her feet indicates the way 'the church treadeth underfoot whatsoever is mutable, and inconstant, with all corrupt affections and such like'. For Newton, the woman is the primitive Church; when Constantine obtained control, she became tainted, symbolized by her flight into the wilderness (Wainwright 1993: 71). Milton sees her attire as a sign of the bliss of the saints: 'Attired with stars we shall for ever sit' ('On Time' 21). In similar vein, the singer of an African-American spiritual admonishes: 'Don't toucha my starry crown,/Good Lord I'm gwine home' (Johnson and Johnson 1954: ii.70).

THE WOMAN AS THE BLESSED VIRGIN MARY

The association of the woman with the Blessed Virgin Mary has a long history. The earliest explicit and exclusive reference is in the work of Oecumenius in the sixth century (in LeFrois 1954: 45), though there are earlier hints in Andrew of Caesarea's commentary (*Comm.* 33) and Epiphanius (*Pan.* 78.11.3–4; also Primasius in Matter in Emmerson and McGinn 1992: 44; cf. Zindras-Swartz in Stein 2000: 276; Milhou in Stein 2000: 24). The Woman Clothed with the Sun is a key text in the development of doctrine and iconography about Mary (Prigent 1959; Gabara and Bingemeyer 1989; Warner 1985), and imagery from Rev 12 (including the moon under the woman's feet and stars in her crown) appears frequently in artistic portrayals of Mary, as in the examples cited earlier in this chapter.

Visions of the Virgin Mary played a significant role in the indigenization of Christianity in Latin America. Most important of these is the one commemorated at Guadeloupe, in Mexico, where in December 1531 Juan Diego had three visions of Mary, who imprinted her image on his cloak, now kept in a magnificent basilica near the sight of the apparition. The iconography has typical features of Rev 12:1 (see D. Thompson 1996: 181). Also important is the shrine of Nossa Senhora Aparecida do Norte in southern Brazil, where local fishermen discovered a small image of a black virgin.

OTHER INTERPRETATIONS OF THE WOMAN

Indebted to this Marian tradition are texts in the Jewish Kabbalah where astrological imagery, combined with Christian theology, is used to speak of Israel, wife and virgin (*Sefer ha-Mashiu*, MS Jerusalem-Mussayoff 24, fol. 34b; MS Jerusalem-Mussayoff 5, fol. 120 in Idel in McGinn 2000: 209). One of the most remarkable interpretations of all is Joanna Southcott's identification of herself with the Woman Clothed with the Sun, the 'New Eve'. In 1814, as a woman over 60, she claimed to be pregnant with the messiah, Shiloh. She died shortly after her apparent pregnancy, but her prophecies were written down and sealed, like an apocalyptic prophecy (cf. Rev 22:10), and had an enormous impact on popular culture (cf. Harrison 1979: 24–134; Hopkins 1982: 20, 33). Earlier, Ann Lee, the founder of the Shakers, was identified by her followers as the Woman Clothed with the Sun (Stein in Stein 2000: 113; Garrett 1987: 55–6, 161–8, 216).

The following words of Joanna Southcott, under the inspiration of the Holy Spirit, not only indicate the fulfilment of Joel's prophecy that women would prophesy as well as men, but also reflect her belief in her calling to be the Woman Clothed with the Sun which would eventually lead her to believe that she was to give birth to the messiah (Joanna Southcott, *A Continuation of Prophecies* (1802), 55):

> And Joel's words must come true
> before I make an end;
> the revelations to your view
> must make the learned bend
> the woman clothed with the sun
> you'll find must first appear;
> the marriage of the lamb must come;
> my seal it must appear.

The war in heaven

As has been noted, from an early period Rev 12 was seen to offer insight into the larger cosmic struggle between God and the forces of darkness, and it was often cited as evidence for a pre-mundane fall of Satan. For Victorinus the war in heaven is the beginning of the advent of the Antichrist (1916: 114.7–8), but Origen seems to relates the story to the fall of the dragon (Satan) into materiality at the beginning of creation (*Comm. Jo.* i.97–8; Origen here cites Job 40:14, but his use of the word 'dragon' suggests that he also has Rev 12 in mind; cf. *Hom. Gen.* 1.1–2; Anselmetto 1980: 265). Andrew of Caesarea (*Comm.* 34) sees a twofold reference: first, the casting out of the devil from the angelic order for his pride and envy and, secondly, his defeat by the cross of Christ (linking the text with John 12:31, in Averky 1985: 139).

The Apocalypse presents Michael as the protagonist of the war in heaven (12:7). Commentators, embarrassed by the relegation of such an important role to an archangel, tried ever so valiantly to identify him with Christ; so, for example, Bullinger: 'we affirm Christ to be figured and signified to us under the type of Michael' (*A Hundred Sermons* 356 in Patrides in Patrides and

Wittreich 1984: 230, 237, n. 90). One justification offered for this was given by Edward Leigh: 'the composition of the word of three Hebrew particles, *mi-ca-el*, meaning, who is like unto the Lord?, that is only Christ' (*Annotations upon all the New Testament* (1650) 597; cf. Thomas Taylor, *Christ's Victorie over the Dragon* (1633) 341–2). Napier proposed another possibility: 'Michael meaneth the Holy Spirit' (*A Plaine Discovery* 205 in Patrides and Wittreich 1984: 230; cf. *Watchtower Bible* 181; Daniélou 1964: 117–45).

Bunyan reflects the ancient view that Michael is the advocate and guardian of the people of God (cf. Dan 12:1). His pilgrim gives thanks for Michael's help in his battle against the powers of evil (1967 edn 106). Milton, who sees the war in heaven as taking place before creation, deals with the christological problem by introducing Christ coming to the aid of the archangels (*Paradise Lost* i.41–9, 609–12, 738–51; ii.689–95; iv.37–41; v.582–3; *Paradise Regained* iv.618–21 in Patrides in Patrides and Wittreich 1984: 229; cf. Langland, *Piers Plowman* xviii.311–31; Hildegard of Bingen, *Scivias* ii and vi Hart and Bishop edn 73, 288, 317, 431). Several scenes in *Paradise Lost* contain descriptions of cosmic or personal battles inspired by Rev 12:

> Oh for that warning voice, which he who saw
> Th' Apocalypse heard cry in Heav'n aloud,
> Then when the Dragon, put to second rout,
> Came furious down to be revenged on men,
> Woe to the inhabitants on earth! That now,
> While time was, our first parents had been warned
> The coming of their secret foe, and 'scaped
> Haply so scaped his mortal snare; for now
> Satan, now first inflamed with rage, came down,
> The tempter ere th' Accuser of mankind,
> To wreck on innocent frail man his loss
> Of that first battle, and his flight to Hell.
>   (iv.1–12; cf. vi.686–8, vi.44–6)

The symbiotic relationship between heavenly and earthly battles is high-lighted in the Trier Apocalypse, where a line divides what is happening in heaven (the dragon pursuing the woman) and what is occurring on earth, where John is pursued by armed soldiers (in Mayr-Harting 1991: 20; cf. Van der Meer 1978: 97; see plate 7 below). A similar juxtaposition of heavenly and earthly events is found in a wall-painting in the church in Saint-Pierre-les-Églises where the adoration of Magi is set over against Michael's battle with dragon (Emmerson and McGinn 1992: 109, plates 6a and b; and Klein in Emmerson and McGinn 1992: 168–9).

Plate 7   The Woman Clothed with the Sun (Rev 12:1–6). Trier Apocalypse, Stadtsbibliothek, Trier.

Historical actualizations

There have been many identifications of figures in Rev 12 with specific historical people. For Hippolytus the seven-headed dragon of 12:3–4 indicates the kings of Persia, the Medes, Assyria and Babylon (*Antichrist* 25–7, 49; *Daniel* iv.3–12 in Prigent 1973: 323–4). Victorinus refers the seven heads of the dragon to seven Roman emperors from Galba to Nerva (end of first century CE), who is linked to the Antichrist (1916: 100.7; 118.5–10; 110.7–8). According to Rupert of Deutz, the seven kingdoms are those through which the dominion of the Antichrist will be established (*Commentary on Revelation*, PL 169:106B in Rusconi in McGinn 2000: 296). Frederick II, writing in 1239, identified Pope Gregory as the great dragon who leads the world astray (Rev 12:17; in Rusconi in McGinn 2000: 175).

Rev 12:3 provided the inspiration for one of Joachim of Fiore's *figurae*, which encapsulate imagery from the Apocalypse in diagrammatic form (see plate 8). His dragon has seven heads, identified as Herod, Nero, Constantius, Muhammad, Mesemoth, Saladin and one to come. The final Antichrist, indicated by the tail of the dragon, is Gog (20:8). Between the long necks of the dragon's heads appear captions detailing the seven persecutions of the Church:

> Herod. The First Persecution, that of the Jews. The Time of the Apostles.
> Nero. The Second Persecution, that of the Pagans. The Time of the Martyrs.
> Constantius. The Third Persecution, that of the Heretics. The Time of the Doctors.
> Muhammad. The Fourth Persecution, that of the Heretics. The Time of the Virgins.
> Mesemoth. The Fifth Persecution, that of the Sons of Babylon in the Spirit and not in the letter. The Time of the Conventuals.
> Saladin. The sixth persecution has begun.
> The Seventh King is symbolized by the tail.
> Gog is the final Antichrist.
> (Tr. in McGinn 1979: 136–7; see plate on 142 and Joachim of Fiore 1953: plate 14; Reeves and Hirsch-Reich 1972: plate 21 and 146–52; cf. Rusconi in McGinn 2000: 302)

Saladin, the contemporary tyrant, is represented as a larger head. The seventh, even larger head represents the last and greatest Antichrist still to come. The sixth and seventh heads are joined at the neck, explained in one of the accompanying notes: there must be seven persecutions, but the seventh is included in the sixth period so that the seventh, the sabbath of history, has no tribulation. Joachim sees the final persecution performed by a pseudo-pope inside the church in an unholy alliance with the infidel from outside.

The space between the menacing seventh head and the curled tail labelled Gog expresses Joachim's belief that victory over the Antichrist will be followed by the sabbath age of history, the third *status* of illumination and liberty, which will last until the appearance of Gog heralds the end of the world. After this millennial period of peace, Satan will be released (Rev 20:7); the flick of the

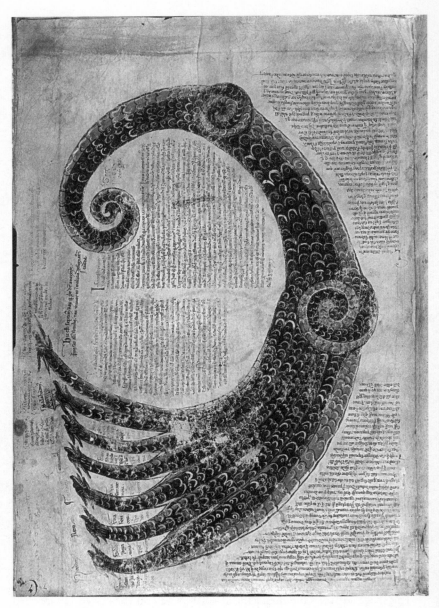

Plate 8 Joachim of Fiore, figura of the dragon with seven heads (Rev 12–13). Corpus Christi College, Oxford.

dragon's tail will mark the prelude to the Last Judgement. Even the peace and liberty of the seventh, sabbath age, must deteriorate, for it must never be confused with the perfection of the eighth age (in McGinn 1979: 136–41; cf. Patrides and Wittreich 1984: 5; Lee, Reeves and Silano 1989: 4; Wainwright 1993: 51; Emmerson 1981: 67). Elsewhere, Olivi following Joachim, correlates the seven ages of the Church with the seven general *aetates* of world's history:

Adam to Noah;
Noah to Abraham;
Abraham to Moses;
Moses to David;
David to Christ;
Christ to Antichrist;
Antichrist to the end of the world.

(*Lectura* 698f; cf. *Lectura* 718 in
Lee, Reeves and Silano 1989: 21)

John Bale reads the chapter typologically and historically: the dragon's first head is a serpent because of the temptation of Eve and the Fall; the second is a calf because of the beginning of idolatry under Nimrod. Four heads signify four monarchies: the lion for the Assyrians, the bear for the Persians, the leopard for the Greeks, and the strange beast for the Romans. The seventh head is that of a man and signifies the carnal lust of the papacy (Bale 1849: 406–7). Further, the serpent's head depicts the resistance of Judaism to Christ; the calf's head, the persecutors of Christianity; the lion's head, the heretics of the early Church; the bear's head, the hypocrites and usurpers of empire, the founders of the papacy and Muhammadanism; the leopard's head signifies the sects; the head of a strange beast, the wicked governors and tyrants responsible for the slaying of the witnesses [cf. Rev 11]. The head of the man symbolizes the worldly polity and falsehood as found in the Roman Church (Bale 1849: 407–8; Firth 1979: 51). In the interpretation of the German Calvinist Alsted, the woman, child, dragon, beast and lamb recapitulate events from Christ's birth to 1517 (in Wainwright 1993: 68).

In the Tudor period in England there was a spate of contemporary applications. For Edmund Spenser, Elizabeth I was the Woman Clothed with the Sun, and it was a 'Red Cross Knight' who has to fight the dragon. He combines images from Rev 12:3 and 13:1–6 to describe the beast, who represents the false church, wearing the triple crown of the papacy (*Faerie Queene* 1.7.16 in Sandler in Patrides and Wittreich 1984: 163; cf. Emmerson in McGinn 2000: 434; Emmerson 1981: 204–5). According to Cowper, the pope is the great dragon, and therefore the Antichrist (in Frederick in McGinn 2000: 89; cf. Cowper, 1934 in Newport 2000: 36). A contrasting interpretation is that of the Roman Catholic Bossuet, who sees the child of 12:5 as Constantine, whose establishment of the Church meant the triumph of Christianity over paganism (in Newport 2000: 72; similarly, Mede, in Armogathe in McGinn 2000:194; cf. Firth 1979: 221).

Contrasting political interpretations are offered from the 'right' (the dragon refers to opponents of the Stuarts, according to John Dryden, in Wainwright 1993: 167) and the 'left' (the dragon is George III, according to Blake: *America*, plate 4, and *Europe*, plate 11 in Burdon 1997: 186). In a marginal note to Watson's *Apology* in 1799, Blake says that in the present oppressive and reactionary political situation 'the Beast and the Whore rule without control' (Blake 1972: 388). To Hal Lindsey, the woman menaced who sprouts 'two wings of a great eagle and flies off into the wilderness' (12:14) indicates the US Air Force jets transporting Jews beyond the Antichrist's clutches (1970: 32–47; cf. 1973: 123, 178–9, in Boyer 1992: 212).

Images of the life of soul and spirit

An example of an allegorical reading that relates the text to the spiritual life is found in Methodius, who uses the eschatological imagery to refer to the struggle of the soul with evil powers in the present time, and specifically as an inspiration to virgins to lead a celibate life. In Discourse 8, put in the mouth of the virgin martyr Thecla, he explains that the Woman Clothed with the Sun in 12:1–6 is 'our mother' the church, who gestates the spiritual seed sown by Christ and labours to bring forth spiritual progeny (*Banquet* viii.4–6, ANF vi.335–7). Methodius explicitly rejects the idea that the male child brought forth in 12:5 is Christ, pointing out that he became incarnate long before the Apocalypse was written. The maleness of the child is a symbol of Christians rejecting the passions and the 'weakness of women' and growing strong in 'manly virtue' as they receive the masculine Word (*Banquet* viii.7, ANF vi.337). The moon on which the woman stands is the faith of Christians and the laver of baptism, since the baptized shine with a new light. The great red dragon of 12:3 is the devil 'who lies in wait to destroy the Christ-accepted mind of the baptized, and the image and clear features of the Word which had been brought forth in them' (*Banquet* viii.10, ANF vi.338). The snatching up of the newborn to the throne of God in 12:5 means that the devil is not permitted to destroy those who turn towards heaven. The stars 'swept down' in 12:4 indicate various heretical groups, called stars because they are 'dark, obscure, and falling'; 'one-third' refers to their straying from orthodox belief about the Trinity. The wilderness into which the Church is cast (12:6) is the garden of virtue,

which is 'unfruitful of evils, and barren of corruption, and difficult of access
... to the multitude', but easy of access for the holy (*Banquet* viii.11, ANF
vi.338). The wings on which the woman ascends in 12:14 are the 'wings of
virginity'.

In addition to representing the church, the woman is also a model for Christian virgins, who are exhorted to imitate their mother in not being troubled
by the afflictions of this life or the attacks of the devil. They are to 'bravely
prepare for the battle, armed with the helmet of salvation, and the breastplate,
and the greaves' (Eph 6:17; *Banquet* viii.12, ANF vi.339). The seven heads of
the dragon in 12:3 represent the 'seven great struggles of chastity' against the
devil – that is, against such evils as incontinence, cowardice and unbelief – and
the ten horns are demonic opposites to the Ten Commandments. By winning
these battles, the Christian gains the seven diadems from the heads of the
dragon (12:3), as 'crowns of virtue'. Victory is assured, because Christ has
already weakened and overcome the beast (*Banquet* viii.12–13, ANF vi.340).

Hildegard of Bingen allows the images of Rev 12 to be the currency of her
own visionary experience, which reflects an ecclesiological perspective: 'After
this I saw the image of a woman as large as a great city, with a wonderful crown
on her head and arms from which a splendor hung like sleeves, shining from
Heaven to earth. Her womb was pierced like a net with many openings, with
a huge multitude of people running in and out' (*Scivias* ii.3, Hart and Bishop
edn 169). A manuscript of Augustine's *City of God* in the Bodleian Library (MS
Laud Misc. 469 fol. 7v) depicts themes from Rev 12. Below the enthroned
Christ on the left is a Christ-like Michael who drives Satan and his host from
heaven. On the right is the church, symbolized by the Woman Clothed with
the Sun, who protects a newly baptized soul against the attack of Satan, the
dragon, while the 'old', dead body of the baptized soul (cf. Rom 6:3–11),
lies on a bed below (Emmerson and McGinn 1992: 116, plate 14; Klein in
Emmerson and McGinn 1992: 174). Similar is the exegesis of Francis Lambert,
where the seven heads of the dragon are a type of all the arts and crafts of Satan
(in Bauckham 1978: 260). Bunyan's Monster, who 'propounded conditions
to men', owes much to Rev 12 (1967 edn 346–7).

Jung sees in the vision of the woman of Rev 12 the epitome of archetypes
that have been repressed by the conscious or doctrinal mind. Here primitive
vital forces, for which the Jewish and Christian world-view has no official place,
are resurgent: John's unconscious turns to the myths of Leto and Apollo and
of Tammuz or Adonis, while his conscious mind tries unsuccessfully to assim-
ilate this to the scheme of the war of the Lamb and the army of martyrs (cf.
Rev 14:5; 19:14). The wrathful Lamb itself (Rev 6:16), which Jung calls an
'aggressive and irascible ram', is the resurgence of an archetype repressed by
the unbearable light of the teaching of divine love (in Burdon 1997: 213).

The flight of the woman (12:13–17)

Victorinus refers the flight of the woman in the second half of Rev 12 to the flight in the last days of the 144,000 (cf. 7:4 and 14:1) who receive the faith through the preaching of Elijah (1916: 112.1–10; ANF vii. 356). Apparently he has mainly Jews in mind (in Bousset 1999: 29, 215). In the Trinity Apocalypse the woman who is the Church is nourished by the eucharist in a desert place (fol. 14 in Van der Meer 1978: 159).

The situation of the woman in the wilderness recalls and reverses the casting out of Hagar in Genesis 16. In George Eliot's story *Romola*, the title character sets out to sea in a small boat, paralleling the woman in Rev 12:13–17, who takes refuge in the wilderness when the serpent sends forth a flood to carry her away. Eliot's boat perhaps also suggests a tabernacle or ark from which Romola will emerge once again as a living symbol of charitable love (in Carpenter and Landow in Patrides and Wittreich 1984: 317).

Ancient Literary Context

The influence of Daniel 7 is evident here, as in earlier parts of the book – for example, in John's call vision in 1:9–20 – and in 11:7 and 17:3. The beast from the sea of 13:1 recalls the four beasts arising from the sea in Dan 7:1–8, though John's beast is single, with multiple heads, so four of Daniel's beasts are here merged into one. In Dan 7 the beasts represent four kingdoms and function (as does Nebuchadnezzar's vision of the statue in Dan 2) as a kind of philosophy of history, explaining the necessity of an inexorable, pre-ordained succession of world empires before the 'fifth monarchy', the kingdom of God, is revealed. John's vision is altogether more immediate. Its political character is evident (Brady 1983), drawing as it does on Daniel, but its existential impact relates more to the social cost of nonconformity (13:17) and its call to endurance (13:10; 14:12), themes also occurring in Daniel (see the tales of the lions' den and the burning fiery furnace in Dan 3 and 6). The Apocalypse follows the gospels, rather than Daniel, in not relating the reign of the human figure ('Son of Man') directly to struggle with the beast(s), (though there is a sense of political conflict between the Son of Man and the ruling elite in Jerusalem in passages like Mark 8:31). In Rev 13:3 (cf. 13:12, 14) there is an indirect influence of the Son of Man figure/Lamb on the description of the beast's head as bearing the marks of slaughter.

In 2 Esdras 13 it is a man, not a beast, who arises from the sea 'inspiring terror in all on whom he looks'. Although he is unarmed, he emits 'a blast of fire' from his mouth, which consumes the hostile crowd (Hamilton 1999: 19 considers the importance of 2 Esdras for interpreters in the sixteenth century). The description of the second beast in Rev 13:11, with the signs and wonders it performs (13:13), is reminiscent of the treatment of false prophecy in Deut 13:1–5, a text that is important for the Apocalypse (cf. Rev 19:20, and on prophecy see Horbury 1998: 111–27).

The Interpretations

Of all the texts which have been a happy hunting ground for decoders of the Apocalypse (Brady: 1983), pride of place must go this chapter, which contains the solitary example of a practice known by its Hebrew name, *gematria*, whereby a numerical significance is given to a particular word. This is made possible in Greek and Hebrew because of their use of letters for numbers (a = 1, b = 2, etc.). A widespread interpretation of the number 666 in 13:18 is that it represents the sum of the letters of 'Nero Caesar' in Hebrew (נרון קסר = NRWN QSR), a view supported by the alternative reading 616, known to Irenaeus, which is the sum of the letters if Nero if spelled without the n (n = 50).

The two beasts have been variously identified. Links with Rome, whether ancient, ecclesiastical or eschatological, dominate, particularly in the early modern period, as Protestantism sought to establish itself. Interpretations of this chapter epitomize the different approaches to the Apocalypse: eschatological prediction, historical calculation, contemporary actualization and spiritual exhortation. The two beasts are understood either diachronically or synchronically. In the former interpretation we find the Roman Empire being succeeded by another form of Roman imperium, the Roman Catholic Church, while in the synchronic view the beasts represent two types of opposition to God's ways, one political and one religious. The synchronic view is more natural to Rev 13, whereas the beasts in Dan 7 (cf. Dan 2) clearly refer to a historical sequence of empires. Often Daniel is taken as an important hermeneutical clue for the interpretation of the chapter.

Interpretations of the Beast as a general symbol of evil

A more general understanding of the Beast (in contrast to identifications with specific figures or institutions) was set in train by Tyconius and established by Augustine. Tyconius contrasted the 'city of God' with the 'city of the devil', both existing at the same time. The city of God is present in the church, but 'the devil's city' is present in worldly powers, symbolized by the beasts of the Apocalypse (in Beatus 1930: ix.3 in Wainwright 1993: 35; cf. Bauckham 1978: 57; note that all references in this section are to Tyconius material preserved in Beatus, *Comm.*). His comments on this chapter exemplify his interpretative method. One of his seven basic hermeneutical principles, called 'the devil and his body', holds that Scripture often moves back and forth among different senses of a word:

> But in the narrative of our text it must be understood what part of the beast he means, since the beast itself is one body but it has many separate members. For sometimes he [John] calls the devil the 'beast', and sometimes his body, that is the infidels, i.e. those who lack baptism, and sometimes [he calls the beast] one of the heads of the beast himself, which, as if slain, was resurrected, which is an imitation of true faith, that is, evil Christians inside the church, and sometimes he calls the beast only the leaders, that is bishops or priests, who live a carnal life inside the church. All these parts are one body. (vi.3.15–16, tr. J. Kovacs)

The horns of the beast mean power or pride; the heads are the princes of the world, whereas the crown is the name of Christianity. The second beast of 13:11 Tyconius locates within the church. Its two horns are the law and the gospel, which the beast preaches, pretending to be just like the Lamb (Beatus, *Comm.* v.19). Making fire come down in 13:13 refers to wicked priests who baptize and ordain priests and cause the Holy Spirit to leave the church. Thereby, 'they seduce not those who dwell in the sky but those who dwell on the earth and they make themselves to be an image of the first beast and because of them antichrist reigns in the church'. So, whatever future eschatological power is exercised by the Antichrist, it also at work in the church of Tyconius' day (Beatus, *Preface* 17–20; *Comm.* vi.3.1–6, 15–19; cf. Bede, *Explanatio Apocalypsis*, PL 93:169.21–6).

For Augustine, non-Christians belong to the earthly city, which is the beast from the sea (*City of God* viii.24; xiii.16; xv.1, 7; xx.9; cf. Wainwright 1993: 37). The figure of the beast also appears in the Quran: 'We will bring forth the Beast from the earth to speak upon them' (Q-27:82). According to Rupert of Deutz, the seven heads of the dragon and beast from the sea are 'the seven kingdoms spoken of in sacred scripture, through which the gradual establishment of the dominion of the Antichrist will be established' (*Commentary on Revelation* in Rusconi in McGinn 2000: 296).

For Saint John of the Cross the seven heads make war against the soul as it climbs the seven steps of love, freeing itself from 'sensual things' and entering into 'purity of spirit' (1979: 1.101–2 in Wainwright 1993: 203). To Bunyan, all persecution was a mark of the Antichrist, and the Beast is an agent of persecution. Giant Maul (persecution) is far more dangerous in Part II of *the Pilgrim's Progress* than Giant Pope in Part I (1967 edn 218, 244–5, 311 in Hill 1988: 218, 311). Christina Rossetti regards the seven heads of the Beast as the seven deadly sins (*The Face of the Deep* 406 in Wainwright 1993: 209). According to Shelley, on Anarchy's forehead the mark of the Beast (Rev 13:16) parodies the inscription borne by the messianic rider of Rev 19:11: 'On his brow this mark I saw – "I AM GOD, AND KING, AND LAW"' ('The Mask of Anarchy' 36–7 in Paley 1999: 240; cf. Blake's 'Antichrist' figure Urizen, who pronounces 'one King, one God, one law' in 'The First Book of Urizen' 2.40).

Eschatological interpretations

Much more common are eschatological interpretations. The first beast is Rome 'fallen but now eschatologically revived', according to Hippolytus, (Hippolytus, *Antichrist* 50 in Dunbar 1983: 330; Prigent 1973: 326–8). For Gregory IX the emperor is the Antichrist's associate (cf. Rev 13:11, in McGinn 2000: 88). In the sixteenth century, at the height of the controversy between Protestantism and Catholicism, Ribera interprets the beast with seven heads eschatologically (1593: 35, 184–208, 284–301, 303, 374–8, 385 in Wainwright 1993: 61–2).

Joachim believed that the Antichrist had multiple manifestations. The sequence of the heads of the dragon of Rev 12:3 (which gave its authority to the beast, in 13:2) is a series of political manifestations of evil with the worst still to come. The Roman Empire, a head of the dragon, in its last phase was to be identified with Babylon. The two beasts in Rev 13, both manifestations of the Antichrist, were to arise at the end of the second status, or time of the sixth seal, the beast from the sea as a political leader and the beast from the land as a religious leader (*Expos*, fols 5r, 8r, 24v, 166v in Reeves in Patrides and Wittreich 1984: 51; cf. Lee, Reeves and Silano 1989: 4).

In his commentary on the Apocalypse, Peter Olivi challenged contemporary notions of the Church as a static, unchanging body and portrayed it as an institution in process. At the coming of the Antichrist the powers of darkness would gain control of the papacy, and a minority who had insight would defend the faith against their own leaders. In the fifth age, the Church had become big and powerful, but there had been a gradual decline until it turned into a new Babylon. The sixth period of church history had begun around the beginning of the thirteenth century with Joachim of Fiore, and continued with the advent of Francis of Assisi. The world was on the brink of a new, spiritual age. Olivi predicted that those who held power under the old dispensation, including popes supported by secular rulers, would persecute those committed to the new age until Christ came to destroy the great Antichrist ('Commentary on Cecidit, cecidit, Babylon', *Lectura*, fols 107r–108v; cf. Joachim, *Expositio*, fols 200r–202r in Lee, Reeves and Silano 1989: 23, and below, 182–3 on Rev 17). Needless to say, the hierarchy were scandalized by the suggestion that they would be on the side of the Antichrist. Olivi says the beast ascending from the sea signifies the bestial life of carnal and secular Christians; since the end of the fourth period it has had many heads, carnal princes and prelates.

> In this sixth period Francis' evangelical state has almost killed one head; for the more the higher, more widely practiced and more perfectly evangelical poverty and perfection is impressed upon and magnified within the church, the more powerfully the head of earthly cupidity and vile carnality is killed. But now this head, almost destroyed, is reviving so much that carnal Christians admire and follow its carnal glory. When, however, the apostate beast from the earth (13:11) ascends on high with its two horns of pseudo-religious and pseudo-prophets falsely resembling the true horns of the lamb, the most powerful temptation of the mystical Antichrist will occur. . . . The pseudo-christians and pseudo-prophets will cause the cupidity and carnality or earthly glory of the secular beast to be adored by all, and will offer great signs [see 13:13–15] to this end: first, of its ecclesiastical authority, contradiction of which will seem to be disobedience, contumacy and schismatic rebellion; second, of the universal opinion of all its masters and doctors and of the whole multitude or common opinion of all, contradiction of which will seem foolish, insane, and even heretical; third, of arguments and falsely twisted scriptures, as well as of some superficial, ancient and multiform religion confirmed and solemnized through long succession from antiquity. Thus with these signs they will seem to make the fire of divine wrath descend on those who contradict them . . . and will decree that whoever does not obey should be anathematized, ejected from the synagogue, and, if necessary, turned over to the secular arm of the former beast [13:1]. They will make the image of the beast – that is, the pseudo-pope raised up by the king of the first beast – adored in such a way that he is believed in more than Christ and his gospel and honoured as if he were the god of this world. (*Lectura* in David Burr, www.fordham/edu/halsall/source/olivi, from the critical edition by Lewis 1976; cf. Lee, Reeves and Silano 1989: 78–9)

Specific identifications of the two beasts

With regard to the ten horns (13:1) Lactantius writes:

> I will describe how it will take place so that you do not think that it is incredi-
> ble. First of all, the empire will grow but the supreme directing power will weaken
> and will be scattered and divided among many. Then civic quarrels will contin-
> ually spread abroad and there will be no end of deadly wars until ten kings will
> emerge simultaneously. They will divide the world to destroy and not to govern
> it. (*Institutes* vii.16 in McGinn 1979: 5)

For Victorinus, the beasts of Rev 13 and 17 symbolize both the kingdom of
the Antichrist and the Antichrist himself (1916: 116.10–11; 118.11–13; ANF
vii.356), but principally the latter. According to Rev 17:9–10 the seven-headed
beast (cf. 13:1) symbolizes seven kings. Victorinus interprets the sixth of the
seven kings as Nero, as both past and future persecutor of the saints (1916:
118.10–120.19), for Rome is Babylon, the persecutor whose judgement is
coming (1916: 86.11–12; 130.14–16; many modern scholars would agree with
this last interpretation). Victorinus suggests that the second beast in 13:11 is
Nero's false prophet who is associated with Jewish corruption and will cause a
golden image of the Antichrist to be placed in the Jerusalem temple (1916:
128.5–6, quoting Dan 11:4–5). To Dionysius the description of the beast in 13:5
suggests the emperor Valerian (in Eusebius *HE* vii.10.2). The notes in the
Geneva Bible define the first beast as the Roman Empire and also engage in
anti-Roman Catholic polemic (in Hill 1990: 4).

More specific identifications of the beasts include events under Julian Apostate (Bossuet in Newport 2000: 72), 'Frederick called emperor', according to
Gregory IX (in McGinn 1998: 174); the 'beast wounded to death' is Frederick
II in the fourteenth-century Franciscan *Breviloquium* (Lee, Reeves and Silano
1989: 117). The beasts – the leopard, lion and bear (alluded to 13:2) – signify
'the Macedonians, Persians & Chaldeans whom the Romans overcame' (*Geneva
Bible*). According to Herder, the beast from the sea is the rebel leader Simon
ben Gurion in the Jewish War, and the beast from the land is his subordinate
Johannan ben Levi (*Werke* 9:167–84 in Wainwright 1993: 126). For Lewis
Mayer, the first beast was a symbol of the Roman Catholic Church, while the
second was Napoleon (in Newport 2000: 176–7; cf. Burdon 1997: 102). Hal
Lindsey sees the Common Market and the trend toward unification of Europe
as the beginning of the ten-nation confederacy predicted by the Apocalypse
(1970: 94; cf. Boyer 1992: 249). Some twentieth-century North American interpreters think that the 'mark of the Beast' refers to misguided programmes for
social and economic betterment that are inspired by the devil (in Boyer 1992:

95). There are even more esoteric identifications on offer (e.g. Chosroes, the son of a Persian king, according to Alexander Minorita, *Expositio* 234, 273–92, 407, 427–8 in Wainwright 1993: 54; cf. W. Bousset 1999: 254–5).

The Beast in Protestant–Roman Catholic debate

One indication that the anti-Roman Catholic interpretation was well established in radical groups long before the Reformation is Ubertino of Casale's identification of both the angel of the abyss (Rev 9:11) and the beast from the sea (13:1) with Pope Boniface VIII (in Potesta in McGinn 2000: 114–18). According to the Lollards, the Apocalypse reveals the nature of the Antichrist. In one of his two tracts against the papacy, Wyclif concluded that the pope is the Antichrist here on earth, for he is 'agens crist bothe in lef and in lore' ('De Papa' in Wyclif 1929: 66–74 in Firth 1979: 7). For Calvin the Antichrist is not a single pope, but a succession of popes (in Firth 1979: 35).

Bale argued that the lamb-like Beast of 13:1 was a general symbol of Roman Catholicism, and that the second beast (13:11) is a more specific picture of this church, or of her hierarchy (1849: 422; Newport 2000: 176). His anti-Catholic sentiment is apparent in his interpretation of the names of blasphemy (13:5–6) as 'Pope, Cardinal, Patriarch, Legate, Metropolitan, Primate, Archbishop' (1849: 422; Wainwright 1993: 60). A similar point is made in the *Geneva Bible*'s comment on 'They worshipped the beast' (13:12): 'By receiving the features, ordinances, decrees, ceremonies, & religion of Romaine empire'. The second beast is the pope. The two horns (13:11) signify the priesthood and the kingdom, so there are 'in his arms two keys. The Pope in ambition, cruelty, idolatry, and blasphemy does follow & imitate the ancient Romans.' William Fulke argued that the beast is the 'head of the persecuting malignant church, having seven heads and ten horns [13:1], and is the same which afterward in the 17 chapter beareth the great whore Babylon' ('A Sermon preached at Hampton Court' in Bauckham 1978: 327).

According to Napier, the first beast is the pope 'because of his presumption to the two swords exemplified by Boniface VIII' (in Firth 1979: 145). For Brightman the two beasts together symbolize the papacy and its political operations: 'the first arrogated to himself the supreme spiritual power, the second, beginning with Boniface VIII, assumed temporal power' (*Rev. of Rev.* 430 in Firth 1979: 169). John Dove draws on Rev 13 in his general description of the Antichrist: He is the 'adversary of the truth' and is divided into political Rome (the beast of 13:1 and of Rev 17) and ecclesiastical Rome, which is 'the state of Popes reigning in the place of Emperors' (in Bauckham 1978: 100–3). For Tyndale, the mark of the Beast (13:16) is 'bishops and priests that preach not, or that preach aught save God's word, [who] are . . . servants of the Beast, whose mark they bear'. It is impossible to preach Christ, Tyndale said, 'except thou preach against Antichrist; that is to say, [those] which with their false doctrine and violence of sword enforce to quench the true doctrine of Christ' (*Doctrinal Treatises* 42–3, 185–6, 232–52 in Hill 1990: 42).

Edmund Spenser's 'Monstrous beast', on which the harlot Duessa sits, mixes the dragon (12:4), the seven-headed beast (13:1) and the scarlet beast of 17:3 (*Faerie Queene* 1.7.18 in Emmerson in McGinn 2000: 434; cf. Durham, *Commentarie* 573 in Newport 2000: 36). According to Bullinger, 'For if we account from the setting forth of the Apoc. six hundred threescore and six years [cf. 13:18], we shall come to the year of our Lord 763. To the same time I (say) wherein the Bishop of Rome, forgetting his humility, simplicity, poverty and also his office and ministry set his mind to bear rule' (in Bauckham 1978: 310).

Winstanley, radical of the English Civil War period in the seventeenth century, uses the word 'Antichrist' to describe everything that is 'Catholic' in theology and that is associated with the State Church in politics. The universities 'wander after the Beast' because they produce the ideologies which offer support for the political system (Sabine edn 47, 67, 214, 474; Hill 1990: 141). In *The Family Bible* the name of blasphemy (cf. 13:4–5) is 'the papal hierarchy' (Philip Doddridge, *The Family Bible Expositer* 1434 in Newport 2000: 61). James Bicheno identified Louis XIV with the beast from the earth (13:11). But while the papacy and the French monarchy were the fullest expression of evil, he thought that the Antichrist was also evident in British society: for example, in the slave trade and in commercial greed (in Oliver 1978: 47; cf. Wainwright 1993: 174).

By contrast, for the Roman Catholic Ribera, the beast with seven heads is not the Rome of his own day, but a future Rome under the power of the Antichrist: 'In those days the church will commit apostasy, but the pope will not lose faith even though the forces of the Antichrist will drive him from Rome' (1593: 35, 184–208, 284–301, 303, 374–8, 385 in Wainwright 1993: 61–2; cf. Elliott 1851: iv.466–8). According to the Roman Catholic *Douay Bible*:

This first beast with seven heads, and ten horns, is probably the whole company of infidels, enemies and persecutors of the people of God, from the beginning to the end of the world. The seven heads are seven kings, that is, seven principal kingdoms or empires, which have exercised, or shall exercise tyrannical power over the people of God; of those, five were then fallen, viz. the Egyptian, Assyrian, Chaldean, Persian, and Grecian monarchies: one was present, viz. the empire of Rome; and the seventh and chiefest was to come, viz. the great Antichrist and his empire. (Douay Bible, 1809 edn 264 in Newport 2000: 78)

In Adventist interpretation the seven heads of the Beast represent the specific religious bodies of 'western civilization', one of which, with the deadly
wound that was healed (13:3), was a symbol of the papacy. That wound was
inflicted by the reforms of Martin Luther and by the imprisonment of Pius VI
in 1798. This latter point is especially emphasized in Seventh-Day Adventism.
The other six heads represent Protestantism as six groups from which, according to Houteff, all Protestant denominations ultimately spring (in Newport
2000: 208). According to Koresh, the first beast is to be understood as a com-
posite symbol of worldly and religious powers. The scarlet beast of 17:3 is
America, supporting the Whore of Babylon: that is, the consummation of all
religious error. This phase of America is also symbolized by the beast of Rev
13:11 (in Newport 2000: 219).

The mortal wound that was healed (13:3)

Other interpretations of the deadly wound in 13:3 include Victorinus' view that
it refers to Nero's suicide and subsequent resurrection and restoration (1916:
120.7–10), which are antitypes of Christ's sacrificial death and resurrection.
The *Geneva Bible* comments on the wounded head: 'This may be understood
of Nero, who moved the first persecution against the Church, and after slew
himself, so that the family of the Caesars ended in him.' The wound that was
healed is the Roman Empire as established by Vespasian. For Joachim, the seven
heads are Herod, Nero, Constantius, Muhammad, Mesmoth (meaning uncertain, but perhaps an Islamic leader) and Saladin. After a few years, the wound
to the Beast/dragon will be healed, and the king in charge (whether it be Saladin
or another in his place) will gather a much larger army, before the final appearance of the Antichrist (in McGinn 1998: 137).

Olivi attributes to Joachim the view that to adore the dragon (13:4) is to
adore that king in whom the devil particularly resides (*Lectura*, fol. 90v in Lee,
Reeves and Silano 1989: 24–5). Olivi concludes that Frederick II is the wounded
head, and that in the time of the mystic Antichrist he will be revived in
someone from his seed (*Lectura*, fol. 93r in Lee, Reeves and Silano 1989: 25).
According to Bale, the wound took place at the Reformation, when the Roman
Catholic Church's power was challenged, but it was healed when Mary I
restored Catholicism in England (1849: 426 in Wainwright 1993: 60; cf.
Bauckham 1978: 73). John Cotton thought that Henry VIII and Elizabeth 'cut
off the head of the Beast', but they preserved its body in the canons of their
church, and 'an unsafe principle in their hearts' (in Hill 1990: 43). Tom Paine
rejoices in the 'death-wound' dealt to 'the affectation of mystery' by courts

(*Rights of Man* 208–9). He asserts that 'Burke, by seeking to disprove Paine's *The Rights of Man*, proves to be of the beast; and consequently, proves that government is a beast' (*Rights of Man* 195 in Burdon 1997: 126). Hildegard interprets the head of the Beast as 'the deceiver . . . surrounding the holiness of the saints . . . with many vices' (*Scivias* iii.11.32, Hart and Bishop edn 505).

The beast from the land (13:11)

The beast from the land is Pope Benedict XI according to Ubertino of Casale (Rusconi in McGinn 2000: 305). For Mede this beast is a symbol of pagan Rome and/or the Holy Roman Empire, and it becomes a symbol of papal Rome, which has taken over the role of the Antichrist from its predecessor (Newport 2000: 175). In Adventist interpretation the beast with horns like a lamb (13:11) is the United States, which fulfils the prophecy when it enforces Sunday observance, which 'Rome' claims as acknowledgement of her supremacy (in Newport 2000: 185–7, 209). Similarly, the Jehovah's Witnesses interpret the Beast as 'The Anglo-American World Power', described as 'the organization

Plate 9   'Television is the image of the beast' (Rev 13:15). A familiar advertisement in twenty-first-century São Paulo, Brazil. C. Rowland.

proposed, promoted, and supported by Britain and the United States and known initially as the League of Nations' (*Watchtower Bible*, 194–5).

The number 666 (13:18)

According to Irenaeus, the number indicates that the Beast sums up and con-centrates in himself all the apostasy that has taken place in the 6,000 years of the world's history (*AH* v.28.2). The three 6's also demonstrate that he will recapitulate Nebuchadnezzar, whose statue had a height of 60 cubits and a breadth of six cubits, and also the 600 years of Noah, when the flood came as a punishment for apostasy (*AH* v.29.2). The 6's stand for 'the recapitulations of that apostasy, taken in its full extent, which occurred at the beginning, during the intermediate periods, and which shall take place at the end' (*AH* v.30.1, ANF i.558).

The practice of *gematria* is illustrated by another passage from Irenaeus, where he notes three possible specific names of the Antichrist, all names whose letters add up to 666: Evanthus, Teitan and Lateinos. He suggests that if Lateinos is intended, it could be a synecdoche for the Roman Empire and con-cludes that the Holy Spirit has deliberately not given a clear revelation of the Antichrist's name. As already mentioned, he recognizes that in some manu-scripts the reading is 616 (*AH* v.30.1–4; ANF i. 558–60; cf. Daley in McGinn 2000: 9). Victorinus says that in Latin the number of the Beast is DICLUX, and Diclux, like Teitan, means that the Antichrist calls himself light, and the same holds for Lucifer (1916: 124.7–15, ANF vii.356–7 in Matter in Emmerson and McGinn 1992: 40). According to the *Geneva Bible*, this number 'signifieth Latei-nus, or Latin, which noteth the Pope or Antichrist who useth in all things the Latin tongue . . . because Italy in old time was called Latinum, the Italians are called Latini, so that hereby he noteth of what country chiefly he should come'. The Catholic elements in the innovations of Laud in the 1630s convinced a sig-nificant number of hitherto conformist Puritans that the Antichrist was to be found in England. In 'An anonymous Speech against the Judges' (1640), there is a contemporary manuscript note calculating that VVILL LAUD equals 666 (Hill 1990: 68–9).

Bale thinks that 666 indicates a Greek word transliterated as 'arnume', meaning 'I deny' (1849: 448; Firth 1979: 52). Gill suggests the Latinized 'Ludovicus' as the numerical equivalent of 666: 'Hence we have a further key. Antichrist, Rome, will fall when a King by the name of Louis is on the throne of France' (*Exposition* 3:797, Newport 2000: 58; cf. Burdon 1997: 92). In a later period, it was widely noted, for example, that if the letter A is given the value 100, B 101, C 102, and so on, the name HITLER adds up to 666 (Boyer in Stein

2000: 163). According to the Jehovah's Witnesses 'Just as six fails to measure up to seven, so 666 – six to the third degree – is a fitting name for the world's gigantic political system that fails so miserably to measure up to God's standard of perfection' (*Watchtower Bible* 196–7). Their ways of refusing to accept the mark of the Beast include not accepting blood transfusions and remaining unemployed in order not to compromise the laws of God.

Other interpreters link the number with dates. According to Olivi, 600 represents the six ages of the world, the 60 represents the six periods of this sixth world age, and the 6 represents the sixth period. In another interpretation, he suggests that 666 represents the number of years the Saracens will reign, from CE 635, when they defeated the Persians, until 1300. There are 666 years from the year 648, when they took Africa, to the beginning of the fourteenth century, which is 1,290 years from the death of Christ (*Lectura* 732–3 in Burr 1993: 143; cf. Lee, Reeves and Solano 1989: 21).

According to Foxe, 666 was 'the year when Mohammedans effectively began to seek power' (1583: 1:354 in Firth 1979: 96). In the context of the upheaval in England after the execution of Charles I in 1649, George Foster suggested that 'all forms and ways of worship, rules and government which is the wisdom of the flesh' were the Beast and should be destroyed. Parliament was the beast with ten horns, as cruel as the king, and would be overthrown 666 days after the execution of Charles I – that is, at the end of November 1650. It is no wonder, then, that there was an intense expectation of the kingdom of God following the execution of Charles I and a consequent intense disappointment when the commonwealth disappointed the hopes for change (in Hill 1990: 110).

Popes

In the light of the interpretations we have already encountered, it will come as no surprise that the Beast's number was applied to the pope. In the thirteenth century there was a long struggle between several popes and Emperor Frederick II, who was excommunicated by Gregory IX in 1227, and then again in 1239, when Gregory IX identified him with the Beast of Rev 13:1. Frederick in return identified Pope Gregory with the horseman of Rev 6:4 and the dragon of Rev 12:9, polemic which was returned in kind by Frederick and his supporters. One of Frederick's propagandists responded by demonstrating that *Innocencius papa* adds up to 666 (in McGinn 2000: 89; D. Thompson 1996: 73). Foxe initially identified the number 666 with Muhammad because his death had been near 666, but later he described the Antichrist as both the Turks and the Pope (in Firth 1979: 97–9). The Apocalypse's numerology probably

inspired Dante's equally enigmatic reference: 'stars already close at hand/
... will bring a time/in which, dispatched by God, a Five/Hundred and Ten
and Five, will slay the Whore/together with that giant who sins with her' (*Purgatorio* 33.40–5). Here the Latin letters DVX, taken as numbers, make up the
word 'leader', which Dante, inspired by Joachite prophecy, sees as a future world
leader who will bring peace and restoration. His identity would only be apparent on his appearance (in Herzman in Emmerson and McGinn 1992: 401, 412).

Artistic representations

In the Wellcome Apocalypse (Wellcome Library, London) the Antichrist commands that books be burned (fol. 10v), and the Velishav Bible (fol. 135r) shows
him personally stoking flames filled with books of theology (in Emmerson
1981:131). The iconography of the Antichrist, therefore, illustrates his false
preaching, his blasphemy against the name of Christ, and his opposition to the
law of God (cf. Gulbenkian Apocalypse, Gulbenkian Library, Lisbon, fol. 36v
in Emmerson 1981: 131, which also illustrates Rev 9:1 by showing a winged,
devilish figure with a scroll inscribed 'Ego sum Christus', fol. 20v). In the
Flemish Apocalypse (Paris BN neerl. 3, c.1400; Van der Meer 1978: 222) the
minions of the Antichrist, dressed in Franciscan habits with heads of leopards,
lead astray king, bishop and mendicants as they are marked with the beast.
Other friars (Dominicans and Franciscans) struggle under the banner of the
cross. This may reflect the struggles in the Franciscan order. In the Trinity
Apocalypse (mid-thirteenth century) contemporary figures also appear: the
picture of judgement in Rev 20 has Dominic, Francis and Benedict, with a
queen (probably Eleanor wife of Henry III); and a queen, a nun, a Benedictine
and a lay brother struggle against the Beast of Rev 13 (in Van der Meer 1978:
152–9; cf. James 1931: 52; Carey 1999: 84).

In the woodcut based on Rev 13 by Dürer there is a contrast between God
enthroned and the two beasts (in Van der Meer 1978: 300). A bishop is being
deceived by the beast, and in the juxtaposition of the sword and the cross
(which incorporates elements from Rev 14) two ways are graphically depicted
(in Smith 2000: 66; cf. Carey 1999: 1137). In the print by the late eighteenth-
century cartoonist James Gillray the images of the Apocalypse become identi-
fiable political figures, Edmund Burke among them (British Museum, London,
in Carey 1999: 247).

Ancient Literary Context

As in chapter 7, a gathering takes place, though here the Lamb is explicitly mentioned as well as Mount Zion, the temple mountain in Jerusalem, which makes the text more closely related to 2 Esdras 13, where the human figure who rises from the sea assembles a throng on a mountain. The new song which the 144,000 sing (14:3) echoes Rev 5:9. The rapid transition from earth to heaven and back again is common in prophetic and apocalyptic texts (Lowth 1753; Bengel 1740/1857; Burdon 1997: 51, 76). Themes of purity and election suggest the tradition of holy war (Deut 23:9–14; 1 Sam 21:5; 2 Sam 11:9–13; *1QM* 7:3–9; *11QTemp* 58:17–19; cf. Lev 15:18; 15:31; and Ex 19:15, where sexual relations are to be avoided when approaching the holy mountain; see Bauckham 1993b: 94), and also the marking of the elect in a period of crisis (Ezek 9:4). The vision of the eschatological harvest echoes Joel 2:1, already reflected in the trumpet blasts (Rev 7:6–9:20; 11:15–19). Verse 8 contains the first mention of Babylon, whose destruction will be the focus of a later vision

(Rev 17). The contrast between followers of the Lamb, described in this chapter, and those marked by the Beast (14:9) resembles the two-way doctrine found in the opening chapters of the *Didache* and the *Epistle of Barnabas* 18–20, among other early Christian texts.

The Interpretations

This vision represents one of the starkest contrasts in the whole book between the way of life and the way of death. The identity of the special group and the meaning of the virginity of its members (14:4) attract the attention of commentators, as do the angels and the proclamation of the eternal gospel. The prediction of Babylon's fall forms part of a contrast between the way of the Lamb and the way of the Beast. In 14:14, as in Rev 10:1, judgement is exercised by a figure resembling Christ, whose identity prompts discussion among commentators.

The 144,000 standing with the Lamb on Mount Zion (14:1–5)

According to Victorinus, the 144,000 'virgins' in 14:4 stand for the totality of Jewish Christians in the Church (1916: 49.82 in Wainwright 1993: 28). The 'Acts of the Gallican Martyrs' (cited in Eusebius *HE* v.1.10) adapts a phrase from 14:4 to describe the courageous martyr Vettius Epagathus, who 'follows the Lamb wherever he goes' (1965 edn i.411; cf. Musurillo 1972: 64). This reference is unusual; while the Apocalypse is concerned with martyrdom (see e.g. Rev 11), references to the book are strangely absent in the earliest martyr acts. Interestingly, recent scholarship on the Apocalypse questions the assumption that it was born in a situation of persecution (L. Thompson 1990; cf. Rowland 1982: 403–12).

For Origen and Methodius (*Banquet* iii), the virgins are a spiritual elite within the Church. Origen begins his *Commentary on the Gospel of John* by quoting from Rev 7:2–5 and 14:1–5 (the descriptions of the 144,000), claiming that since the number is much larger than the Jewish believers in Christ, these must be the Gentile Christians (*Comm. Jo.* i.1–7, Trigg edn 104–5). He interprets 14:4 as a call to pursue perfection: the 'virgins' – that is, the celibate – are also called the 'first-fruits'. Origen implies that Ambrose, his patron, is such a person, since he is 'hastening to be spiritual and no longer human' (*Comm. Jo.* i.9, Trigg edn 106). While ordinary Christians are symbolized by the tribes of Israel, devoted students of Scripture such as Ambrose and Origen himself are 'levites and priests':

Among us, the followers of Christ's teachings, most people spend the majority of their time on the affairs of everyday life and dedicate few of their actions to God. These could be [in John's image] the members of the tribes who have little in common with the priests and who give slight attention to the service of God. But it will be quite appropriate to call those who are dedicated to the divine word, and who live truly for the service of God alone, levites and priests, because of the special chararacter of their efforts in this domain. (*Comm. Jo.* i.10, tr. J. Kovacs)

These 'priests' are the 'first-fruits' and the gifts they offer to God are the 'first-fruits out of many first-fruits' (*Comm. Jo.* i.12), a point Origen uses in service of the main theme of his preface, the interpretation of Scripture. As the gospels are the 'first-fruits' of the Scriptures and the Gospel of John is the 'first-fruits of the gospels' (*Comm. Jo.* i.23), so the 'first-fruits' of Origen's own exegetical endeavour will be a commentary on this book (*Comm. Jo.* i.12–13).

Cyprian regards 14:1 as a promise that the sign of the cross brings salvation to those marked with it on their foreheads (*Test.* ii:22). The virginity of the multitude indicates the importance of continence and virginity (cf. *Vir.* iv). In the Coptic *Apocalypse of John*, the seer himself is described as a 'holy virgin', and the *Second Apocalypse of John* speaks of humans who live like angels in this age (i.e. without sexual relations, see Luke 20:34–6), although without direct reference to Rev 14:4 (in Court 2000: 47). In the fourteenth century Margery Kempe regrets that she is in a sense a 'second class citizen' because she is no longer a virgin (*The Book of Margery Kempe* i. 22).

In the *Geneva Bible*, in line with its anti-Roman perspective, the multitude is interpreted symbolically as 'a great and ample Church'. The Lamb is Jesus Christ who 'ruleth in his Church to defend and comfort it, though the beast rage never so much: and seeing Christ is present ever with his Church, there can be no vicar: for where there is a vicar, there is no Church'. In the clear distinction between this group and others, John Foxe sees a discourse on the nature of the true and false churches (1587: 276 in Firth 1979: 105–6; cf. Bale 1849: 450). This may also be the basis of the two standards in Ignatius of Loyola's *Spiritual Exercises*, where the retreatant is offered allegiance to two opposing armies, one of Christ and the other of Satan (Puhl 1950: §137).

The *Watchtower Bible* suggests that the multitude are not physically virgins, but people who have not defiled themselves spiritually. Followers of Selivanov in nineteenth-century Russia, however, have interpreted this literally and related it to the 'fiery baptism' of castration (in Clay in Stein 2000: 308).

The new song (14:3)

Hildegard alludes to the new song in *Scivias* ii.5 (Hart and Bishop edn 206), as does Bunyan in *Pilgrim Progress* (1967 edn 319). Milton portrays John seeing 144,000 male virgins singing a new song before the Lamb ('Damon's Elegy' 214). In *Paradise Lost* he imagines the content of the song:

> Shaded with branching palm, each order bright,
> Sung triumph, and him sung victorious King,
> Son, heir, and Lord, to him dominion giv'n,
> Worthiest to reign: he celebrated rode
> Triumphant through mid-heav'n.
>
> (vi.885–9)

The angels (14:6–9, 15, 17–19)

According to Cyprian, the angel announcing judgement in 14:6 is not a harbinger of the Last Judgement, but a sign that God alone can be worshipped (*Fort.* ii). The three angels in 14:6–9 signify protests against idolatry (*Fort.* iii). For Victorinus the angelic proclamation of the gospel to the nations (14:6) is both a past and a future event, relating to the two comings of Christ. The angel flying through heaven is Elijah, whose prophecy anticipates the kingdom of the Antichrist (1916: 49.82, 112, 140; ANF vii.357 in Wainwright 1993: 28).

Reformation polemic dominates in the *Geneva Bible*'s interpretation of the angel from the altar in 14:18 as Christ 'who is also the altar, the Priest and sacrifice', while other angels are explained as 'the true ministers of Christ who preach the Gospel faithfully'. Other identifications of the awesome angelic figures have been proposed. To Alexander Minorita the angel of verse 6 was Boniface, the missionary to the Germans, and the angel with the sickle of 14:17–19 is the emperor Charlemagne (*Expositio* 112, 153, 157, 162, 197, 299, 310, 384–5, 408–9 in Wainwright 1993: 54). For Johann Bugenhagen, who preached the sermon at Luther's funeral, the angel of 14:6 is Luther (in Pelikan in Patrides and Wittreich 1984: 74, 88 n. 1). Mede saw the angels of 14:6–9 as protesting against idolatry: the first makes image worship a crime, the second damns the author of idolatry (Rome), and the third its followers (in Murrin in Patrides and Wittreich 1984: 132). Frederick Thruston takes the second angel to refer to the Calvinist Church, while the third angel is the Church of England, which is 'pure and permanent' (in Burdon 1997: 102). Brightman interprets the avenging angel with the sickle (14:14) as Thomas Cromwell, and the angel who comes out of the altar (14:18) as Thomas Cranmer (*Rev. of Rev.* 503–4 in Firth 1979: 170).

The eternal gospel (14:6)

In the preface to his *Commentary on John*, Origen continues the exegesis of Rev 14 summarized above (see on 14:1–5), focusing on the phrase 'eternal gospel', which he understands as a warrant for the spiritual exegesis he will explore in this commentary. Origen thinks that the 'eternal gospel' is implied but not fully embodied in the letter of the Scripture. Even the Gospel of John, the most advanced of the written gospels, is incomplete, because it belongs to sensible reality. The revelation of Christ consists of three stages: first the law (the Old Testament), then the gospel (the New Testament as a whole), then the 'eternal gospel', which is the spiritual understanding and personal appropriation of the gospel by the interpreter. This 'eternal gospel' completes and surpasses the written gospels, even as the New Testament completes the 'shadows' revealed in the Old Testament:

> Just as there is a 'law' which contains the 'shadow of good things to come' (Heb 10:1) which are revealed by the law when it is proclaimed according to the truth, in the same way the gospel, which all who read it think they understand, teaches a shadow of the mysteries of Christ. And as for that which John calls an 'eternal gospel', which could properly be called 'spiritual', for those who understand directly all the things about the Son of God it gives a clear presentation of the mysteries revealed in his teachings and the realities of which his actions were symbols. (*Comm. Jo.* i.39–40, tr. J. Kovacs)

The method of interpretation usually referred to as 'allegory', Origen called 'spiritual interpretation', because it entails the spiritual transformation of the interpreter. No one can grasp the deeper meaning of John's Gospel unless he reclines on Jesus' breast (John 13:23) and becomes 'another John' (*Comm. Jo.* i.22). In other words, only a person who becomes like Christ will be able to go beyond the letter of the gospel and begin to understand the 'eternal gospel'. While Origen's commentary aims to glimpse the 'eternal gospel', he recognizes that it will be fully revealed only at the end-time. At the end of his preface he introduces a quotation from Rev 14:6–7: 'But at the end of time, an angel flying through the air with a gospel will announce the good news to every nation' (*Comm. Jo.* i.83–4, tr. J. Kovacs). In *First Principles* iii.6.8 Origen uses the phrase 'eternal gospel' to describe the perfect law of heaven, and in *Comm. Rom* 1.14 it is a title of the Son (in Monaci 1978: 148). 'The Everlasting Gospel', Blake's

most explicitly antinomian work contains a bitter satire of conventional religion. Here the phrase 'the everlasting gospel' is a defiant title indicating another
type of religion which proclaims that 'Empire is no more'.

Separating from Babylon (14:8–13)

Victorinus identifies Babylon with Rome the persecutor, which will be
destroyed (1916: 86.11–12; 130.14–16). In the *Geneva Bible* 'Babylon is fallen'
(14:8) refers to the Church of Rome:

> For as much as the vices which were in Babylon, are found in Rome in greater
> abundance, as persecution of the Church of God, confusion, superstition, idol-
> atry, impiety, and as Babylon the first Monarchy was destroyed, so shall this
> wicked kingdom of Antichrist have a miserable ruin, though it be great &
> seemeth to extend throughout all Europe.

A remarkable example of the use of 14:9–11 is to be found in a narrative
about the emergence of Broad Mead Baptist Church in Bristol in the middle
of the seventeenth century. Dorothy Hazzard was one of the 'professors of the
city' who 'began to lead the way out of Babylon' and decided to separate themselves from 'hearing Common Prayer, not knowing whither they went; but at
the command of God, they went out as it is said of Abraham, Heb xi.8'. This
move was not unproblematic for Hazzard, as her husband was the local clergyman (though one 'savouring of a puritanical spirit, preaching against the
Debauchery of the people and priests'). Her growing conviction that the
Baptist and Anabaptist reformation had much to commend it meant separat-
ing from her husband's pattern of worship and attracting the opprobrium of
contemporaries, who made accusations similar to those endured by her
younger contemporary Anne Wentworth. Nevertheless, the Apocalypse
emboldened her to take the decisive step to a different church polity, more in
line with what she considered to be the spirit of the early church:

> Opening her Bible to read, [she] happened upon that place in Rev. xiv, 9, 10, 11
> if any man worship the Beast and his image and receive his mark . . . the same
> shall drink of the wine of the wrath of God. . . . This struck such terror in her
> soul, that she dreaded to go; and thereupon presently (without admitting or hear-
> kening to any more Reasoning) she resolved in the strength of the Lord never to
> go more to hear common prayer. (In Hayden 1974: 84–96; cf. the critique of the
> Church of England in writings of the Leveller John Lilburne, *A Worke of the Beast*
> (1639) and *Come out of Her My People* (1639); cf. Haller 1979)

This religious separatism perhaps confirms common suspicions of the effects of the Apocalypse. This example also brings out, however, the way in which the text emboldens those, including women, who doubt the ecclesial and political arrangements of the day. The focus in this narrative on the Church should not disguise its intensely political character, as a group finds itself rebelling against a religious culture that does not sit easily with a different vision of the religious life. This in turn attracted calumny from the majority. The story resonates with the experience of pre-Constantinian Christians whose determined nonconformity led them into the role of being 'professors' at regular intervals (Kreider 2001).

Their works follow them (14:13)

'For their deeds follow them' is used in Brahms' *German Requiem*, which eschews a specifically Christian content and gives the blessing of the dead in 14:13 a universal character. This accords with significant threads in the Apocalypse, where belonging to a church looms less large than in other New Testament texts. 'For their deeds follow them' is also quoted in Patience's apology for the poor in Langland's *Piers Plowman*, which contains a critique of the way in which basic Christian values are ignored by professed Christians and is a stern warning to the rich about how wealth interferes with the exercise of Christian charity and humility. The poor man presses ahead 'with a pack on his back', but this is not a burden, for he is unencumbered by status and wealth (*Piers Plowman*, Passus xiv.213).

The harvest and the winepress (14:14–20)

The awesome harvest and the winepress, not surprisingly in the light of the similar imagery in 1:13–14, is interpreted by Joachim in a christological sense and also as a reference to a future order of perfect men who preserve the life of Christ and the apostles (in McGinn 1998: 136). The *Geneva Bible* says that the command to the one sitting on a cloud with a sickle to reap (vv. 15–16) 'is spoken familiarly for our capacity, alluding unto an husbandman, who suffereth himself to be advertised by his servants when his harvest is ripe, and not that Christ hath the need to be told when he should come to judgement for the comfort of his Church and destruction of his enemies'. The blood as high as a horse's bridle (14:20) is interpreted as the consequence of the bloodshed of human oppression: 'By this similitude he declareth the horrible confusion of the tyrants and infidels, which delight in nothing but wars, slaughters, persecutions and effusion of blood.' A historicizing approach to the reaping of the grapes in 14:19 is found in the comment of Bossuet who refers to invasions by Attila the Hun (in Wainwright 1993: 64).

Imagery from 14:20 is used by Shelley in Ahasuerus's discourse: 'Drunk from the wine-press of the Almighty's wrath' ('Queen Mab' 218 in Paley 1999: 231). Elsewhere the poet tells how 'blood-red rainbows' transform the covenant into a harbinger of further massacres (*Prometheus Unbound* iv.227–31 in Paley 1999: 229).

The verse is also reflected in the general historical predictions found in Blake's 'the sons and daughters of Luvah at the winepresses as they tread the Last Vintage of the nations' (Plates 25, 27 of *Jerusalem* in Blake 1991–5), which also recalls Isa 63 (in Fisch 1999: 221, 290). A typically idiosyncratic interpretation of 14:14–20 is evident in Blake's painting of William Pitt, *The Spiritual Form of Pitt Guiding Behemoth* (Tate Gallery, London), which is paired with *The Spiritual Form of Nelson Guiding Leviathan*. Seeing the war with France as an apocalyptic event, Blake interprets the two figures as agents of the divine will, like Assyria in Isa 10:1 or Cyrus in Isa 45. He sees Pitt as the destroying angel of 14:14. Remarkably, given Blake's political inclinations, Pitt and Nelson are not portrayed as particularly demonic but are (albeit unknown to themselves) agents of judgement (this is a theme which runs through his often complicated Continental prophecies, *America* and *Europe*). An earlier poem of Blake's links the imagery of 14:19–20 with the French Revolution and with the Duke of Burgundy: 'from his mountains, /an odour of war, like ripe vineyard, /rose from his garments' (*The French Revolution* 82–4 in Paley 1999: 47).

Lawrence disparages the 'fire and brimstone' morality of John:

> This [earlier views of the after life] was not good enough for the brimstone apocalyptist and John of Patmos. They must have a marvellous, terrific lake of sulphurous fire that could burn for ever and ever, so that the souls of the enemy could be kept writhing . . . this is the vision of eternity of all Patmossers. They could not be happy in heaven unless they *knew* their enemies were unhappy in hell. (Lawrence 1931: 75–6).

Ancient Literary Context

Interpretations of this brief chapter focus on the Exodus imagery and questions of theodicy, provoked by the Song of Moses, 'Just and true are your ways, King of the nations' (15:3). The hymn in 15:3–4 reflects Ex 15, the song sung after the Israelites have passed through the Red Sea and the army of Pharaoh has been destroyed, especially the praise of God in the opening verses. As in the Exodus passage, there are echoes of the Psalms, especially Ps 111:2 and 145:17.

The 'temple of the tent of witness' in 15:5 reflects the idea that there is a heavenly model for the earthly temple in Jerusalem (cf. Ex 25:9 and Heb 8:2). The probable background to the bowl (vial) image, mentioned in 15:7 and dominating the following chapter, is the vessels of the temple (Ex 27:3).

The threat posed by what seemed like heavenly water (15:2) is a familiar feature of early Jewish mystical texts. Those who would ascend to heaven to learn the divine mysteries are warned about the sight of what *appears* to be water but turns out to be part of the ice-like walls of heaven (Morray-Jones 2002).

The Interpretations

This chapter, like other parts of the Apocalypse, brings us close to Christian liturgical tradition and, at least indirectly, to the heart of the celebration of Easter, since Exodus 15 forms one of the readings for the Easter Vigil. The explicit mention of Moses and the parallel to the Song at the Sea connects this passage to a rich vein of Jewish interpretation: for example, the ancient Jewish interpretation of Exodus, the *Mekilta of R. Ishmael* (1956), much of which is roughly contemporary with the Apocalypse.

The sea of glass (15:2) and the temple (15:5–8)

Morel at the end of the sixteenth century identifies the sea of glass mixed with fire with the defeat of the Armada, seen as the first vengeance against the Antichrist (in Bauckham 1978: 176). Keats may be drawing on imagery from 15:5–8 in *The Fall of Hyperion*, especially in i.95–107, which deals with the priest Moneta's ministrations before the altar (in Paley 1999: 284).

Exodus imagery: the song of Moses (15:3–4)

Hippolytus notes that Exodus imagery abounds in this chapter (Prigent 1972: 409; cf. the interpretation of Exodus in *ExodusR* 23.7 and *Mekilta of R. Ishmael*). Andrew of Caesarea, noting the reference to the song of Moses *and* of the Lamb, notes that hymns are sent up to God by 'those justified before grace under the law' as well as by Christians: 'It is fitting for those who are celebrating the last most important victory over the enemy to remember the first successes of their battle such as in the history of the chosen people of God' (*Comm.* 45 in Averky 1985: 160). For Bede 15:5–16:21 represents the fifth age of seven plagues that will infest the earth (PL 93:129–34 in Matter in Emmerson and McGinn 1992: 47; cf. Bonner 1966).

    The song of 15:3–4 is quoted by Milton on several occasions: for example, in *Samson Agonistes* (1671) the chorus adds the words 'Just are the ways of God' to the memorial of God's saving purposes and Israel's willingness to enjoy 'bondage with ease [rather] than strenuous liberty' (line 293). In *Paradise Lost* x.644 it echoes in the heavenly host's response, 'as the sound of seas', to the Almighty's declaration of eschatological deliverance through the Son.

In the textual commentary surrounding the engraved version of William Blake's *Job* sequence, 15:3 figures in the comment on Job 42:12 (along with Ps 51:16). Blake's portrayal of Job is reminiscent of one understanding of the conversion of Paul, seen as a change from a religion dominated by law to one determined by grace. To Blake, the religion of law and sacrifice is diabolical, and the remote God of such religion needs to be dethroned. He interprets Job's vision of God in the whirlwind as a vision of Jesus Christ. Exploiting the space offered by a text which is 'not too explicit', he reads the book of Job as a conversion account (in Blake 1981: i.697–717; cf. Rowland in Tuckett and Horrell 2000), not, as most modern commentators have done, as a profound disquisition on the problem of evil (a reading which has to ignore significant parts of this enigmatic text). Starting as an adherent of a religion of the letter, Job is overwhelmed by apocalypse and converted to a religion of the spirit. Blake's quotation of Rev 15:3 at this point could be intended simply as a statement about divine justice, but for Blake, things are always more suggestive. The hymn of praise in Rev 15 comes after the tribulation of the people of God as they survive the ordeal of the sea of glass mingled with fire. Blake appears to relate this to Job's ordeal as he moves from a self-satisfied religion to an altogether more creative and dangerous world of vision and divine immediacy.

The song of Moses is an important text for Bauckham's argument that the book of Revelation expresses a universalistic hope for the salvation of all people. He understands the prediction that 'all nations' shall worship God (15:4) as a deliberate modification of the song of Moses in Ex 15, which celebrates God's deliverance of only the nation of Israel:

> In Exodus 15 God's mighty act of judgment and deliverance inspires terror in the pagan nations. This is indeed, in the context, a recognition of his incomparable deity, but its significance remains rather negative. John has reinterpreted it in a strongly positive sense, as referring to the repentance of all the nations and their acknowledgment and worship of the one true God. . . . In this way John has interpreted the song of Moses in line with the most universalistic strain in Old Testament hope: the expectation that all the nations will come to acknowledge the God of Israel and worship him. (Bauckham 1993: 100–1)

Ancient Literary Context

The Apocalypse contains three series of sevens which focus on the eschato-logical catastrophes (seals, 6:1–17; 8:1–2; trumpets, 8:2–9:21; 11:15–19; bowls/vials, 16:1–21). Such schematization of plagues was a standard compo-nent of Jewish and Christian expectations of the future. The third series is introduced as the 'last plagues' (15:1) indicating finality, and suggesting a sequential, rather than a recapitulative, reading. Chapter 16 is replete with imagery from the Egyptian plagues (cf. Ex 9:8–12; 7:14–25), and the drying up of the Euphrates may be a contrast to the drying up of the Red Sea in Ex 14. The mount of Meggido (= *har Meggido*) in 16:16 is deeply rooted in Jewish hope and fears (cf. Judg 5:19; 2 Kings 23:29–30; Ezek 38–9; Zech 12:11).

The Interpretations

Similar hermeneutical issues emerge in this chapter as with the seven seals and seven trumpets. A link with Exodus is frequently mentioned (cf. 15:3, the Song of Moses). Interpretations range from the general and hortatory to historically specific identifications. Critical moments in a society's life are linked with the various plagues described in this chapter. The keyword 'Armageddon' (NRSV: Harmagedon) pervades modern popular imagination about global cataclysm. The site of Josiah's defeat according to 2 Kings 23:29, it has become an image of the ultimate conflict. Alongside applications to public events, we find new visions of doom or challenges to action, in which images from the Apocalypse are reused, just as themes from Exodus and the prophetic books had pervaded John's visionary world. A modern Orthodox interpretation, rooted in resistance to re-education in the Communist labour camps, uses Armageddon in a transferred sense to refer to spiritual struggles with the forces of evil: 'The human heart is the Armageddon of this aeon' (Marculescu 2000: 241–3).

General, hortatory applications

In the chapters on the seals and trumpets, the question was raised as to whether the plague sequences should be read sequentially, or whether the trumpets and the bowls in some way recapitulate the first sequence. Victorinus thinks that the bowls recapitulate the trumpets, but with more detail: (1916: 84.14–86.12; cf. Wainwright 1993: 29).

The Franciscan *Breviloquium* sees the angels with vials (bowls) as preachers, which reflects the effect of popular preaching after the Joachite/Franciscan revolution (*Breviloquium* 238–9 in Lee, Reeves and Silano 1989: 142). The interpreters of the *Geneva Bible* link the text with the Hebrew Bible (cf. Hippolytus, *Antichrist* xii and Irenaeus *AH* v.35.2 in Prigent 1972: 409), and interpret it as a criticism of the Roman Church: the first bowl was like the first plague of Egypt, 'which was sores and boils or pox: and this reigneth commonly among Canons, monks, friars, nuns, Priests and such filthy vermin which bear the mark of the beast'. According to Charles Wesley, the first six bowls are directed to the Beast and its followers, and only the last at the impious on earth ('Letter of C. Wesley' in Newport 2000: 146). In line with a long tradition of Jewish and Christian interpreters, he sees a fixed period of woes and disasters on earth before the 'blessed days shall begin'.

Poetic evocations

Echoes of the terrible disasters of the bowls are found in two medieval texts. In the first we find a response from nature (Kind) to Conscience:

> Kind heard Conscience then and came out of the planets
> And sent forth his foragers, fevers and fluxes,
> Coughs and cardiac ailments, cramps and toothaches,
> Rheums and running sores and rankling scurvy,
> Boils and blisters and burning agues,
> Frenzies and foul disorders; foragers of Kind
> Had pricked and preyed upon people's skulls.
> (Langland, *Piers Plowman* xx.80–6)

A poem in Old High German speaks of the 'Muspilli', which appears to mean the end of the world:

> The moon will fall, and the earth will burn,
> No stone will be left standing,
> Then the day of judgement will drive through the land,
> Travelling with fire as a visitation on the people.
> Then can no relative help another in the face of the Muspilli!
> (in McGinn in McGinn 2000: 383)

Christina Rossetti makes indirect use of awesome texts from the Apocalypse to describe the inner spiritual life. In response to the image of the sun in 16:8–9, she says: 'Though the sun smite us by day and the moon by night, yet to us let the Sun of Righteousness arise with healing in his wings. Though Thou destroy our flesh, save our spirit.' The fleeing of the islands and disappearance of the mountains (16:20) prompts her prayer: 'When all faileth, save Thou, fail us not Thou; Thou Who never failest them that seek Thee. Lord, give us grace to seek and find Thee' (*The Face of the Deep* 381–4 in Wainwright 1993: 211). A similar psychologizing interpretation of Armageddon's storms (16:18) may be reflected in Shakespeare's *King Lear* III.iv.12, where Lear refers to the storm on the heath as 'this tempest in my mind' (in Wittreich in Patrides and Wittreich 1984: 189).

Historical actualizations

A typical interpretation of the sequence of trumpets and bowls as predicting specific events in history is offered by the late sixteenth-century interpreter, John Napier:

first trumpet (8:7) and bowl (16:2) refer to the destruction of Jerusalem in
    CE 71.
second trumpet (8:8) and bowl (16:3) is the translation of the Empire to the
    East in CE 316 (under Constantine and Pope Sylvester).
third trumpet (8:10) and bowl (16:4) signify Totila burning Rome in 561.
fourth trumpet (8:12) and bowl (16:8) refer to Charlemagne's installation as
    Emperor in 806.
fifth trumpet (9:1) and bowl (16:10) indicate the rise of the heretical Turks,
    specifically Zadok.
sixth trumpet (9:13) and bowl (16:12) is Osman, in 1296.
seventh trumpet (11:15) and bowl (16.17) is the Reformation in 1541.
(Summarized from *A Plaine Discovery* 8 in Firth 1979: 143–4)

In a similar vein, Bossuet sees the bowls as referring to a series of events
from the second century CE until the capture of Rome by Alaric the Goth (in
Wainwright 1993: 64). Alsted associates the bowls with a sequence of events in
the years 1517–1694 (in Wainwright 1993: 68), while Brightman refers them
to events that began under Elizabeth in 1560 (*Rev. of Rev.* 150 in Firth 1979:
170).

An interpretation similar to Napier's but reflecting upheavals at the end of
the eighteenth century is that of Joseph Galloway. The first four bowls are:

the destruction of the French ancient regime
the end of papal Rome
the pollution of the rivers of Germany
judgement on 'the Sun', meaning Louis XVI of France.

The last three bowls indicate events that are soon to come, including the
destruction of the French atheistic republic, the Ottoman Empire (signified by
'the great river Euphrates', v.16) and, finally, all the remaining enemies of God
at Armageddon (*Brief Commentaries* 223–306 in Burdon 1997: 100–1).

Euphrates and Armageddon

Olivi says that because of the constant battles among kingdoms of the Roman
Church, the size and strength of their armies will be weakened (signified by
the drying up of the Euphrates in 16:12), which will prepare for a destruction
of the carnal Church to be carried out by the ten kings and the eleventh who
presides over them (in McGinn 1998: 204; cf. Joachim, *Expositio*, fols 190r–v,

209 and *Breviloquium* 209 in Lee, Reeves and Silano 1989: 140–2). In the sixteenth century Samuel Sewall understands the drying up of the river Euphrates as the destruction of the Spanish Empire in the Americas (*Phaenomena Quaedam Apocalyptica Ad Aspectum Novi Orbis Configurata* in Stein in Patrides and Wittreich 1984: 275). A hortatory note is struck by the *Geneva Bible*, in criticism of Catholicism: 'By Euphrates which was the strength of Babylon, is meant the riches, strength, pleasures and commodities of Rome the second Babylon.' According to Foxe, the drying up of the Euphrates and the admission of the kings of the East is a reference to the Saracens and the twelve Ottoman Turks (1583; 4:102 in Firth 1979: 94–5).

Some take Armageddon (16:16) to refer to past historical events: for Herder it is the siege of Masada in CE 70 (*Werke* 9:195–6 in Wainwright 1993: 132), for Bossuet the defeat of the emperor Valerian by the Persians (third century CE; in Wainwright 1993: 64), and for Grotius, Constantine's defeat of Maxentius at the Milvian Bridge in 312 (*Opera* 2:2 in Wainwright 1993: 132). But for many interpreters Armageddon is a symbol of the ultimate cataclysmic threat and refers to World War III (Lindsey 1970: 152–7; cf. Boyer 1992: 124). In the Cold War period Armageddon expressed fear of a nuclear holocaust, a view reinforced by the more explicit 2 Pet 3:10 (Boyer in Stein 2000: 170).

Armageddon forms part of the complex eschatological scenario popular among many conservative Protestants, particularly in North America. In the last days there will be an increase of disasters and apostasy, culminating in the great tribulation; then Christ will defeat the Antichrist at Armageddon, restore the Temple in Jerusalem, and establish the millennial kingdom (Boyer in Stein 2000: 143, cf. LaHaye and Jenkins 1995–2002; Lindsey 1970 and 1973; Boyer 1992; Mojtabai 1987; McGinn 2000: 166–8).

Visionary reimaginings of the text

The chapter has also inspired new prophecy. For example, Hildegard appropriates features of 16:12–16 in a vision of a vile monster (*Scivias* ii.7, Hart and Bishop edn 294). The 'trumpet song' of the early Anabaptist martyr Anna Jansz sounds an apocalyptic note of foreboding (Snyder and Huebert-Hecht 1996: 340). Replete with imagery from the Apocalypse (14:3, 19–20; 16:17; 19:17; 21:9) as well as other biblical passages (e.g. Matt 25:6), it illustrates the great influence of apocalyptic themes in the earliest phase of Anabaptism. Jansz urges Anabaptists to take up their new song, expecting imminent vindication in the face of the persecution they suffered from both Roman Catholics and other Protestants:

At Bosra and Edom, so the author has read
The Lord is preparing a feat
From the flesh of kings and princes,
Come all you birds,
Gather quickly
I will feed you the flesh of princes.
As they have done, so shall be done to them.
You servants of the Lord, be of good cheer.
Wash your feet in the blood of the godless.
This shall be the reward for those who robbed us.
Be pleased therefore, rejoice and be glad.
Play a new song on your harps;
Delight in God
All you who foresee vengeance.
The Lord comes to pay
And to revenge all our blood [Rev 16:17]
His wrath is beginning to descend
We are awaiting the last bowl.
Oh bride, go to meet your Lord and King.
Arise Jerusalem, prepare yourself.
Receive all your children alike.
You shall spread out your tents.
Receive your crown, receive your kingdom.
Your King comes to deliver.
He brings his reward before him.
You shall rejoice in it.
We shall see his glory in these times.
Rejoice, Zion, with pure Jerusalem.

> (In Snyder and Huebert-Hecht 1996: 340)

Revelation 17

Ancient Literary Context

At the heart of this vision is the earlier vision of the beasts from the sea and the land (Rev 13), which are themselves derived from Dan 7. In the Hebrew Bible, Israel is a harlot because 'she' rebels against God and is attracted to other divinities and cultures. Hence harlotry is a metaphor for false religion and all the social practices involved in it (Hos 1–2; Jer 2–3; Ezek 16; 23). That the harlot is drunk with blood in 17:6 echoes 6:9–10, and the Apocalypse contrasts Babylon and Jerusalem (21:9, 19, 24). The extraordinary vision of Babylon enthroned on the Beast includes a feature which is unusual in John's apocalypse. While the book of Daniel is full of explanations of its dreams and visions, by either the inspired seer (as in Dan 2) or an angelic interpreter (Dan 7–11), John's images usually remain without interpretation. Rev 17 offers a notable exception (cf. Rev 1:20; 4:5). The heads of the Beast on which Babylon is seated are said to represent seven mountains and seven kings. Ancient Jewish writers engaged in similar allusive reference to Roman emperors (e.g. *Sibylline Oracles* 5:12).

The Interpretations

In the interpretations of this vision we find general warnings as well as anti-Jewish readings and the identification of 'Babylon' with Turkey, but dominating the reception of chapter 17 is the understanding of Babylon and the Beast as Rome, both as empire and then, pervasively from the sixteenth century; onwards, as the Roman Catholic Church (especially prevalent in artistic representations, particularly in the sixteenth century; Scribner 1994). A Roman link is deeply ingrained in the text itself, particularly in 17:9. It is tempting to suppose that the interpretation as a critique of the Roman Church originates in the great ecclesiastical and political upheaval at the Reformation, when, despite his misgivings about the Apocalypse, Martin Luther came to find in this text a ready aide in his polemic against the Roman Catholic Church (Backus 2000). In actuality, the suspicion of the papacy and Roman practices had its origin in the late medieval period, when both radical Franciscans and Wycliffites initiated a critique which drew on this chapter.

General warnings, contrasts and criticisms of wealth

Cyprian offers an early example of a general moral application which is closely tied to anti-Jewish polemic. He sees the Whore not as an eschatological figure but rather as a symbol of Jewish religious corruption, as is clear from his comment on the waters upon which the Whore sits (17:1, 15). These are gentile nations, the Church which has now replaced the Jews as the Lord's spouse, because of the Jews' 'harlotry'. He sees the gentile water, mixed with the pure eucharistic wine of the chalice, as a symbol of Christ's marriage with the Church (*Letter* 63.12; for modern examples that link this chapter with Jerusalem rather than Rome, see Massyngberde-Ford 1975: 282–93 and Barker 2000: 279–301). Tertullian uses the example of Babylon in giving advice to Christian women to dress modestly, unlike the Whore of Babylon, and also in a general exhortation about seeking heavenly crowns, not earthly ones (*Dress* xi.12.2; *Test.* iii.36). In another work he likens Babylon to the idolatrous public life of Rome, in contrast to what is required of Christ's followers (*The Chaplet* xiii.3–4). He sees the ten horns (17:3, 16–17) as ten kingdoms, which will replace the one empire (Tertullian, *Resurr.* xxiv). For Hippolytus (*Daniel* iv.23.6) the sixth and seventh heads (17:10) are an indication that there is still time to come before the consummation of all things. The Beast and the Whore are the mystical body of Satan according to Tyconius (in Bauckham 1978: 57). For Andrew of Caesarea (*Comm.* 53) the harlot is the earthly kingdom, represented as it were in one body, which is to reign even until the coming of the Antichrist (in Averky 1985: 173).

In the seventeenth century John Bale used this chapter and Rev 12 to indicate two contrasting communities, Jerusalem and Babylon (Bale 1849: 453–92, cf. Firth 1979: 50–1). Bunyan's *The Holy City* (1665) describes the Whore of Babylon as 'this gentlewoman', and in the posthumous 'Of Antichrist and his Ruin' he calls the Antichrist a 'gentleman' (Hill 1989: 215, 329). In *Pilgrim's Progress* there appeared to Stead-fast, Madam Bubble, 'the mistress of the world' (1967 edn, 373), and also a monster with seven heads and ten horns which was governed by a woman (1967 edn 346–7).

Milton's use of imagery from the chapter links ecclesiastical and economic abuses (*Paradise Lost* i.680–4, 690–2, 713–37 in Hill 1989: 225). In 1660 Hester Biddle calls on the women of London to turn their eyes to the plight of the poor, or run the risk of being no better than Babylon: 'yet thou canst pass by them in thy gaudy apparel, and outstretched neck, with thy face decked with black spots, which are the marks of the Whore, the beast, and the False Prophet, which is not the attire of Sarah, Abraham's wife' (in Hobby 1988: 43).

The image of Babylon seated on the seven-headed beast appears on the title-page of William Blake's illustration of Edward Young's *Night Thoughts* of 1797 (Blake 1981: i.344), made at a time when the war with France had caused suspicion of revolutionary ideas and repression of radicals. Indeed, Blake writes in a marginal note to 'Watson's Apology': 'To defend the Bible in this year 1798 would cost a man his life. The Beast and the Whore rule without control.' In 'Night VIII' Blake very pointedly depicts the heads of the Beast as contemporary military, royal, legal and ecclesiastical powers. (see plate 10). This very much resembles how his radical predecessor, Gerrard Winstanley, uses the Beast to describe the oppressive aspects of contemporary political and economic power, seeing private property as the curse, gained by oppression or murder. The professional ministry, kingly power, the judiciary, and the buying and selling of the earth are incarnations of the four oppressive beasts in Daniel 7, which are reflected also in John's Apocalypse (Hill 1983: 234–5 and Bradstock and Rowland 2002: 132–4).

Specific identifications of Babylon and the Beast, especially with Rome, the papacy and the Roman Catholic Church

EARLY CHRISTIAN WRITINGS

The identification of the Whore with Rome has a long pedigree. Irenaeus (*AH* iii.23.7; v.28.2) and the author of the 'Acts of the Gallican Martyrs' (in Eusebius *HE* v.1.57 in Musurillo 1972: 49) describe the Beast as a manifestation

Plate 10 Babylon seated on the Beast (Rev 17:3–8). William Blake's illustration of 'Night VIII' of Edward Young's *Night Thoughts*. British Museum, London.

Plate 11 The Angel announces the Fall of Babylon (Rev 17–18). Great East Window, York Minster.

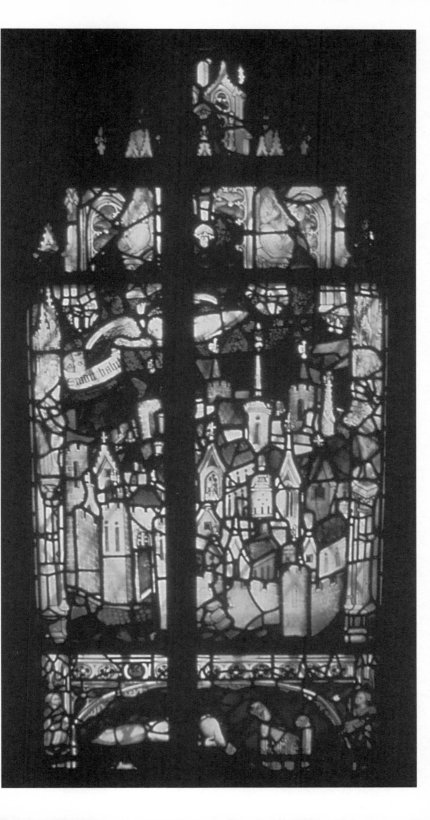

of Satan, but later in Irenaeus' writing it is linked with the empire (*AH* v.30.3; cf. Tertullian, *Resurr.* xxiv; *Against the Jews* ix.15; *Dress* ix.12.3). Elsewhere, however, Tertullian seems to follow Rom 13:4 in regarding the empire as a servant of God (*Scorpion's Sting* xiv.1). Lactantius says that the chapter refers to the decline of the empire (*Institutes* vii.15 in McGinn 1979: 58).

For Victorinus, the Beast of Rev 13 and 17 is both the kingdom of the Antichrist and the Antichrist himself (1916: 116.10–11;118.11–13), but principally the latter. The Beast, a Roman emperor who will reappear, most likely Nero, because of Rev 13:3 (1916: 118.12–15; 120.7–10), calls himself God, and his death is a parody of Christ's. The seven hills and the Whore are Rome (1916: 118.1–2; 120.5; 130.17–132.4). When the Antichrist, Nero, marches out to make war upon the saints, he will launch his attack from Rome (1916: 118.17–120.1). But while Rome is Babylon of Rev 17 and 14:8, Sodom in 11:8 is Jerusalem, and the Antichrist will insist on circumcision of his followers. The seven heads of 17:9 are the Roman emperors from Galba to Nerva (1916: 118.5–10). The seven kings, 'five of whom have fallen and one is and one yet to come', Victorinus understands as a reference to the time in which the Apocalypse was written; the five are the emperors Titus, Vespasian, Otho, Vitellius, and Galba (ANF vii.358). This means that Domitian is the one who remains, and the one to come is Nerva. Also providing a general link with the Antichrist legend is the following appropriation:

> And there being no man available, a polluted woman shall reign in the [city of the] seven hills, and defile the holy altars of God, and standing in the midst of the seven hills shall cry out with a loud voice, saying: Who is God, but I, and who shall resist my sway? And forthwith the seven hills shall be shaken and all life cast into the deep. (*Greek Apocalypse of Daniel* in W. Bousset 1999: 70)

JOACHIM AND OTHER MEDIEVAL WRITERS: THE CHURCH,
THE POPE AND THE TURKS

As we have seen, one of Joachim of Fiore's *figurae* relates to the interpretation of the beast with seven heads in Rev 12:3 (cf. 17:3; see above, p. 142). Joachim is not clear about Babylon and its relationship to the Roman Church, though he seems to suggest that the 'King of Babylon' is the emperor who will persecute the Church (in McGinn 1998: 316). Olivi implies a link between the Roman Church and Babylon. In the struggle that would inaugurate the kingdom of God he saw the forces of evil concentrated in the carnal Church (*ecclesia carnalis*), which is identified with the Whore of Babylon ('Commentary on Cecidit, Babylon', *Lectura*, fol. 95r in Lee, Reeves and Silano 1989: 23). The 'merchants' and 'businessmen' of the new Babylon (18:11–19) are interpreted as various types of carnal clerics. The carnal Church is 'a synagogue of

Satan' (Rev 2:9) because of its rejection of evangelical poverty (ibid., fols 107r–108v; cf. Joachim, *Expositio*, fols 200r–202r in Lee, Reeves and Silano 1989: 23).

Many of Olivi's Joachimist disciples recognized John XXII as the mystic Antichrist who had completed the transformation of the Church into the Whore of Babylon. This is a response to John's condemnation of the Franciscan radicals' ideal of poverty, which Olivi had himself upheld in *De usu paupere* (in Lee, Reeves and Silano 1989: 60; cf. Burr 1989 and 2001). Olivi observes that when the church fathers called the great Whore 'Rome', they referred not to the 'church of the just' sojourning within it, but to the reprobate who attack the pilgrim Church. The Whore stands for the Roman people and the Roman Empire during the pagan state and also later in Christianity (*Lectura* 819–31 in Burr 1993: 93–8; Emmerson and McGinn 1992: 89). Dante likewise denounced the corruption and degeneracy of the papacy in language based on Rev 17:1–2:

> It was shepherds such as you that the Evangelist had in mind when she that sitteth upon the waters was seen by him committing fornication with the kings: she that was born with the seven heads, and from the ten horns had her strength, so long as virtue pleased her spouse. (*Inferno* 19.106–11 in Herzman in Emmerson and McGinn 1992: 410–11)

Langland also evokes the Whore of Babylon in describing the spiritual discernment required to follow the path of true religion. He sees a vision of a deceptively appealing woman:

> I looked on my left side as the lady told me
> And was aware of a woman wonderfully dressed.
> Her gown was faced with fur, the finest on earth;
> Crowned with a coronet – the king has none better.
> Her fingers were filigreed fancifully with gold,
> And rich rubies on them, as red as hot coals,
> And diamonds most dear of cost, and two different kinds of sapphires,
> Pearls and precious water-stones to repel poisons.
> Her robe was most rich, dyed with red-scarlet,
> With ribbons of red gold and with rich stones.
> Her array ravished me – I'd seen such riches nowhere.
> I wondered who she was and whose wife she might be.
> 'Who is this woman,' said I, 'so worthily attired?'
> (*Piers Plowman*, ii: 7–19)

Other commentators find apocalyptic significance in the threat from Turkey and Islam. Aytinger, in his *Commentary on Pseudo-Methodius*, remarks on 17:7

that through the woman John meant Turkey, which was drunk with the blood of the saints and martyrs of Jesus. The Beast is Muhammad, and the seven mountains in 17:9 signify seven successive Turkish emperors (in McGinn 1998: 275). Occasionally one finds this link with Muhammad and Islam in illuminated manuscripts of the Apocalypse. Whereas in one type of illustration the Whore of Babylon is depicted as a woman in traditional garb seated on a throne above diverging streams (a scene straightforwardly based on the text), another type ignores the waters and seats her in oriental majesty on a divan of stacked cushions, wearing a richly ornamented crown (in Williams in Emmerson and McGinn 1992: 231; cf. Seidel in McGinn 2000: 474; Reeves in Patrides and Wittreich 1984: 44).

THE REFORMATION AND THE EARLY MODERN PERIOD: THE ROMAN CHURCH, THE POPE AND THE KING

Brightman is typical of many who interpret the Whore in 17:5 as the Roman Church (in Newport 2000: 36). Bullinger likewise writes of the 'proud whore, that false new start-up Romish Church, who extolling herself braggeth more of her outward apparel than of inward furniture' (in Bauckham 1978: 311). To Dent the ten kings of 17:16 are Protestant princes allied against the pope (in Bauckham 1978: 178). William Fulke takes a longer perspective, interpreting the seven hills of Rome and the seven heads of the beast as a series of Roman rulers: (1) kings, (2) consuls, (3) *decemviri*, (4) dictators, (5) *triumviri*, (6) Caesars or emperors, (7) popes (in Bauckham 1978: 334). According to Nicholas Ridley, by Babylon John meant 'the whole trade of the Romish religion . . . which is contrary to the only rule of all true religion, that is, God's word' (in Firth 1979: 72).

In the marginal notes of the *Geneva Bible* we read: 'The beast signifies the ancient Rome.' The mystery of the seven heads concerns ancient Roman history:

> For after this the empire was decayed in Nero, Galba, Otho, Vithius, Vespasian & Titus died in less than fourteen years and reigned as kings: Domitian then reigned, and after him Cocceius Nerva which was the seventh. Even the eighth means Trajan the emperor who was a Spaniard & adopted by Nerva, but because he persecuted the faithful, he goeth also to perdition.

The woman that sits on the Beast is the new Rome, which is the papacy, whose cruelty and bloodshed are indicated by the word 'scarlet'. The beauty of Babylon stands only in its 'outward pomp & impudence and craft', which resemble those of 'a strumpet'.

Edmund Spenser's Duessa who is the Whore/Queen of Scots, which reflects the embattled state of Elizabethan England, is influenced by 17:1–3 (*Faerie Queen* 1.7.18 in Sandler in Patrides and Wittreich 1984: 150; cf. Emmerson in McGinn 2000: 434; cf. Milton, 'A Masque presented at Ludlow Castle' (1637) 51–2). In his *Antichrist Stormed* of 1689 Keach states that 'most of our Eminent Protestant Writers, both Ancient and Modern, do affirm without the least doubt, that the Church of Rome is the great Whore spoken of [in] Rev 17:28' (in Newport 2000: 10; cf. Knowlys in Newport 2000: 30). The following lines by a Puritan theologian epitomize the Protestant interpretation

> Loe with ten hornes a dragon red,
> The harlot hereupon doesth ride,
> With purple robes, and crowne on head,
> A deadly cup she hath beside.
> To her euen kings do bow the knee,
> Thus Antichrist deciphered see
> As if in marble grauen were hee.
> He sits at Rome, where was times past
> Th'empire, of him kings hold in fee,
> With heresie he the world doth waste,
> A bloudie one, yet God would be.
> The city with seauen hilles beset,
> Is Rome it selfe, to be seene yet.
> Who sitt'h in Church, and claims Christs place,
> And roome to haue, and glad would raigne,
> Who doth Gods word so much disgrace,
> By Tiber sitt'h, as did Sibill faine,
> His bonnet white, *Pontifex* his name?
> The Pope him selfe, that thinkes it no shame:
> Whome doth Gods word already wound,
> And feare none other weapons need:
> The Pope, whome Gospell doth confound,
> God graunt his truth may with all speede,
> This mistic darkenes away chace,
> And when he com'th, him vtterly deface.
> (Andrew Willet, *Sacorum emblematum centuria una* in Emmerson 1981: 205–6)

Roman Catholic commentators naturally reacted against such interpretations. For Ribera the whore is not contemporary Rome but future Rome under the power of the Antichrist (1593: 35, 184–208, 284–301, 303, 374–8, 385 in Wainwright 1993: 61–2). Similarly, Suárez suggested that Babylon is not Christian Rome but a 'renewed pagan Rome to come at the end of time' (in

Armogathe in McGinn 2000: 189). Protestant apocalyptic expectations were ridiculed in Ben Jonson's play *The Alchemist* (1610): for instance, when Ananias accuses Surley of looking like the Antichrist because he is dressed as a Spaniard (IV.vii.55). This mocks the commonplace English identification of Catholicism with the Spanish threat and of Armageddon with the Armada (in Emmerson in McGinn 2000: 412; cf. Emmerson 1981: 205–20; for further sixteenth- and seventeenth-century examples see Newport 2000: 10, 30, 38, 130).

A good example of how the text is used in a specific historical context comes from John Milton. The execution of Charles I in 1649 led to a spate of political writing, including Milton's *The Tenure of Kings and Magistrates*, in which he explored whether various biblical passages supported monarchy. In his *Eikonoklastes* ('Image Breaker') he responded to a hagiography of the 'martyred' king Charles I called *Eikon Basilike* ('Royal Image') which had portrayed Charles offering an apologia for his actions. The work had attracted enormous support for the royal ideology. Milton responds by using images from the Apocalypse to predict the end of the monarchy of the Beast and of Babylon (*Eikonoklastes* 226–7 in Milton 1962: 597–9).

FROM THE SEVENTEENTH CENTURY TO THE PRESENT: OTHER IDENTIFICATIONS OF THE WHORE

Coleridge's *Conciones ad Populum* of February 1795 opens with a satirical 'letter from Liberty to her dear Friend Famine', in which Liberty approaches first Gratitude, then the Court, and finally, Religion in general:

> but alas! Instead of my kind Mistress, horror-struck I beheld 'a painted patched up old Harlot'. She was arrayed in purple and scarlet colour, and decked with gold and precious stones and pearls, and upon her Forehead was written 'MYSTERY' [cf. Rev 17:4–5]. I shriek'd, for I knew her to be the Dry-nurse of that detested Imp, Despotism. (In Burdon 1997: 115; cf. Paley 1999: 143)

In a similar vein, he writes: 'I am concerned that the Babylon of the Apocalypse does not apply to Rome exclusively; but to the union of Religion with Power and Wealth, whereof it is found' (Coleridge 1993: 89 in Paley 1999: 113). Elsewhere Coleridge calls the empress of Russia 'the "insatiate Hag" of the Apocalypse' ('Ode to the Departing Year' 93 in Burdon 1997: 131).

For Tillinghast the war between the Lamb and the kings in 17:14 is the English Civil War. After this the millennium (20:1–6) would follow in 1701 (in Hill 1990: 113). John Cotton also saw the tumultuous events in England in a prophetic context, defending the military actions of the Lord General and speaking of Cromwell and his army as 'chosen and faithful' (Thomas Hutchinson, ed., *A Collection of Original Papers Relative to the History of the Colony of*

Massachusetts-Bay 235 in Stein in Patrides and Wittreich 1984: 270). Winstanley sees in the Whore all that is associated with the state church. The universities are 'the throne of the Beast' because they produce the ideologies which justify an unjust social system. Even if they are themselves good men, university-trained parsons and ministers who receive tithes are bound to become corrupt (in Hill 1990: 141).

For the eighteenth-century prophets Blake and Brothers, Babylon is London (in Hamilton 1999: 290; cf. Mee 1992), a view reflected also in the Martin brothers' pictures of the destruction of Babylon and London (in Carey 1999: 265, 268). In the mid-nineteenth century the temptation for Anglo-Catholics to convert to Roman Catholicism is pictured as a serious threat to the Church of England, as is evident in a poem of 1854 entitled 'God send her swift deliverance', which asks for deliverance for clergy who may be tempted by 'the drunken bliss of the strumpet kiss of the Jezebel of Rome' (Moultrie, 'Altars Hearths and Graves' in Walsh 1898: 371–2).

According to the *Scofield Reference Bible*, there are two 'Babylons' which are to be distinguished in the Apocalypse: ecclesiastical Babylon, which is apostate Christendom, headed by the papacy, and political Babylon, which is the Beast's confederated empire, the last form of gentile world dominion. Ecclesiastical Babylon is 'the great whore', and is destroyed by political Babylon (Rev 17:15–18), so that the Beast alone may be the object of worship (cf. 2 Thess 2:3, 4; Rev 13:15, Scofield 1917: 1346–47).

Jehovah's Witnesses think the Whore of Babylon must be a world-wide religious entity (cf. Rev 17:15, 18), the entire world empire of false religion, linked with the League of Nations and the United Nations (*Watchtower Bible* 235, 240–1). Hal Lindsey points out that the 'one-world religious system is not described in delicate terms. A harlot, or a prostitute, is one who is unfaithful' (1970:128–9, 117, 123, cf. Boyer in Stein 2000: 163). David Koresh follows conventional Adventist exegesis, saying that the Whore of Babylon is a supremely blasphemous religious system that takes in all the errors of Roman Catholicism and apostate Protestantism. This conspiracy needs a host, as the woman needs a beast to ride, and that host, says Koresh, is latter-day America (Newport 2000: 221–2, 231).

The identification of the Whore with ancient Rome has come to dominate the approach to this chapter in modern historical scholarship (Aune 1998b: 905; Bauckham 1993a: 123). The general connection is clearer than the detailed interpretation, however. The seven mountains may point to Rome, but the seven kings have been variously identified (A. Y. Collins 1984: 54–83). If one begins with the first emperor, the 'five kings' would be Augustus, Tiberius, Caligula, Claudius and Nero, and we come to CE 68, the year of the three soldier-emperors (Galba, Otho, Vitellius) as the time of the author (on theories of the dating and origins of the Apocalypse, see Aune 1997: lxi–ixix and cxx–cxxxiv). But this involves a major discrepancy with the earliest witnesses, who date the Apocalypse to the reign of Domitian (Irenaeus *AH* v.30.3; Eusebius *HE* iii.17.1). Other ways of computing have been suggested. For example, the five kings who have fallen are understood as the emperors who persecuted the people of God, omitting Augustus and Claudius and including Vespasian and Domitian. A similar list of emperors is found in another eschatological text, *Sibylline Oracles* 5:12, here starting with Julius Caesar and including the soldier-emperors. This would suggest a date in the late 60s for Rev 17 and the Apocalypse as a whole (Rowland 1982: 403–12), though, of course, it is not impossible that the final form of the Apocalypse was promulgated 30 years later, during or just after Domitian's reign.

The problematic nature of the image of 'the whore of Babylon'

One contribution of modern study of the Bible has been increased attention to the medium in which its message is communicated. This has led some to question biblical images of women, with the Apocalypse seen as more problematic than any other New Testament book outside the Pastoral Epistles (Pippin 1992; A. Y. Collins 1993). It projects images of women who are either active, wrong-headed Jezebels (2:20–3; cf. ch. 17) or passive wives and mothers (19:7–8; 21:2, 9; cf. ch. 12). Male celibacy is commended (14:4; on male imagery see Moore 1996), and woman is portrayed as harlot (ch. 17).

It should be noted, however, that there are negative male figures such as Balaam, who embodies the false prophet (2:14). In addition, the harlot of chapter 17 is seated on the Beast, suggesting that the initiative for her immoral behaviour lies with the Beast which 'supports' and then cruelly abandons her (17:3, 16). Babylon is not the active partner in the 'fornication' but merely the object of the attentions of the kings of the earth who have made Babylon what she is (17:2; 18:3, 9). The imagery suggests the complexity of oppression. Babylon is deceived and culpable, but ultimately at the mercy of the Beast.

In addition, Revelation, as a prophetic book, has offered space for women as well as men to flourish, even within a patriarchal society. Female prophets and mystics down the centuries have been inspired by it to explore the inner life and also to exercise a public role that society would deny them (Elm 1994: 32; Jantzen 1995; Mack 1992). Perpetua and Felicity, Teresa of Avila and Hildegard of Bingen found in this authoritative visionary text a licence to transgress convention and function in a male domain. Anna Trapnel, one of a large number of women visionaries and prophets in seventeenth-century England, uses imagery from the Apocalypse in describing a heavenly court populated with herself and her women companions. Her prophecy offers an example of the important role women have played in social movements. She makes an explicit claim to be included in the apocalyptic promises: 'John thou wilt not offended be / That handmaids here should sing / That they should meddle to declare / The matters of the King' (in Hobby 1988: 33–4). Certainly no all-male, apocalyptic world is conceived of here!

This is not to deny that the medium may all too easily detract from the message (Freire 1972), so that a text like Rev 17, instead of impressing on us the grim reality of our world, itself becomes an obstacle. So Blake, finding the Bible used as an instrument of oppression rather than as an inspiration for the imagination, evolved his own mythology, rooted in the symbols and images of the biblical prophecies and apocalypses, to express a more humane conception of life. He sought to enable Scripture's imagery to be reborn by word, picture, myth and artistic ingenuity, so that the Scriptures and the spiritual experiences of previous generations could become present truth and words of life.

It is in this context that we can best understand one of the most intriguing comparisons in interpretations of this chapter, both from late seventeenth-century England, one by Hanserd Knowlys and the other by Anne Wentworth (see above, p. 7). Knowlys repeats many of the conventional eschatological and anti-Catholic sentiments of Protestant exegesis of his day (*Exposition* 169 in Newport 2000: 31). Wentworth, on the other hand, turns to the Apocalypse to deal with a critical moment in her life, when she has been abused by her husband and ejected from her house. The image of Babylon offers a language to articulate the intensity of her anger and the weight of the oppression she feels, along with her hope for deliverance:

> Mercy and Judgment they did meet,
> And with a holy Kiss each other greet:
> Justice and Equity took Mercies part,
> And Mercy stabbed Babylon to the heart:
> That Babylon did bleed unto death;
> Then the Lord put his Sword in his sheath.
> When this monstrous Whore is dead and gone,
> That would not leave a Saint not one;
> Makes her self drunk with the Saints Blood,
> This great Whore did never do any good;
> But doth all the mischief, that she can;
> And the people makes a God of proud Man.

> (*The Revelation of Jesus Christ* in Bradstock
> and Rowland 2002: 154–6; Hobby 1988: 50)

Revelation 18

Ancient Literary Context

The prophetic critique of Babylon is rooted in Jeremiah's dirge over the city (Jer 51) and Ezekiel's lament over Tyre (Ezek 27–8) and reflects a common prophetic form. The antiphon of lament and rejoicing in 18:18–19 is John's witness to the contrasting reactions to Babylon's demise, which parallels how biblical prophets, privy to the discussions of the heavenly court (1 Kings 22:19–23; Isa 6; 21:1–10; 40:1–13; cf. Job 1–2), share what they have seen and heard. The personification of a great city opposed to the ways of God is common in the prophets (e.g. Babylon in Isa 14 and Tyre in Ezek 27–8). There are many echoes of prophetic texts in this chapter, and several word-for-word quotations: e.g. Rev 18:2: 'fallen, fallen is Babylon' (cf. Isa 21:9); Rev 18:4: 'come out from [Babylon]' (cf. Isa 48:20; 52:1); and Rev 18:21: the throwing of a stone (cf. Jer 51:63–4).

The Interpretations

The destruction of Babylon is greeted with contradictory reactions. Voices oscillate between cries of triumph at Babylon's fall and searing laments at the demise of its sophisticated culture (Schüssler Fiorenza 1993: 132). The following examples of interpretation illustrate two major approaches. The first section describes general moral applications, in which the proclamation of Babylon's fall is met with either glee or remorse. The second group of interpretations link Babylon's fall with particular events, ranging from the end of the historical Babylon in the sixth century BCE, through the destruction of Jerusalem and its temple in CE 70, to the shaking of the foundations of the Roman Catholic Church, which for many, in the late medieval period, beginning was the incarnation of the spirit of Babylon.

Moral paraenesis

Cyprian cites the passage to prove that the Christian should flee from pagans, lest he share in their faults and their punishment (*Test.* iii.34). For Tyconius, Babylon is the world in opposition to the church (in Bauckham 1978: 18–19). Olivi regarded practically the whole church as corrupted and thrown into disorder, and turned into a new Babylon (*Lectura* 52 in Burr 1993: 93–8). This picks up on the Apocalypse's lack of any strong sense of the church as a real alternative against the influences of the Beast and Babylon (O'Donovan 1995: 62). According to Milton, the haunt of demons is the domain of Satan, destroyed by the unarmed Son of God (cf. 18:2; *Paradise Regained* iv.628).

Shelley's description of the 'Pageant of Anarchy' as 'drunk as with detoxication / Of the wine of desolation' (in Paley 1999: 240–1) echoes 18:3 and 17:2 (cf. Ezek 23:33). Coleridge applies the text to his contemporaries: 'We have been drinking with a riotous thirst / Pollutions from the brimming cup of wealth, / A selfish Lewd, effeminated race' (*Fears in Solitude* 55–7 in Paley 1999: 138). The perspective of the persecuted minority, evident especially in 18:13, 20, and 24, is echoed in quarters as diverse as the early Adventists, abolitionists and feminists (Butler in Numbers and Butler 1987: 207; cf. Kraditor 1969).

Bunyan's Vanity Fair uses images of trade and luxury from Rev 18 to represent the Church of Rome and the power of Mammon:

> EVANGELIST: . . . Almost five thousand year agone, there were Pilgrims walking to the Celestial City, as these two honest persons are; and Beelzebub, Apollyon, and Legion, with their companions, perceiving by the path that the Pilgrims

made that their way to the City lay through this town of Vanity, they contrived here to set up a fair; a fair wherein should be sold all sorts of vanity, and that it should last all the year long. Therefore at this Fair are all such merchandise sold as houses, lands, trades, places, honours, preferments, titles, countries, kingdoms, lusts, pleasures, and delights of all sorts, as whores, bawds, wives, husbands, children, masters, servants, lives, blood, bodies, souls, silver, gold, pearls, precious stones, and what not. (1967 edn 137 in Hill 1989: 225; cf. Milton, *Paradise Lost* i.680–4, 690–9, 713–37)

The twentieth-century South African interpreter Allan Boesak says that when readers find themselves identifying with the sorrow of the merchants, 'they share the viewpoint which is so typically the one of those who do not know what it is like to stand at the bottom of the list' (Boesak 1987: 121–2).

Historical linkages

According to Joachim of Fiore, this section of the Apocalypse (16:18–19:21) deals with the crucially important penultimate, sixth period. The fall of this 'Babylon' corresponds to the fall of ancient Babylon, and Jerusalem in 21:2, 10 to the return of the exiles led by Zerubbabel and Joshua, reflecting Joachim's use of correspondences between Old and New Testaments to illuminate the Apocalypse and other parts of Scripture (*Expositio* fols 191–3 in Daniel in Emmerson and McGinn 1992: 81; see above, 47, for the importance that Joachim attaches to the Apocalypse as a key to Scripture). Babylon is understood as the churches of the Greeks, as well as all those members of the Latin Church who are reprobate.

The fall of Babylon, according to the fifteenth-century Czech Taborites, is a prophecy of the fall of Prague with its supporters of Sigismund (the rich), which would herald the New Jerusalem with its classless society (in Cohn 1957: 209). According to Alexander Minorita, the angel in 18:21 is Godfrey of Bouillon, ruler of Jerusalem after the city's capture by the Crusaders (*Expositio* 112, 153, 157, 162, 197, 299, 310, 384–5, 408–9 in Wainwright 1993: 54). In popular propaganda of the Reformation period the angel in 18:1–2 who proclaims the fall of Babylon is linked with Luther, as part of the extraordinary hagiography which gave him the kind of apocalyptic status earlier given to Francis (in Scribner 1994: 19–20).

The *Watchtower Bible* relates 18:24 to suppression of Jehovah's Witnesses in Bavaria on 13 April [1933]. The Catholic Church is said to share responsibility for consigning thousands of Witnesses to concentration camps: its hands are stained by the life-blood of hundreds of Witnesses who were executed (*Watchtower Bible* 270–1). An alternative view is that the fall of Babylon refers not to Rome but to the destruction of Jerusalem in CE 70 (Herder, *Werke* (1877–1913) l9:195–6 in Wainwright 1993: 132; cf. Barker 2000).

Ancient Literary Context

The vision of the rider on the white horse echoes, without exactly paralleling, biblical passages where God is portrayed as the divine warrior, girded with weapons of war (Ex 15:3; Isa 59:17–19), as well as John's opening vision of the 'one like the Son of Man' (1:12–20; cf. 14:14–20), and particularly the first of the 'horsemen of the Apocalypse' in 6:2. The 'sword to smite the nations' parallels messianic passages like Isa 11:4; 2 Esdras 13:9–11; 2 Thess 2:8 (cf. *Psalms of Solomon* 17:24:

Rev 2:12, 16	These are the words of him who has the sharp, two-edged sword. . . . I will come to them and make war against them with the sword of my mouth. cf. 1:16: from his mouth came a sharp, two-edged sword . . .
Rev 19:15, 21	From his mouth comes a sharp sword with which to strike the nations . . . And the rest were killed by the sword

of the rider on the horse, the sword that came from his mouth . . .

Isaiah 11:4   With righteousness shall he judge the poor, and decide with equity for the meek of the earth; he shall strike the earth with the rod of his mouth and with the breath of his lips he shall kill the wicked.

2 Esdras 13:9–10   When he saw the hordes advancing to attack, he did not so much as lift a finger against them. He had no spear in his hand, no weapon at all; only, as I watched, he poured out what appeared to be a stream of fire from his mouth, a breath of flame from his lips with a storm of sparks from his tongue. These . . . fell on the host prepared for battle and burnt them all up.

2 Thess 2:8   And then the lawless one will be revealed, whom the Lord Jesus will destroy with the breath of his mouth, annihilating him with the manifestation of his coming.

Most of these passages suggest that judgement in the context of an eschatological battle comes by the power of the Word of God rather than through force of arms.

The Interpretations

While the opening of the chapter continues themes of exultation from Rev 18, the climax is the vision of the rider on the white horse whose interpretation in music, poetry and art is the main focus of the following interpretations. The christological focus is very much to the fore, but identifications with other historical figures have been suggested.

The songs of acclamation

The songs of exultation in 19:1–8, modelled on hymns in the Hebrew Psalter, have themselves inspired further paeans of praise, as exemplified by the use of 19:1 in Thomas Weelkes' 'Alleluia! I heard a voice from heaven'. Charles Wesley's hymn 'Lift your heads, ye friends of Jesus' refers to the marks of Christ's death in 19:13 (in Newport 2000: 143; see above, 90–1). For the *Geneva Bible* the acclamations signify that God's judgements are 'true and just, and that we ought to praise him evermore for the destruction of the Pope'. Milton alludes to 19:17 in 'To his celestial consort us unite' ('At a Solemn Music' 27, 1980: 16). Similar paeans of praise are found in *Paradise Lost*: 'No voice exempt, no voice but well could join / Melodious part, such concord is in heaven. / Thee Father first they sung omnipotent [cf. 19:1]' (iii.370–2; cf. x.641–3; v.872–3). The wedding of the Lamb in 19:6–9 contributes to 'the unexpressive nuptial Song' in 'Lycidas' (174–81 in Patrides in Patrides and Wittreich 1984: 220). It also forms part of Bunyan's description of the welcome offered to Christian when he arrives in the heavenly court (1967 edn 214).

Verse 6 provides the opening line for the climactic chorus which ends Part 2 of Handel's *Messiah*: 'Hallelujah, for the Lord God Omnipotent reigneth, Hallelujah!' To this the librettist had added a line from a hymn in 11:15 ('The kingdom of this world is become the Kingdom of our Lord and of His Christ, and He shall reign for ever and ever'), before concluding with another verse from 19:16: 'King of Kings and Lord of Lords'.

The rider on the white horse

According to Cyprian, Christ's coming in marriage to his bride the Church (19:7) occurred already at his first coming, and it bore fruit in the Spirit-filled children of God (*Test.* ii.19). He compares 19:11 to John 1:14 (*Test.* ii.30; cf. John 1:1), and says that the battle of this chapter refers to the Incarnation, which brings judgement on Israel and salvation to the gentiles (*Test.* ii.3). Origen cites 19:11–16 more than any other text in the Apocalypse, which reflects the strong christological focus of his exegesis. He emphasizes the revelatory function of the Son (19:11; *Comm. Jo.* vi.173), takes the robe dipped in blood (19:13) as a symbol of Christ's incarnation and sacrifice (*On Martyrdom* 50), and speaks frequently of Christ as judge (*Comm. Jo.* i.252) and king of kings (19:16; *Hom. Num.* xi.4; xii.2; *Comm. Jo.* xiii.397; in Monaci 1978: 146–7). Andrew of Caesarea (*Comm.* 58) sees here a reference to the vesture of the Word of God in his most pure and incorrupt flesh and blood during the time of his sufferings (in Averky 1985: 191).

The images from 19:11–16 also pervade Bunyan's description of the promise to Christian from 'the Shining Ones': 'There also you shall be clothed with glory and majesty, and put into an equipage fit to ride out with the King of Glory' (*Pilgrim's Progress*, 1967 edn 213).

Blake sees Christ in this image:

> One Man Jesus the Saviour. Wonderful! Round his limbs
> The clouds of Oblon folded as a Garment dipped in blood
> Written within and without in woven letters: and the writing

Is the Divine Revelation in the Litteral [sic] expression:
A Garment of War, I heard it namd the Woof of Six Thousand Years.
(*Milton* 45[44]:11–15 in Paley 1999: 87)

Elsewhere Blake speaks of the winepress of Los (cf. 19:15), the embodiment of prophetic power and 'mental fight' (*Milton* 26[24]), that is the disturbing work of poetic Imagination, which may lead to revolutionary consequences (in Fisch 1999: 267). Milton alludes to 19:15 in a portrayal of the star falling from the sky (Rev 8:10–11), interpreted as Lucifer being 'trod' by a Saviour: 'But thou, Infernal Serpent, shalt not long / Rule in the clouds; like an autumnal star / Or lightning thou shalt fall from heav'n trod down / Under his feet' (*Paradise Regained* iv. 618–21).

The epithets 'King of kings' and 'Lord of lords' from 19:16 are widely taken up. In Milton's *Paradise Regained* Jesus rebukes Satan: 'The kingdoms of the world to thee were given! . . . If given, by whom but by the King of kings' (iv.185). Another example is the following line from Charles Wesley's hymn mentioned at the beginning of this chapter: 'Christ to all believers precious, Lord of Lords, shall soon appear' (in Newport 2000: 142–3; see above, 90–1).

Modern historical criticism is dominated by the interpretation of 19:11–16 as a reference to Christ's second coming (Bauckham 1993b: 104). The rider's robe is white but dipped in blood before the final battle has taken place. That juxtaposition is seen as a sign of the 'conquering' messiah whose triumph comes through suffering and death (cf. Rev 5:5–6). Indeed, in some theological readings this christological focus then determines how the more abhorrent images in the final verses are understood, as showing the consequence of human sinfulness in the light of the cross of Christ (Sweet 1979: 282).

Historical actualizations of the rider

The Beguin visionary Na Prous Boneta sees in the rider on the white horse an image of her own prophetic inspiration:

> Again, that horse which the blessed John says in the book of Revelations he saw is Na Prous herself, and he who sits on this white horse is Jesus Christ. Also one time the Lord leapt on her neck and fashioned a white horse with a man on it, saying, See how this man controls this horse just as he wishes. Thus I am above all nature, and I rule you as I will, and I am with you wherever you are.

From that moment on, she claims, the entire Holy Trinity was with her in spirit (in May 1965; cf. Potesta in McGinn 2000: 119; Burr 2001:230–6).

The sixteenth-century English Puritan George Gifford emphasizes 'the word of God' in 19:13, suggesting that preachers play a role in the last battle, alongside the military activity of princes and soldiers (*Sermons upon the whole booke of the Revelation* 380 in Bauckham 1978: 175, 357). Spain and the Jesuit mission are the two major weapons of the Antichrist against Protestant England, but their future defeat is assured (in Bauckham 1978: 352, 357; cf. Thruston, *England Safe and Triumphant* 2:358 in Wainwright 1993: 168). At the height of the English Revolution in 1649 the Fifth Monarchist Mary Cary saw an active role for the saints in the establishment of God's kingdom on earth, since Christ had ascended to heaven. The rider on a white horse of 19:11 leads the armies of the saints in the last battle ('The Little Horn's Downfall' 120–1, cf. Capp 1972: 133–41, 174–90; Hill 1972; Mack 1992: 101–18; Hobby 1988: 30; N. Smith 1989: 73–104). According to the Tudor interpreter Morel, the blood in which the rider's robe is dipped (19:13) is the 'literal blood of Christ's enemies, to be slain by the armies of the Protestant alliance' (in Bauckham 1978: 176).

In an early writing of Blake, the winepress of the wrath of God (19:15; cf. 14:19–20) is the Duke of Burgundy (the last duke died in 1714), apparently because of the link between the red wine and blood shed in war. He makes Burgundy the mouthpiece for the English conservative politician Edmund Burke: 'red as wines / From his mountains, an odour of war, / like ripe vineyard, rose from / his garments' (*The French Revolution* 82–4 in Paley 1999: 47). There is also a possible allusion in Byron, *Childe Harold's Pilgrimage* iii.174–5 in Paley 1999: 194).

On 13 December 1996 (several years after the cataclysm at Waco) the Branch Davidians expected David Koresh to return as the rider on the white horse, to lead his followers in the mass slaughter of the wicked. When Koresh did not return, this was regarded as one final act of God to test the faith of the righteous (Newport 2000: 225).

The angel standing in the sun (Rev 19:17)

In *Paradise Lost* Uriel is the 'angel standing in the sun', who confronts Satan as he wanders around the fringes of the globe:

> For [the devil's] sight no obstacle found here . . . and the air,
> Nowhere so clear, sharpened his visual ray
> To objects distant far, whereby he soon
> Saw within ken a glorious angel stand,
> The same whom John saw also in the sun:
> His back turned, but not his brightness hid;

Of beaming sunny rays, a golden tiara
Circled his head, nor less his locks behind
Illustrious on his shoulders fledge with wings
Lay waving round; on some great charge employed
He seemed, or fixed in cogitation deep.
    (iii. 615–29 in Patrides in Patrides and Wittreich 1984: 227)

Turner's graphic evocation of the angel in the sun (Tate Gallery, London) complements his *Death on a Pale Horse* (Carey 1999: 227; for Blake's depiction see above, 96; on the image in medieval iconography, see Klein in Emmerson and McGinn 1992: 168). A historical referent is found in the work of Francesco Eixemenis, a leading fifteenth-century Catalonian interpreter of the Apocalypse who saw references in Revelation to monastic leaders. Linking Francis with 19:11, he hails him as a 'standard bearer of Christ' whose advent would reform a decaying Church (in Lee, Reeves and Silano 1989: 86).

The lake of fire and the defeat of the false prophet

The beast thrown into lake of fire (19:20) is a Saracen king, according to Alexander the Minorite (*Expositio* 234, 273–92, 407, 427–8 in Wainwright 1993: 54). For the Methodist preacher Thomas Taylor the false prophet is Muhammad (in Newport 2000: 111). The 'lake of fire' of 19:20 is echoed in Milton's 'burning lake' of Hell (*Paradise Lost* ii.575–81; cf. 'In Quintum Novembris' 7).

Hildegard of Bingen develops the image of the defeat of the false prophet in *Scivias* iii.11.7. This interpretation echoes the presumption of the kings of Babylon and Tyre (Ezek 27–8; cf. W. Bousset 1999: 149).

The unremitting fierceness of the language of judgement reaches its climax in this chapter. Blake interprets the image of the lake of fire as a fiery furnace, whose function is to purge and renew. At the end of *Jerusalem*, a work which challenges Britain (or Albion as Blake describes it) to recognize the departure from its vocation, the poet describes Albion's recognition of the need for moral renewal in a furnace which turns out to be the waters of life (Rev 22:1): 'Do I sleep amidst danger to Friend! O my Cities and Counties / Do you sleep! rouze up! rouze up. Eternal Death is abroad / So Albion spoke & threw himself into the Furnace of afflication / All was a Vision. All a Dream: the Furnaces became / Fountains of living Water flowing from the Humanity Divine' (*Jerusalem* 96: 35–7).

Revelation 20

Ancient Literary Context

This chapter caused problems for later interpreters, but its distinctive theme of the millennium, the thousand-year period during which the saints are to share Christ's rule on earth (20:4–6), occasioned many of the earliest extant references to the Apocalypse. The expectation of an earthly kingdom was the norm in Jewish hope and was also typical of Christian hope in the first century (Dale 1991; cf. Gilbertson 1997; McKelvey 1999). There are hints of the millennium, or at least of God's reign on earth, elsewhere in the New Testament (Mark 14:25; 1 Cor 6:9; 15:25), though with no mention of a precise period. Papias of Hierapolis (early second century) recalled a saying of Jesus that the creation would return to and exceed the perfection of the original creation (see p. 203), a view found also in the *Apocalypse of Baruch* 27. The two-stage eschatology in Rev 20–1, in which an intermediate this-worldly messianic period precedes the further eschatological events of resurrection, judgement and descent of the New Jerusalem, has parallels in the *Apocalypse of Baruch* and 2 Esdras, suggesting that this two-stage eschatological hope was a feature of late first-

century CE hope. Beliefs about a this-worldly messianic kingdom were probably widespread in Asia Minor, as shown for example by the expectation of an
earthly New Jerusalem among the Montanists, a Christian renewal movement
of the mid-late second century (Trevett 1995).

At the end of the thousand years Satan is released (20:7). The nations, described
as Gog and Magog, are deceived, and they attack the saints and 'the beloved city'
(20:9), only for fire to descend from heaven to destroy them. This passage draws its
inspiration from Ezek 38–9, a passage also alluded to in Rev 19:21.

The judgement scene in 20:11–14 has close links with Dan 7:9–10 with its
heavenly court scene and books opened for scrutiny. The notion of heavenly
books containing the secrets of heaven and earth appears elsewhere in ancient
Jewish literature: for example, in *1 Enoch* 81 and the *Testament of Abraham*,
Rec A 12. The criterion for judgement in Rev 20:11 is works: 'the dead were
judged according to their works'. Like Matt 25, this text challenges the assumption that quality of belief is what counts. Resistance to the Beast and Babylon
can be discerned in all those who instinctively do what is required of them by
God (cf. Rom 2:13–14).

The theme of judgement pervades biblical books from Noah's flood in
Genesis, through the repeated predictions of judgement on a recalcitrant
people in the books of Kings and prophets to the gospels, Paul and the Apocalypse. Most judgement texts in the Hebrew Bible are not strictly speaking
eschatological. The prophets, however severe their predictions, usually con-
template continued life on earth after the cataclysm of judgement, not a final
assize after which there would be no future on earth. The idea of a final judgement appears relatively late in Jewish history, in Dan 12:1 (second century
BCE), and in the earliest parts of the Enochic corpus, e.g. *1 Enoch* 10 (probably third century BCE). In Dan 7 and 12 we have a judgement scene that is
largely replicated in the Apocalypse. Elsewhere in the New Testament only
occasionally is there description of a final assize (Matt 25:31–45; cf. Rom 2:5),
even though the theme of judgement appears frequently. Paul looks forward
to a personal assize (Rom 2:3–10; 14:10; 2 Cor 5:14) and also one when the
saints will judge the world (1 Cor 6:9).

The Interpretations

The millennium

The words 'millennial', 'millenarian', and 'chiliastic' are used in a variety of ways.
All have their roots in the Latin or Greek words for 'one thousand' and refer

to the thousand-year messianic reign on earth, though often they are used for expectation of an earthly kingdom without any specific reference to its length. 'Millennial' and 'chiliastic' frequently describe that earliest phase of Christian hope when an earthly kingdom of God was earnestly expected. 'Millenarian' is widely used in the sociology of religion to characterize groups which expect a radical change in history and an earthly reign of the saints or the downtrodden (Wilson 1973). 'Chiliasm' is also used in sociological discussion to describe the pattern of behaviour of people like Thomas Muentzer and Gerrard Winstanley who believed their action would implement the new age (Mannheim 1960; Rowland 1988). In some forms of modern eschatological expectation we find a distinction between pre-millennialism, which holds that Christ's second coming will take place before the messianic reign on earth (often linked with a cataclysmic eschatology which envisages a divine irruption into history), and post-millennialism, according to which Christ's appearance will take place only at the end of the millennium (often linked with gradualist, evolutionary, views of history inexorably moving towards its eschatological goal). The term 'amillennialism' means rejection of the hope of the messianic reign on earth, either because of a belief that this event has already happened in the cross and resurrection or the emergence of the Church, or because the description in Rev 20:4–6 is taken as purely symbolic. Augustine's interpretation in the *City of God* is often seen as an example of the former; such amillennialism is characteristic of much Christian eschatology.

BARNABAS, JUSTIN, IRENAEUS AND TERTULLIAN

An early Christian parallel to Rev 20 is found in the *Epistle of Barnabas* (a text roughly contemporary with the Apocalypse and unlikely to be dependent on it):

> 'He finished in six days' [cf. Gen 2:1]. This implieth that the Lord will finish all things in six thousand years, for a day is with Him a thousand years. And He Himself testifieth, saying 'Behold today will be as a thousand years' [2 Pet 3:8]. Therefore, my children, in six days, that is, in six thousand years, all things will be finished. (xv.3–5, ANF i.146)

The notion of six ages of creation plus a final sabbath age recurs regularly in other early Christian writings (e.g. Lactantius, *Institutes* vii.14.7 in Daley 1991: 68, 239 and in McGinn 2000: 19). It fits neatly into the sevenfold scheme found in the Apocalypse, particularly the sequence of seals which ends with a period of silence (8:1–2).

Jewish Christians in the latter part of the first century CE held explicit this-worldly hopes. Indeed, Papias quotes a saying of Jesus which predicts that the whole of creation will be restored to its pristine condition and be even more glorious than at the beginning (in Irenaeus *AH* v.33.3–4). Papias was criticized by the fourth-century church historian Eusebius for holding that the kingdom of God would be set up on earth (*HE* iii.39.11; cf. Cerinthus in *HE* iii.28.2), but in the second century chiliastic views were very popular, especially in Asia Minor. Justin uses Rev 20 in his *Dial.* 80; his primary interest in the Apocalypse is its millennialism, just as the Montanists looked to Rev 21 for their idea of an earthly kingdom (Trevett 1995: 95–104; see also Eusebius *HE* v.18.1). Irenaeus believes in two different resurrections, exactly as Rev 20 indicates: first, the resurrection of the just and then the resurrection of all people according to their works. He describes the state between them as 'the Kingdom of the Son' (cf. 1 Cor 15:24; *AH* v.36.3; 32.1). In one text he says that the millennial binding of Satan is already accomplished by the salvific incarnation of Christ (*AH* ii.23.7). Elsewhere, however, in his polemic against the spiritualizing tendencies of the Gnostics, Irenaeus defends at some length, on the basis of many Scripture texts, the idea that the just will reign in a literal earthly kingdom (*AH* v.32.1–36.3).

Tertullian defends a literal millennial belief in *Against Marcion* iii. 24, in a text reminiscent of surviving fragments of Montanist teaching. What is striking is how Rev 20 is here interpreted in the light of the New Jerusalem in Rev 21:

> For we also hold that a kingdom has been promised to us on earth . . . This will last for a thousand years, in a city of God's making, Jerusalem sent down from heaven which the apostle designates as 'our mother from above' [Gal 4:26] . . . Ezekiel knew that city, and the Apostle John saw it [Rev 21:1], and the Word of the New Prophecy which dwells in our faith witnesses to it so that it even foretold the appearance of the likeness of that city to serve as a sign before its manifestation before men's eyes. In fact this prophecy was just lately fulfilled in the course of the eastern expedition. For . . . in Judea a city was suspended from heaven for a short space in the early morning during a period of forty days . . . We say that this is the city designed by God for the reception of the saints at the [first] resurrection, and for their cherishing with all abundance of goods, spiritual goods to be sure, in compensation for the goods we have despised or lost in this age. . . . This is the purpose of that kingdom; which will last a thousand years . . . and then when the resurrection of the saints is completed, the destruction of the world and the conflagration of judgement will be effected; we shall 'change in a moment' [1 Cor 15:52–3] into the angelic substance, by the 'putting on of incorruption', and we shall be transferred to the celestial kingdom. (Bettenson 1982: 164)

The emphasis on the enjoyment of this-worldly goods is an important part of much pre-Constantinian hope for the future, found also in Lactantius (in McGinn 1979: 17–80). In another work Tertullian includes the 'first resurrection' and the 'judgement of universal resurrection' in a summary of the eschatological scheme laid out in John's Apocalypse (*Resurr.* 25).

HIPPOLYTUS CYPRIAN AND VICTORINUS

In his *Commentary on Daniel*, one of the oldest extant biblical commentaries, Hippolytus affirms that the reign of the Antichrist and the end of the world will occur 6,000 years after creation (a view echoed by later commentators such as the early Augustine, in Daley 1991: 131). The end is not to come until 500 years after Christ's birth (iv.23–4). After this will come a sabbath (cf. Heb 4:9–10), when the saints will reign with Christ, as described by John in the Apocalypse (iv.23). Hippolytus interprets Rev 17:10, 'five have fallen, one is living, and the other has not yet come' to refer to the seven ages of creation (*Daniel* 4 in Daley 1991: 38–41). The millennium itself is not to be measured in literal calendar years; when John saw the glory of that day, he used the number 1,000 to indicate perfection. Hippolytus addresses a difficulty interpreters down the centuries have found in Rev 20: the presence of two resurrections. He interprets them by referring to the 'many mansions' of John 14:2; they indicate not two separate events but two different orders of merit (in Prigent 1972: 404). The loosing and subsequent defeat of the devil in 20:7–10 is a public demonstration of just judgement (in Gwynn 1888: 402–4; cf. Prigent 1973: 320; Prigent 1972: 403). Cyprian suggests that the 6,000 years of the devil's attack on humanity are almost finished (*Fort.* pref. 2).

The earliest extant commentary on the Apocalypse, written by Victorinus of Poetovio around 260 (see above, 15), shared the chiliastic interpretation of Justin, Irenaeus and Tertullian to a large extent (Victorinus 1997: 40–1). Victorinus thinks the description of the millennial rule of the saints in 20:4–6 recapitulates the seventh trumpet in 11:16–18, and that the 'first resurrection' of 20:6 is anticipated already in 14:1–4 (the Lamb standing with the 144,000). He teaches explicitly about two resurrections (cf. 20:4, 13), which he develops by comparing texts from Paul. The first resurrection, which takes place at the parousia of Christ, is indicated by the trumpet in 1 Thess 4:15–17; the second by the *last* trumpet mentioned in 1 Cor 15:52. It is not clear, however, whether he sees a clear chronological distinction between the two, since the just are already glorifed at the first resurrection, and eternity begins with it (in Dulaey 1993: i.211–12). The binding of Satan means that the just are protected from satanic seduction; after 1,000 years he is released in order to lead the nations who remained enslaved to him to perdition (in Dulaey 1993: i.211–12).

ORIGEN, METHODIUS, LACTANTIUS AND EUSEBIUS

Origen, who is well known for his symbolic interpretation of Scripture, rejects the idea of a literal millennium (*First Principles* ii.11.2; *Comm. Matt.* vii.35 in

Daley 1991: 49), a view also reflected in the work of his pupil Dionysius (Eusebius *HE* vii.24–5). He suggests that the millennium may refer to the time before the more efficacious prayer of the Christian era:

> And if the whole of this age is 'today' perhaps 'yesterday' is the preceding age. I have come to suppose that this is what is meant in Psalms and in Paul's letter to the Hebrews. In Psalms it says, 'A thousand years in your sight are but as yesterday when it is past' (Ps 89:4). Perhaps this is the famous millennium that is compared to 'yesterday' and distinguished from 'today'. (*On Prayer* xxvii.13, Greer, tr., 144)

The chaining of Satan (Rev 20:2) begins at the time of creation, Origen says in a comment on the abyss in Gen 1:2, which he identifies as the abyss where

Plate 12   Kip Gresham, *The Key to the Great Abyss* (Rev 20:1–3).

the devil and his angels are (*Hom. Gen.* 1.1; in the Latin translation the verb is in the future, but Doutreleau, in Origen 1976: 26, n. 1, assumes the tense was present in the lost original; cf. Anselmetto 1980: 265). Origen compares this with Luke 8:31, where demons beg Jesus not to send them into the abyss (cf. *Hom. Gen.* 1.2). Satan is released in order to crucify Christ, after which he is again banished to the abyss. The period of apocalyptic catastrophe, suffering and punishment (cf. Rev. 20:7–10) is that of Jesus' crucifixion and the ensuing destruction of Jerusalem. The divine fire which consumes the forces surrounding the beloved city (20:9) refers to the fire that destroys Jerusalem (cf. *Comm. Jo.* i.86; *Comm. Matt.* 40). The first resurrection (20:4–5) is not a physical removal to the intermediate state, but Christian baptism (*Hom. Jer.* 11.3 in Anselmetto 1980: 266). Origen suggests that there is a double baptism, one in the Logos and the other in fire. The first is joyful, but the second is sorrowful and reserved for sinners.

According to Methodius, the millennium has its precursor in the feast of Tabernacles; it is celebrated after the harvest of the earth's fruits which symbolizes the completion of God's work in the world. The Jewish celebration is a shadow of the true eschatological feast, the new creation where there will be no more pain (cf. Rev 21:4; *Banquet* ix.1). According to Lactantius, the world has grown old and is crumbling to ruin; it is now in the sixth and final millennium of its history. During this final age, after a period of continuing injustice and instability, Roman rule will come to an end and will be succeeded by the rule of ten tyrants. These will be overthrown by an enemy from the north during whose time the cosmos will suffer devastation, and all the living will be made to pass through a fire of judgement. The victory of Christ over all evil will then usher in an age of peace. After a judgement of believers the just will rule in this world with Christ (*Institutes* vii. 14–17, a vision influenced by Virgil's 'Fourth Eclogue' and *Sibylline Oracles* 8, in Daley 1991: 66–8; cf. McGinn 1979: 73).

As already noted, Eusebius of Caesarea finds chiliasm objectionable. Calling Constantine pious, a lover of virtue and of God, who has victoriously cleansed the world of hatred of God (*HE* x.9.8), he cannot accept the threat to the established order posed by the anti-Roman sentiments of the Apocalypse, and so unequivocally condemns a this-worldly millennium (*HE* iii.39.12).

TYCONIUS AND AUGUSTINE

A new type of interpretation emerges in the fourth century, though in some ways it has been anticipated by Cyprian and Origen. According to Tyconius, the millennium is the whole age of the Church's history, from the passion of the Lord until his second coming (in Beatus, *Comm.* ii.5.9). Humanity currently finds itself in the last days, since during this period Christ was born, suffered and rose again. What is left of this last period is also called the 1,000 years of the first resurrection, during which believers have received their spiritual bodies through baptism. Baptism is the first resurrection (20:5), the Christian's rebirth through dying to sin (Tyconius, *Rules* iii.4; cf. Beatus, *Comm.* ii.5.3). The Son of Man – that is, the Church – has come and, during this last day and final hour, has risen from the dead; Satan is now bound (20:2), and the thousand-year reign of the saints progresses on earth, through the Church (in Fredriksen in Emmerson and McGinn 1992: 28; cf. Daley in McGinn 2000).

Augustine's interpretation resembles that of Tyconius on many points, but he often explains in more detail what Tyconius only hints at, and to some extent his similar interpretations (e.g. of the two resurrections) were developed independently. He only read Tyconius' *Commentary* when he started work on the last books of his *City of God* (Dulaey 1986). Augustine once believed that the first resurrection described in Rev 20:4–6 would be bodily, and that the sabbatical rest of the saints would last for a literal 1,000 years (*Serm.* 259.2; cf. Daley 1991: 133). But, as he points out in *The City of God* xx.7, even then he had held that the saints' delights would be of a spiritual character, in contrast to those who thought that the resurrected dead would spend their rest in 'the most unrestrained material feasts, in which there will be so much to eat and drink that those supplies will break the bounds of moderation, but also of credibility' (1969: 285). By the time he writes *The City of God*, he has come to think that the binding of Satan (20:1–3) which begins the millennium, has already taken place, with the first coming of Christ. This binding – which means Satan's confinement to the hearts of unbelievers – is repeated whenever men and women are converted to the Christian faith (xx.7–8).

In book 20 of *The City of God* Augustine discusses Rev 20 in some detail. He takes 20:1–6 to refer to events already in process, while 20:7–15 speak of future events: the persecution of the saints in the last days (20:7–10) and the final judgement of God (20:11–15). Augustine draws in many other New Testament texts to elucidate the words of the Apocalypse. In particular, he compares John 5:25–9 (which he assumes was written by the same author), where he sees the same mixture of present and future, thus clarifying the meaning of the 'first resurrection' and 'second death' in Rev 20:6, 14. The 'first resurrection' that begins the millennium is spiritual, as is suggested by John 5:25: 'Very truly, I tell you, the hour is coming, *and is now here*, when the dead will hear the voice of the Son of God, and those who hear will live'. 'This first resurrection', Augustine says, 'is not that of the body, but of the soul. For souls, too, have their own death, in irreligion and sin' (*City of God* xx.6, Greene edn vi. 275;

cf. xx.9). As further evidence that 'death' and 'resurrection' have a symbolic meaning here, he cites 2 Cor 5:14–15. The first resurrection, Augustine says, 'is only for those who are to be blessed forever' (xx.6, Greene edn vi.277), but both blessed and wretched take part in the second resurrection, the resurrection of the flesh, described in Rev 20:12–15 and in John 5:28–9. The 'second death' of Rev 20:6, 14 is the 'resurrection of condemnation' in John 5:29.

Augustine follows Tyconius in relating the chaining of the devil in Rev 20:1–3 to the binding of the strong man in Matt 12:29 (xx.7–8). The power of the devil, the strong man, is restrained, and his house is plundered as the gospel takes hold in the world. Restrained from seducing God's elect, the devil is cast into the 'pit' of unbelievers' hearts. The 'nations' whom Satan is not allowed to deceive (Rev 20:3) are the nations out of which the Church is formed. This means that the devil is not allowed to rage with full power against God's elect, not that he is totally excluded from the Church, as Augustine points out in an interpretation of the sealing of 20:3: 'And the added words "put a seal upon him," seem to me to mean that God wished it to be unknown who belonged to the devil's party and who did not. For in this world this is indeed unknown, since it is uncertain whether he who seems to stand is about to fall' (xx.7, Greene edn vi.289).

Suggesting a symbolic interpretation of the number 1,000 (xx.7; cf. xx.5), Augustine refers the millennial kingdom of 20:4–6 to the period of the Church between the first and second comings of Christ: 'Accordingly the church even now is the kingdom of Christ and the kingdom of heaven. And so even now his saints reign with him' (xx.9, Greene edn vi.307–9). In particular, the thrones of 20:4 indicate the 'sees of the administrators and the administrators themselves by whom the church is now directed' (xx.9, Greene edn vi.311). But while Augustine celebrates the power of the gospel and of the Church in which it has taken hold, his is not an easy triumphalism. He sharply contrasts the present reign of the Church, in which there are 'tares' along with the good 'wheat' (Matt 13:24–9), with the reign of the saints in the eschatological kingdom (Matt 25:34), and he presents the church as a *regnum militiae*: that is, a kingdom on the march against the devil: John speaks 'about this kingdom militant, in which there is still conflict with the foe, and battles must sometimes be fought, against vices that make war on us . . . until that most peaceful kingdom is attained where our King shall reign without a foe' (xx.9, Greene edn vi.309). In the Church both righteous and unrighteous will remain mixed together until the final judgement. Although Satan has been restrained, he is still a formidable foe, for whose final assault the Church must prepare herself. Before the Last Judgement the devil will be released (Rev 20:7), 'so that the City of God may perceive how strong an adversary it has vanquished, to the great glory of its Redeemer, Helper, Deliverer' (xx.8, Greene edn vi.297).

Augustine's interpretation of the millennial kingdom as the time of the Church was to be very influential. It picked up an emphasis of the New Testament on the 'already' rather than the 'not yet' (see e.g. Mark 1:15; Luke 17:21; John 5:24–5; 3:19; Rom 3:21). Repudiation of chiliasm (belief in a literal millennium) was confirmed by the Council of Ephesus in 431, and Augustine's allegorical and non-historical exegesis of the Apocalypse became the standard interpretation in the early Middle Ages (Fredriksen in Emmerson and McGinn 1992: 29–35).

JEROME, ANDREW AND BEDE

Similarly, Jerome asserts that the saints will in no way have an earthly kingdom, but only a celestial one: 'thus must cease the fable of one thousand years' (Jerome, *Commentary on Daniel* in Lerner in Emmerson and McGinn 1992: 51). In the preface and conclusion he added to Victorinus' commentary (CE 398) Jerome says that the thousand-year kingdom is a symbol of the life of virginity, in which the ascetic 'reigns' with Christ while the devil remains 'bound' through renunciation (text in Victorinus 1997: 124–31; cf. Daley in McGinn 2000: 28). He interprets Rev 20:1–6 as an image of the peace and growth of the Church after the time of persecution. Andrew of Caesarea (*Comm.* 60 in Daley 1991: 198) writes that the 1,000 years means the whole time from the Incarnation to the coming of the Antichrist. With the coming of the incarnate Son of God on earth, Satan was bound, paganism was cast down, and there came the reign of Christ. The number 1,000 is used in place of an indefinite number to signify the long period of time until the second coming of Christ (in Averky 1985: 197). Beatus interprets the number as a symbolic reference to this world, and to the reign of the Church throughout time (1930: 605 in J. Williams in Emmerson and McGinn 1992: 223).

Despite the enormous influence of Augustine's interpretation of Rev 20, eschatological millenarianism is anticipated in some early medieval commentaries. A period of peace after the upheavals caused by the Antichrist is espoused by Bede (following Jerome). This time was to be of relatively short duration, a sabbath period on earth, paralleling the 'silence in heaven for half an hour' (Rev 8:1 in Lerner in Emmerson and McGinn 1992: 55–7).

JOACHIM OF FIORE AND THE JOACHITE TRADITION

Joachim played a central role in rekindling speculation about a this-worldly fulfilment of eschatological hopes, even though the millennium of Rev 20 plays relatively little part in his developing apocalyptic perspective. He hinted that, alongside the Augustinian interpretation, the passage might also refer to a future sabbath for the Church and the world, though this period would be short (in Lerner in Emmerson and McGinn 1992: 58). This sabbath is indicated in the silence of Rev 8:1, which allows for 'divine space' on earth. During that time the dragon will be imprisoned in the abyss: that is, in the remaining nations which are at the ends of the earth. The number of years, months and days of that time are known only to God. When they have been completed, Satan again will be released from his prison to persecute God's elect, symbolized by the tail of the dragon. Gog is the Antichrist at the end of the third status, or age (in McGinn 1998: 138; cf. Bauckham 1978: 20; Daley in McGinn 2000: 79).

Alexander Minorita interpreted the thousand years literally to refer to the Church's earthly reign from its triumph under Constantine and Pope Sylvester until the Last Judgement anticipated in 1326 or soon thereafter (*Expositio* 1:114–15, 412–13, 443, 445, 450, 509 in Lerner and Burr in Emmerson and McGinn 1992: 60, 99). Only 70 years remain, after which the reign of the Antichrist can be expected at any moment (cf. Gerard of Poehlde and Gerloh of Reischerberg in McGinn 1998: 100, 113).

Peter Olivi refers the millennium to three different episodes in history: Christ's death and resurrection, Constantine's Christianization of the Roman Empire, and the seventh period following the Antichrist's death. Thus, whereas Joachim had accepted Augustine's interpretation of Rev 20, Olivi raised the possibility that there would be a sabbath (cf. Heb 4:9) lasting for an extended period, possibly as Rev 20 suggested, for 1,000 years. He did not exclude a view that the sabbath would begin in the fourteenth century and last for either a century or seven years (in Lerner in McGinn 2000: 351). Because he was under suspicion of heresy, Olivi raised these possibilities only as matters for debate, but he lavished such attention on them that his preference was clear to later readers (in Lerner in Emmerson and McGinn 1992: 62).

Rupescissa, a follower of Olivi, conceded that Olivi's literal reading of Rev 20 was contrary to the 'glosses and sayings of the saints' and that Augustine had opposed it in *The City of God*. Nevertheless, he swore that he had been granted privileged knowledge of its truth by means of an 'intellectual vision', vouchsafed to him 'in the twinkling of an eye' (cf. 1 Cor 15:52), while he was in captivity in 1345. As in the case of Joachim and Hildegard (see above, 15; 61), his interpretation begins in a charismatic experience. It was revealed to him that the war with the Antichrist, the thousand-year sabbath, and the final loosing of Satan were successively foretold in Rev 16–20. While he conceded that Augustine had interpreted the thousand years 'mystically', Rupescissa concluded that Augustine had 'not been given to understand' the true meaning of the binding of Satan (*Liber secretorum eventuum* 74, 84 in Lerner in Emmerson and McGinn 1992: 67). Suggesting that the sabbath would last for a thousand years, Rupescissa, along with Lactantius, was responsible for the spread of a literal expectation of a thousand-year period of bliss into European eschatology (ibid. 68).

THE MILLENNIUM IN THE EARLY MODERN PERIOD

None the less, the difficulties of a literal reading of Rev 20:4–6 were widely recognized (see Tyndale 2000: 157). The critique of chiliasm developed in post-Constantinian Christianity re-emerges with Beza, who concludes that there is no resemblance between the hedonistic earthly paradise postulated by Cerinthus and the 'thousand years' of the Apocalypse (Backus 2000: 27–8). He mentions that Justin, Irenaeus and Hippolytus were all chiliasts, thus acknowledging ante-Nicene millennialism without supporting it himself. He thought that the Apocalypse was a continuation and compendium of Old Testament prophecies, and that, like them, it was obscure and difficult to understand. The prophecies of the Apocalypse were for the most part already fulfilled, and the thousand years were to be understood as the whole of the history of the Church (Backus 1998: 664 and 2000).

In John Bale's interpretation the devil was bound for 1,000 years, from Christ's birth to CE 1000, when he was set loose by Pope Sylvester II. Since then, all the doctors of the Church had erred (in Fairfield 1976: 65, 71). In England, Satan was released through Dunstan, archbishop of Canterbury (tenth century), and the Antichrist's fall is the overthrow of papal power (Bale 1849: 560–1 in Bauckham 1978: 21, 26–8, 73). The millennium signifies eternity, and the first resurrection a rising from sin to repentance and from ignorance to knowledge. This is being fulfilled in the work of the Reformation (Bale 1849: 567 in Firth 1979: 55). Mede agreed with the sixteenth-century German interpreter Alsted, that 'the Saints of the First resurrection should reign on Earth during the Millennium, and not in Heaven', though he says that this state belongs to the parousia of Christ rather than preceding it (*Works*, ed. Worthington (1664) 2:944–5 in Firth 1979: 222). It is the time of judgement (in Wainwright 1993: 68). According to Thomas Brightman, Satan's binding began with Constantine's becoming the first Christian emperor of Rome (306) and ended in 1300, with the invasion of the Ottoman Turks; it refers to the absence of persecution by pagan enemies. Christ's millennial reign began with the Reformation of Wyclif and will end in the Day of Judgement a thousand years later (in 2300). The spiritual reign of Christ had already started, and it continued in the successors of the saints and martyrs 'in the church militant' on earth (in Smolinski in Stein 2000: 38; cf. Foxe 1583: 1:292; 4:103; Capp in Patrides and Wittreich 1984: 96; Firth 1979: 92, 238).

The *Geneva Bible* offers a christological interpretation of the chapter. The angel represents the order of the apostles, and 'may signify Christ, who should tread down the serpent's head'. The key 'meaneth the Gospel'. The 1,000 years reaches from Christ's nativity until the time of Pope Sylvester II. The first resurrection means 'to receive Jesus Christ in true faith, & to rise from sin in newness of life'. When Satan is loosed, 'the true preaching of God's word is corrupt'. Gog and Magog, however, are interpreted historically as the enemies of the Church of God, such as the Turks and others.

In the chequered career of Francisco de la Cruz in the Spanish Americas in the sixteenth century we find an apocalyptic perspective tinged with millennialist ideas, already hinted at in expectations surrounding Columbus's mission (in Milhou in Stein 2000: 4–5). De la Cruz predicted the coming of an idyllic society free from the attacks of Satan, who would remain in chains for a thousand years. The millennium was the ideal model of a colonial society ruled by a morally liberal Creole aristocracy. The encomienda system, in which indigenous people would work for the colonizers in return for the protection of Spain, would continue within a hierarchical society. Polygamy would be legalized, as would the marriage of priests; the descendants of the Inca dynasty would be deposed, with black slavery and the Indian masses in a state of submission (in Smolinski in Stein 2000: 22). We see here a subtle interplay of ideas from the Apocalypse with circumstances that produced not subversion (except in the implications for a European-dominated ecclesiastical establishment) but an ideology for the good life of the elite in colonial Peru.

Along with other Roman Catholic commentators in the sixteenth century, Ribera did not think that the millennium was literally a thousand years, but rather the period between Christ's death and the coming of the Antichrist. The millennial rule is enjoyed in heaven, not, as Augustine had suggested, on earth. It is the blessed state of the souls of the faithful departed (in Newport 2000: 76; cf. Wainwright 1993: 61–2). According to Robert Bellarmine, the Antichrist is an individual Jew, reigning in Jerusalem for three and a half years (the loosing of Satan spoken of in Rev 20:7), which will precede 'destruction and the dawn of the perfect age' (in Newport 2000: 76). For Bossuet the millennium begins with the ministry and passion of Christ and ends with the Last Judgement (*Écriture* 326–70). The coming of Gog and Magog is partially fulfilled by heretics like Luther, but ultimate fulfilment is reserved for the end of time (*Écriture* 305–70 in Newport: 2000: 73; cf. Wainwright 1993: 64, 73).

Isaac Newton echoed the this-worldly views of the earliest Christians:

> But I, and as many as are Christians, in all things right in their opinions, believe both that there shall be a resurrection of the flesh, and a thousand years life at Jerusalem, built, adorned, and enlarged. Which is as much as to say, that all true Christians in that early age received this prophecy: for in all ages, as many as believed the thousand years, received the Apocalypse as the foundation of their

opinion: and I do not know one instance to the contrary. (*Works* 5:446 in Paley 1999: 9–10)

The theological history of the English-speaking colonies in North America is pervaded with apocalypticism (R. Bloch 1985; Smolinski in Stein 2000: 36–71) and dominated by a split between those who interpreted the first resurrection in Rev 20:4 symbolically of the conversion of men and women, and those who, following Alsted, interpreted it literally (Smolinski in Stein 2000: 39; on a parallel divide in English apocalypticism at the end of the eighteenth century, see Mee 1992). This points to the later divisions between pre- and post-millennialists and to a deep divide in political theology, evident up to the present. Some, like John Eliot (1604–90), were essentially Fifth Monarchists (looking forward to the earthly reign of Christ after the four earthly kingdoms of Dan 2 and 7), a view that embarrassed the leaders of the fledgling New England society.

According to Coleridge, Satan bound means the containment of religious persecution, but fanaticism is found among 'the miserable covenanters of Scotland' (*Biographia Literaria* i:198 in Paley 1999: 152; cf. Shaffer 1972: 98). For the *Scofield Reference Bible* the thousand years is 'the duration of the kingdom of heaven in its mediatorial form' (i.e. the kingdom of Christ on earth after the rapture, p. 1349). For Jehovah's Witnesses the thousand years is the time when God's people will reign in paradise; they will be tested when Satan returns and can choose whether to stay in paradise or not (*Watchtower Bible* 290–3).

Historical actualizations of millennial images

The optimism of the triumph of Constantine is evident in the interpretation of the chapter by the radical Franciscan Arnold of Villanova. Pope Sylvester I bound the dragon of Rome so that worldly idolatry should cease and the spiritual progress of the faithful be fostered (in Lee, Reeves and Silano 1989: 99). Alexander the Minorite thought that the devil was only partly bound under Constantine and Pope Sylvester I, but he is completely bound in the reign of the emperor Henry V, who opposed Pope Calixtus II in the early twelfth century. The Beast is Saladin (*Expositio* 234, 273–92, 407, 427–8 in Wainwright 1993: 54). The mysterious figures of Gog and Magog (20:8–9), which derive from Ezekiel 38–9, are also linked with Islam and Islamic leaders. To Joachim of Fiore they are the Saracens (in Hamilton 1999: 43); for Luther, Gog is the Turks (*Preface to the Revelation of St. John* II, in *Works* 35:404–5, 409). Foxe refers this theme to a period of great trouble for the Church (in Bauckham 1978: 223; cf. Burdon 1997: 92).

Anti-Catholic applications are found also. The Jesuits and seminary priests, dispersed in all countries, were linked with the armies of Gog and Magog, which compass about the tents of the saints and the beloved city (Gifford, *Sermons* in Bauckham 1978: 354). Magog is Satan, and also at other times the pope, according to Luther (in Firth 1979: 12). At the end of the seventeenth century Keach sees the binding of Satan as the arrival on British soil of the Protestant King William and the subsequent driving out of the Catholic King James II; the millennial kingdom dawns in 1688 (in Newport 2000: 13, 41). For Mayer the bottomless pit is the French nation and the anarchy which was taking place (in Burdon 1997: 102). Kershaw thought the millennium would take place in 2000, citing among other evidence that the temple of Jerusalem was destroyed 'utterly' in CE 74. If one adds 666 (13:18) and 1260 (11:3), a total of 2000 is reached (in Newport 2000: 107).

The Last Judgement (20:11–15)

The Last Judgement is a central component of Christian theology, referred to often in the New Testament (e.g. Rom 2:5; 14:10; 2 Cor 5:10; Matt 10:15; John 5:29; 1 John 4:17; Heb 10:25–7; 2 Pet 2:9), though Rev 20:11–15, along with Matt 25:31–45, offers one of the few explicit descriptions. The subject has had widespread influence on Christian theology, worship and art (Klein in Emmerson and McGinn 1992: 164–5; Binski 1996), though it is not always clear if a reference to the Day of Judgement has been inspired directly by the Apocalypse. Only a few examples can be mentioned here.

As noted earlier in this chapter, Augustine used Rev 20 in his description of the consummation of history (*City of God* xx.11–15). Just before the final judgement, the devil will be unchained (Rev 20:7–9); that is, he will be allowed to rage against the Church, which will suffer intense persecution (*City of God* xx.11–12). The 'holy city', the Church expanding throughout the world, must be persecuted by the 'city' of the devil, symbolized by Gog and Magog. For Augustine, as for Tyconius, the release of the devil signifies the reign of the Antichrist, immediately before the parousia; this contrasts to chiliastic belief, where the Antichrist comes before the millennial rule (the Antichrist is one of two possible interpretations Augustine gives to the 'false prophet' of 20:10 in *City of God* xx.14). The fire from heaven which destroys the devil's troops (Rev 20:9) is the troops' own internal rage, provoked by the sight of the firmness of the saints in persecution.

The final judgement of the devil and the hostile 'city' is described in Rev 20:10. The beast who is thrown into the lake of fire refers to unbelievers hostile to believers, while those who carry the image of the beast (20:4) are false Christians (*City of God* xx.9, 14). The Last Judgement takes place at the time of the second resurrection of the dead, which, in contrast to the spiritual first resurrection, is of the body. The 'books' that are opened in Rev 20:12 are the Old and New Testaments, which reveal the commandments that provide the basis for judgement. In addition, there is 'another book, which is of the life of each one' (Augustine's reading for the 'book of life' in 20:12). The opening of this book is a miraculous process in which human deeds will be recalled, in an instant, so that the conscience of each person will be made aware of his deeds, good and evil (*City of God* xx.14). Augustine distinguishes this book from the 'book of life' of Rev 20:15, which he takes as a symbol of divine prescience and recollection.

Lactantius draws on extra-biblical sources to sketch a fairly literalistic picture of the last assize, an event reserved for those who had revered God, since those who had refused to recognize him are judged already. There is a critical point at which the balance is tipped between good and bad deeds (*Institutes* 7:20; cf. *Testament of Abraham*, Rec B 10 in Charlesworth 1983: 1. 900). The modern commentator R. H. Charles wrestled with the Apocalypse's emphasis on judgement by works, as opposed to justification by faith, and concluded that 'works' in Rev 20:14 refers to 'moral character, from which action in the world originates' (1920: cv).

In the Joachite tradition the Last Judgement is overshadowed by preoccupation with earlier phases in the divine economy when the crucial eschatological action would take place, action in which God's faithful servants should be ready to participate (Lee, Reeves and Silano 1989: 320; Reeves and Hirsch-Reich 1972: 232–48; Burr 1993: 179–97). Thomas Muentzer echoes the realized eschatology evident in New Testament passages like John 5:24 when he sees the lake of fire (Rev 20:10) and the trials of judgement as already having come upon the people of the world. This is a feature of several radical writers who relate the apocalyptic traditions to their actions in the present time (Muentzer 1988: 137, 366; cf. Winstanley, Sabine edn 120, 149, 226; Cohn 1957: 252–80).

The *Geneva Bible* interprets the opened books as 'every man's conscience'. There is only a cross-reference to Phil 4:3 to explain the book of life. In the related note to 2 Cor 5:10, judgement's consequence for the elect is either glory or shame, rather than damnation, thus implying their ultimate salvation. In another related marginal note, to Matt 25:35, any notion that salvation depends on works is repudiated. For Bale the books that were opened in Rev 20:12 are 'the consciences of men', but the 'book of life' of the same verse is the record of all those predestined to salvation. There are thus two modes of judgement, according to works for those without faith and according to faith, and consequent inclusion in the book of life, for believers (Bale 1849: 577–8). Milton alludes to the sequence of events in Rev 20–1 in the divine prophecy of 'the dread tribunal' (*Paradise Lost* iii.323–43). Blake, in a commentary on his painting *Vision of the Last Judgement* (1810; Blake 1981: plate 870), set down the criteria for attaining eternal life as whether people 'have spent their lives in curbing and governing other people by various arts of poverty and cruelty of all kinds' (in Blake 1972: 615). His painting shows a scroll of judgement rather than 'books', probably because of Blake's suspicion of any religion in which the Bible was treated as a book of rules and regulations rather than as the gateway for the imagination.

Representations in art, literature and song

The images of chapter 20 pervade the iconography of medieval art, not least the ubiquitous evocations of the Last Judgement which adorned Gothic churches (Klein in Emmerson and McGinn 1992: 165) and continued to influence works such as Michaelangelo's paintings in the Sistine Chapel and William Blake's depictions (Blake 1972: 604; for further examples of artistic representations see McDannell and Lang 1988, especially plates 16, 17 and 71).

There is an interesting analogy between the book of life in 20:11–15 and the *Doomsday Book*. Both are exact registers of the inhabitants of a kingdom, the former of the kingdom associated with the Last Judgement and the latter with the England of William the Conqueror. The name 'Doomsday' suggests a connection between the English king and the divine judge and king (in Szittya in Emmerson and McGinn 1992: 375).

References to the binding of Satan (20:2) in literary works include Langland's: 'And he took Lucifer the loathsome who was lord of hell / And bound him as he is bound with bonds of iron' (1990: xix.56–7) and *Paradise Lost* (i.40–8; ii.405; iv.963–7; xii.453–5). In *Paradise Lost* x.635–7 Milton pictures death and hell cast into the lake of fire (Rev 20:10; cf. 'On the Morning of Christ's Nativity' xviii.168; 'In Quintum Novembris' in 1980: 139). The heavenly assize plays a central role in the poetic outrage which the Protestant Milton expressed at the bloody massacre of the Waldensians in Piedmont: 'Forget not: in thy book record their groans' ('Sonnet xv: On the Late Massacre in Piedmont' (1655) 5). He thinks the record of salvation is not fixed for eternity but alterable according to the deeds of those written in the book: 'Though their names in heavenly records now, / Be no memorial, blotted out and razed / By their rebellion, from the books of life' (*Paradise Lost* i.361–3, where the reference is to angels, not humans). Of the awesome moments of judgement Quarles writes:

> I see brimstone sea of boiling fire,
> And fiends with knotted whips of flaming wire,
> Torturing poor souls, that gnash their teeth in vain,
> And gnaw their flame-tormented tongues for pain.
>
>   (In Emmerson in McGinn 2000: 427)

In Bunyan's *Pilgrim's Progress* Pilgrim's dream is full of apocalyptic images from this section of the Apocalypse (1967 edn, 80–1).

The imagery of Rev 20 is also taken up in the poetry and prose of the eighteenth and nineteenth centuries: for example, it pervades Blake's own idiosyncratic myths: 'Urizen unloos'd from chains / Glows like a meteor in the distant north' (*Europe* 3:11–12 in Paley 1999: 63). The influence of 20:11–15 is evident in his *The French Revolution*: 'And the bottoms of the world were open'd, and the graves of arch-angels unseal'd; / The enormous dead, lift up their pale fires and look over the rocky cliffs' (lines 301–2 in Paley 1999: 51). Blake portrays the binding of Satan by the angel (1981: i.585) as a struggle which evokes both Gen 32 (Jacob's wrestling with the angel) and Job's night vision (Job 7:14). In this struggle Blake recognized the bondage placed upon his life by a religion of law and prohibition. He thought the subjection of Satan would be more a subordination of law to grace and imagination than a denial of the law.

Also indebted to Rev 20:1–3 is Shelley's 'Great France sprang forth / And seized, as if to break, the ponderous chains / Which bind in woe the nations of the earth' (lines 470–2 of 'The Serpent Is Shut Out from Paradise' in *The Revolt of Islam* in Paley 1999: 255). Elsewhere he combines images from various parts of the Apocalypse:

> A golden-winged Angel stood
> Before the Eternal Judgement-seat:
> The Father and the Son
> Knew that strife was now begun,
> They knew that Satan had broken his chain,
> And, with millions of demon in his train,
> Was ranging over the world again.
> Before the Angel had told his tale,
> A sweet and creeping sound
> Like the rushing of wings was heard around;
> And suddenly the lamps grew pale –
> The lamps, before the archangels seven,
> That burn continually in heaven.
>
>   (From an untitled fragment published
>   posthumously, *The Poetical Works of Percy
>   Bysshe Shelley*, ed. William Michael Rossetti,
>   2:299 in Paley 1999: 274)

A spiritualizing interpretation of the awesome apocalyptic imagery is offered by Christina Rossetti: the devil in the pit shows how 'prayer is a chain apt presently to bind him, and which he cannot snap' (*The Face of the Deep* 459 in Wainwright 1993: 209).

Erasmus Darwin evokes Rev 20:2 and 7 to describe France on the eve of its revolution in 1789:

> Long had the Giant form on GALLIA's plains
> Inglorious slept, unconscious of his chains;
> Round his large limbs were wound a thousand strings
> By the weak hands of Confessors and kings;
> O'er his closed eyes a triple veil was bound,
> And steely rivers lock'd him to the ground;
> Whole stern Bastille with iron cage in thralls
> His folded limbs, and hems in marble walls.
> – Touch'd by the patriot-flame, he rent amazd
> The flimsy bonds, and round and round him gazd;
> Starts up from earth, above the admitting throng
> Lifts his colossal form.
> (*The Botanic Garden* 377–88; in Paley 1999: 54)

Charles Wesley refers to 'that long and blessed Period when peace, right-eousness and felicity, are to flourish over the whole earth'. Then 'Christ the Lord of hosts shall reign in Mount Sion, and in Jerusalem and before his Elders gloriously'. The 'long and blessed period' is probably the millennium, the period of peace and joy which was the hope of many (in Newport 2000: 129). Joseph Priestley interprets the millennium as 'earthly but not literally of one thousand years: perhaps the prophet meant to signify 365,000 years'. Whereas Wesley had thought that the millennium might last a very long time because it would take God so long to judge many millions of souls, Priestley extends the time because he reckons that, although progress in science is now more rapid, a thousand years would be scarcely sufficient to bring the world to its 'mature state' (in Burdon 1997: 113).

African-American spirituals often look forward to the Day of Judgement. They portray the 'book of life' of 20:12, 15 as both a future and a present reality:

> De Angels in heab'n gwineter write my name . . .
> Yes write my name wida golden pen . . .
> Write my name in de Book of life . . .
> Yes write my name in de drippin' blood
> (Johnson and Johnson 1954: ii.128–9)

My Lord's a writin' all de time,
And take me up to wear de crown [Rev 2:10; 3:11] . . .
Jesus rides in de middle of de' air.
My Lord's a writin' all de time.
Sees all you do. He hears all you say.

(Ibid.: i.123)

Ancient Literary Context

Two themes pervade this vision. First, there is the new heaven and earth, which emphasizes discontinuity, in contrast to the more organic sense of change in eschatological passages such as Rom 8:22, which speaks of the liberation of the creation. The last chapters of Isaiah (65:17; 66:2) suggest a similar radical disjunction, which some think reflects a period of growing despair among apocalyptic visionaries about the possibility that this world is a fit arena for God's future (Hanson 1974; cf. Cook 1995). This is paralleled in 2 Pet 3:13 where fire rather than flood (as in the story of Noah) will mark the ultimate destruction of the cosmos.

Secondly, there is the vision of the New Jerusalem in all its glory, which incorporates the kind of details that John's visionary ancestor, Ezekiel, had been privileged to learn when conducted, in a vision, through the different quarters of the new city (Ezek 40–8). The closest parallel is Ezek 40:3–41:20, the culmination of Ezekiel's prophecy with a vision of the New Jerusalem and its 'measuring' (cf. Rev 11:1). The main point of this vision is the return of the glory

`*Revelation 21* 221`

of the Lord to the temple in Jerusalem. This coincides with a central theme of the Apocalypse whereby the divine glory located in heaven now returns to earth in a Jerusalem which resembles Eden (22:1–4). In 21:3 the throne of God is found on earth and not in heaven as it was in 4:1–11 (cf. 7:9–17; 8:1–5; 11:15–19; 15:2–8; 19:1–6).

Both Ezekiel and the Apocalypse have a counterpart in the *Temple Scroll* from Cave 11 at Qumran, which purports to be a vision of Moses at Sinai. Drawing on biblical legislation, it offers an outline of the new city and the qualities of its inhabitants; it approximates a utopian text in the detail that is lavished on all aspects of the city's life and architecture (Goodwin and Taylor 1982). The Apocalypse differs from these precedents in the presence of the Lamb (21:9, 22) and also in the absence of a temple. In this it reflects an idea found in other early Christian texts, that the earthly temple is transcended in lives of obedience, service and worship, wherever two are three are gathered together in the name of Jesus (Matt 18:20; cf. Mark 14:58; John 4:25; Acts 7:48; Rom 12:1; 1 Cor 3:19; Minucius Felix, *Octav.* 32).

Despite differences in the form of their visions, 2 Esdras shares with the Apocalypse an eschatological sequence: woes, messianic kingdom, resurrection, judgement and new age. In particular, the juxtaposition of a this-worldly messianic reign of a limited duration with judgement, resurrection and an eternal kingdom are common to both, suggesting a particular development in apocalyptic tradition at the end of the first century CE, for there is little evidence of a transcendent kingdom in earlier Jewish texts (on 2 Esdras, see Stone 1990).

Coming at the end of the book, Rev 21 draws together themes from throughout the book: for example, in 21:5 the command to John to 'write' recalls the beginning in 1:19, and the title 'Alpha and Omega' recalls 1:8; 'those who conquer' in 21:7 echoes the promises of the messages in Rev 2–3 (2:7, 11, 17, 26; 3:5, 12, 21), and the end of sorrow and thirst in 21:4, 6 recalls promises to those 'robed in white' in 7:16. As we saw in the Introduction (see above, 5–6), the Apocalypse shares themes with many other New Testament books. Here the end of death in 21:4 echoes 1 Cor 15:26, and the heavenly Jerusalem is alluded to briefly in both Gal 4:26 and Heb 12:22. The Apocalypse reflects the ambivalence evident throughout the Bible towards Zion (Jerusalem) as both a focus of hope and a place of rebellion (evident from Rev 11:8).

The Interpretations

This chapter is popular because of its offer of consolation and hope, which puts it, along with chapters 1 and 4, 5, 7 and 12, in a different category from much of the rest of the Apocalypse. In the interpretations which follow there is, relatively speaking, a lack of the kind of historical actualizing that we have found in the interpretations of the earlier chapters. This is not to deny that the New Jerusalem may in some sense be a present possibility, as Alexander the Minorite and William Blake suggest, and as Christopher Columbus believed his explorations were, in a way, bringing this new world into being. Some of the earliest interpretations of the chapter use it to understand the saving work of Christ in the past and the life of the Church in the present. But in general what we find is more evocative and hopeful, rather than a view of the text as already actualized in the present.

The poetic and literary works discussed here demonstrate how that 'new heaven and the new earth' have pervaded literary culture. That influence is selective. A glance at the recent *Revised Common Lectionary* (1992) reveals how an editorial hand has adapted the Apocalypse's angular text to modern religious sensibilities. The negative sentiments of 21:8 and 27 are omitted (as also they are left out of Roland Bainton's ethereal treatment of Rev 21 in his choral piece 'And I saw a new heaven'), suggesting that those responsible did not fear John's awesome statement in 22:19: 'if any one takes away from the words of the prophecy of this book, God will take away that person's share in the tree of life and in the holy city, which are described in this book'. Such editing produces a more acceptable book (a feature of interpretation down the centuries, of course).

The examples which follow consider the nature of the New Jerusalem and its relationship to human society. The chapter contains more detail about the future age than any other biblical text, Ezek 40–8 apart, and the most memorable interpretation is perhaps the diagrammatic description of Joachim of Fiore, which portrays a monastic-inspired heaven on earth, lived in community. This evocation did not remain at the level of the ideal but was translated into the practical politics of church life in the religious orders established in the thirteenth century (the Franciscans and the Dominicans). In the struggle over their identity and their interpretation of the historical context in which they emerged, the Apocalypse had a central role.

The New Jerusalem, the bride of the Lamb, as a present and future reality

Much writing inspired by this chapter is orientated towards the future. For Origen, however, the 'new heaven and new earth' of 21:1 has already begun, when Christ rose on the third day (in Mazzucco 1983: 60, citing *Comm. Jo.* x.35). The Church is the city of God (*Hom. Jer.* ix.2 in Anselmetto 1980: 264),

and Christ is the door to this city, through which enter the saints, now puri-
fied of all idolatry (*Hom. Num.* xxv.3, alluding to 21:27, in Mazzucco 1978: 71).
Origen explicitly rejects the chiliastic view (*First Principles* ii.11.2). Instead of
a place of earthly delights, the New Jerusalem is an image of increased knowledge of, and devotion to, God. There, in a school for souls where instruction
continues even after this life, the saints will eat the 'bread of life' (John 6:35),
that is, divine wisdom:

> The mind, when nourished by this food of wisdom to a whole and perfect state,
> as man was made in the beginning, will be restored to the 'image and likeness'
> of God [Gen 1:26]; so that, even though a man may have departed out of this
> life insufficiently instructed, but with a record of acceptable works, he can be
> instructed in that Jerusalem, the city of the saints, that is, he can be taught and
> informed and fashioned into a 'living stone', a 'stone precious and elect' [1 Pet
> 2:4–6] because he has borne with courage and endurance the trials of life and
> the struggles after piety. There, too, he will come to a truer and clearer knowl-
> edge of the saying already uttered here, that 'man does not live by bread alone,
> but by every word that proceedeth out of the mouth of God' [Matt 4:4]. (*First
> Principles* ii.11.3, Butterworth tr. 149)

Cyprian regards Christ as the spouse of a universal, fruitful Church which is
the New Jerusalem (*Test.* ii.19). The marriage of the bride described in 21:9–11
has already happened and has borne fruit.

As we shall see, interest in the design of the city, with its mathematical pre-
cision and symmetry, pervades literature and art. Irenaeus interprets the New
Jerusalem as the Church, in a typological comparison of Christ with Jacob: 'In
a foreign country were the twelve tribes born, the race of Israel, inasmuch as
Christ was also, in a strange country, to generate the twelve-pillared foundation [21:14] of the Church' (*AH* iv.21.3, ANF i.493). Victorinus comments that
the gates of the city are to be open always, and the twelve apostles of 21:14 are
the means whereby Jesus Christ, the true foundation, was revealed to the world.
He links the vision of the New Jerusalem closely with the millennium in 20:4–6,
for the descent of the New Jerusalem takes place during the millennium (1916:
154.6–7), and he interprets the state of the new heaven very literally (ANF
vii.359; 1916: 146.2–148.2 in Wainwright 1993: 29).

According to Tertullian, the kingdom is at first an earthly kingdom for a
thousand years; after this it becomes a heavenly kingdom (*Against Marcion*
iii.24). Unlike many other interpreters, he takes account of the negative note
in verses like 21:8 and 27. The eight categories of sinners are not pagans, he
says, but fallen Christians (*Concerning Flight in Persecution* vii).

In a rare actualizing interpretation, Eusebius, in his *Life of Constantine* iii.13,
suggests that the church of the Holy Sepulchre erected by Constantine in

Jerusalem may be the New Jerusalem predicted by the 'prophets' – apparently referring to Rev 21, along with other biblical texts. Similarly, in *HE* x.4.2 he praises Paulinus, the bishop of Tyre, as the king of a 'new and better Jerusalem' who, by rebuilding the church in Tyre, restored God's house for Christ and for Christ's holy bride (cf. Rev 21:9).

Augustine popularized the notion found in Tyconius that the New Jerusalem was not just the Church of the saints in the past nor the heavenly reward to come; it was also the Church of today, which is a mix of sinners and saints (in Armogathe in McGinn 2000: 187). In the extant fragments of his *Commentary* Tyconius applies all of Rev 21 to the life and doctrine of the Church (in Bauckham 1978: 18). In a comment on 21:4, appropriated by Beatus, Tyconius says that the chapter refers to both the present and the future of the Church:

> This Jerusalem . . . is the church, which [John] sums up (*recapitulat*) from the passion of Christ up to the day in which it rises again and will be crowned unvanquished in glory with Christ. He mixes together two times, now present, now future, and it is more fully declared with how much glory the church is taken up by Christ and separated from all attacks of evil. (In Beatus, *Comm.* 12.2.1, tr. J. Kovacs)

The 'spring of the water of life' in 21:6 is baptism: 'Hence the apostle also says that the dead will rise uncorrupted and the saints will be changed into glory [cf. 1 Cor 15:52]. That is, to those who wish it I will give remission of sins by the fount of baptism' (In Beatus, *Comm.* 12.2.11, tr. J. Kovacs).

In contrast to other parts of his commentary (see above, 15–17), Tyconius here emphasizes the positive aspect of the church, not its being a mixed body. The high mountain (21:10) is Christ. In its descent from heaven (21:2, 10) the New Jerusalem, situated on this mountain, replicates the Lamb. Just as the Son of God descended in humility, so the heavenly city descends daily from God, following the footsteps of Christ, the Son of God. This contrasts with the Beast, which 'ascends' rather than descends according to Rev 13:1 (in Beatus, *Comm.* 12.2.24, 28–30). The 12 gates (20:12) are the 12 apostles and also the 12 prophets made firm in Christ, who is the one door (cf. John 10:7); they also symbolize the doctrine of the Trinity proclaimed to the four corners of the world (in Beatus, *Comm.* 12.2.42, 50). The gold measuring rod of 21:15 and the 'city of gold, clear as glass' of 21:18 symbolize the Church, which is fragile but golden (in Beatus, *Comm.* 12.2.53). The gold symbolizes wisdom, and the clear glass the Church's faith in the truth: 'because that which is seen outside is also inside and there is nothing pretended, and not clear, in the saints of the church' (in Bede, PL 93:197.21–6, tr. J. Kovacs). Of Rev 21:23 ('And the city does not need sun or moon to shine on it') Tyconius writes that this is 'because the church is ruled not by light or the elements of the world, but with Christ its eternal sun it is led through the darkness of the world' (in Bede, PL 93:203.39–41, tr. J. Kovacs). Augustine, who takes Rev 20:1–6 to refer to the period of the Church and Rev 20:11–15 to the Last Judgement, understands the New Jerusalem of Rev 21 as both the Church in the present age and the 'world to come' where the saints will enjoy eternal life (*City of God* xx.17):

> This city is said to come down out of heaven because the grace by which God made it is heavenly . . . And it has been coming down from heaven from its beginning, since its citizens grow in number continually to the end of the present age by the grace of God which comes down from above through the new birth of baptism with the Holy Spirit sent down from heaven. But by the judgement of God, which will be the last judgement, through his son Jesus Christ, its splendour will appear by God's grace in such strength and newness that no traces of age will remain; since even our bodies will pass from their old decay and mortality into the exemption from decay and death. (Greene edn vi.347)

Verses 1 and 4, Augustine says, clearly speak of a future time. He relates the 'new heaven' and 'new earth' to Paul's statement that the 'present form of this world is passing away' (1 Cor 7:31), and sees here a reference to a general conflagration. This will purify the substance of our bodies, so that 'the world, renewed for the better, may be fitly furnished with men who have been renewed even in the flesh for the better' (*City of God* xx.16, Greene edn vi.345). The sea will be no more (21:1) because 'the roughness and stormy weather of human life in this age shall be no more'. The promises of 21:4 for life without tears or sorrows or pain, Augustine says, cannot refer to the present, millennial age, where these woes are still evident. He connects the promise that 'death will be no more' with the end of sin, by citing 1 Cor 15:55–6, where Paul associates death with sin and predicts the end of both. Thus he concludes: '[John] is so clearly speaking of the world to come and of immortality and of the everlasting life of the saints (for only then and only there shall these things be nonexistent), that if we think these expressions obscure we ought not to seek clarity or read it anywhere in the sacred Scriptures' (*City of God* xx.17, Greene edn vi.351).

Hildegard, echoing earlier interpretations which see the descent of the New Jerusalem as a present reality, sees its coming in the renewal of the inner life (*Scivias* iii.10.31, Hart and Bishop edn 488–9). She is one of the few interpreters to pick up on the oscillations between the positive and the negative images in Rev 21 (*Scivias* iii.10.30; Hart and Bishop edn 488; cf. Tertullian, discussed above).

Hope for a better future within history

The vision of the New Jerusalem has figured in the 'pursuit of the millennium' in which future hope becomes intertwined with practical politics (Cohn 1957; Rowland 1988). This is a feature of the Joachite interpretation of the Apocalypse. Alexander Minorita promotes a view that has had wide currency: namely, that Jerusalem must be built by the good deeds of the elect before the last day. The New Jerusalem symbolizes the hope he attaches to the new Franciscan and Dominican orders (*Expositio* 449–50, 453–4, 469 in Wainwright 1993: 54; Burr 1993: 32, 184–5; note the particular importance of the third age in Joachite exegesis, and see the *figura* of Joachim of Fiore discussed below, 228–9). Olivi sees the coming new age as one of greater illumination and insight (*Lectura* 960 in Burr 1993: 117–18), and sees in the gates of 21:21 a reference to the new teaching orders of learned monks ('doctors', *Lectura* 968–9 in Burr 1993: 117–18).

John Bale stresses the importance of human initiative in bringing the New Jerusalem:

> The apostle John, in the Apocalypse, doth say
> He saw a new heaven, and a new earth appearing . . .
> A New Jerusalem, the said John also see [sic]
> As a beautiful bride, prepared to her husband.
> Our true faithful church is that same fair city,
> Whom we have cleansed by the power of our right hand . . .
> Now we have destroyed the kingdom of Babylon,
> And thrown the great whore into the bottomless pit,
> Restoring again the true faith and religion.
>
> (*Dramatic Writings* 72, 74 in
> Fairfield 1976: 61; cf. Bale 1849: 582)

The journals of Christopher Columbus witness to his sense of vocation to 'reveal' the new heaven and the new earth, not as some heavenly revelation, but as something hidden on earth: 'Of the New Heaven and earth which our Lord made, as St John writes in the Apocalypse, after he had spoken it by the mouth of Isaiah, he made me the messenger thereof and showed me where to go' (Morison 1965: 291; cf. Milhou in Stein 2000: 3–12; Keller 1996: 159).

The establishment of the New Jerusalem in Münster in 1534–5 is one of the few violent 'actualizations' of the Apocalypse. Here visionary experience, not subjected to critical scrutiny, resulted in bizarre and occasionally violent behaviour designed to purge the New Jerusalem of infidels (Cohn 1957: 261–80; G. H. Williams 1962: 362–86; Stayer 1972). The theme of the New Jerusalem pervaded the preaching of Münster's Anabaptist leaders. Bernard Rothmann wrote of prophets in their midst who summoned Anabaptists from the surrounding region to 'come to the holy Jerusalem, to Zion, and to the new temple of Solomon' (in Baring-Gould 1891: 266, 273; Cohn 1957: 262–70; Arthur 1999: 61).

Hopes for human co-operation in bringing in the kingdom of God are also evident among Fifth Monarchists in the middle of the seventeenth century, both in England and in the American colonies (R. Bloch 1985). The hope for a fifth kingdom, based on Dan 2, was linked with the Apocalypse's New Jerusalem and used to inform practical politics. Thus John Tillinghast in his *Generation-work*, published in 1653, includes 'the pulling down of high and lofty things, and persons, that oppose Christ' as part of what is required to bring the new Jerusalem about (in Froom 1946–54: ii.570–3). In *The Cry of a Stone* Anna Trapnel laments the lost opportunity for a rule of the saints in a New Jerusalem which the Bare Bones Parliament offered (Trapnel 2000: 63, 68). Contemporary with Trapnel, Mary Cary, in *A New and More Exact Mappe or Description of the New Jerusalem* (1651) appears to equate the New Jerusalem of Rev 21 with the millennium of Rev 20. She predicts 'that kings, nobles and mighty men, are to be subjected to his saints', who will seek 'the public weal, and safety and happiness, and salvation of all' (in Hobby 1988: 30; Capp cf. 1972; Trapnel 2000: xxvii). For William Blake, 'mental fight' and prophetic activity contribute to the building of Jerusalem, as expressed in his 'Preface to Milton': 'until we have built Jerusalem in England's green and pleasant land' (1972: 480–1).

Post-millennialist optimism inspired by Rev 21 is reflected in Jonathan Edwards' convictions about America (on post-millennialism see above, 201–2). In Christianity's spread to the New World, God has prepared the way 'for the future glorious times of the church, when Satan's kingdom shall be overthrown throughout the whole habitable globe, on every side, and on all continents'. America was the land where God could begin 'a new world in a spiritual respect, when he creates the new heavens and new earth' (in Edward Johnson, *Wonder-Working Providence and Jonathan Edwards* in Abrams in Patrides and Wittreich 1984: 357; cf. R. Bloch 1985: 16–20; Boyer 1992: 226).

These ideas are echoed in Blake's prophecy *America*, which harbours hopes for the nascent American nation over against a tired Europe. Similar apocalyptic sentiments are expressed by Herman Melville, alluding to Rev 21:24 ('the nations shall walk in its light'):

> We Americans are the peculiar chosen people – the Israel of our time; we bear the ark of the liberties of the world. God has given to us, for a future inheritance, the broad domains of the political pagans, that shall yet come and lie down under the shade of our ark. The rest of the nations must soon be in our rear. We

are the pioneers of the world, the advance guard, sent on through the wilderness
of untried things, to break a new path in the New World that is ours. (Hayford
edn 151; cf. Smolinski in Stein 2000: 68)

The words 'See, I am making all things new' in 21:5 have encouraged a sense
of anticipation and the hope for progress within history. Not surprisingly, this
verse is appealed to by the Marxist philosopher Ernst Bloch (Hudson 1982),
whose *magnum opus The Principle of Hope* is punctuated with references to
John's vision, mediated through a Joachite lens. Bloch's this-worldly eschatology contrasts with Karl Barth's roughly contemporary rejection of such human
initiative (1958: iv.268). For Bloch creation and apocalypse are contrary principles, the former summed up in the phrase, 'And behold, it was very good!'
(Gen 1) and the latter in the phrase, 'See, I am making all things new!' It is the
latter principle that leads out of the world as it is into the better world fore-
seen by John. Apocalypse is 'the a priori of all politics and culture' and represents an 'awakening into totality' (in Zindras–Swartz in Stein 2000: 288; cf.
Bloch 1972: 33–4).

The *Geneva Bible*, on the other hand, repudiates any idea that the new age
is a threat to the established political order. That the descent of the New
Jerusalem is an act of grace is emphasized in its comment on 21:10: 'It is said
to come down from heaven, because all the benefits that the Church hath, they
acknowledge it to come of God through Christ.' The presence of the kings of
the earth in 21:24 is evidence against egalitarianism: 'Here we see as in infinite
other places the Kings & Princes (contrary to that wicked opinion of the
Anabaptists) are partakers of the heavenly glory, if they rule in the fear of the
Lord – Isa 60,11. Phil 4,4, chap. 3, 5. & 10,11.' Similarly, the sixteenth-century
Jesuit Francisco Ribera says that the New Jerusalem is not earthly but heavenly,
an eternal state of blessedness (1593: 498–548 in Wainwright 1993: 62).

John's vision of the holy city coming down from heaven prompted Joachim
of Fiore's *figura* entitled *Dispositio novi ordinis pertinens ad tercium statum ad
instar novi Hierusalem* (see plate 13), which is a plan for the new society of the
third age surrounded by explanatory text (1953: plate 12; Reeves and Hirsch-
Reich 1972: plate 31). In the centre it has the four-square pattern of John's city
(21:16), with additional suburbia. The arms of a cross contain four oratories
for the monastic residents in the city; each is associated with one of the four
living creatures of Rev 4:6–7. On the left, the seat of Pope Leo, lies the oratory
of Peter and all the apostles, where the older and weaker brethren are situated.
On the right is the oratory of St Paul and all the doctors of the Church (*viri
eruditi*). At the bottom is the oratory of St Stephen and the martyrs. At the top,
presided over by the eagle, is the oratory of John and all virgins (contemplatives of both sexes). At the centre of this holy society is the oratory 'of the Holy

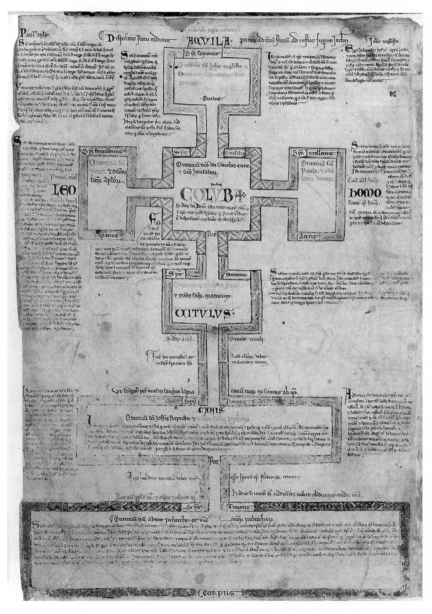

Plate 13 Joachim of Fiore, *figura* of the New Jerusalem (Rev 21–2). Corpus Christi College, Oxford.

Mother of God and of Holy Jerusalem', the throne of God, where the 'spiritual father' presides over and rules the whole order which lives under the wings of the dove (*columba*). The diagram makes clear that for Joachim, the contemplative life was supreme. Nevertheless, the life of the wider world is incorporated into this new society. At the foot of the diagram, admittedly outside the wall of the city, lies the oratory of John the Baptist and all prophets. Here are the clergy who live under their own rule and serve the secular community. Finally, below this is the oratory of the lay flock gathered under Abraham and all the patriarchs, which lies at a distance of about three miles. Here, as the accompanying text explains, live the married with their sons and daughters, sharing a life in common:

> They will sleep with their wives for the sake of having children rather than for pleasure. At set times or days they will abstain from them by consent to be free to pray, taking account of the physical constitution and age of the young people lest they be tempted by Satan [1 Cor 7:5] . . . They will have food and clothing in common . . . No idle person will be found among these Christians . . . Let each one work at his own craft, and the individual trades and workers shall have their own foremen . . . Food and clothing will be simple as befits Christians. . . . Honest and approved women will spin wool for the need of Christ's poor. . . . They will give tithes of all that they possess to the clerics for the support of the poor and strangers, and also for the boys who are studying doctrine . . . so that there may be no one in need among them but all things held in common. (Tr. McGinn 1979: 147–8)

This picture, with its practical details of food and clothing and religious practices as well as its spatial measurements, is quite down-to-earth. In Joachim's New Jerusalem, people live in their own homes but according to a lay religious rule, fasting, working with their hands, giving to the poor and obeying their spiritual fathers. In its recognition of the importance of the laity, this vision was prophetic of future developments when in the age of the friars there were 'third orders' and lay fraternities of various kinds. This picture of a future society including secular clergy and laity, along with monks, and friars, is echoed many times in Joachim's writing. It might be called utopian were it not that Joachim clearly believed that such a state of bliss on earth was not just a possibility but a clear future reality (in McGinn 1979: 297, n. 12; McGinn notes that the historian and philosopher of utopianism, Ernst Bloch, described Joachim as 'the spirit of revolutionary Christian social utopianism'; see E. Bloch 1971: 137; cf. Moltmann 1996: 143, 157, 186–90).

The nearest analogue is the *Temple Scroll* from Qumran (Vermes 1997: 190) from the late Second Temple period (first century BCE) with its detailed prescriptions regarding the organization and geography of the (probably) eschatological community. One could also compare the prescriptive *Law of Freedom* of the Digger writer Gerrard Winstanley, in which, after the end of the communist experiment, Winstanley appeals to Oliver Cromwell. It contains a detailed prescription for an ideal society based on the values of the Digger community which has parallels to actual societies being set up in the American colonies at about the same time (Sabine edn 501; cf. Mary Cary, *A New Mappe* 270, 307–10; Hinds 1996: 213–18; Capp 1972 and in McGregor and Reay 1984: 187–8; R. Bloch 1985). The founders of New Haven, Connecticut, set out to create a utopian settlement, based on nine squares (Atwater 1851), a plan still visible in the design of the modern city. In the nineteenth century a utopian project in north-eastern Brazil, that of Antonio Conselheiro at Canudos, was popularly known as 'the New Jerusalem' (Levine in Stein 2000: 181–90; da Cunha 1944).

Given the appearance of cultic motifs throughout John's vision, it comes as a surprise to read in 21:22 that John saw no temple in the New Jerusalem. The rest of the New Testament suggests that this should not surprise us, however. The veil of the Temple is rent at Jesus' death (Mark 15:38); heaven and earth no longer meet in tabernacle or Temple. Peter Olivi echoes such sentiments, pointing out that the Church has been bound neither to a physical location like the Jerusalem temple nor to a ceremonial law such as the Torah. In the imminent eschatological age a new form of religiosity will be worked out: 'in the Church of the seventh period, however, this will be fulfilled even more fully inasmuch as it will not need many earlier doctrines, since Christ's spirit will teach it all truth without mystery of external voice and book' (*Lectura* 979 in Burr 1993: 117–18).

Literary allusions

Allusions to Rev 21 abound in literary texts. Dante's *Divine Comedy* and Bunyan's *Pilgrim's Progress* describe the journey of the soul to the celestial city. So too as Chaucer's pilgrims draw near to Canterbury, the poet suggests that theirs is a journey to the New Jerusalem:

> And Jhesu, for his grace, wit me sede
> To shew you the wey, in this viage,
> Of thilke parfit glorious pilgrimage
> That highte Jerusalem celestial.
> (*Canterbury Tales*, fragment X,
> lines 48–51 in Emmerson
> in McGinn 2000: 408)

One of the most distinctive appropriations of the Apocalypse is the fourteenth-century work 'The Pearl'. In it the reader is offered a vision of the heavenly Jerusalem. There is a succession of explicit links with the Apocalypse, especially its detailed description of the celestial city (Finch 1993: 91–9; Fowler 1984: 171–80).

At the very start of Shakespeare's *Antony and Cleopatra*, Antony uses the image of the new heaven and earth to express the boundless character of the bonds that exist between lovers:

CLEO. If it be love indeed, tell me how much.
ANT. There's beggary in the love that can be reckon'd.
CLEO. I'll set a bourn how far to be belov'd.
ANT. Then must thou needs find out new heaven, new earth.
(i.14–17)

In another text Shakespeare makes a surprising link of Rev 21–2, where the division between heaven and earth is overcome, with the fiery judgement:

Let the vile world end,
And the promised flames of the last day
Knit earth and heaven together!
Now let the general trumpet blow his blast,
Particularities and petty sounds
To cease!
(*Henry VI Part 2*, v.ii.40–5)

Images from 21:5, 18 pervade Henry Vaughan's address to God in 'L'Envoy':

Arise, arise!
And like old cloaths fold up these skies,
This long work veyl: then shine and spread
Thy own bright self over each head,
And through thy creatures pierce and pass
Till all becomes thy cloudless glass'
(lines 7–12 in Emmerson in
McGinn 2000: 428)

According to Saint John of the Cross, the waters from the fountain of life in 20:6 are 'the inmost love of God' (*Complete Works* 2:311 in Wainwright 1993: 203).

John Donne uses the contrast between the Bride of the Lamb (21:9) and the 'richly painted' Whore of Babylon (Rev 17) to contrast the Reformed Church and Catholicism, and he explores how God's true Church could suddenly awake after sleeping a thousand years during the 'dark ages' of Catholicism:

> Show me, dear Christ, Thy spouse so bright and clear.
> What! Is it she which on the other shore
> Goes richly painted? Or which, robbed and tore,
> Laments and mourns in Germany and here?
> Sleeps she a thousand, then peeps up one year?

('Holy Sonnet XVIII' in Emmerson in McGinn 2000:
409; cf. Emmerson 1981: 207–9)

William Cowper develops the imagery about 'nations' and 'kings' of 20:24:

> Bright as a sun the sacred city shines;
> All kingdoms and all princes of the earth
> Flock to that light; the glory of all lands
> Flower into her; unbounded is her joy,
> And endless her increase . . .
> Eastern Java there
> Kneels with the native of the farthest west;
> And Æthiopia spreads abroad the hand,
> And worships. Her report has travell'd forth
> Into all lands. From ev'ry clime they come
> To see thy beauty and to share thy joy, O Sion!
> An assembly such as earth
> Saw never, such as heav'n stoops down to see.

('The Task', lines 80–4, 810–17 in Cowper
1934, in Paley 1999: 16–17)

In Bunyan's *Pilgrim's Progress* the pilgrim Christian uses Rev 21 in describing to Pliable the glorious reward that awaits them at the end of their journey: 'There shall be no more crying, nor sorrow; for he that is owner of the place will wipe all tears from our eyes' (1967 edn 56; cf. Bunyan, *Christian Behaviour* 185–6 and *A Discourse of the Building of the House of God* (1688) in Hill 1988: 220). A rather different view of such expectations is that of D. H. Lawrence, who mocks the priggish, virginal, 'bourgeois' view of the New Jerusalem and the 'brimstone Patmossers' knowing their enemies' torment in the lake of fire (*Apocalypse* 75 in Burdon 1997: 211).

Coleridge, in 'Dejection', describes the union between the human soul and the natural world as having apocalyptic character, giving revelatory insight beyond the comprehension of those dominated by the senses rather than the imagination:

Joy, Lady! is the Spirit and the power,
Which wedding Nature to us gives on dower
A new Earth and New Heaven,

Undreamt of by the sensual and the proud.
(lines 67–70 in Burdon 1997: 139)

Blake and his mentor Milton both drew on Rev 21–2 in their epic poems *Jerusalem* and *Paradise Lost*. Milton uses the imagery of these chapters to describe the bliss of heaven from which Satan has departed (*Paradise Lost* i.682; ii.1049–50; iii.363–4, 594–605, 506–7; iv.590; v.644–7; x.381, 647–8; xi.901; 'On the Morning of Christ's Nativity' ii.13; 'Lycidas' 181). At the close of *Paradise Lost* Michael, assuming the role of John's angel (cf. Rev 1:1 and 22:6) as the 'seer blest', sets out the story of Christianity's initial glory and corruption, culminating with Christ's coming

. . . to dissolve
Satan with his perverted world, then raise
From the conflagrant mass, purged and refined
New Heav'ns, new Earth, ages of endless date,
Founded in righteousness and peace and love,

To bring forth fruits, joy and eternal bliss'
(xii. 546–51)

It is worth noting that Milton's 'raise from the conflagrant mass, purged and refined' suggests a continuity between the new creation of Rev 21:1 and the old creation. This recalls Gen 1:2, where the creation comes about as the result of the taming of chaos by God's creative act.

The influence of Rev 21–2 is particularly evident in Blake's vision of Golgonooza in the early chapters of *Jerusalem*. Golgonooza, the city of 'Art and manufacture' (*Milton* 24:50) is a four-square city (cf. Rev 21:16) which resembles the New Jerusalem (*Jerusalem* 12:45–8 and 13:1–5; cf. *Four Zoas* viii.109). Blake imagines himself and Los (a mythic, prophetic figure, whose imaginative activity seeks to create a new world) standing on the banks of the Thames seeking to build Golgonooza by their 'mental fight' (*Jerusalem* 10:17; cf. 53:15), and to extend their influence to the whole of Britain (*Jerusalem* 14:16–24; cf. *Milton* 6:1–7; cf. Bunyan's Mansoul (*Pilgrim's Progress* 1967 edn 247), discussed by Korshin in Patrides and Wittreich 1984: 256; on the influence of the New Jerusalem on Keats, see Paley 1999: 286).

Blake conceives the new earth to be in this world, but it comes about only through a 'mental fight':

I know of no other . . . Gospel than the liberty both of body and mind to exercise the Divine Arts of Imagination. . . . What is the Joy of Heaven but Improvement in the things of the Spirit? What are the Pains of Hell but Ignorance, Bodily Lust, Idleness and devastation of the things of the Spirit? . . . To labour in Knowledge is to Build up Jerusalem. (*The Marriage of Heaven and Hell* 2:14; cf. *Jerusalem* 77:50 cf. 'Preface to Milton', 1991–5: 212–13)

Blake's this-worldly expectation has its parallels in early Christian chiliasm (discussed above, 202–3; see e.g. Irenaeus *AH* v.36.1–2). He describes the blessed future: 'The Lamb of God reciev'd [*sic*] me in his arms he smil'd upon us: / He made me his Bride & Wife [cf. Rev 21:9]: he gave thee to Albion' (Blake, *Jerusalem* 20:39).

In his painting *The Waters of Life* (Tate Gallery, London) Blake evokes the New Jerusalem, depicting wide boulevards of running water (Rev 22:2), probably implying a contrast with the cramped conditions that confronted him in the streets of London in his day (Hamlyn and Phillips 2000: 144). Such use of the vision of the New Jerusalem in a critique of contemporary society was evident a century earlier in Cotton Mather, who says that Jerusalem's golden streets indicate that righteousness will prevail in that city, where the 'Golden Rule' will govern all activity in the marketplace. In New England, in contrast, there was an 'abundance of cheating through short measures of tea, salt, cheese, wood, and hay as well as robbery of the public treasury by deception and false report' (in Stein in Patrides and Wittreich 1984: 277). A very different use of the New Jerusalem image is that of Dryden, who portrays the new London as a present rather than a future good: 'Me-thinks already, from this Chymick flame, / I see a City of more precious mold: / Rich as the Town which gives the Indies name, / With Silver pav'd, and all divine with Gold' ('Annus Mirabilis' 1169–72 in Patrides in Patrides and Wittreich 1984: 252).

The New Jerusalem in church architecture, liturgy and song

The image of the New Jerusalem coming down out of heaven has influenced the architecture and decoration of churches. A striking example of this is the large chandeliers, called Jerusalem crowns, that were placed in churches in Germany and France beginning in the eleventh century, often in the apse or over tombs (Schiller 1990: 192–5). These consisted of a golden circle or polygon representing the walls of the holy city, adorned with images taken from Rev 21:10–27: towers and gates (usually numbering 12 and open on all sides, reflecting 21:25), figures of prophets (apparently an interpretation of the 12 tribes of Israel mentioned in 21:12), the 12 apostles (Rev 21:14) and precious stones (21:11, 18–21). A large number of candles (48, 72, or 96) convey the splendour of the light from God that illuminates the city (21:23). Inscriptions make clear the symbolic meanings: for example, one explains the angelic and human figures (prophets, apostles, bishops, warriors and saints) as overseers of the heavenly city, who encourage the worthy and shut out the unworthy. A dedicatory inscription for a Jerusalem crown erected by the emperor Frederic Barbarossa calls it an image of 'the heavenly Jerusalem, glistening as it descends from the far regions which are illuminated by the stars, shining with much gold and gleaming with precious stones' (in Schiller 1990: 194).

Perhaps related to the Jerusalem crowns is the use of imagery from Rev 21 in medieval liturgies for dedicating new churches and for annual commemorations of a church's dedication. Flanigan cites a responsory for these occasions which draws on 21:2–3:

'I saw the holy city, the new Jerusalem, descending from heaven, prepared by God. And I heard a voice from the throne saying "Behold the tabernacle of God with men, and it will dwell with them" (Flanigan in Emmerson and McGinn 1992: 333–4).

Versicles that alternate with this in the liturgy include the following:

And he who was sitting on the throne said 'Behold I make all things new' (21:5).
I saw the new heaven and the new earth, and the holy city Jerusalem descending from the heavens (21:1–2).

I saw the city of Jerusalem descending from heaven, adorned as a bride for her groom (21:2). (Flanigan in Emmerson and McGinn 1992: 334)

The chapter continues to influence Christian worship, particularly in hymns. An African-American spiritual declares: 'I want to be ready . . . to walk in Jerusalem just like John'; another says of heaven: 'De streets up dere are paved wid gold' (Rev 21:21, in Johnson and Johnson 1954: ii.58–9; ii.140–1). A sixteenth-century text, 'Jerusalem my happy home,' set to an American folk tune, includes these verses:

> Jerusalem, my happy home,
> when shall I come to thee?
> When shall my sorrows have an end?
> Thy joys when shall I see?
> Thy saints are crowned with glory great [cf. Rev 2:10];
> they see God face to face [Rev 22:3];
> They triumph still [Rev 3:21], they still rejoice
> in that most happy place.
>
> (*The Hymnal 1982*: 620)

Another hymn is based on a Latin text by Peter Abelard (d. 1142):

> O what their joy and their glory must be,
> those endless Sabbaths the blessed ones see;
> crown for the valiant, to the weary ones rest;
> God shall be all [cf. 1 Cor 15:28], and in all ever blest.
>
> Truly 'Jerusalem' name we that shore,
> city of peace that brings joy evermore;
> wish and fulfillment are not severed there,
> nor do things prayed for come short of the prayer.
>
> There, where no troubles distraction can bring [cf. Rev 21:4],
> we the sweet anthems of Zion shall sing;
> while for thy grace, Lord, their voices of praise,
> thy blessed people eternally raise.
>
> Now, in the meanwhile, with hearts raised on high,
> we for that country must yearn and must sigh,
> seeking Jerusalem, dear native land,
> through our long exile on Babylon's strand.
>
> (*Hymnal 1982*: 623; cf. 624: 'Jerusalem the golden', with a text
> based on the twelfth-century poetry of Bernard of Cluny)

Ancient Literary Context

The chapter begins with the climax of John's vision of the New Jerusalem begun in 21:1; the concluding verses then offer admonitions and testimonies about the importance of the book. The emphasis on the role of John and on the prophetic book given to him recalls the opening chapter, as does the appearance of the angel to John (cf. 1:1). In 22:1–5 the city where the throne of God and of the Lamb will be found is described in terms reminiscent of the garden of Eden in Gen 2–3, with its river (Gen 2:10–14) and 'tree of life' (Gen 2:9). Absent is the serpent of Gen 3; in Rev 22:3 'nothing accursed will be found', in contrast to Gen 3:14: ('cursed are you among all animals'). The chapter emphasizes John's role as prophet (22:6, 9, 10, 18, 19), inviting comparison with the prophets of the Hebrew Bible. In particular, the images of 22:1–5 recall Ezekiel's vision of the renewed temple, from which water will gush out, bringing great fertility (Ezek 47:1–12). The 'tree of life' found 'on either side of the river' whose leaves will heal the nations (Rev 22:2) resembles the many trees of Ezek 47:12 whose 'fruit will be for food, and their leaves for healing'. When the prophet John meets the angel in 22:8–11, he responds as did Ezekiel when granted a vision of the divine throne-chariot, by falling on his face (Ezek 1:28; cf. the prophet Daniel's response to the angel Gabriel in Dan 8:17 and John's to the vision in Rev 1:17).

The Apocalypse began with an appearance of the awesome 'one like the Son of Man' in 1:9–20, followed by his words to the seven churches (2:1–3:22). Here at the end, John again hears words of Christ (22:12–13, 16, 20), who repeats his earlier promises to come soon (1:3, 7–8; cf. 2:16; 3:11). The descriptions of Christ also echo Rev 1: he is 'the Alpha and the Omega' (22:13; cf. 1:8; 21:6) and 'the first and the last' (1:17; cf. 2:8).

The Interpretations

Early interpreters of the chapter focus especially on its relevance for christology, an interest reflected also in later appropriations. Poetic evocations of the water and trees of paradise (22:1–5, 14, 17, 19) abound. The dialogue in 22:9–11 between John and the angel, who calls John his 'fellow servant', finds echoes in other conversations between angels and humans. John's strong words about the authority of his book (22:18–19) have served as a model for later authoritative claims, but they have also provoked questioning of the prophet's authority and the relative value of allusive texts like the Apocalypse as compared with biblical works that are more comprehensible. The concluding invocation 'Come, Lord Jesus!' (22:20) has been used in public and private prayer. The coming which it anticipates can be understood in cosmic and eschatological terms, or in more local and immediate terms, which reminds us of the general ambiguity between present and future in the Apocalypse as a whole which is so evident in the history of interpretation.

Christ, the Alpha and Omega (22:13) and the morning star (22:16)

For Cyprian the tree of life (22:2) is the cross, which gives life to those who have its mark on their foreheads (22:4; *Test.* ii.22). Christ is the slain Lamb and King, who came to deliver humanity and conquered the Antichrist with his 'tree of life' (*Test.* iii.23). Eusebius thinks the eschatological war between the Beast and the servants of Christ is already under way, not a matter of the indefinite future. Verse 11 ('Let the evildoer still do evil, and the filthy still be filthy, and the righteous still do right') is carried out in the cruel desecration of the bodies of Christian martyrs by their persecutors, who cast them to dogs (*HE* v.1.58–9; Eusebius may have in mind the word 'dogs' in 22:15).

For Origen 22:13 summarizes the identity of the Son as revealer and bringer of salvation. An extended discussion of this verse in his *Commentary on John* illustrates Origen's close attention to the individual words of Scripture. He argues that the three phrases 'Alpha and Omega', 'the first and the last', and 'the beginning and the end' express different aspects of Christ (*Comm. Jo.* i.209). 'The beginning and the end' indicates that the Son is 'the beginning of all that exists', because he is Wisdom, the principle or pattern of all that comes to be (i.116, commenting on John 1:1; cf. i.210–21). The phrase also describes how the Son brings salvation:

> The Only begotten is indeed 'all in all' [1 Cor 15:28] since he is the 'beginning' in the man he assumed [the human Jesus], the 'end' in the last of the saints [to achieve salvation] and also in every person in between. Or [in another interpretation] he is 'beginning' in Adam and 'end' in his sojourn among us, as it is written 'the last Adam became a life-giving spirit [1 Cor 15:45]'. (*Comm. Jo.* i.225, tr. J. Kovacs)

Or, as Origen says elsewhere, the Son is called 'the beginning and the end' because he sums up in himself all significant moments in salvation history (*Schol Ap* 4, TU 38:22; *Comm. Rom.* ix.39, PL 14: 1239C in Monaci 1978: 147). The title 'first and the last' shows that Christ has taken on the nature of all rational beings (cf. Col 3:11), from the highest angels down to humans, and perhaps even extending to the demons (*Comm. Jo.* i.209–20). This presupposes the common patristic idea that the Saviour must assume the nature of everything to be saved (*Comm. Jo.* i.224). The 'Alpha and Omega' Origen understands as a reference to the many different christological concepts (in Greek, *epinoiai*) contained in Scripture: for example, titles such as 'beginning' and 'Word' in John 1:1. The exploration of these titles is the main subject of book 1 of Origen's *Commentary on John*:

> If there are letters of God, as indeed there are, which the saints decipher when they say that they have read what is in the heavenly tablets [cf. *1 Enoch* 81.2], these letters, which exist so that heavenly things may be read through them, are concepts about the Son of God which are divided up into alpha and the other letters up to omega. (*Comm. Jo.* i.221, tr. J. Kovacs)

Just as the written word can be understood only by knowing the whole alphabet, so it is only by understanding all the titles ('concepts') of the Son revealed in Scripture that one can acquire all spiritual knowledge (cf. *Comm. Rom.* i.14).

According to Primasius, the verse shows the consubstantiality of the Father and the Son, and their unity with the Holy Spirit, the third person of the Trinity. He finds a reference to the Holy Spirit in the letters Alpha and Omega, since they have the same numerical value as *peristera*, the Greek word for dove, the form in which the Holy Spirit appeared in the baptism of Jesus (in Matter in Emmerson and McGinn 1992: 44; cf. Daley 1991: 210).

The Alpha and Omega are featured in two of Joachim of Fiore's *figurae* (1953: plates 11a and 11b, cf. Reeves and Hirsch-Reich 1972: plate 26, discussed above, 46–7; 1953: plate 13, cf. Reeves and Hirsch-Reich 1972: plate 27, discussed above, 63; on Arnold of Villanova's use of Alpha and Omega, see Lee, Reeves and Silano 1989: 35–6). The sense of infinity is captured in Milton's 'In height or depth, still first and last will reign' (*Paradise Lost* ii.324). The images from 22:13 have quite a different force in a late seventeenth-century inscription from Poitiers, where they convey a sense of foreboding about the day of wrath:

> Alpha and Omega. The Beginning and the End.
> For all things become every day worse and worse,
> For the end is drawing near.
> > (In McGinn 2000: 379)

The christological focus is also evident in the *Geneva Bible*, which explains the middle of the street in 22:2 thus: 'that Christ who is the life of his Church, is commune to all his and not peculiar for any one sorte of people.' The image of the 'morning star' is a messianic title in 22:16 (cf. 2:28 and Num 24:17); elsewhere in the Bible the star refers to the enemy of the people of God (the 'Day Star' in Isa 14:12). Drawing on both types of symbolism, Milton presents Satan-Lucifer as an inadequate parody of Christ who gives misleading instruction to his minions.

> . . . for great indeed
> His name, and high was his degree in heaven;
> His countenance, as the morning star that guides
> The starry flock, allured them, and with lies
> Drew after him the third part of heaven's host.
> > (*Paradise Lost* v.706–10; cf. v.699–715;
> > i.294; iii.201)

Images of paradise (22:1–5)

According to the *Geneva Bible*, in the pure river of 22:1 'John alludeth to the visible paradise to set forthe more sensibly the spiritual: and this agreeth with that which is written, Ezek 47,1'. Poets are fond of the imagery of these verses, especially the river of the 'water of life' that flows from the throne of God (22:1, 17) and the 'tree of life' (22:2, 14, 19). In Spenser's *The Faerie Queene* the Red Knight is replenished during battle by the Well of Life and the Tree of Life (canto ii in Sandler in Patrides and Wittreich 1984: 150). In Bunyan's *Pilgrim's Progress*, as Pilgrim and Hopeful are close to the end of their arduous journey, having crossed safely through the River of Death, their angelic companions use images from Rev 22:1–5 to describe the heavenly Jerusalem they are approaching (1967 edn 212–13). Earlier in the narrative the pilgrims drink from the 'River of the Water of Life' and delight in the fruit of the trees on its banks (Rev 22:1–2; 1967 edn 215).

Also reflecting imagery of 22:1–2 is Milton's 'And drink thy fill of pure immortal streams' ('Sonnet XIV' (1646) 14). He imagines his drowned friend Lycidas in a happier place: 'Where other groves, and other streams along, / With nectar pure his oozy locks he laves' ('Lycidas' (1637) 174–5; cf. *Paradise Lost* v.652; xi.79). Echoing 22:5, Milton speaks of the heavenly 'courts of everlasting day' which the Son of God forsook in order to come to earth to redeem humankind ('On the Morning of Christ's Nativity' 13). An African-American song says 'Dat heab'nly home is bright an' fair' (Johnson and Johnson 1954: ii.105). Another spiritual celebrates the promise of the tree of life in 20:2 (cf. 2:7): 'You got a right, I got a right, / We all got a right, to the tree of life' (ibid. i.183–4).

In Byron's 'Childe Harold III' the natural world is seen as proleptically eschatological: 'then to see Thy valley of sweet waters, were to know Earth paved like Heaven' (in Paley 1999: 195). In the 'Conclusion' to his *Ecclesiastical Sonnets*, written in 1820, Wordsworth compares his Lakeland idyll to the bliss of the millennium. He imagines cyclical time sleeping 'as a snake enrolled, / Coil within, coil at noontide', while the river of 'living waters' rolls towards 'the eternal City' (in Paley 1999: 154). In 'The Excursion', Wordsworth describes the fall of the Bastille in eschatological terms, combining the image of new heaven and new earth from Rev 21:1 with the tree of 22:2:

> I beheld
> Glory – beyond all glory ever seen,
> Confusion infinite of heaven and earth,
> Dazzling the soul. Meanwhile, prophetic harps
> In every grove, were ringing, 'War shall cease;
> Did ye not hear that conquest is abjured?
> Bring garlands, bring forth choicest flowers, to deck
> The tree of Liberty'.
>
> ('The Excursion', in *Ecclesiastical Sonnets, Poetical Works* iii. 719–26 cf. ii.827–81 in Paley 1999: 154)

In a nationalistic vein, Frederic Thruston, writing during the Napoleonic Wars at the beginning of the nineteenth century, speaks of an England which is 'the river of life which, for ages almost without end, beautifies, and gladdens, and supports, the Holy Catholic Church, of the New Jerusalem' (*England Safe and Triumphant* 2:383 in Wainwright 1993: 168).

Humans and angels in the plan of God (22:8–11)

According to 22:8–9, John falls down to worship his angelic interpreter but is rebuked: 'for I am thy fellow servant, and of thy brethren the prophets'. A similar temptation overcomes Dante, who tries to kneel before a fallen 'Roman Shepherd' (a sinful pope), whom he encounters in purgatory, and is told: 'Don't be mistaken; I, with you and others, am but a fellow-servant of one Power' (*Purgatorio* 19.127–34; for such ideas in Jewish tradition, see Stuckenbruck 1995). Milton also stresses the privileged position of humans, in that they have a unique place in the story of redemption. The archangel Raphael, appearing to Adam in the garden of Eden, tells him:

> Nor less think we in heaven of thee on earth
> Than of our fellow servant, and inquire
> Gladly into the ways of God with man:
> For God we see hath honoured thee, and set
> On man his equal love
> (*Paradise Lost* viii.224–8).

The authority of 'the words of this prophecy' (22:10, 18–19)

As has been indicated at various points in this commentary, Hildegard is implicitly and explicitly indebted to John's inspiration in her own visions. In a vision of the glorious eschatological time, she appeals explicitly to John and cites Rev 22:5 (*Scivias* iii.12, Hart and Bishop edn 520). In another passage she claims authoritative character for her book through an allusive paraphrase of 22:18–19. Hildegard hears a voice from heaven crying out:

> And therefore, if anyone rejects the mystical words of this book, I will draw My bow against him and transfix him by the arrows from my quiver; I will knock his crown from his head, and make him like those who fell in Horeb when they murmured against Me. And if anyone utters curses against this prophecy, may the curse that Isaac uttered come upon him. (*Scivias* iii.13.16, Hart and Bishop edn 536; cf. Dronke 1984: 148)

Just before Francis of Assisi died on 3 October, 1226, he dictated a 'testament' which was to become the subject of controversy between the various wings of the Franciscan order. To underline its authority (something denied by Pope Gregory IX in 1230), he alludes to words from the Apocalypse:

> And the brothers must not say, 'This is another rule', for it is a recollection, admonition, exhortation and my testament which I, poor brother Francis, make for you my brothers, so that we may observe the rule we have promised to God in a more Catholic manner. And the general minister and all other ministers and custodians are bound by obedience not to add or subtract from these words [cf. Rev 22:18–19] . . . And whoever observes them will be filled in heaven with a blessing of the most high Father and on earth he will be filled with the blessing [cf. 22:14] of his beloved Son, with the Holy Spirit the Comforter and all the powers of heaven and all the saints. And, I brother Francis, your servant insofar as I can be, internally and externally confirm for you this holy blessing.

The *Geneva Bible*, in the comment on 22:10 ('Do not seal up the words of the prophecy of this book'), contrasts the Apocalypse with Daniel: 'This is not then as the other Prophecies which were commanded to be hid until the time appointed, as in Daniel 12,4, because then these things should be quickly accomplished, & did now begin.' The comment serves to indicate the relative importance of the last book of the Christian Bible. Luther, on the other hand, points to John's assertions in 22:18 as reason for suspecting the worth of a book whose author could make such assertive claims:

> And so I think of it almost as I do of the Fourth Book of Esdras, and I can in nothing detect that it was provided by the Holy Spirit. Moreover, he seems to be going much too far when he commends his own book so highly, – more than any other of the sacred books do, though they are much more important. (*Preface to New Testament* 1522)

The allusiveness of the text, which made it open to a variety of intepretations, contrasted with the desire of Reformers for a more literal, less complex exegesis. So William Tyndale, who was suspicious of allegorical exegesis, admits: 'The Apocalypse or Revelations of John are allegories whose literal sense is hard to find in many places' (2000: 156).

On the other hand, the Nonconformist minister James Bicheno welcomes 'the very lack of the precise reference' and believes that John 'otherwise often provides the words more rather than less effective, since they can be associated with a whole range of situations in his hearers' experience and imagination and imbue them and possible moral responses to them with a biblical authority' (*A Word in Season* 53 in Burdon 1997: 120). Similarly, Blake writes to an enquirer about his own apocalyptic works and the value of similar allusive texts (though in this passage he does not mention the Apocalypse):

> You say that I want somebody to elucidate my ideas. But you ought to know that what is grand is necessarily obscure to weak men. That which can be made explicit to the idiot is not worth my care. The wisest of the ancients consider'd what is not too explicit as the fittest for instruction, because it rouzes the faculties to act. I name Moses, Solomon, Esop, Homer, Plato . . . Why is the Bible more Entertaining & Instructive than any other book? Is it not because they are addressed to the Imagination, which is Spiritual Sensation and but mediately to the understanding or reason? ('Letter to Trusler' in Blake 1972: 793–4)

'Come, Lord Jesus!' (22:20)

The invocation in the book's penultimate verse 'Amen. Come, Lord Jesus!' occurs in one of the earliest Christian liturgies, in *Didache* 10.6. Probably also reflective of worship is the same phrase in its Aramaic form in 1 Cor 16:20: 'Let any one be accursed who has no love for the Lord. Maranatha!' The Aramaic 'Maranatha' is ambiguous and could be translated 'Our Lord has come' or 'Come Lord!' A similar ambiguity is found in the Apocalypse: the Lord's coming is both cosmic and eschatological (as in 19:11) and local and immediate (as in 3:3, 11, 20). The present coming juxtaposed with a future coming epitomizes the oscillation in interpretations of the Apocalypse between present, immediate, application and future hope.

At the end of the sermon cited earlier in this chapter Bicheno appeals in prophetic style to an audience beyond the immediate:

> O ye nations! Ye nations! Prepare to meet your God. He cometh in his power, to rejudge the cause of the dead. He will break his enemies with a rod of iron, and dash them to pieces like a potter's vessel. Then ye servants of God, ye afflicted followers of Christ, look up, and lift up your heads, for your redemption draweth nigh. He that testifieth these things saith, surely I come quickly, amen. Even so, come lord Jesus. (*A Word in Season* 53 in Burdon 1997: 120)

One tendency in interpretation of the Apocalypse that has been emphasized in this commentary is the present application of its images, the attempt to articulate what they mean for, and demand of, the individual or society. So, 'Surely I come quickly' (22:20) is interpreted as an exhortation in The *Geneva Bible*: 'Seeing the Lord is at hand, we ought to be constant and rejoice, but we must beware we esteem not the length nor shortness of the Lords coming by our own imagination, 2. Pet. 3,9.' There are various understandings of how the heavenly vision can be anticipated on earth. For Charles Wesley it is in 'Love, the earnest of our heaven, / Love our full reward shall be, / Love shall crown us', the anticipation of the moment when 'We his open face shall see [cf. Rev 22:4]' ('Lift your heads, ye friends of Jesus' in Newport 2000: 43). For Blake, however, that future bliss can be glimpsed in art which 'is the Tree of Life', whereas 'Science is the Tree of Death' and 'Good and Evil are Riches and Poverty a Tree of Misery propagating Generation and Death' ('Laocoon' in Blake 1972: 777; cf. *Jerusalem* 86:18; 14:2 in Burdon 1997: 198). It is appropriate that the last word of this commentary should be given to one whose own visionary and prophetic life was inspired by the Bible's prime visionary text, and who demonstrated how the wider culture could be drawn into an apocalyptic message that is as inspirational as it is illuminating.

Few readers of the Apocalypse will dispute the fact that something rather different is going on in this text as compared with the rest of the New Testament. Even if, as has been hinted from time to time in the foregoing pages, the differences in underlying thought patterns between early Christian writers and their descendants are probably less than is often alleged, the problem remains of how one is to judge among the quite different readings of this book. We have pointed to a division in the interpretations between those that attend to the detail of the text, relating it to persons and events, past, present or future, and those where the apocalyptic images are used time and again to illuminate situations or to prompt new visionary experiences. In the former we have a close reading of the text; in the latter there is less detailed explanation and more concern with how the apocalyptic images can inform the present reality of an individual or a group. This commentary has emphasized readings in which interpreters are drawn into the visionary world of the Apocalypse, in such a way that their own prejudices and preferences and those of their contemporaries are confronted with an alternative perspective on divine and human affairs. Such juxtaposition of the book's images and the reality of the present is not too far removed from the position of the mature Luther, who wrote in in his later *Preface to the New Testament* that readers 'ought to read this book and learn to look upon Christendom with other eyes than those of reason'. Christians are to understand contemporary realities by holding them up along-side images from the Apocalypse.

Of course such readings are not without their problems. It is partly because of the peculiar character of many of the actualizations of the Apocalypse that it has provoked a mixture of incomprehension and distaste, as opponents are demonized and, very occasionally, imaginations are stirred to imitate the vio-lence the book describes. Its catalogue of disaster and destruction, apparently sanctioned by God, its cries for vengeance, and its terrible gloating over the fall of Babylon, all seem so contrary to the spirit of Jesus.

One thing that becomes clear from a survey of the history of the reception of the Apocalypse is that it is not so easy to pin down one original meaning of the text and then use that to evaluate the later interpretations, for the exegesis of such an allusive text is always going to resist the desire for an authoritative interpretation. Ultimately, the question of how to adjudicate among varying readings belongs to the interpretative community. Within the Christian com-munity, viewed in the broadest sense, what has been primarily determinative in making sense of the disparate collection we know as the Bible has been the fourfold story of Jesus. In this respect one may agree with Luther (though not with the way he minimizes the importance of figurative language for Christian theology), when he writes concerning the Apocalypse: 'it befits the apostolic office to speak of Christ and his deeds without figures but to teach Christ is the thing which an apostle above all else is bound to do, as He says in Acts 1: Ye shall be my witnesses. Therefore I stick to the books which give me Christ clearly and purely' (Luther, *Preface to the New Testament* 1522). The gospel stories constitute the framework for understanding what counts as faithfulness to Jesus. It is the memory of Jesus which is to be invoked, shared and wrestled with in the articulation of a contemporary faith. While Paul's writings may be chronologically prior, Christian faith is given shape by the gospels, not by the epistles (or for that matter the Apocalypse). The rest of the New Testament bears witness to a creative exploration of what faith may mean in new situations that are removed from the particularity of Jesus' circumstances.

If one were to expound the Apocalypse in such a way that its images led to a practice at odds with the pattern of Jesus' life, death and resurrection as found in the gospels, there would be an incompatibility with the gospel. That would apply just as much to Luther or other mainline interpreters as to the Mün-sterite Anabaptists. However imperfectly the Christian Church in its various branches has kept to this standard in practice, it has been unable to shake off the fact that the fundamental story which shapes its life is of a crucified messiah who refused armed struggle as a way of inaugurating the kingdom of God (Matt 26:53; John 18:36). Conformity to Christ (1 Cor. 11:1) depends on the indwelling Spirit who brings to mind the words of Jesus (John 15:26; cf. 1 Cor 3:16, Rev 1:10; 2:7; 4:2; 19:10; 21:10), as well as on engagement with the four-fold story of Jesus' career. The witness of Jesus in life and death is evident in the Apocalypse and must pervade interpretations of it. A Christian reading of the Apocalypse has its key in the person of Christ, the Lamb in the midst of the divine throne, standing as if it had been slaughtered (Rev 5). The orien-tation is towards Christ who is the faithful witness (Rev 3:14). Any inter-pretation which ends up in revolutionary violence, naïve complacency or self-congratulatory celebration misses the point, just as one that 'baptizes' the status quo and ignores the element of judgement in both the gospels and the Apocalypse. This means not only an ongoing struggle to identify and overcome the demons in ourselves but also confronting them in the institutions of Church and State.

Prophecy plays an important role in both Old and New Testaments, and the questions of how to evaluate the claim to prophetic insight which character-izes many of the appropriations of the Apocalypse is raised already in the Bible, as passages like 1 Kings 22, Jer 23 and 1 John 4:1 indicate. According to Deut 13, the false prophet is one who seeks to persuade hearers to worship other gods and be just like the other nations. John's apocalyptic prophecy obviously did not stand alone in the churches of his day, nor is it likely to have been unchallenged. By its nature, prophecy is not subject to control by neatly defined regulations. The difficulty of testing the prophetic spirit is made particularly clear in the book of Jeremiah (Jer 14:14; 23:9 and 27:9), as Jeremiah is con-fronted with prophets who proclaim peace and security, probably appealing to deeply ingrained religious sentiments about Zion, God's holy dwelling place. The prophet is often vindicated only by hindsight (Jer 26:18). Jeremiah's prophetic ministry found a parallel in Jesus' view that the true prophet can expect to suffer for his message (Luke 11:49), echoed also in the experience of Paul (2 Cor 11:23–33), who himself evokes Jeremiah's call to describe his own prophetic vocation (Gal 1:15; cf. Jer 1:5). Jeremiah's experience of persecution and rejection led to some of the most remarkable outbursts of the prophetic tradition, which link the prophet's obedience to his experience of negative social and psychological consequences. The prophet can expect to suffer because he or she has to utter the words of God to nations, peoples and lan-guages (Jer 1:10; cf. Rev 10:11).

The story of Jesus offers the world an alternative story. It gives the per-spective of the victim, of the Abels of this world who otherwise remain silent. One way of reading the Apocalypse is as revealing the true nature of a world in which violence and destruction are prevalent. The story of the Lamb who is slain offers a critique of human history and of our delusions, of the violence we use to maintain the status quo, and of the lies with which we disguise the oppression of the victim (Rowland 1998: 503–13).

In addition, from the very first explicit reference to the Apocalypse, by Justin in the middle of the second century, interpreters have recognized the importance of this book as a witness to the horizon of hope for Christian life and thought. In its hope the book transcends the focus of many New Testament writings on the individual or the small early Christian communities, continuing the great themes of prophetic hopes and also Jesus' proclamation of the kingdom of God. The Apocalypse is the foundation text for 'the principle of hope', to quote the title of Ernst Bloch's major study (1986). Those who look for the better world it promises find encouragement to engage in the task that features so prominently in the Apocalypse: bearing witness. To return to an example with which we began this study, from late twentieth-century Latin America: many who have experienced situations parallel to that of John on Patmos, of tribulation requiring endurance and wisdom, find that the Apocalypse speaks to them. They find in this prophecy a source of insight into situations of oppression and evil and also of new hope for the working out of God's gracious purposes for the whole world.

actualization. The reading of the biblical text in relation to new circumstances.

Alcázar, Luís de (1554–1613). A Jesuit who pioneered a reading of the Apocalypse linking its prophecies to the period of the early Church.

Alcuin (c.740–804). An English theologian and administrator.

Alexander Minorita (d. 1271). A Franciscan commentator from north Germany who pioneered a way of interpreting the images of the Apocalypse as a historical sequence. Influenced by Joachim of Fiore, he saw the rise of the Franciscan and Dominican orders as fulfilling Joachim's predictions.

Alsted, J. H. (1588–1638). A German in the Calvinist tradition who saw the sequences in the Apocalypse as referring to different periods in the history of the Church. He thought the millennium would begin at the end of the seventeenth century.

Anabaptists. A sixteenth-century movement which stressed that baptism was a personal pledge of faith of a committed believer. They rejected what they saw as the corrupt doctrines and practices of the Roman church, and the only partial reformation of the new Protestant churches, and sought to establish Christian communities based on their understanding of the early New Testament congregations. They were regarded as enemies of the state and hunted down, imprisoned or executed.

modern Mennonites, Hutterites and Amish trace their origins to sixteenth-century Anabaptism.

Andrew of Caesarea (late sixth and early seventh centuries). Author of a commentary, who helped ensure a place for the Apocalypse in Eastern Christianity. Influenced by Origen, he interpreted the Apocalypse in terms of the moral life.

Andrews, J. N. (1829–83). A Millerite and leader of the Seventh-Day Adventists. He suggested that the lamb-like Beast of Rev 13 was linked with the USA.

Anselm of Havelberg (twelfth century). An interpreter of the Apocalypse who expounded the seven seals as the seven periods of the church's history.

apocalypse. A text that purports to offer disclosure of heavenly secrets by vision, dream or audition.

apocalyptic. An adjective referring to that which is linked with revelation or the Apocalypse, the book of Revelation, often used as an alternative way of referring to apocalypticism.

Apocalypticism. A phenomenon in religion which is defined by either the form of the apocalypse (q.v.) or the contents of the various apocalypses. According to the first definition, apocalypticism is the religion characterized by ecstatic visionary experience in which divine mysteries beyond human understanding are communicated to humans. According to the latter definition, apocalypticism is a cluster of ideas corresponding to the contents of the Apocalypse (catastrophe, hope for a new world, and stark contrasts between good and evil).

Aquinas, Thomas (c.1225–74). A Dominican and the Christian church's major systematic theologian.

Arnold of Villanova (c.1240–1311). An interpreter in the Joachite tradition of Apocalypse interpretation.

Augustine of Hippo (354–430). The most influential theologian of Western Christianity, who first accepted the expectation of a this-worldly kingdom of God but in his classic *The City of God* adopted Tyconius' ecclesial interpretation and injected a note of agnosticism about the date and character of the future.

Aytinger, W. (fl. 1496). A German commentator on the revelations of Pseudo-Methodius.

Bale, John (1495–1563). A Renaissance interpreter of the Apocalypse who adopted the Augustinian contrast between two different communities modelled on Jerusalem and Babylon, and who found in the Roman Catholic Church (along with Islam) the latest manifestation of Babylon.

Beatus of Liébana (eighth century). A Spanish commentator who is an important resource for reconstructing the views of earlier commentators like Tyconius and whose commentaries prompted a tradition of illuminated manuscripts of the Apocalypse.

Bede (early eighth century). Chronicler of English Christianity, whose commentary on the Apocalypse relied heavily on earlier interpreters such as Tyconius and pioneered a sevenfold division of the text.

Bellarmine, Robert (1542–1621). A Jesuit interpreter who challenged sixteenth-century Protestants who used the Apocalypse to promote anti-Catholic views.

Bengel, J. A. (1687–1752). A German Pietist and distinguished biblical exegete, whose commentary on the

New Testament (*Gnomon Novi Testamenti*) had wide influence, including on John Wesley.

Berengaudus (c. ninth century). The first interpreter to explain the Apocalypse as a guide to the whole of history.

Bernard of Clairvaux (1090–1153). A monastic reformer and abbot of one of the chief centres of the Cistercian order.

Beza, Theodore (1519–1605). A Calvinist theologian, textual scholar and Calvin's successor in Geneva.

Bíblia Sagrada, São Paulo (1990). A Bible in Portuguese, which in the marginal notes of the pastoral version reflects many of the ideas of Latin American liberation theology.

Bicheno, James (d. 1831). A Nonconformist minister in southern England who linked the Apocalypse with the events surrounding the French Revolution.

Blake, William (1757–1827). An English artist, poet and visionary whose illuminated books represent a distinctive appropriation of the apocalyptic tradition. He was on the fringe of radical movements in London at the time of the French Revolution.

Boesak, Allan (1945–). A Reformed minister, president of the World Alliance of Reformed Churches, founder of the United Democratic Front, and a leader of the anti-apartheid struggle in South Africa in the 1980s.

Bonaventure (1221–74). A Franciscan who mediated between the radical Franciscans, who wished to take Francis's Rule literally, and those who sought a more realistic compromise. His views were influenced by Joachim of Fiore, and he shared a conviction about the eschatological significance of Francis inspired by the Apocalypse.

Bosch, Hieronymus (c.1450–1516). A painter who depicted John on Patmos and whose pictures are pervaded with the ethos of the Apocalypse.

Bossuet, J.-B. (1627–1704). A French Roman Catholic preacher who rejected anti-Catholic interpretations of the Apocalypse and found in it prophecies relating to the first five centuries of the Church's existence.

Botticelli, Sandro (1444–1510). An Italian painter whose depiction of the nativity of Christ is linked with the fulfilment of the prophecies of the Apocalypse at the time of Savonarola (q.v.).

Breviloquium. A fourteenth-century Joachite interpretation of the Apocalypse influenced by Peter John Olivi and Arnold of Villanova.

Brightman, Thomas (1562–1607). An Anglican Calvinist who reproached the churches of the Reformation for the inadequacy of their reforms.

Brothers, Richard (1757–1824). Prophet and interpreter of the Apocalypse who on his own authority linked its prophecies with late eighteenth-century England. He thought of himself as messiah and was part of the rich prophetic tradition at the end of the eighteenth century in England.

Browning, Robert (1812–89). An English poet who, like Blake, was influenced by the Apocalypse (e.g. in his poem *Sordello*) and who reacted against the effects of higher criticism of the Bible.

Buldesdorf, Nicholas (d. 1446). The author of *Testimonies of the Holy Spirit in Prophecies* who was much influenced by Joachite ideas. He was burnt at the stake after the Council of Basel.

Bullinger, Heinrich (1504–75). A Swiss reformer, follower of Zwingli, and the major commentator on the Apocalypse among the magisterial reformers. His sermons on the Apocalypse were translated into English in 1561.

Bunyan, John (1628–88). A preacher and member of an independent congregation in Bedford, and opponent of the Catholic tendencies in the Church of England, who was imprisoned for his beliefs. His spiritual classic *The Pilgrim's Progress* reflects the narrative direction of the Apocalypse.

Byron, George, Lord (1788–1824). An English poet.

Calvin, John (1509–64). A theologian and reformer whose pioneering theological polity paved the way for Reformed Christianity.

Cary, Mary (1621–c.1663). A Fifth Monarchist who regarded the saints on earth as the agents of Christ's eschatological victory in setting up his kingdom on earth.

Cerinthus (fl. c.100). A Christian teacher whose views are known only through the reports of church fathers such as Irenaeus; he apparently held that the world was created not by the supreme God but by an inferior being.

Chiliasm. *See* **millennialism**.

Coleridge, Samuel Taylor (1772–1834). An English poet and theologian, whose early poetry reflects a willingness to use the Apocalypse to interpret the events of the French Revolution. He mediated the new German biblical criticism while being critical of its reductionist tendencies.

Constantine (d. 337). The first Christian emperor, whose rule began in 306.

Cowper, William (1731–1800). An English poet.

Cranach, Lucas (1472–1553). An illustrator of the Apocalypse for Luther's Bible of 1522.

Cruz, Francisco de la (d. 1578). An early millenarian interpreter in the context of the Americas.

Cyprian (d. 258). A Latin church father who used the Apocalypse to interpret the life of the Church and the crises of his day.

Dante, Alighieri (1265–1321). An Italian poet and political theorist whose *Divine Comedy* is infused with apocalyptic elements and who was influenced by the Joachite ideas current in his day.

Darby, John Nelson (1800–82). An Anglican priest who became a leader of the Plymouth Brethren and interpreted the prophecies of the Apocalypse as referring to future events (including the millennium).

Darwin, Erasmus (1731–1802). Physician, poet and scientist; grandfather of Charles Darwin.

Decoding. The presentation of apocalyptic images in another, less allusive form, thereby claiming to show by detailed explanation what the text *really* means.

Deissmann, Adolf (1866–1937). A professor of New Testament at the University of Berlin, whose support for the German cause in the First World War shocked Karl Barth.

Dell, William (fl. 1649). A chaplain to the New Model Army in the English Civil War and supporter of the radical cause.

Deutz, Rupert of (c.1075–1129). Abbot of Deutz in Germany and exponent of a historical exposition of the Apocalypse, which did not link it closely with events of his own day.

Dionysius of Alexandria (third century). A pupil of Origen and bishop who disputed the chiliastic interpretation and challenged the apostolic authorship of the Apocalypse.

Donne, John (1571–1631). An English priest and poet.

Durden, Ralph (fl. 1585). A man who received an apocalyptic vision and a vocation to be Elijah and the Lamb who could open the sealed book of the Apocalypse.

Duvet, Jean (c.1485–1561). An engraver who produced a series of woodcuts on the Apocalypse.

Edwards, Jonathan (1703–58). A North American Puritan preacher and revivalist.

Eichhorn, Johann Gottfried (1752–1827). An early historical interpreter of the Apocalypse who relates the text to the events of the first century.

Eixemenis, Francesco (1827–1409). A Franciscan writer an theology and philosophy from Catalonia.

Eliot, George (1819–80). An English novelist.

Eliot, John (1604–90). The 'apostle to the Indians', translator of the Bible into Algonquian and proponent of Fifth Monarchy ideas.

English Civil War. A struggle between supporters of Charles I and Parliament that embraced most parts of the British Isles between 1642 and 1649. It led to the king's defeat and execution in 1649.

Epiphanius of Salamis (d. 403). Writer of *Panarion*, a large-scale description and rebuttal of ancient Christian heresies.

Felgenhauer, Paul (1593–1677). Interpreter of apocalyptic writings, mystic and critic of ecclesiastical authorities in Germany.

Fifth Monarchists. A group particularly active in the mid-seventeenth century who believed that the fifth kingdom of God or Christ, predicted in Daniel 2 and 7, would succeed the evil empires of the world, and that it might be set up by the violent intervention of the saints.

Foster, George (fl. 1650). A visionary inspired by the Apocalypse whose message linked him with Winstanley and the Levellers.

Foxe, John (1516–87). An apologist for the English Reformation (in his *Acts and Monuments*) who related the Apocalypse to events happening in church and society.

Francis of Assisi (1182–1226). Founder of the Franciscan order. His uncompromising commitment to the way of life of Jesus of Nazareth led to a rigorous Rule for his order which became the subject of controversy after his death. One group, the Spiritual Franciscans, sought to be faithful to the letter of the Rule of Francis, particularly in not owning property, and argued against the practices of more moderate Franciscans. Chief among the radical Franciscans was Peter John Olivi, who wrote in support of the Spirituals' position, as well on the Apocalypse.

Frederick II (1194–1250). Holy Roman emperor, excommunicated by Pope Gregory IX for linking the pope with figures from the Apocalypse.

Fulke, William (1538–89). An English Puritan and apologist for Protestantism.

Galloway, Joseph (1730–1803). A lawyer born in Maryland who devoted himself to the study of biblical prophecies.

Geneva Bible. A sixteenth-century Calvinist translation of the Bible into English. Its marginal notes often relate the text of the Apocalypse to the religious upheavals of its own time.

Gifford, George (1548–1600). A Puritan and translator of William Fulke's commentary on the Apocalypse from Latin, whose preaching reflects events round about the time of the Spanish Armada.

Gill, John (1698–1771). A Baptist commentator.

Gillray, James (1756–1815). A satirist and painter of *Presages of the Millenium* [*sic*].

Gnosticism. A blanket term to describe a variety of texts and movements from about the second century CE onwards. Some of these involve revealed knowledge (*gnosis*) through apocalypses, often involving a complex mythological explanation of the origin of both God and the world. The Nag Hammadi gnostic documents indicate a great diversity among the texts and groups.

Grotius, Hugo (1583–1645). A theologian and lawyer, who advocated an interpretative approach to the Apocalypse which linked the images with the first century CE.

Hazzard, Dorothy (d. 1674). Founding member of Broad Mead Baptist Church in Bristol. Her support for Anabaptism led her to separate from the Church of England.

Herder, J. R. (1744–1803). A poet and literary critic who shared the historicist approach to the Apocalypse while at the same time looking for ways in which its vision could illuminate the present life of the reader.

Hildegard of Bingen (1098–1179). An abbess and prophet whose writings, especially the visionary *Scivias* (completed in 1151), are pervaded with imagery from the Apocalypse.

Hippolytus (d. 235). A leader and later schismatic bishop of the Church in Rome, who collected eschatological material from Scripture in *On the Antichrist*, and whose commentary on Daniel is the earliest on an apocalyptic text. In both works there is little attempt to relate the Scriptures to contemporary events.

Hoffman, Melchior (c.1500–c.1543). An Anabaptist sympathizer who influenced those who established the apocalyptic commonwealth in Münster.

Hölderlin, Johann Christian Friedrich (1770–1843). German lyric poet.

Houteff, Victor (1885–1955). A Seventh-Day Adventist leader and supporter of Ellen White's vocation as a prophet.

Hugo, Victor (1802–55). A French novelist.

Hus, Jan (1369–1415). A Czech reformer put to death at the Council of Constance. He was influenced by Wyclif.

Innocent III (1160–1216). A pope who was intimately involved with the promotion of the Dominican and Franciscan orders.

Irenaeus of Lyons (late second century). Early Christian bishop who was an early exponent of chiliasm, or millennialism, which sees the fulfilment of God's purposes in a this-worldly millennium.

Irving, Edward (1792–1834). Early nineteenth-century preacher and founder of the Catholic Apostolic Church.

Jacopone da Todi (1230–1306). A poet and supporter of the Franciscan Spirituals who became a Franciscan lay brother.

Jansz, Anna (d. 1539). An Anabaptist martyr who was influenced by its early apocalypticism. *En route* to her untimely death at the stake, she left a moving testament to her infant son.

Jerome (c.340–420). The biblical scholar who was responsible for the Vulgate, the Latin translation of the Bible, and reviser of Victorinus' (q.v.) commentary. His position on the Apocalypse largely parallels that of Augustine.

Joachim of Fiore (c.1135–1202). Arguably the most influential interpreter of the Apocalypse, he saw the book as the key to Scripture and the whole of history. He opened up the possibility of a this-worldly application, which had a decisive influence on late medieval politics and spirituality.

John of the Cross (1542–91). A mystic and exponent of a reading of the Apocalypse which related it to the spiritual life.

Jonson, Ben (1572–1637). A sixteenth-century playwright.

Jost, Ursula (c.1539). An Anabaptist visionary and contemporary of Melchior Hoffman.

Jung, C. J. (1875–1961). A pioneer psychoanalyst who interpreted the differences between the Apocalypse and the other Johannine writings as indicating a change in John's psychology.

Justin (mid-second century). An early Christian theologian and apologist who expected the coming of God's kingdom on earth and based this on Rev 20. He offers one of the earliest witnesses to the apostolic authority of the book.

Justinian (485–565). Roman emperor from 527 who sought to establish the political and religious unity of the empire.

Keach, Benjamin (1640–1704). An interpreter who saw in the advent of William of Orange a sign of the last things and the beginning of the ultimate opposition to Rome.

Keats, John (1795–1821). An English poet.

Kempe, Margery (c.1373–1438). Author of an early English spiritual autobiography (*The Book of Margery Kempe*).

who was suspected of sympathy with the Lollards.

Kershaw, James (c.1730–97). A Methodist who believed that the end of the present age would come in 2000.

Knowlys, H. (1598–1691). An independent Baptist writing around 1688 when there was fear of a return of Roman Catholicism in England.

Koresh, David (Vernon Howell, 1959–93). Leader of the Branch Davidians, who was killed when the sect's compound was stormed by US federal troops in 1993. Coming from an Adventist background, he seems to have claimed to be one of the eschatological agents found in the Apocalypse. His change of name involves a claim to messianic status based on Isaiah 45.

Lactantius (c.250–325). A Christian apologist and author of the *Divine Institutes* who espoused a this-worldly eschatological expectation.

LaHaye, T. (1926–) and **Jenkins, J. B.** (1949–). Authors of the 'Left Behind' series of novels, which draw heavily on the interpretation of the Apocalypse and other eschatological texts from the Bible in the *Scofield Reference Bible*.

Lambert, Francis (c.1486–1530). A reformer from Hesse and later a follower of Zwingli, who wrote one of earliest Reformation commentaries on the Apocalypse, which he saw as a prediction of the triumph of the just within history.

Langland, William (c.1330–1400). English author of *Piers Plowman*.

Lawrence, D. H. (1885–1930). An English novelist who devoted the later years of his life to the study of the Apocalypse, which he regarded as the product of 'a second-rate mind'.

Lead, Jane (1624–1704). A mystic and visionary whose revelations use the Apocalypse to describe the soul's journey to be reunited with the divine Wisdom (Sophia).

Lee, Anne (1736–84). The leader of the Shakers (q.v.). A revivalist movement which originated in England but moved to North America. She was believed by her followers to be the Woman Clothed with the Sun of Rev 12.

Lindsey, Hal (1930–). An American evangelist whose *The Late Great Planet Earth* has sold hundreds of thousands of copies. He relates late twentieth-century persons and events to the symbols of the Apocalypse, following an interpretative approach similar to that in the *Scofield Reference Bible*.

Lollards (c.1382–1430). A late medieval reform movement, based on the writings and teachings of the Oxford theologian John Wyclif. The term 'Lollard' was an abusive term for heretical religious views.

Lllul Raimon (c.1233–c.1315). Spanish lay philosopher, mystic and missionary who wanted to convert Muslims to Christianity.

Luther, Martin (1483–1546). An Augustinian monk who became the leader of the Reformation in Germany. He initially challenged the authority of the Apocalypse in his 1522 *Preface to the New Testament*, but in the 1546 *Preface* he took a much more positive approach and welcomed its different perspective on the church and the world.

Mather, Cotton (1663–1728). A Boston minister and millennial preacher.

Matthijs, Jan (c.1500–1534). Anabaptist leader in Münster, along with Jan van Leiden. Matthijs died while leading what appears to have been a suicidal sortie, seemingly at divine prompting.

Mayer, L. Composer of a pamphlet in 1803 which related the images of the Apocalypse to England's struggle with France in the Napoleonic Wars.

Mede, Joseph (1586–1638). Fellow of Christ's College, Cambridge, who was a proponent of a recapitulative reading which sees the different sequences of the Apocalypse as overlapping in time. Though he was not involved in politics, the implicit imminent expectation of his minute exegetical calculations gave an impetus to future hope in the seventeenth century.

Melville, Herman (1819–91). An American novelist.

Memling, Hans (c.1440–94). Painter of the altar-piece in the Hospital of Saint John, Bruges.

Methodius of Olympus (d. 311). An interpreter who used the Apocalypse to promote the ascetical life.

Methodius, Pseudo- (late seventh century). The anonymous author of a commentary on the Apocalypse, mistakenly attributed to the fourth-century bishop Methodius is of Olympus, which reflects on the rise of Islam.

Meyer, Sebastian (1465–1546). A leader of the Reformation in Bern who published a commentary on the Apocalypse in 1539, following the tradition of Francis Lambert except in its rejection of Joachim's influence. He influenced John Bale.

Miller, William (1782–1849). Founder of the Seventh-Day Adventists, who predicted the return of Christ in 1843–4. The mutation of the group's shattered hopes offers a paradigm for the way in which an eschatologically orientated group deals with disappointment.

Millennialism, or **chiliasm**. The view that the millennium, the 1000-year kingdom promised in Rev 20, will be established on earth.

Milton, John (1609–74). Poet, Nonconformist, anti-monarchist and apologist for the Commonwealth in England from 1649 to 1660.

Montanus (mid-second century). Founder of a prophetic movement in Phrygia (in modern Turkey). which claimed inspiration by the Spirit-Paraclete and expected the New Jerusalem in Phrygia.

Moulin, Pierre du (1558–1658). A French Reformed theologian whose book *The Fulfilment of Prophecies* (1624) predicted the date 1689 as the end of the Beast's reign.

Münster. The site of an Anabaptist apocalyptic commonwealth (1533–5), led by Jan Matthijs (d. 1534) and Jan Bockelson (1509–36, also known as John of Leiden). which was brutally repressed.

Muentzer, Thomas (c.1485–1525). A radical reformer, whose mix of mysticism with the practice of revolutionary change led him to participate in the Peasants' Revolt, in which he was defeated and executed in 1525.

Muggleton, Ludowick (1609–98). English founder of a sect in 1652; he and John Reeve claimed to be the witnesses of Rev 11.

Napier, John (1550–1617). A Scottish mathematician whose systematization of the images in the Apocalypse had a wide circulation.

Newton, Isaac (1642–1727). A distinguished and influential mathematician from Trinity College, Cambridge, who looked in biblical *prophecy* for the same kind of providential arrangement of history and eschatology that he found in the laws of nature.

Olivi, Peter John (c.1248–98). A philosopher, theologian and leader of the radical Franciscans who identified Francis as the angel of the sixth seal. He initiated the critique of Rome that was to have widespread influence in subsequent centuries.

Origen (c.185–235). A leading third-century theologian and exegete, based in Alexandria and later in Caesarea, who was tortured for his faith. Rejecting this-worldly hopes, he explored the christology of the Apocalypse and its relevance for the spiritual life.

Paine, Tom (1737–1809). An English rationalist, political reformer, and campaigner who had great influence on revolutionary politics in France and North America.

Papias. An early second-century Christian bishop of Hierapolis and early witness to the chiliastic tradition in second-century Christianity. Fragments of his work are preserved by Irenaeus and Eusebius.

Pareus, David (1548–1622). A professor at Heidelberg, a Calvinist who applied the Apocalypse to the contemporary Church, especially the papacy.

Pirie, Alexander (fl. 1794). A writer who connected the Apocalypse with the French Revolution.

Priestley, Joseph (1733–1804). A Unitarian and a scientist (the discoverer of oxygen), who related the Apocalypse to the French Revolution.

Primasius of Hadrumetum (mid-sixth century). A commentator who was dependent on Tyconius (q.v.).

Prous Boneta, Na (c.1297–c.1325). A member of the Beguins, a lay religious movement often suspected of heresy (as evidenced by the trial of Marguerite Porete), and follower of Peter Olivi, who opposed the church's hostility to the radical Franciscans. A visionary, she was burnt at the stake.

Quarles, Francis (1592–1664). An English poet.

Raphael, Sanzio (1483–1520). An Italian painter.

Reeve, John (fl. 1652). An English visionary who believed he was commissioned, along with Ludowick Muggleton, to be one of the two witnesses of Rev 11.

Ribera, Francisco (1537–91). A Jesuit from Salamanca, who proposed a futurist interpretation of the Apocalypse to counteract its contemporary application by many Protestant exegetes who linked Babylon with the Roman church.

Ridley, Nicholas (c.1500–55). An English bishop and martyr.

Rossetti, Christina (1830–94). A poet and part of the Pre-Raphaelite circle in nineteenth-century England, whose poetry often reflects the Apocalypse.

Rupescissa (or Roquettillade, d. 1362). An interpreter of the Apocalypse in the Franciscan Spiritualist tradition who entered the Minorite order in 1322.

Saladin (1137–93). Sultan of Egypt who captured Jerusalem.

Savonarola, Girolamo (1452–98). An apocalyptic visionary and Dominican preacher in Florence, who was put to death in 1498. He predicted a time of trial and hardship for the Church, which would later be reformed.

Scofield Reference Bible. An edition of the Bible with marginal notes by Cyrus Scofield, which largely followed the approach of John Nelson Darby (q.v.).

Sewall, Samuel (1652–1730). A New England magistrate who corresponded with Cotton Mather about the interpretation of the Apocalypse and its applicability to the New England settlements.

Shakers. A radical Protestant group which emerged in England in the eighteenth century and transferred to America, led by Anne Lee (q.v.).

Shelley, P. B. (1792–1822). An English poet, whose *Prometheus Unbound* reflects the influence of the Apocalypse.

Southcott, Joanna (1750–1814). A visionary who made an enormous impact on early nineteenth-century England when, at the age of 64, she claimed to be the Woman Clothed with the Sun and the one to bear the messiah, Shiloh. Her self-understanding and her prophecies were pervaded by the imagery of the Apocalypse.

Spenser, Edmund (1552–99). Author of *The Faerie Queene* and member of the fledgling Protestant Elizabethan state.

Stringfellow, William (1928–85). A civil rights activist, lawyer and theologian, who spoke of the struggle between Jerusalem and Babylon in the context of protests against the war in Vietnam.

Suárez, Francisco (1548–1617). A Spanish Jesuit theologian.

Sutcliffe, Joseph (1762–1856). An early Methodist who related the symbols of the Apocalypse to the events of the late eighteenth century.

Swedenborg, Emanuel (1688–1772). A visionary and voluminous writer who discussed interrelations between the human and the divine, and claimed to have visionary insight into the spiritual world.

Sylvester. Name of two different popes, the first from the fourth century, who was a contemporary of Constantine, the first Christian emperor, and the second from the tenth century.

Taborites. The radical followers of Jan Hus, who in the fifteenth century sought to establish God's reign on earth by violent means.

Taylor, Thomas (1738–1816). An early Methodist preacher.

Tertullian (c.160–c.220). An early Christian theologian, writing in Latin, who became a member of an apocalyptic sect, the Montanists. Like Justin and Irenaeus, he rejected attempts to spiritualize the Christian hope and asserted the this-worldly fulfilment of the divine promises.

Thruston, Frederic (fl. 1812). An Anglican priest whose interpretation of the Apocalypse gave a salvific role to England and the Church of England in the fulfilment of the divine promises.

Tillinghast, John (1604–55). An interpreter who read the Apocalypse as a sequence of events from the apostolic times to the end of the world.

Towers, Joseph (fl. 1790). Interpreter of the Apocalypse in the context of the French Revolution and in support of liberal causes. His writing on biblical prophecy was suppressed by the British Prime Minister William Pitt.

Trapnel, Anna (fl. 1654). A Fifth Monarchist (q.v.) whose visions, inspired by the Apocalypse, reflect political dissatisfaction with the Commonwealth.

Turner, J. M. W. (1775–1851). An English painter.

Tyconius (d. c.400). A member of the Donatist Church in North Africa and leading biblical exegete whose *Book of Rules* influenced Augustine. His influential commentary on the Apocalypse, which emphasizes the contemporary more than the eschatological import of the visions, is no longer extant, but it is quoted by later commentators, including Beatus of Liébana and Bede.

Tyndale, William (c.1492–1536). A biblical translator.

Ubertino of Casale (c.1259–c.1330). A leading Franciscan Spiritual and follower of Olivi who identified Pope Boniface VIII (1294–1303) with the Antichrist.

Valerian (193–260). Roman emperor.

Velasquez, Diego de Silvay (1599–1660). A Spanish painter.

Victorinus (d. 304). Bishop in Slovenia and author of the first surviving commentary on the Apocalypse. He looked for a this-worldly millennium but also saw the images as having a relevance for the church of his day.

Waldensians. A group founded by Peter Waldo in the twelfth century which challenged the practices of the church.

Ward Howe, Julia (1819–1910). Poet, reformer and author of 'The Battle Hymn of the Republic'.

Wentworth, Anne (fl. 1679). A Baptist who used the Apocalypse to interpret her ejection from her family home by her husband.

Wesley, Charles (1707–80). An Early Methodist theologian and hymn writer, brother of John.

Wesley, John (1707–88). An Anglican priest, evangelist and founder of Methodism.

Whiston, William (1667–1732). Professor of mathematics at Cambridge, following Isaac Newton, who translated the works of Josephus. He believed that a pre-millennial period would begin in 1716 and that the world would end in 2000.

White, Ellen (1827–1915). An Adventist prophet, esteemed by Branch Davidians, who asserted that the USA was the second beast of Rev 13.

Whitefield, George (1714–71). An English Methodist preacher who also preached widely in North America.

Wilkinson, Henry (fl. 1640). A preacher of the English Civil War period.

Willet, Andrew (1562–1621). A Puritan theologian and biblical commentator.

Winstanley, Gerrard (1609–76). A leader of the Digger commune in Surrey. He believed that the Beast and Babylon were manifest in the monarchy, the magistracy, the army and the Church.

Witham, R. (d. 1778). A Roman Catholic commentator whose *Annotations on the NT* (1733) included refutation of anti-Catholic readings of the Apocalypse.

Wordsworth, William (1770–1850). An English poet.

Wyclif, John (c.1324–1384). An English theologian who attacked abuses in the church and a forerunner of the later Reformation. His writings influenced Jan Hus in Bohemia.

Yoder, John Howard (1927–97). A Mennonite theologian who was in large part responsible for the renewal of interest in the Anabaptist tradition in the late twentieth century.

Primary Sources

Alexander Minorita 1955: *Expositio in Apocalypsim*, ed. A. Wachtel. Weimar: Boelhaus.

The Ante-Nicene Fathers, 1994: ed. A. Roberts and J. Donaldson, 10 vols. Peabody, Mass.: Hendrickson.

Augustine 1957–72: *The City of God against the Pagans*, ed. and tr. William Chase Greene, 7 vols. Loeb Classical Library. Cambridge, Mass.: Harvard University Press.

—— 1984: *The City of God against the Pagans*, ed. H. Bettenson, intro. by D. Knowles. Harmondsworth: Penguin.

Bale, J. 1849: *Select Works of Bishop Bale*. Cambridge: Cambridge University Press.

Beatus of Liébana 1930: *In Apocalypsin Libri Duodecimi*, ed. H. A. Sanders. Rome: American Academy.

Bettenson, H. 1982: *The Early Christian Fathers*. Oxford: Oxford University Press.

Blake, W. 1972: *The Complete Writings*, ed. G. Keynes. Oxford: Oxford University Press.

—— 1981: *The Paintings and Drawings of William Blake*, ed. M. Butlin, 2 vols. New Haven: Yale University Press.

—— 1991–5: *William Blake's Illuminated Books*, gen. ed. D. Bindman, 6 vols. London: Tate Gallery Publications/William Blake Trust. M. Paley (ed.), *Jerusalem*; A. Lincoln (ed.), *Songs of Innocence and of Experience*; M. Eaves, R. N. Esssick and J. Viscomi (eds), *The Early Illuminated Books*; D. Doerrbecker (ed.), *The Continental Prophecies*; R. Essick and J. Viscomi (eds), *Milton: a Poem*; and D. Worrall (ed.), *The Urizen Books*.

——2000: *The Complete Illuminated Books*, ed. D. Bindman. London: Thames and Hudson.

The Book of Common Prayer According to the Use of the Episcopal Church 1977: The Church Hymnal Corporation.

The Book of Common Prayer and Administration of the Sacraments. Oxford: Oxford University Press.

Bradstock, A. and Rowland, C. 2002: *Radical Christian Writings: A Reader*. Oxford: Blackwell.

Bunyan, J. Brothers, Richard 1795: *A Revealed Knowledge of the Prophecies and the Times*. Philadelphia: Bailey.

Bunyan, J. 1862: *The Whole Works of John Bunyan*, ed. K. Offor, 3 vols. London.

——1967: *Pilgrim's Progress*. London: Dent.

Charlesworth, J. H. 1983–5: *The Old Testament Pseudepigrapha*, 2 vols. New York: Doubleday.

Coleridge, S. T. 1912: *The Complete Works of Samuel Taylor Coleridge*, ed. E. M. Coleridge, 2 vols. Oxford.

——1993: *Poems*, ed. J. Beer. London: Dent.

Cowper, W. 1934: *The Poetical Works of William Cowper*, ed. H. S. Milford. Oxford: Oxford University Press.

Dante Alighieri 1995: *The Divine Comedy*, ed. A. Mandelbaum. London: Dent.

Davies, L. E. 1995: *The Prophetic Writings of Lady Eleanor Davies*, ed. E. S. Cope. Oxford: Oxford University Press.

Deuschler, F., Hoffeld, J. and Nickel, H. 1971: *The Cloisters Apocalypse*, vol. 1: Facsimile; vol. 2: Commentaries. New York: The Metropolitan Museum of Art.

The Divine Office 1974: *The Liturgy of the Hours According to the Roman Rite as Renewed by Decree of the Second Vatican Council and Promulgated by the Authority of Pope Paul VI*. London: Collins, vol. 2.

Eusebius 1965: *Ecclesiastical History*, ed. Kirsopp Lake, 2 vols. Cambridge, Mass.: Harvard University Press.

Foxe, J. 1583: *Actes and Monuments of Matters Most Speciall and Memorable*, 8 vols. London.

——1587: *Eicasmi seu meditationes in sacram Apocalypsin*. London: Byshop.

The Geneva Bible 1578: London: Barker.

Grubb, N. 1997: *Revelations: Art of the Apocalypse*. New York: Abbeville.

Hildegard of Bingen 1990: *Scivias*, eds and trs C. Hart and J. Bishop, intro. by B. Newman. New York: Paulist.

——1997: *An Anthology*, ed. and tr. F. Bowie. Oxford: Lion Giftlines.

Hugo, Victor 1996: *Les Misérables*. Harmondswerth: Penguin.

The Hymnal 1982, according to the use of The Episcopal Church [USA]. New York: The Church Hymnal Corporation.

Hymns Ancient and Modern: New Standard 1983: Beccles: Hymns Ancient and Modern.

Joachim of Fiore 1953: *Il Libro delle Figure dell' Abate Gioachino da Fiore*, vol. ii, ed. L. Tondelli, M. Reeves and B. Hirsch-Reich. Turin: Società editrice internazionale.

John of the Cross 1979: *The Collected Works of St John of the Cross*, tr. K. Kavanaugh and O. Rodriguez, 2 vols. Washington, DC: ICS Publications.

Kempe, M. 1985: *The Book of Margery Kempe*, ed. B. Windeatt. Harmondsworth: Penguin.

Kerssenbrock 1891: Extracts from chronicle of events in Münster 1534–5 in English tr. in Baring-Gould 1891: 195–371.

Lactantius 2003: *Divine Institutes, Translated with Notes and Introduction*, ed. A. Bowen and P. Garnsey. Liverpool: Liverpool University Press.

LaHaye, T. and Jenkins, J. B. 1995: *Left Behind*. 1996: *The Tribulation Force*. 1997: *Nicolae*. 1998: *Soul Harvest*. 1999: *Apollyon*. 1999: *Assassins*. 2000: *The Indwelling*. 2000: *The Mark*. 2001: *The Desecration*. 2002: *The Remnant*. Wheaton: Tyndale House.

Lake, K. 1912: *The Apostolic Fathers*. London: Heinemann.

Langland, W. 1990: *Piers Plowman: An Alliterative Verse Translation*, ed, E. T. Donaldson. New York: Norton.

Lectionary for Mass for Use in the Dioceses of the United States 1998: Second typical edition. Washington, DC: Confraternity of Christian Doctrine.

Lee, H., Reeves, M. and Silano, G. 1989: *Western Mediterranean Prophecy: The School of Joachim of Fiore and the Fourteenth Century* Breviloquium. Toronto: Pontifical Institute of Medieval Studies.

The Library of Nicene and Post-Nicene Fathers 1994: ed. P. Schaff, series 1: 14 vols; series 2: 14 vols. Peabody, Mass.: Hendrickson.

Lilburne, J. 1971: *Come out of Her My People*. The Rota, University of Exeter: Menston (reprint of British Museum edn of 1639).

Lindsey, H. 1970: *The Late Great Planet Earth*. London: Lakeland.

——1973: *There's a New World Coming*. New York: Bantam Books.

Llull, Ramón 1993: *Doctor Illuminatus: A Ramón Llull Reader*, ed. A. Bonner. Princeton: Princeton University Press.

McGinn, B. 1979: *Apocalyptic Spirituality: Treatises and Letters of Lactantius, Adso of Montier-en-Der, Joachim of Fiore, the Franciscan Spirituals, Savonarola*. London: SPCK.

Mede, J. 1632: *Clavis Apocalyptica*. Cambridge: Buck.

——1650: *The Key of Revelation*, tr. R. More. London.

Mekilta of R. Ishmael 1956: ed. J. Z. Lauterbach. Philadelphia: Jewish Publication Society of America.

Melville, Herman 1970: *The Writings of Herman Melville*, ed. H. Hayford. Evanston, Ill.: Northwestern University Press.

Milton, J. 1962: *The Complete Prose Works*, ed. D. M. Wolfe. New Haven: Yale University Press.

——1980: *The Complete Poems*, ed. B. A. Wright, intro by G. Campbell, new edn. London: Dent.

——1991: *Milton: Political Writings*, ed. M. Dzelzanis. Cambridge: Cambridge University Press.

Muentzer, T. 1988: *The Collected Works of Thomas Müntzer*, ed. and tr. P. Matheson. Edinburgh: T&T Clark.

Musurillo, H. 1972: *Acts of the Christian Martyrs*. Oxford: Clarendon Press.

Origen 1966: *On First Principles*, tr. G. W. Butterworth. New York: Harper & Row.

——1976: *Homélies sur la Genèse*, ed. L. Doutreleau. SC 23. Paris: Du Cerf.

——1979: *An Exhortation to Martyrdom, Prayer, First Principles; Book IV, Prologue to the Commentary on the Song of Songs, Homily 27 on Numbers*, tr. R. A. Greer. The Classics of Western Spirituality. London: SPCK; New York: Paulist.

——1998: Selections from his works, in Joseph Trigg (ed. and tr.), *Origen*. London: Routledge, 67–240.

Revelation: its grand climax at hand! 1988: New York: Watchtower Bible and Tract Society.

Revised Common Lectionary 1992: Consultation on Common Texts. Nashville: Abingdon.

Ribera, F. 1593: *In Sacram Beati Ioanni Apostoli et Evangelistae Apocalypsin Commentari*. Lugduni.

Schmidt, F. 1938: *Das Buch mit sieben Siegeln: aus der Offenbarung des Johannes*. Vienna: Universal.

Scofield, C. I. 1917: *The Scofield Reference Bible: The Holy Bible with a New System of Connected Topical References to all the Greater Themes of Scripture, with Annotations, Revised Marginal Renderings, Summaries, Definitions, Chronology, and Index to which are added helps at hard places, explanations of seeming discrepancies, and a new system of paragraphs*. Oxford: Milford, Oxford University Press.

Shelley, P. B. 1960: *The Complete Poetical Works of Percy Bysshe Shelley*, ed. T. Hutchinson. Oxford: Oxford University Press.

——1977: *Shelley's Poetry and Prose*, ed. D. H. Reiman and S. B. Powers. New York: Norton.

Sheppard, G. T. 1989: *The Geneva Bible* (The Annotated New Testament, 1602 edition). New York: Pilgrim.

Spenser, E. 1980: *The Faerie Queene*, ed. A. C. Hamilton. London: Longman.

Trapnel, A. 2000: *The Cry of a Stone*, ed. H. Hinds. Tempe: Arizona University Press.

Tyconius 1963: *The Turin Fragments of Tyconius' Commentary on Revelation*, ed. F. LoBue. Cambridge: Cambridge University Press.

——1989: *The Book of Rules*, tr. W. S. Babcock. Atlanta, Ga.: Scholars Press.

Tyndale, William 2000: *The Obedience of a Christian Man*, ed. D. Daniell. Harmondsworth: Penguin.

Van Braght, T. J. 1950: *Martyrs Mirror*. Scottdale, Pa.: Herald Press.

Vermes, G. 1997: *The Complete Dead Sea Scrolls*. Harmondsworth: Penguin.

Victorinus 1916: *In Apocalypsin*, in *Victorini episcopi Petavionensis opera*, ed. J. Haussleiter. CSEL 49: Vienna: F. Tempsky.

—— 1997: *Sur l'Apocalypse: Introduction, texte critique, traduction, commentaire*, ed. M. Dulaey, SC 423. Paris: Du Cerf.

Walton, W. 1931: *Belshazzar's Feast*. Oxford: Oxford University Press.

Wesley, J. 1975: *The Works of J. Wesley*, ed. A. C. Outter. Oxford: Clarendon Press.

Williams, J. 1991: *A Spanish Apocalypse: the Morgan Beatus Manuscript*. New York: George Braziller.

—— 1994: *The Illustrated Beatus: A Corpus of the Illustrations of the Commentary on the Apocalypse: Introduction*. London: Harvey Miller.

Winstanley, G. 1941: *Works*, ed. G. H. Sabine. Ithaca, NY: Cornell University Press.

Wordsworth, W. 1966–7: *The Poetical Works*, ed. E. de Selincourt and H. Darbishire. Oxford: Clarendon Press.

Wyclif, J. 1929: *Select English Writings*, ed. H. E. Winn. Oxford: Oxford University Press.

Websites

Note: The following addresses indicate a few of the resources relevant to the subject of this book that are available on the world-wide web, especially for artistic representations and for primary texts not readily available in book form. Bracketed addresses give the home page for the previous item. Given the ever-changing nature of web resources, some addresses may not remain current.

Art, Images, Music and Materials related to the Book of Revelation, compiled by Felix Just, SJ, Loyola Marymount University: http://bellarmine.lmu.edu/~fjust/

Beatus of Liébana, Codex Urgellensis (tenth-century illustrated manuscript): http://casal.upc.es/~ramon25/beatus/index_eg.htm

A Celebration of Women Writers: http://digital.library.upenn.edu/women/_generate/1601–1700.html [http://digital.library.upenn.edu/women]

Center for Millennial Studies, Boston University: http://www.mille.org

Darby, John Nelson (1800–82), *Synopsis of the Books of the Bible*, 'The Revelation', at Christian Classics Ethereal Library: http://www.ccel.org/d/darby/synopsis/Revelation.html [http://www.ccel.org/d/darby]

Early Church Fathers: http://www.ccel.org/fathers2 [http://www.ccel.org]

Joachim of Fiore: http://www.centrostudigioachimiti.it/Gioacchino/GF_Tavoleeng.asp [http://www.centrostudigioachimiti.it/Benvenuti/Benvenutieng.asp]

Joanna Southcott: www.joannasouthcott.com/unpublished.htm

Journal of Religion and Film (*See also* Ostwalt, C.): http://www.unomaha.edu/~wwwjrf

Lead, Jane, writings of: http://www.passtheword.org/jane-lead/revelatn.htm [http://www.passtheword.org/jane-lead]

Links to Revelation, Apocalyptic and Millennial Websites and Materials by Prof. Felix Just, SJ, Loyola Marymount University: http://bellarmine.lmu.edu/~fjust/apocalyptic_links.htm

Luther's writings: http://www.wls.wels.net/students/coursematerial/reformationhistory/lutherreadings.htm

Medieval Women's Monasticism: http://www.faculty.de.gcsu.edu/~dvess/ids/medieval/medwomen.html [http://www.faculty.de.gcsu.edu/~dvess]

Na Prous Boneta: http://www.fordham.edu/halsall/source/naprous.html [http://www.fordham.edu/halsall]

Olivi, Peter: http://www.fordham.edu/halsall/source/olivi.html [http://www.fordham.edu/halsall]

Ostwalt, C. 'Visions of the end: secular Apocalypse in recent Hollywood film.' *Journal of Religion and Film*, vol. 2, no. 1 (April 1998) (on films *Waterworld* and *Twelve Monkeys*): http://www.unomaha.edu/~wwwjrf/OstwaltC.htm [http://www.unomaha.edu/~wwwjrf]

PBS Frontline, 'Apocalypse! the evolution of apocalyptic belief and how it shaped the western world': http://www.pbs.org/wgbh/pages/frontline/shows/apocalypse

Shaker Manuscripts Online: http://www.passtheword.org/shaker-manuscripts

Wentworth, Anne, 'The Revelation of Jesus Christ': http://chaucer.library.emory.edu/wwrp

Women Writers Online, at Brown University (for Mary Cary, Anna Trapnel): http://www.wwp.brown.edu/texts/wwoentry.html [http://www.wwp.brown.edu]

Secondary Sources

Abrams, M. H. 1973: *Natural Supernaturalism: tradition and revolution in Romantic literature*. New York: Norton.

Achelis, H. 1897: *Hippolytstudien*. Leipzig: Hinrichs.

Adorno, T. 1974: *Minima Moralia*. London: Verso.

Alexander, P. J. 1980: The diffusion of Byzantine apocalypses in the medieval West and the beginnings of Joachism. In M. Reeves and A. Williams (eds), *Prophecy and Millenarianism*, Harlow: Longman, 53–106.

Alison, J. 1997: *Living in the End Times: the last things re-imagined*. London: SPCK.

Allo, E. B. 1921: *L'Apocalypse de Saint Jean*. Paris: Lecoffre.

The Alternative Service Book 1980: Services authorized for use in the Church of England in conjunction with The Book of Common Prayer. London: Hodder.

Anselmetto, C. 1980: La Presenza dell'Apocalisse di Giovanni nelle Omelie di Origene. In H. Crouzel and A. Quacquarelli (eds), *Origeniana Secunda*, Rome: Ateneo, 255–66.

Argyriou, A. 1981: *Les Exegèses grecques de l'Apocalypse à l'époque turque (1453–1821)*. Thessalonica: Society of Macedonian Studies.

Arthur, A. 1999: *The Tailor King: the rise and fall of the Anabaptist kingdom of Münster*. New York: Dunne.

Ashton, J. 1991: *Understanding the Fourth Gospel*. Oxford: Oxford University Press.

—— 1994: *Studying John*. Oxford: Oxford University Press.

—— 2000: *The Religion of Paul the Apostle*. New Haven: Yale University Press.

Aston, M. 1984: *Lollards and Reformers: images and literacy in medieval religion*. London: Hambledon.

Atwater, E. E. 1851: *History of the Colony of New Haven and its Absorption into Connecticut*. New Haven: privately printed.

Aulen, G. 1931: *Christus Victor*. London: SPCK.

Aune, D. 1983: *Prophecy in Early Christianity and the Ancient Mediterranean World*. Grand Rapids, Mich.: Eerdmans.

—— 1997: *Revelation 1–5*. Word Biblical Commentary 52a. Dallas: Word.

—— 1998a: *Revelation 6–16*. Word Biblical Commentary 52b. Nashville: Nelson.

—— 1998b: *Revelation 17–22*. Word Biblical Commentary 52c. Nashville: Nelson.

Averky, Archbishop 1985: *The Apocalypse of St. John: An Orthodox Commentary*. Platina: Valaam Society.

Backus, I. 1998: The church fathers and the canonicity of the Apocalypse in the sixteenth century: Erasmus, Frans Titelmans, and Theodore Beza. *Sixteenth Century Journal*, 29, 651–65.

—— 2000: *Reformation Readings of the Apocalypse: Geneva, Zurich and Wittenberg*. Oxford: Oxford University Press.

Balás, D. and Bingham, D. J. 1998: Patristic Exegesis of the Books of the Bible. *The International Catholic Bible Commentary*, ed. William R. Farmer. Collegeville, Minn.: Liturgical Press.

Ball, B. W. 1975: *A Great Expectation: eschatological thought in English Protestantism to 1660*. Leiden: Brill.

Baring-Gould, S. 1891: *Freaks of Fanaticism and Other Strange Events*. London: Methuen.

Barker, M. 2000: *The Revelation of Jesus Christ*. Edinburgh: T&T Clark.

Barnes, R. B. 1988: *Prophecy and Gnosis: apocalypticism in the wake of the Lutheran Reformation*. Stanford, Calif.: Stanford University Press.

Barolsky, P. 1995: The visionary experience of Renaissance art. *Word and Image*, 11, 174–81.

Barrett, L. E. 1977: *The Rastafarians*. London: Heinemann.

Barth, K. 1933: *The Epistle to the Romans*, 1919, tr. E. C. Hoskyns. London: A&C Black.

—— 1958–62: *Church Dogmatics*. Edinburgh: T&T Clark.

Barton, J. 1986: *Oracles of God*. London: Darton, Longman and Todd.

Bauckham, R. 1976: The martyrdom of Enoch and Elijah: Jewish or Christian? *Journal of Biblical Literature*, 95, 447–58.

—— 1978: *Tudor Apocalypse: sixteenth-century apocalypticism, millenarianism and the English Reformation*. Sutton Courtenay: Appleford.

—— 1993a: *The Climax of Prophecy: studies in the Book of Revelation*. Edinburgh: T&T Clark.

—— 1993b: *The Theology of the Book of Revelation*. Cambridge: Cambridge University Press.

—— 1998: *A Gospel for all Christians: rethinking the Gospels' audiences*. Edinburgh: T&T Clark.

Beale, G. K. 1999: *The Book of Revelation*. Grand Rapids, Mich.: Eerdmans.

Becker, J. C. 1980: *Paul the Apostle: the Triumph of God in Life and Thought*. Edinburgh: T&T Clark.

Beer, J. 1994: Blake's changing view of history: the impact of the Book of Enoch. In S. Clark and D. Worrall (eds), *Historicizing Blake*, Basingstoke: Macmillan, 159–78.

Bell, K. 1992: *Stanley Spencer*. London: Phaidon.

Bengel, J. A. 1857: *Gnomon of the New Testament*, 1740. Edinburgh: T&T Clark.

Benjamin, W. 1970: Theses on the philosophy of history. In H. Arendt (ed.), *Illuminations*, London: Cape, 245–55.

Bentley, G. E. Jr 2001: *The Stranger from Paradise: a biography of William Blake*. New Haven: Yale University Press.

Berger, K. 1976: *Die Auferstehung des Propheten und die Erhöhung des Menschensohnes*. Göttingen: Vandenhoeck und Ruprecht.

Bethea, D. M. 1989: *The Shape of the Apocalypse in Modern Russian Fiction*. Princeton: Princeton University Press.

Biale, D. 1982: *Gershom Scholem: Kabbalah and counter-history*. Cambridge, Mass.: Harvard University Press.

Binski, P. 1996: *Medieval Death: ritual and representation*. London: British Museum Press.

Blackburn, B. J. 1999: The Virgin in the sun: music and image for a prayer attributed to Sixtus IV. *Journal of the Royal Musical Association*, 124, 157–95.

Bloch, E. 1971: *Man on His Own*. New York: Herder.

—— 1972: *Atheism in Christianity: the Religion of the Exodus and the Kingdom*. New York: Herder.

—— 1986: *The Principle of Hope*. Oxford: Blackwell.

Bloch, R. 1985: *Visionary Republic: millennial themes in American thought 1756–1800*. Cambridge: Cambridge University Press.

Bloomfield, M. 1962: *Piers Plowman as a Fourteenth-Century Apocalypse*. New Brunswick, NJ: Rutgers.

Bockmuehl, M. 1990: *Revelation and Mystery in ancient Judaism and Pauline Christianity*. WUNT 2.36. Tübingen: J. C. B. Mohr.

Boesak, A. 1987: *Comfort and Protest*. Edinburgh: St Andrews.

Bonhoeffer, D. 1965: *No Rusty Swords*. London: Collins.

Bonner, G. 1966: *Saint Bede in the Tradition of Western Apocalypse Commentary*. Newcastle upon Tyne: J&P Bealls.

Bornkamm, H. 1983: *Luther in Mid Career 1521–30*. London: Darton, Longman and Todd.

Bossuet, J.-B. 1690: *L'Apocalypse: avec une explication*. Paris: Marbre Cramoisy.

Bousset, W. 1896: *Die Offenbarung Johannis*. Göttingen: Vandenhoeck und Ruprecht.

—— 1999: *The Antichrist Legend: a chapter in Jewish and Christian folklore*. Atlanta, Ga.: Scholars Press.

Boxall, I. 1999: Who is the woman clothed with the sun? In M. Warner (ed.), *Say Yes to God: Mary and the Revealing of the Word Made Flesh*, London: Tufton Books, 142–58.

—— 2002: *Revelation: vision and insight*. London: SPCK.

Boyarin, D. 1994: *Radical Jew: Paul and the politics of identity*. Berkeley: University of California Press.

Boyer, P. 1992: *When Time Shall Be No More: prophecy belief in modern American culture*. Cambridge, Mass., and London: Belknap Press of Harvard University Press.

Brading, D. A. 2002: *Our Lady of Guadalupe: image and tradition across five centuries*. Cambridge: Cambridge University Press.

Bradstock, A. 1997: *Faith in the Revolution: the political theologies of Müntzer and Winstanley*. London: SPCK.

Brady, D. 1983: *The Contribution of British Writers between 1560–1830 to the Interpretation of Revelation 13.16–18*. Tübingen: J. C. B. Mohr.

Brightman, F. E. 1895: *Liturgies Eastern and Western*. Oxford: Clarendon Press.

—— 1915: *The English Rite*, 2 vols. London: Rivington.

Brown, F. 2002: *A Woman Clothed with the Sun*. Cambridge: Lutterworth.

Bull, M. 1995: *Apocalypse Theory*. Oxford: Blackwell.

Burdon, C. 1997: *The Apocalypse in England 1700–1834: the Apocalypse unravelling*. London: Macmillan.

Burkitt, F. C. 1894: *The Book of Rules of Tyconius*. Cambridge: Cambridge University Press.

—— 1914: *Jewish and Christian Apocalypses*. Schweich Lectures. London: For the British Academy by Oxford University Press.

Burr, D. 1976: The persecution of Peter Olivi. *Transactions of the American Philosophical Society*, 66 (new series), 3–98.

—— 1989: *Olivi and Franciscan Poverty: the origins of the Usus Pauper controversy*. Philadelphia: University of Pennsylvania Press.

—— 1993: *Olivi's Peaceable Kingdom: a reading of the Apocalypse Commentary*. Philadelphia: University of Pennsylvania Press.

—— 1997: Na Prous Boneta and Olivi. *Collectanea Franciscana*, 67, 477–500.

—— 2001: *The Spiritual Franciscans: from protest to persecution in the century after Francis*. Philadelphia: University of Pennsylvania Press.

Butler, M. 1981: *Romantics, Rebels and Reactionaries*. Oxford: Oxford University Press.

Caird, G. B. 1966: *The Revelation of Saint John the Divine*. London: A&C Black.

—— 1980: *The Language and Imagery of the Bible*. London: Duckworth.

Calí, P. 1971: *Allegory and Vision in Dante and Langland*. Cork: Cork University Press.

Capp, B. 1972: *The Fifth Monarchy Men: a study in seventeenth-century millenarianism*. London: Faber.

Carey, F. (ed.) 1999: *The Apocalypse and the Shape of Things to Come*. London: British Museum Press.

Cerrato, J. A. 2002: *Hippolytus between East and West: the commentaries and the provenance of the corpus*. Oxford: Oxford University Press.

Charles, R. H. 1910: *Studies in the Apocalypse*. Edinburgh: T&T Clark.

—— 1920: *A Critical and Exegetical Commentary on the Revelation of Saint John*, 2 vols. Edinburgh: T&T Clark.

Cohn, N. 1957: *The Pursuit of the Millennium*. London: Paladin.

Collins, A. Y. 1976: *The Combat Myth in the Book of Revelation.* Missoula, Mont.: Scholars Press.

—— 1979: *The Apocalypse.* Wilmington, Del.: Michael Glazier.

—— 1984: *Crisis and Catharsis.* Philadelphia: Westminster.

—— (ed.) 1986: *Early Christian Apocalypticism: genre and social setting.* Decatur, Ga.: Scholars Press.

—— 1993: Feminine symbolism in the Book of Revelation. *Biblical Interpretation,* 1, 20–33.

—— 1996. *Cosmology and Eschatology in Jewish and Christian Apocalypticism.* Leiden: Brill.

Collins, J. J., (ed.) 1979: *Apocalypse: the morphology of a genre. Semeia,* 14, Society of Biblical Literature. Missoula, Mont.: Scholars Press.

—— 1984: *The Apocalyptic Imagination.* New York: Crossroads.

——, (ed.) 2000: *Encyclopedia of Apocalypticism,* vol. i. New York: Continuum.

Cook, S. L. 1995: *Prophecy and Apocalypticism: the post-exilic setting.* Minneapolis: Fortress.

Corsini, E. 1983: *The Apocalypse: the perennial revelation of Jesus Christ.* Wilmington, Del.: Michael Glazier.

Court, J. M. 1979: *Myth and History in the Book of Revelation.* London: SPCK.

—— 2000: *Revelation and the Johannine Apocalyptic Tradition.* Sheffield: Sheffield Academic Press.

Cowley, R. W. 1983: *The Traditional Interpretation of the Apocalypse of St. John in the Ethiopian Orthodox Church.* Cambridge: Cambridge University Press.

Crum, W. E. 1913: *Theological Texts from Coptic Papyri.* Oxford: Clarendon Press.

da Cunha, E. 1944: *Rebellion in the Backlands (Os Sertões).* Chicago: University of Chicago Press.

Daley, B. 1991: *The Hope of the Early Church.* Cambridge: Cambridge University Press.

Daniell, D. 2003: *The Bible in English.* New Haven: Yale University Press.

Daniélou, J. 1964: *The Theology of Jewish Christianity.* London: Darton, Longman and Todd.

Deanesly, M. 1951: *The Significance of the Lollard Bible.* London: Athlone Press.

—— 1978: *The Lollard Bible and Other Medieval Biblical Versions.* New York: AMS.

Deppermann, K. 1987: *Melchior Hoffmann.* Edinburgh: T&T Clark.

Dobroruka, V. 1997: *Antônio Conselheiro, o beato endiabrado de Canudos.* Rio de Janeiro: Diadorim.

Douie, D. 1978: *The Nature and the Effect of the Heresy of the Fraticelli.* New York: AMS.

Dronke, P. 1984: *Women Writers of the Middle Ages: a critical study of texts from Perpetua to Marguerite Porete.* Cambridge: Cambridge University Press.

Drury, J. 1999: *Painting the Word: Christian pictures and their meanings.* New Haven: Yale University Press.

Dulaey, M. 1986: L'Apocalypse: Augustin et Tyconius. In A. M. Bonnardière (ed.), *Saint Augustine et la Bible,* Paris: Beauchesne, 369–86.

—— 1993: *Victorin de Poetovio: premier éxègete latin,* 2 vols. Paris: Institut d'études augustiniennes.

Dunbar, D. 1983: Hippolytus of Rome and the eschatological exegesis of the early Church. *Westminster Theological Journal*, 45, 322–39.

Elliott, E. B. 1851: *Horae Apocalypticae; or, A Commentary on the Apocalypse, Critical and Historical*, 4 vols. London: Seeley.

Ellul, J. 1977: *Apocalypse*. New York: Seabury.

Elm, S. 1994: *Virgins of God: the making of asceticism in late antiquity*. Oxford: Oxford University Press.

Emmerson, R. K. 1981: *Antichrist in the Middle Ages: a study of medieval apocalypticism, Art and Literature*. Manchester: Manchester University Press.

Emmerson, R. K. and Herzman, R. B. (eds) 1992: *The Apocalyptic Imagination in Medieval Literature*. Philadelphia: University of Pennsylvania Press.

Emmerson, R. K. and McGinn, B. (eds) 1992: *The Apocalypse in the Middle Ages*. Ithaca, NY: Cornell University Press.

Engels, F. 1959: On the history of primitive Christianity. In L. Feuer (ed.), K. Marx and F. Engels, *Basic Writings on Politics and Philosophy*, London: Fontana/Collins, 209–35.

Erdman, D. V. 1977: *Blake: Prophet against Empire*. Princeton: Princeton University Press.

—— 1980: *William Blake's Designs for Edward Young's* Night Thoughts. Oxford: Clarendon Press.

Esler, P. L. 1995: *The First Christians in their Social Worlds*. London: Routledge.

Fahey, M. 1971: *Cyprian and the Bible: a study in third-century exegesis*. Tübingen: J. C. B. Mohr.

Fairfield, L. 1976: *John Bale: mythmaker for the English Reformation*. West Lafayette, Ind.: Purdue University Press.

Farrer, A. 1949: *A Rebirth of Images*. Westminster: Dacre.

—— 1964: *The Revelation of St. John the Divine*. Oxford: Clarendon Press.

Finamore, S. 1997: God, Order and Chaos: a history of the interpretation of Revelation's plague sequences and an assessment of the value of R. Girard's thought for the understanding of these visions. DPhil. thesis, Oxford University.

Finch, C. 1993: *The Complete Works of the Pearl Poet*. Berkeley: University of California Press.

Firth, K. 1979: *The Apocalyptic Tradition in Reformation Britain 1530–1645*. Oxford: Oxford University Press.

Fisch, H. 1999: *The Biblical Presence in Shakespeare, Milton and Blake*. Oxford: Clarendon Press.

Fishbane, M. 1985: *Biblical Interpretation in Ancient Israel*. Oxford: Clarendon Press.

Flood, D. 1972: *Peter Olivi's Rule Commentary*. Wiesbaden: Steiner.

Forey, M. 1994: Apocalypse in Spenser and Milton. DPhil. thesis, Oxford University.

Fowler, D. C. 1984: *The Bible in Middle English Literature*. Seattle: University of Washington Press.

Frankfurter, D. 1992: *Elijah in Upper Egypt: the Apocalypse of Elijah in early Egyptian Christianity*. Minneapolis: Fortress.

Fredriksen, P. 1982: Tyconius and the end of the world. *Revue des études augustiniennes*, 28, 59–75.

Freire, P. 1972: *Pedagogy of the Oppressed*. Harmondsworth: Penguin.

French, T. 2002: *York Minster: The Great East Window*. Oxford University Press.

Freschkowski, M. 1995–7: *Offenbarung und Epiphanie*, 2 vols. Tübingen: J. C. B. Mohr.

Froom, L. E. 1946–54: *The Prophetic Faith of Our Fathers*, 4 vols. Washingtosn, DC: Review and Herald Publishing Association.

Funk, R. W. (ed.) 1969a: *Apocalypticism. Journal for Theology and the Church*, 6. New York: Herder and Herder.

——— 1969b: The apostolic parousia. In W. R. Farmer, C. F. D. Moule and R. Niebuhr (eds), *Christian History and Interpretation*, Cambridge: Cambridge University Press, 249–68.

Gabara, Y. and Bingemeyer, M. C. 1989: *Mary Mother of God, Mother of the Poor*. Tunbridge Wells: Burns and Oates.

Gager, J. 1975: *Kingdom and Community: The Social World of Early Christianity*. Englewood Cliffs, NJ: Prentice-Hall.

Garrett, C. 1973: *Respectable Folly: millenarians in the French Revolution in France and England*. Baltimore: Johns Hopkins University Press.

——— 1987: *The Origins of the Shakers: from the Old World to the New World*. Baltimore: Johns Hopkins University Press.

Garsted, E. S. 1973: *The Rise of Adventism*. New York: Harper & Row.

Gilbertson, M. 1997: *The Meaning of the Millennium*. Cambridge: Grove.

Girard, R. 1987: *Things Hidden since the Foundation of the World*. London: Athlone Press.

Goodenough, E. R. 1935: *By Light, Light: The Mystic Gospel of Hellenistic Judaism*. New Haven: Yale University Press.

Goodwin, B. and Taylor, K. 1982: *The Politics of Utopia*. London: Routledge.

Gorringe, T. J. 1999: *Karl Barth: against hegemony*. Oxford: Clarendon Press.

Gruenwald, I. 1980: *Apocalyptic and Merkavah Mysticism*. Leiden: Brill.

Gwynn, J. 1888: Hippolytus and his 'Heads against Caius.' *Hermathena: a series of papers on literature, science and philosophy by members of Trinity College, Dublin*, 6, 397–416.

Haller, W. 1979: *Tracts on Liberty in the Puritan Revolution 1638–1647*. New York: Octagon.

Halperin, D. 1988: *Faces of the Chariot*. Tübingen: J. C. B. Mohr.

Hamilton, A. 1981: *The Family of Love*. Cambridge: Cambridge University Press.

——— 1988: *Cronica, Ordo Sacerdotis, Acta HN: three texts on the Family of Love*. Leiden: Brill.

——— 1999: *The Apocryphal Apocalypse: the reception of the Second Book of Esdras (4 Ezra) from the Renaissance to the Enlightenment*. Oxford: Oxford University Press.

Hamlyn, R. and Phillips, M. 2000: *William Blake*. London: Tate Gallery.

Hanson, P. D. 1974: *The Dawn of Apocalyptic*. Philadelphia: Fortress.

Happé, P. 1996: *John Bale*. Englewood Cliffs, NJ: Prentice-Hall.

Harrison, J. F. C. 1979: *The Second Coming: popular millenarianism 1780–1850*. London: Routledge, Kegan and Paul.

Hayden, R. 1974: The records of a church of Christ in Bristol 1640–1687. *Bristol Record Society*, 27, 84–96.

Heller, R. 1983: 'Kandinsky and Traditions apocalyptic.' *Art Journal*, 43, 19–26.

Hellholm, D. (ed.) 1989: *Apocalypticism in the Mediterranean World and the Near East*, 2nd edn. Tübingen: J. C. B. Mohr.

Helms, C. 1991: The Apocalypse in the Early Church: Christ, eschaton and the millennium. DPhil. thesis, Oxford University.

Hemer, C. J. 1986: *The Letters to the Seven Churches in their Local Setting*. Sheffield: Sheffield Academic Press.

Hill, C. E. 1992: *Regnum Coelorum: patterns of future hope in early Christianity*. Oxford: Clarendon Press.

Hill, C. 1972: *The World Turned Upside Down*. London: Penguin.

——(ed.) 1983: *Winstanley: the law of freedom and other writings*. Cambridge: Cambridge University Press.

——1989: *A Turbulent, Seditious and Factious People: John Bunyan and his church*. Oxford: Oxford University Press.

——1990: *The Antichrist in Seventeenth-Century England*. London: Verso.

——1993: *The English Bible and the Seventeenth-Century Revolution*. Marmondsworth: Penguin.

Hinds, H. 1996: *God's Englishwomen: seventeenth-century radical sectarian writing and feminist criticism*. Manchester: Manchester University Press.

Hobby, E. 1988: *Virtue of Necessity*. London: Virago.

Hopkins, J. K. 1982: *A Woman to Deliver her People: Joanna Southcott and English millenarianism in an era of revolution*. Austin: University of Texas Press.

Horbury, W. 1998: *Jews and Christians in Contact and Controversy*. Edinburgh: T&T Clark.

Hoskier, H. C. 1929: *Concerning the Text of the Apocalypse; collations of all existing available Greek documents with the standard text of Stephen's third edition, together with the testimony of versions, commentaries and fathers; a complete conspectus of all authorities*. London: Quaritch.

Houlden, J. L. (ed.) 1995: *The Interpretation of the Bible in the Church*. London: SPCK.

Howard-Brook, W. and Gwyther, A. 2000: *Unveiling Empire: reading Revelation then and now*. Maryknoll, NY: Orbis.

Hudson, W. 1982: *The Marxist Philosophy of Ernst Bloch*. London: Macmillan.

Hurtado, L. 1998: *One God, one Lord: Early Christian Devotion and Jewish Monotheism*, rev. edn. Edinburgh: T&T Clark.

James, M. R. 1931: *The Apocalypse in Art*. London: British Academy.

Jantzen, G. 1995: *Power, Gender and Christian Mysticism*. Cambridge: Cambridge University Press.

Johns, L. L. (ed.) 2000: *Apocalypticism and Millennialism: shaping a believers' church eschatology for the twenty-first century*. Kitchener, Canada: Pandora.

Johnson, J. W. and Johnson, J. R. 1954: *The Books of American Negro Spirituals*, vols 1 and 2. New York: Da Capo.

Jones, W. 1835: *A Biographical Sketch of E. Irving*. London: J. Bennet.

Jung, C. G. 1959: *Answer to Job*. London: Routledge, Kegan and Paul.

Kaminsky, H. 1976: *A History of the Hussite Revolution*. Berkeley and Los Angeles: University of California Press.

Kamlah, W. 1935: *Apokalypse und Geschichtstheologie: die mittelälterliche Auslegung der Apokalypse vor Joachim von Fiore*. Berlin: Ebering.

Keller, C. 1990: Die Frau in der Wüste: ein feministisch-theologischer Midrasch zu Offb 12. *Evangelische Theologie*, 50, 414–32.

—— 1996: *Apocalypse Now and Then: a feminist guide to the end of the world*. Boston: Beacon.

Kermode, F. 1999: *The Sense of an Ending: studies in the theory of fiction*, 1967. Reprinted with an epilogue, Oxford: Oxford University Press.

Kirschbaum, E. 1968: Apokalypse des Johannes. In H. Aurenhammer (ed.), *Lexicon der christliche Ikonographie*, vol. 1: *Allgemeine Ikonographie*, Vienna: Hollinek (repr. 1994), cols 124–49.

Klassen, W. 1992: *Living at the End of the Ages: apocalyptic expectation in the Radical Reformation*. Waterloo, Ont.: University Press of America.

Knight, J. M. 1996: *Disciples of the Beloved: The Christology, Social Setting, and the Context of the Ascension of Isaiah*. Sheffield: Sheffield Academic Press.

Kolakowski, L. 1978: *Main Currents of Marxism*. Oxford: Clarendon Press.

Kovacs, J. L. 1995: 'Now shall the Ruler of this World be Cast Out': Jesus' death as cosmic battle in John 12:20–36. *Journal of Biblical Literature*, 114, 227–47.

Kraditor, A. S. 1969: *Means and Ends in American Abolitionism: Garrison and his critics on strategy and tactics, 1834–1850*. New York: Pantheon Books.

Kreider, A. 2001: *The Origins of Christendom in the West*. Edinburgh: T&T Clark.

Kretschmar, G. 1985: *Die Offenbarung des Johannes: die Geschichte ihrer Auslegung im ersten Jahrtausend*. Stuttgart: Calwer Verlag.

Labriolle, P. 1913: *La Crise Mantaniste*. Paris: Leraux.

Lane Fox, R. 1986: *Pagans and Christians*. Harmondsworth: Penguin.

Leff, G. 1967: *Heresy in the Later Middle Ages: the relationship of heterodoxy to dissent*, 2 vols. Manchester: Manchester University Press.

Le Frois, B. J. 1954: *The Woman Clothed with the Sun*. Rome: Orbs Catholicus.

Lerner, R. E. 1968: *The Age of Adversity*. Ithaca, NY: Cornell University Press.

—— 1972: *The Heresy of the Free Spirit in the Later Middle Ages*. Berkeley: University of California Press.

—— 1985: Antichrists and Antichrist in Joachim. *Speculum*, 60, 553–70.

Lewis, S. 1995: *Reading Images: narrative discourse and reception in the thirteenth-century illuminated Apocalypse*. Cambridge: Cambridge University Press.

Lewis, W. 1976: Peter John Olivi, prophet of the year 2000: ecclesiology and eschatology in the 'Lectura super Apocalipsim,' introduction to a critical edition of the text. Dissertation, University of Tübingen.

Lieb, M. 1991: *The Visionary Mode: biblical prophecy, hermeneutics and cultural change*. Ithaca, NY: Cornell University Press.

Lieu, J. 1997: *Image and Reality*. Edinburgh: T&T Clark.

Long, T. 1996: A real reader reading Revelation. *Semeia*, 73, 79–107.

Long, T. 1996: Narrator Audiences and Messages: a South African reader response study of narrative relationships in the Book of Revelation. Dissertation, University of Natal.

Lowth, R. 1753: *Lectures on the Sacred Poetry of the Hebrews*. London.

Lubac, H. de 1998: *Medieval Exegesis*, 2 vols. Edinburgh: T&T Clark.

Lührmann, D. 1995: Q: sayings of Jesus or logia? In R. A. Piper (ed.), *The Gospel behind the Gospels: current studies in Q*, Leiden: Brill, 97–116.

Luz, U. 1989: *Matthew 1–7*. Edinburgh: T&T Clark.

Macey, P. P. 1998: *Bonfire Songs – Savonarola's Musical Legacy*. Oxford: Clarendon Press.

Mack, P. 1992: *Visionary Women: ecstatic prophecy in seventeenth-century England*. Berkeley: University of California Press.

Maier, G. 1981: *Die Offenbarung Johannis und die Kirche*. Tübingen: J. C. B. Mohr.

Malina, B. J. and Pilch, J. J. 2000: *Social-Science Commentary on the Book of Revelation*. Minneapolis: Fortress.

Mannheim, K. 1960: *Ideology and Utopia*. London: Routledge, Kegan and Paul.

Marculescu, R. 2000: *Patimiri si Illuminari din Captivitatea Sovietica*. Bucharest: Albatros.

Marsh, C. W. 1993: *The Family of Love and English Society, 1550–1630*. Cambridge: Cambridge University Press.

Marshall, E. 1878: *The Explanation of the Apocalypse by Venerable Bede*. Oxford.

Martin, P. 1983: *Martin Luther und die Bilder zur Apokalypse: die Ikonographie der Illustrationen zur Offenbarung des Johannes in der Lutherbibel 1522–1546*. Hamburg: Wittig.

Massyngberde-Ford, J. 1975: *Revelation*. New York: Doubleday.

Matheson, P. 2000: *The Imaginative World of the Reformation*. Edinburgh: T&T Clark.

May, W. 1965: The confession of Prous Boneta, heretic and heresiarch. In J. H. Mundy et al. (eds), *Essays in Medieval Life and Thought*, New York: Biblo and Tannen, 4–30.

Mayr-Harting, H. 1991: *Ottonian Book Illumination: an historical study*. London: Harvey-Miller.

Mazzaferri, F. 1989: *The Genre of the Book of Revelation from a Source Critical Perspective*. Berlin: de Gruyter.

Mazzucco, C. 1978: Il rapporto tra la concezione del millennio dei primi autori cristiani e l'Apocalisse de Giovanni. *Augustinianum*, 18, 49–75.

—— 1980: L'Apocalisse di Giovanni nel Contro Celso di Origene. In H. Crouzel and A. Quacquarelli (eds), *Origeniana Secunda*, Rome: Ateneo, 267–78.

—— 1983: La Gerusalemme celeste dell'Apocalisse nei Padri. In M. L. G. Perer (ed.), *'La dimora di Dio con gli uomini' (Ap. 21.3): immagine della Gerusalemme celeste dal III al XIV secolo*, Milan: Vita e Pensiero, 49–75.

McClendon, J. W. Jr. 1994: *Systematic Theology: doctrine*. Nashville: Abingdon, ii. 97–102.

McCormack, B. 1995: *Karl Barth's Critically Realistic Dialectical Theology*. Oxford: Oxford University Press.

McDannell, C. and Lang, B. 1988: *Heaven: a history*. New Haven: Yale University Press.

McGinn, B. 1985: *The Calabrian Abbot: Joachim of Fiore in the history of Western thought*. New York: Macmillan.

—— 1992: *The Foundations of Mysticism*. London: SCM Press.

—— 1998: *Visions of the End: apocalyptic traditions in the Middle Ages*. New York: Columbia University Press.

—— (ed.) 2000: *Encyclopedia of Apocalypticism*, vol. ii. New York: Continuum.

McGregor, J. F. and Reay, B. 1984: *Radical Religion in the English Revolution*. Oxford: Clarendon Press.

McInerney, M. B. 1998: *Hildegard of Bingen: a book of essays*. New York: Garland Publishing Co.

McKelvey, R. J. 1999: *The Millennium and the Book of Revelation*. Cambridge: Lutterworth.

McLellan, David 1987: *Marxism and Religion: A Description and Assessment of the Marxist Critique of Christianity*. Basingstoke: Macmillan.

Mee, J. 1992: *Dangerous Enthusiasm*. Oxford: Oxford University Press.

Mesters, C. and Orofino, F. 2002: *Apocalípse de João: esperança, coragem e allegria*. Centro Estudos Bíblicos São Leiopoldo/São Paulo: Paulus.

Mesters, C. 1989: *Defenseless Flower*. London: Catholic Institute for International Relations.

—— 1993: The use of the Bible in Christian communities of the common people. In N. Gottwald (ed.), *The Bible and Liberation*, 2nd edn, Maryknoll, NY: Orbis, 3–16.

Mojtabai, A. 1987: *Blessed Assurance*. Boston: Houghton Mufflin.

Moltmann, J. 1996: *The Coming of God: Christian eschatology*. London: SCM Press.

Monaci, A. 1978: Apocalisse ed escatologia nell'opera di Origene. *Augustinianum*, 18, 139–51.

Moore, S. D. 1996: *God's Gym: divine male bodies of the Bible*. London: Routledge.

Morison, S. E. 1965: *Journals and Other Documents on the Life and Voyages of Christopher Columbus*. New York: Heritage.

Morray-Jones, C. 2002: *A Transparent Illusion*. Leiden: Brill.

Murphy, F. J. 1998: *Fallen is Babylon: the Revelation to John*. Harrisburg, Pa.: Trinity.

Murray, S. 2000: *Biblical Interpretation in the Anabaptist Tradition*. Kitchener, Canada: Pandora.

Mussies, G. 1971: *The Morphology of Koine Greek as used in the Apocalypse of John: a study in bilingualism*. Leiden: Brill.

Myers, C. 1988: *Binding the Strong Man*. New York: Orbis.

Newport, K. E. 2000: *Apocalypse and the Millennium: studies in biblical eisegesis*. Cambridge: Cambridge University Press.

Nickelsburg, G. W. 2001: *1 Enoch: a commentary on the Book of 1 Enoch, chapters 1–36; 81–108*. Minneapolis: Fortress.

Numbers, R. L. and Butler, J. M. 1987: *The Disappointed: Millerism and millenarianism in the nineteenth century*. Bloomington: Indiana University Press.

O'Donovan, O. 1986: The Political Thought of the Book of Revelation. *Tyndale Bulletin*, 37, 61–94.

—— 1995: *The Desire of the Nations*. Cambridge: Cambridge University Press.

O'Leary, S. 1994: *Arguing the Apocalypse: a theory of millennial rhetoric.* New York: Oxford University Press.

Oliver, W. H. 1978: *Prophets and Millennialists: the uses of biblical prophecy in England from the 1790s to the 1840s.* Auckland: Auckland University Press.

Olsen, V. N. 1973: *John Foxe and the Elizabethan Church.* Berkeley: University of California Press.

Ottner, C. 2001: *Apokalypse: Symposion 1999. Studien zu Franz Schmidt* 13. Vienna: Doblinger.

Ozment, S. 1973: *Mysticism and Dissent: religious ideology and social protest in the sixteenth century.* New Haven: Yale University Press.

Paley, M. D. 1986: *The Apocalyptic Sublime.* New Haven: Yale University Press.

—— 1999: *Apocalypse and Millennium in English Romantic Poetry.* Oxford: Clarendon Press.

Patrides, C. A. and Wittreich, J. A. (eds) 1984: *The Apocalypse in English Renaissance Thought and Literature: patterns, antecedents and repercussions.* Ithaca, NY: Cornell University Press.

Patte, D. 1995: *Ethics of Biblical Interpretation: a re-evaluation.* Louisville, Ky.: Westminster.

Patte, D. and Greenholm, C. 2000: *Reading Israel in Romans: legitimacy and plausibility of divergent interpretations.* Romans through History and Culture Series 1. Harrisburg, Pa.: Trinity.

Perrin, N. 1976: *Jesus and the Language of the Kingdom: symbol and metaphor in New Testament interpretation.* London: SCM Press.

Pesce, D. 1997: *Hearing the Motet.* Oxford: Oxford University Press.

Petersen, R. L. 1993: *Preaching in the Last Days: the theme of 'two witnesses' in the sixteenth and seventeenth centuries.* New York: Oxford University Press.

Petroff, E. 1985: *Women's Visionary Literature.* Oxford: Oxford University Press.

Pipkin, W. H. 1989: Seek peace and pursue it: Psalm 34:14. In *Proceedings from the 1988 International Baptist Peace Conference*, Sjovik, Sweden, and Memphis: Baptist Peace Fellowship of North America, 69–76.

Pippin, T. 1992: *Death and Desire: the rhetoric of gender in the Apocalypse of John.* Philadelphia: Fortress.

Polizzotto, L. 1994: *The Elect Nation – The Savonarolan Movement in Florence, 1494–1545.* Oxford: Clarendon Press.

Prigent, P. 1959: *Apocalypse 12: histoire de l'exégèse.* Beiträge zur Geschichte der biblischen Exegese 2. Tübingen: J. C. B. Mohr.

—— 1964: *Apocalypse et liturgie.* Neuchâtel: Delachaux.

—— 1972: Hippolyte, commentateur de l'Apocalypse. *Theologische Zeitschrift*, 28, 391–412.

—— 1973: Les Fragments de l'Apocalypse d'Hippolyte. *Theologische Zeitschrift*, 29, 313–33.

—— 1981: *L'Apocalypse de Saint Jean.* Lausanne: Delachaux.

—— 2001: *Commentary on the Apocalypse of St. John.* Tübingen: J. C. B. Mohr.

Prigent, P. and Stehly, R. 1974: Citations d'Hippolyte trouvées dans le ms. Bodl. Syr. 140, *Theologische Zeitschrift*, 30, 82–5.

Puhl, L. S. J. 1950: *The Spiritual Exercises of St Ignatius*. Chicago: Loyola University Press.

Quispel, G. 1979: *The Secret Book of Revelation*. London: Collins.

Ramsay, W. M. 1904: *The Letters to the Seven Churches*. London: Hodder and Stonghton.

Ratzinger, J. 1956: Beobachtungen zum Kirchenbegriff des Tyconius im *Liber Regularum*. *Revue des études augustiniennes*, 2, 173–85.

Reeves, M. 1999: *Joachim of Fiore and the Prophetic Future*. London: SPCK.

——2000: *The Influence of Prophecy in the Later Middle Ages: a study of Joachimism*. Oxford: Clarendon Press.

Reeves, M. and Gould, W. 1987: *Joachim of Fiore and the Myth of the Eternal Evangel in the Nineteenth Century*. Oxford: Clarendon Press.

Reeves, M. and Hirsch-Reich, B. 1972: *The Figurae of Joachim of Fiore*. Oxford: Oxford University Press.

Ricoeur, P. 1969: *The Symbolism of Evil*. Boston: Beacon.

Roloff, J. 1993: *The Revelation to John*, tr. J. E. Alsup. Minneapolis: Fortress.

Rowland, C. 1979: The visions of God in apocalyptic literature. *Journal for the Study of Judaism*, 10, 138–54.

——1982: *The Open Heaven*. London: SPCK.

——1985: A man clothed in white linen: a study in the development of Jewish angelology. *Journal for the Study of the New Testament*, 24, 99–110.

——1988: *Radical Christianity*. Cambridge: Polity.

——1993: *Revelation*. London: Epworth.

——1996: Apocalyptic, Mysticism and the New Testament. In P. Schäfer (ed.), *Geschichte und Theologie*, Tübingen: J. C. B. Mohr, 1–23.

——1998: *The Book of Revelation*. New Interpreter's Bible xii. Nashville: Abingdon, 503–743.

——(ed.) 1999: *The Cambridge Companion to Liberation Theology*. Cambridge: Cambridge University Press.

Ruether, R. R. and McLaughlin, E. 1979: *Women of Spirit in the Jewish and Christian Traditions*. New York: Book World Promotions.

Rusconi, R. 1996: *Storia e figure dell'Apocalisse fra 500 e 600*. Rome: Viella.

——1999: *Gioacchino da Fiore tra Bernardo di Clairvaux e Innocenzo III*. Atti del 5° Congresso internazionale di studi gioachamiti San Giovanni in Fiore, 16–21 September. Rome: Viella.

Sanders, E. P. 1977: *Paul and Palestinian Judaism*. Philadelphia: Fortress.

——1985: *Jesus and Judaism*. London: SCM Press.

——1992: *Judaism: practice and belief 63 BCE–66CE*. London: SCM Press.

Schiller, G. 1990: *Ikonographie der christlichen Kunst*, vol. 5, part 1: *Textteil*. Gütersloh: Mohn.

——1991: *Ikonographie der christlichen Kunst*, vol. 5, part 2: *Bildteil*. Gütersloh: Mohn.

Schmid, J. 1955–6: *Studien zur Geschichte der griechischen Apokalypse-Textes*. Munich: Zink.

Scholem, G. 1955: *Major Trends in Jewish Mysticism*. London: Thames and Hudson.

—— 1965: *Jewish Gnosticism, Merkabah Mysticism and Talmudic Tradition*. New York: Jewish Theological Seminary.

Schüssler Fiorenza, E. 1993: *Revelation: Vision of a Just World*. Edinburgh: T&T Clark.

—— 1999: *Ethics and the Bible*. Philadelphia: Fortress.

Schweitzer, A. 1961: *The Quest of the Historical Jesus*, 1913. Repr. London: Macmillan.

Scribner, R. W. 1994: *For the Sake of Simple Folk: popular propaganda for the German Reformation*. Oxford: Oxford University Press.

Sevideg, M. J. 1996: *Notorious Voices: feminist biblical interpretation 1500–1920*. New York: Continuum.

Shaffer, E. 1972: *'Kubla Khan' and the Fall of Jerusalem*. Cambridge: Cambridge University Press.

Simonetti, M. 1994: *Biblical Interpretation in the Early Church: an historical introduction to patristic exegesis*. Edinburgh: T&T Clark.

Smith, N. 1989: *Perfection Proclaimed – Language and Literature in English Radical Religion, 1640–60*. Oxford: Clarendon Press.

—— 1994: *Literature and Revolution in England, 1640–1660*. New Haven: Yale University Press.

Smith, R. H. 2000: *Apocalypse: A Commentary of Revelation in Words and Images*. Collegenille, Minn.: Liturgical Press.

Snyder, C. A. and Huebert-Hecht, L. (eds) 1996: *Profiles of Anabaptist Women: Sixteenth-Century Reforming Pioneers*. Waterloo, Ont: Wilfrid Laurier University Press.

Sproxton, J. 1995: *Violence and Religion: attitudes towards militancy in the French civil wars and the English Revolution*. London: Routledge.

Stayer, J. M. 1972: *Anabaptists and the Sword*. Lawrence, Kans.: Coronado.

—— 1991: *The German Peasants' War and Anabaptist Community of Goods*. Montreal: McGill University Press.

Stein, S. 2000: *Encyclopedia of Apocalypticism*, vol. iii. New York: Continuum.

Steinberg, R. M. 1977: *Fra Girolamo Savonarola, Florentine Art, and Renaissance Historiography*. Athens: Ohio University Press.

Steiner, R. 1977: *The Apocalypse of St. John*. London: Rudolf Steiner Press.

Steinhauser, K. B. 1987: *The Apocalypse Commentary of Tyconius: a history of its reception and influence*. Frankfurt: Lang.

Stevenson, J. 1957: The life and literary activity of Lactantius. In K. Aland and F. L. Cross (eds), *Studia Patristica*, Texte und Untersuchungen 63, Berlin: Akademie Verlag, 661–77.

Stone, M. E. 1990: *Fourth Ezra*. Minneapolis: Fortress.

Stonehouse, N. B. 1929: *The Apocalypse in the Ancient Church*. Goes: Oosterbaan & Le Cointre.

Stratton, S. 1994: *The Immaculate Conception in Spanish Art*. Cambridge: Cambridge University Press.

Stringfellow, W. 1973: *An Ethic for Christians and Other Aliens in a Strange Land*. Waco, Tex.: Word.

—— 1977: *Conscience and Obedience*. Waco, Tex.: Word

Stuckenbruck, L. 1995: *Angel Veneration and Christology: a study in early Judaism and in the Christology of the Apocalypse of John.* Tübingen: J. C. B. Mohr.

Sweet, J. 1979: *Revelation.* SCM Pelican Commentaries. London: SCM Press.

Swete, H. B. 1906: *The Apocalypse of St John.* London: Macmillan.

Tannenbaum, L. 1982: *Biblical Tradition in Blake's Early Prophecies: the Great Code of Art.* Princeton: Princeton University Press.

Taushev, A. and Rose, S. 1995: *The Apocalypse in the Teachings of Ancient Christianity.* Platina: St Herman.

Taves, A. 1999: *Fits and Trances and Visions: exploring religion and explaining experience from Wesley to James.* Princeton: Princeton University Press.

Thompson, D. 1996: *The End of Time: faith and fear in the shadow of the millennium.* London: Random House.

Thompson, E. P. 1993: *Witness against the Beast.* Cambridge: Cambridge University Press.

Thompson, L. 1990: *The Book of Revelation: apocalypse and empire.* Oxford: Oxford University Press.

Thomson, J. A. F. 1967: *The Later Lollards.* Oxford: Oxford University Press.

Thrupp, S. 1970: *Millennial Dreams in Action: studies in revolutionary religious movements.* New York: Schocken.

Trebilco, P. 1991: *Jewish Communities in Asia Minor.* SNTSMS 69. Cambridge: Cambridge University Press.

Trevett, C. 1995: *Montanism.* Cambridge: Cambridge University Press.

Troeltsch, E. 1960: *The Social Teaching of the Christian Churches.* New York: Harper.

Tuckett, C. M. and Horrell, D. G. (eds) 2000: *Christology, Controversy, and Community: New Testament essays in honor of David R. Catchpole.* Leiden and Boston: Brill.

Ulmer, R. 1992: *Passion und Apokalypse: Studien zur biblischen Thematik in der Kunst des Expressionismus.* Europäische Hochschulschriften 144. Frankfurt: Lang.

Underhill, E. 1919: *Jacopone da Todi, Poet and Mystic.* London: Dent.

Underwood, T. L. 1999: *The Acts of the Witnesses: the autobiography of Ludowick Muggleton and other early Muggletonian writings.* Oxford: Oxford University Press.

VanderKam, J. C. and Adler, W. 1996: *The Jewish Apocalyptic Heritage in Early Christianity.* Assen: Van Gorcum.

Van der Meer, F. 1978: *Apocalypse: visions from the Book of Revelation in Western art.* London: Thames and Hudson.

Van Oort, J. 1991: *Jerusalem and Babylon: a study into Augustine's* City of God *and the sources of his doctrine of the two cities.* Leiden: Brill.

Viscomi, J. 1993: *Blake and the Idea of the Book.* Princeton: Princeton University Press.

Wainwright, A. 1993: *Mysterious Apocalypse.* Nashville: Abingdon.

Walsh, W. 1898: *The Secret History of the Oxford Movement.* London: Swan Sonnenschein.

Walzer, M. 1985: *Exodus and Revolution.* New York: Harper Collins.

Warner, M. 1985: *Alone of all her Sex: the myth and cult of the Virgin Mary.* London: Picador.

Weinstein, D. 1970: *Savonarola and Florence: prophecy and patriotism in the Renaissance.* Princeton: Princeton University Press.

Weiss, J. 1971: *Jesus' Proclamation of the Kingdom of God.* 1892. London: SCM Press.

Wengst, K. 1987: *Pax Romana and the Peace of Jesus Christ.* London: SCM Press.

Wheelwright, P. 1962: *Metaphor and Reality.* Bloomington: Indiana University Press.

Wiggerhaus, R. 1994: *The Frankfurt School.* Cambridge: Polity.

Williams, A. (ed.) 1980: *Prophecy and Millenarianism.* Harlow: Longman.

Williams, G. H. 1957: *Spiritual and Anabaptist Writers.* London: SCM Press.

—— 1962: *The Radical Reformation.* Philadelphia: Westminster.

Wilson, B. 1973: *Magic and the Millennium.* New York and St Albans: Paladin.

Wink, W. 1984: *Naming the Powers.* Philadelphia: Fortress.

—— 1986: *Unmasking the Powers.* Philadelphia: Fortress.

—— 1993: *Engaging the Powers.* Philadelphia: Fortress.

Woolford, J. and Karlin, D. 1996: *Robert Browning.* London: Longman.

Wright, R. M. 1996: *Art and Antichrist in Medieval Europe.* Manchester: Manchester University Press.

Yeatts, J. R. 2002: *Revelation.* Believers Church Bible Commentary. Scottdale, Pa.: Herald.

Yoder, J. H. 1972: *The Politics of Jesus.* Grand Rapids, Mich.: Eerdmans.

—— 1994: To serve our God and to rule the world. In *idem* (ed.), *The Royal Priesthood*, Grand Rapids, Mich.: Eerdmans, 127–42.

OLD TESTAMENT REFERENCES LISTED IN THE MARGIN OF NESTLE-ALAND 26TH EDITION OF THE GREEK NEW TESTAMEN TEXT OF REVELATION(verse numbers from Revelation followed by Old Testament references)

Chap of Rev	Gen	Exod	Lev Num	Deut	Josh Jud 1,2 Sam	1 Kings	2 Kings	1,2 Chron	Esth Job Neh Ezra	Psa	Prov Song
1	7:28.14	4:3.14 6:19.6, 23.22 10: 19.16		18:32.40					18: J38.17	5:89.28; 89.38; 130.8	
2	7:2.9 3.3 3.22,24	17:16.32	14:N 25.1; 31.16		20: 16.31		20:9.22			6: 139.21 17: 78.24 23:7.10; 62.13 26:2.8f	23: P24.
3		5:32.32						7: J12.14		5:69.29 9:86.9	14: P8.2 19: P3.
4		1:19.24 5:19.16						11: IC29.11	5:Est1.1	1:78.23 2:11.4; 103.19	
5	5:49.9	3:20.4 10:19.6			7,11: 22.19			7: 2C18.18 12: 1C29.11		7:47.9 8:141.2 9:144.9 13: 146.6	20: SS5

ap w	Isaiah	Jer	Lam	Ezek	Dan	Hos	Joel	Amos	Micah Nah Zeph Hab	Zec	Mal
	4:11.2; 41.4 5:40.2 5:55.4 6:61.6 11:30.8 16:49.2 17,19: 44.6; 48.6,12	5:42.5		10: 3.12 13: 1.26; 9.2,11 15:1.24; 43.2 17:1.28	7,13: 7.13; 10.5 9:8.1 14: 7.9; 10.6 17:8.18			1:3.7 8:3.13		7: 12.10 12:4.2	
	12:49.2 17:62.2; 65.15	16: 21.5 23: 11.20; 17.10		7: 31.8 13:12.2 23: 33.27	10: 1.12,14 18: 10.6			1:1.6		10:6.14	
	7:22.22 9:43.4; 49.23; 60.14 14: 65.16 18:55.1			2: 34.4 12: 48.35	5:12.1	17:12.9				11:2.14; 17:11.5	5:3.16
	4:24.23 8:6.2f			2:1.26 5:1.13; 1.27 6:1.5; 1.18; 1.22; 10.12 7:1.10; 14.10	1:2.29 9:4.31; 6.27; 12.7			8:3.13		5:4.2 4:6.11	
	1: 29.11 5:11.1, 10 6,9:53.7 7:6.1 10:61.1,6	6:11.10		1:2.9	1:12.4,9 11:7.10					6:4.10	

Chap of Rev	Gen	Exod	Lev Num	Deut	Josh Jud 1,2 Sam	1 Kings	2 Kings	1,2 Chron	Esth Job Neh Ezra	Psa	Pro Son
6				10: 32.43			6:7.1 10:9.7			10: 79.10	
7	5ff: 35.22ff 6:48.1	14: 19.10, 14	9: L23.40, 43		6:Ju17					11: 97.7 17:23.1f	
8		3: 30.1,3,7 7:9.23f 8:7.20 12: 10.21			2: Jo6.4,6						
9	2:19.28 14: 15.18	2:19.18 3:10.12 13: 27.2; 30.1–3; 40.5 21: 20.13ff		20:32.17	14: Jo1.4		21:9.22		6:J3.21 7: J39.19f 11: J26.6; 28.22 17: J41.10f	11: 88.12 20: 96.5; 135.15– 17	11: P15
10	6:14.19, 22	1:13.21 6:20.11		5:32.40	3:1S 7.10				6:N9.6	3: 29.3; 6:146.6 9: 119.103	

hap ev	Isaiah	Jer	Lam	Ezek	Dan	Hos	Joel	Amos	Micah Nah Zeph Hab	Zec	Mal
	12: 13.10; 50.3 15:2.10, 19,21 15: 24.21; 34.4; 34.12	8:14.12; 15.2f; 21.7 12: 10.22 15:4.29		8: 5.12,17; 29.5; 33.27 12: 32.7; 38.19 14.21		8:13.14 16:10.8	12:2.10; 4.15 17:2.11		17:N1.6	2ff:1.8; 6.1–3 10:1.12	17:3.2
				14: 26.15							
	2:41.25 4:49.6 16f: 49.10	1: 49.36 17: 31.16		1:7.2 3:9.4,6 14: 37.3 15: 37.27 17: 34.23	1:7.2 14:12.1	6:5.3				1:2.10; 6.5	
	5:29.6 10: 14.12 13: 24.17; 26.21	8: 51.25 11:9.14; 23.15		5:10.2 7:5.2,12 38.22	10:8.10	13:4.1	7:3.3	3:9.1 12:8.9	1:H2.20; Z1.7	1:2.17 7:13.9	
	20:2.8; 2.20; 17.8	6:8.3		4:9.4,6	20:5.4,23		2:2.10 7,9:2.4f 8:1.6		20: M5.12 21:N3.4		
		3,11: 25.30 7:25.4 9:33.9		2:2.9 9:2.8; 3.1ff 11:25.2	4:8.26; 12.4,9 5f:12.7 7:9.6,10 11:3.4	3:11.10		3:1.2; 3.8 7:3.7		7:1.6	

Chap of Rev	Gen	Exod	Lev Num	Deut	Josh Jud 1,2 Sam	1 Kings	2 Kings	1,2 Chron	Esth Job Neh Ezra	Psa	Prov Song
11		6:7.17,19 11:15.16 18:15.14 19:9.24			5: 2S 22.9 6:1S4.8 17:2S7.8	19:17.1,6	3:19.2 6:17.1 5:1.10 12:2.11		13:Ez1.2	2:79.1 9:79.2f 5:97.3 10f:105.38 15:2.2 15:10.16 15:22.29; 18:46.7; 61.6; 99.1; 115.13	
12	1:37.9 9:3.1 3.14f 17:3.15	14:19.4	16:N16.30,32	12:32.43 16:11.6		6:17.1–7	6:17.1–7		10:J1.9ff; 2.1ff	1:104.2 12:96.11	
13		4:15.11 16:28.36					13:18.38			4:89.7	

hap ev	Isaiah	Jer	Lam	Ezek	Dan	Hos	Joel	Amos	Micah Nah Zeph Hab	Zec	Mal
	2: 63.18 3:37.2 8:1.9 19:29.6	5:5.14 8:22.8 18: 30.23; 51.25		1: 40.3 8:11.6; 16.46, 49 11: 37.5,10 13: 38.19	7: 7.3,21 13:2.18 15:2.44; 7.14,27		8:4.19	17:3.13; 13	13: Jl.9 15:Ob21 18:M6.9	4:4.3; 4.10,14	
	1,5:7.14 2:26.17 3:14.29; 27.1 2,5:66.7 12: 44.23; 49.13 14: 40.31 1:27.1 16:44.5	9:15.2; 43.11		3: 29.3 14: 17.3,7	3: 7.7,24 4:8.10 7:10.13, 21;12.1 8:2.35; 14:7.25; 12.7 1:7.3; 7.7,24 2: 7.4–6 5,7: 7.8; 7.11; 7.20 6f:7.25; 11.36 7:7.21 8:12.1 11:8.3 15:3.5f	6:2.16 2:13.7			2:M4.10	9f:3.1	

Chap of Rev	Gen	Exod	Lev Num	Deut	Josh Jud 1,2 Sam	1 Kings	2 Kings	1,2 Chron	Esth Job Neh Ezra	Psa	Prov Song
14	10; 19.24				14: 2S12.30			14: 1C20.2		3: 33.3; 40.4; 96.1; 98.1; 149.1 10:11.6; 75.9	
15		3:15.1 3:34.10 5,8: 40.34f	1,6:L 26.21 3:N12.7	3:34.5	3:Jo1.7 Jo14.7		8: 8.10f	8:2C 5.13f		3:111.2; 145.17 4:86.9; 98.2	
16		2:9.10 3f:7.17– 21 10: 10.22 13:8.3 18:9.24			16: Ju5.19	13: 22.21ff	16:9.27; 23.29			1:69.25 4:78.44 5f: 119.137; 145.17 6:79.3 12: 106.9 13: 78.45; 105.30	
17				14: 10.17						14: 136.3 16:27.2 18:2.2; 89.28	

hap f ev	Isaiah	Jer	Lam	Ezek	Dan	Hos	Joel	Amos	Micah Nah Zeph Hab	Zec	Mal
	1:4.5 3:42.10 5:53.9 8:21.9 10: 51.17, 22 11: 34.10 19: 63.2	7:13.16 8: 51.7f 10: 25.15 15: 51.33 18: 25.30	19f: 1.15	1:9.4 10: 38.22	8:4.27 14:7.13		1:3.5 15,18f: 4.13		5:Z3.13	16:5.2f	
	4:2.2 8:6.1,4	3f:10.7 4:11.20; 16.19			5:10.5			3:3.13; 4.13			4:1.11
	1,17: 66.6 6:49.26 9:52.5 10: 8.22 12: 11.15f; 41.2; 41.25; 44.27; 46.11; 51.10 15: 14.13	1:10.25 12: 50.38; 51.36		1:14.19; 23.31	7: 3.27lxx 11:2.18f 18:12.1				1:Z3.8	16: 12.11	
	2:23.17 3:21.1 6:34.7 18: 24.21	1,15: 51.13 2:25.15; 51.7 16: 34.22		4: 28.13 16: 16.39; 23.29; 26.19	12: 7.20,24 14:2.47	16:2.5			2:N3.4 16:M3.3		

Chap of Rev	Gen	Exod	Lev Num	Deut	Josh Jud 1,2 Sam	1 Kings	2 Kings	1,2 Chron	Esth Job Neh Ezra	Psa	Prov Song
18	5:18.20 13:36.6									6:137.8	
19			20:N 16.33	2: 32.43 16: 10.17			2:9.7	6f:1C 16.28, 31		1,3,6: 104.35 2:79.10 4:106.48 5:22.24 115.13; 134.1; 135.1, 20 6:93.1; 97.1; 99.1 7:118.24 11:9.9; 72.2; 96.13; 98.9 19:2.2 20:55.16	

Chap of Lev	Isaiah	Jer	Lam	Ezek	Dan	Hos	Joel	Amos	Micah Nah Zeph Hab	Zec	Mal
8	2: 13.21; 21.9; 34.11, 14 3,23: 23.8, 17 4:48.20; 52.11 6:40.2 7:47.8 8,23: 47.9,14 18: 34.10 22:24.8 23: 34.12	2:9.10 3:25.15; 51.7 4: 50.8; 51.6,9, 45 6:16.18; 50.15 8:50.31, 34 22: 25.10 23:7.34; 16.9 18:22.8 20: 51.48 21: 51.63f 24: 51.49		1: 43.2 3: 27.12, 9f: 26.16f; 27.30ff 11,15: 27.36 12:27.12 15: 27.31 27.12ff 17: 27.27ff 18: 27.32 19: 26.19; 27.30ff 21f: 26.12f; 26.21 24:24.7; 36.18					23:N3.4		
9	3:34.10 8: 61.10 11,15, 21:11.4 12: 62.2f 15:49.2; 63.1–3 15:63.2 20: 30.33	2:51.25		11:1.1 17f: 39.4; 39.17f	1,12: 10.6 20:7.11					6:14.9	

Chap of Rev	Gen	Exod	Lev Num	Deut	Josh Jud 1,2 Sam	1 Kings	2 Kings	1,2 Chron	Esth Job Neh Ezra	Psa	Prov Song
20					8: Jo11.4; Ju 7.12; 1S13.5	11: 10.18	9: 1.10,12; 6.14			9:78.18; 87.2 12:28.4 11: 114.3,7	
21		12: 28.21; 39.14 19: 28.17ff	3,7:L 26.12	17:3.11	7:2S7.14		3:8.27		2:N11. 1,18	3: 95.7 24:68.30 26: 72.10f	
22	1:2.10. 2:2.9		6: N27.16 16:N24. 17	18:4.2 18:13.1; 29.19						1:46.5 4:17.15; 42.3 12:28.4 14:118. 19f	

Chap of Rev	Isaiah	Jer	Lam	Ezek	Dan	Hos	Joel	Amos	Micah Nah Zeph Hab	Zec	Mal
0	3: 24.21 12:4.3	9:11.15; 12.7		8:7.2; 38– 39.16 9:38.22; 39.6	4,11: 7.9,22, 27 11:2.35 12: 7.10; 12.1				9:H1.6		
1	1,4: 65.17, 19; 66.22 2,27: 52.1; 61.10 3:8.8 4f: 35.10; 43.18f; 51.11 6:55.1 11:58.8; 60.1,19 12: 62.6 19: 54.11f 23: 24.23; 60.1; 60.19f 24: 60.5 25f: 60.11 27:4.3; 35.8	3:31.1 4:31.16 6:2.13		3: 37.27 7:11.20 10: 40.1f 11: 43.2f 12f: 40.5; 48.30 −35 15:40.3 16: 43.16; 48.16f 19: 28.13 27: 33.29						3:2.14 6:14.8 7:8.8 16:2.6 25:14.7	
2	5:60.19 7,12: 40.10 11:56.1 17:55.1	2:3.17 12: 17.10		1: 47.1 2: 47.12 11:3.27	5:7.18, 27 11: 12.10		2:1.14			1:14.8 3:14.11	16:3.1

Index of Biblical References (canonical order)

Verses and chapters are in bold, while page numbers are not. Note that any references where the book is mentioned in the text by name, but with no specific chapter or verse, are listed first under the book's title.

General Index